From Megaphones to Microphones

Speeches of American Women, 1920–1960

SANDRA J. SARKELA,
SUSAN MALLON ROSS,
and MARGARET A. LOWE

Westport, Connecticut
London

Library of Congress Cataloging-in-Publication Data

From megaphones to microphones : speeches of American women, 1920–1960 /
Sandra J. Sarkela, Susan Mallon Ross, and Margaret A. Lowe.
    p. cm.
  Includes bibliographical references and index.
  ISBN 0–275–96788–3 (alk. paper)—ISBN 0–275–97772–2 (pbk. : alk paper)
  1. Speeches, addresses, etc., American—Women authors. 2. Women—United States—
History—Sources. I. Sarkela, Sandra J., 1949– II. Ross, Susan Mallon, 1947–
III. Lowe, Margaret A., 1961–
PS663.W65 F76   2003
815'.50809287—dc21   2002025302

British Library Cataloging in Publication Data is available.

Library of Congress Catalog Card Number: 2002025302
ISBN: 0–275–96788–3
     0–275–97772–2 (pbk.)

First published in 2003

Praeger Publishers, 88 Post Road West, Westport, CT 06881
An imprint of Greenwood Publishing Group, Inc.
www.praeger.com

Printed in the United States of America

The paper used in this book complies with the
Permanent Paper Standard issued by the National
Information Standards Organization (Z39.48–1984).

10 9 8 7 6 5 4 3 2 1

We dedicate this book to the faculty and graduates of State Normal Schools and Teachers Colleges, who, without regard to class, race, or sex, teach our children the skills and values of participatory democracy.

Contents

Acknowledgments

The authors thank the many archivists and librarians who helped us locate materials, including Janice Ruth, Jeff Flannery, Bruce Kirby, and Maja Keech at the Library of Congress, and the LOC staff; the Schlesinger Library, notably Sarah Hutcheon; the Sophia Smith Collection at Smith College, especially Kate Weigand, Susan Boone, and Kathleen Banks Nutter; Patrizia Sione, our liaison to the Catherwood Library at Cornell University; Suzanne Gould at the General Federation of Women's Clubs; Shirley Ponomareff at the League of Women Voters; Stuart A. Kollar at the Kelvin Smith Library, Cleveland, Ohio; the staff at the Syracuse University archives; Angela Stockwell at the Margaret Chase Smith Library Center; Wendy E. Chmielewski, Curator, Swarthmore College Peace collection; Carolyn G. Hanneman, Archivist, Congressional Archives at the Carl Albert Center, University of Oklahoma; Vicky Jones, Southwest Collection, Texas Tech University; the Howard University archives; the Beinecke Library at Yale University; Phil Runkel at the University Archives of Marquette University; Patricia Bakunas at the University Library of the University of Illinois at Chicago; and Aaron T. Brown and the staff of the National Archives and Records Administration.

This project was supported by a Research and Creative Endeavors grant from SUNY Potsdam, and a Bridgewater State College Faculty and Library Research Grant. We thank our colleagues at the Bridgewater State College Center for the Advancement of Research and Teaching; the Bridgewater State College History Department; the Department of English and Communication at SUNY Potsdam; and the Crumb Library at SUNY Potsdam. Further, we thank the anonymous reviewers of our manuscript; Michael Leff for his pertinent questions and suggestions; and our editor, Heather Staines, for her support of this project. Student assistants Sarah Costello and Mark Demeo, and proofreader Erin Subramanian were essential in preparing the manuscript.

We also thank our SUNY Potsdam students in COMM 416-Voices of American Women, and Dean Galen Pletcher for his enthusiastic endorsement of the project. At the University of Massachusetts, Kathy Peiss and Joyce Berkman guided our thinking about gender and the public sphere as did the many students enrolled in our courses on women in American history; and Ronald F. Reid and Jane Blankenship focused our attention on the history of American women's public address. Margaret Lowe would like to extend special thanks to her father William D. Lowe and the rest of her family for their constant support as well as the many friends and colleagues who provided much needed intellectual and personal companionship along the way. She is especially grateful to Joan O'Brien, Julia Foulkes, and Maddie Cahill as well as the members of her Bridgewater State College writing group, Ann Brunjes, D'Ann George, Leora Lev, and Laurie Stuhlbarg. Susan Ross thanks her family, academic colleagues, and mentors. In particular, she is grateful to Terry, Kelly, and Casey Ross for steadfast support, her mother for keeping scrapbooks and telling stories, her father for nurturing his daughters' love for learning and teaching, and her sister, Mary, for keeping her mindful that the private sphere has a rich culture, too. She also expresses appreciation to Paula McKenzie for hospitality and research help in Washington, DC, and Teresa Harrison and Mary Lay for guiding and supporting her professional development. Sandra Sarkela is grateful to all of her family, especially Marie and Wiljo Sarkela, generous and supportive parents; the ever-patient listener Patrick Hynes; and Patrick Mazzeo, a bloodhound in the archives, whose help in every way allowed us to complete this project.

Introduction

With the passage of the Nineteenth Amendment to the U.S. Constitution in 1920, American suffragists celebrated their hard-won victory to secure the vote for women. It would be another forty years before Americans would once again witness a clamorous, nationally structured feminist campaign. As a result, the nature and scope of women's public, political activism between 1920 and 1960 is often underestimated. Rather than asking what happens to activist voices once a political movement ends—due to either its success or failure—scholars have tended to jump ahead to the next full-fledged social movement, leaving the intervening years unexamined. Until recently, many had taken a similar approach to women's public activism during the "quiet" decades between 1920 and the vociferous emergence of second wave feminism in the 1960s. In the footsteps of other researchers who began to challenge this neglect, we decided to shift the question. Rather than asking why women were so quiet (or quieted) in public life after 1920, we asked: What in fact were politically active women saying? This book, an anthology of women's public speeches from 1920 to 1960, is the result of our efforts. We hope you will agree that this collection clearly documents that women had much to say and their words deserve close scrutiny. They spoke not with one voice but with many; not on one topic but on every topic; not with one inflection but in multiple tones; not to one audience but before many publics; and not on one platform but through myriad megaphones and microphones all across the nation.

As this collection illustrates, speech making has served as one of the most important mechanisms through which Americans have created or stifled social change. Thus, to overlook women's public speech is to miss a vital contribution to the political life of the nation.[1] Not knowing what we would find, we decided to cast our research net as wide as possible. Our survey of unpublished records in public and private archives, as well as published material in books, newspapers, magazines, and journals of the period, quickly yielded much more than we expected—an astonishing wealth of material, rich in depth and variety. Women from all walks of life, regions, ethnicities, and social classes not only spoke in public but also maintained records of their speeches in the form of notes, manuscripts, publications, and, in some cases, recordings. Though only a first sweep through the numerous collections of speeches delivered by American women from 1920 to 1960, this anthology is an illustrative introduction, just a glimpse, into the lives, history, and speech-giving record of a diverse group of activist women during the middle decades of the twentieth century.

FROM MEGAPHONES TO MICROPHONES

Due to the gendered nature of public life, women public speakers have often had to hold not just the courage of their convictions but also courage of the heart and the body. Just the act of public speaking could provoke outrage. Yet, between 1920 and 1960, women stood before their publics as part of a long tradition of female public speech.[2] Native American women had challenged government agencies, African American women demanded an end to slavery and lynching, Hispanic women led union meetings, Asian American women petitioned Congress, and white women agitated for urban reform.[3] By the 1920s, though, new technologies, new political issues, and historically specific gender, race, and class configurations shaped the context and content of their speeches.

One particularly important development was the radio in the 1920s. As it opened the door to more women's voices and more women listeners, it also altered the dynamics of public speaking in ways that were advantageous to women. First, the radio audience could not see the speaker. They could no longer castigate her as "unfeminine" based on appearance, and those with awkward physical styles or shy mannerisms, could still take over the room with a polished, verbatim text delivered with force in the studio. On the other hand, radio allowed the speaker to converse in a casual tone with her audience. The microphone not only compensated for weak vocal projection, it actually seemed to prefer a more low-key and typically "feminine" style of speech.[4] Finally, the audience did not have to leave home. Women who might not have felt comfortable attending a political rally, or who had little free time due to work and domestic responsibilities, could listen to the radio while cooking, cleaning, and caring for children. India Edwards, for example, who held major positions in the Democratic Party from 1944–1956, explained that she used radio to disseminate women's recorded speeches ("platters") to a national audience:

I was working in the public relations department of the Women's Division, and I started out writing news releases, biographies, but pretty soon I was writing speeches for various and sundry people....We were very dependent upon radio, and that's what I ended up doing for the Women's division. I can't tell you...how many hundreds of platters that we sent out. There were certain speeches that were very effective. For instance, Dorothy Thompson had made a speech that was wonderfully effective, and there were others. And I ended up in charge of all that. And many a time I would leave the Biltmore at 11 o'clock at night with my secretary and we would walk across to the American Express office, which was just nearby, carrying great armloads of these platters and mail them out, because they were used in meetings all over the country.[5]

As the century progressed, other technological developments and cultural conventions would further define and expand women's public speech giving. The exigencies of the Great Depression and World War II upset traditional gender expectations, while suburban life, television sets, and the Cold War shaped the postwar speeches.

The fact that we located so much evidence of women's public speaking, despite its ephemeral nature (often not written, recorded, or saved), suggests that we and other scholars have only begun to scratch the surface of the documentary history of women's public speaking. We know, for example, that civil rights activist Ella Baker gave powerful speeches throughout the 1950s, but she spoke extemporaneously or gave impromptu addresses, and no manuscript, notes, or recordings have yet been discovered for this decade. Furthermore, many of the speeches we located are epideictic or ceremonial speeches which are usually assigned to people with prominent records as speakers or public figures and may be viewed as an indicator of a significant previous record, a sign that much has gone before. Our research suggests that many, many more public speeches do exist waiting to be processed but also that, unfortunately, many speeches were given that will remain "lost to history." Nevertheless, this volume and others illustrate that, contrary to popular belief (and scholarly neglect), women from all walks of life commonly gave public speeches on a regular basis to a variety of audiences.

If so, what did they speak about? Though historians have explored voting patterns and noted some specific gender gaps in women's political interests, women did not enter the political arena between 1920 and 1960 with one unified voice.[6] Instead, they focused on a range of subjects, created assorted political bodies, and organized grass roots political campaigns motivated by their particular socio-economic and intellectual interests. Thus, we find women constantly participating in spirited public debate between 1920 and 1960 on questions of economic policy, social justice, New Deal programs, labor movements, issues of war and peace, corporate power, and international diplomacy. Two topics do recur, however. First, through many twists and turns, women returned again and again to the debate between a definition of equal rights that emphasized women deserved the same rights and the same treatment as men, versus one that advocated certain protections for women and children due to their difference from men. Second, women expressed an explicit self-consciousness about their new status as fully enfranchised citizens. In their public speeches, they set forth various prescriptive ideals and expectations for American women, but all encouraged women to immerse themselves in the political life of the nation, not just in the wake of winning the vote in 1920, but well into the postwar years.

In reviewing women's public speeches, it also becomes clear that throughout the period, American women acquired and honed their ability to maneuver their way through the democratic political process. They mastered the intricacies of local election laws, parliamentary procedure, national party platforms, union tactics, environmental codes, and diplomatic decorum. Reinforcing all of this activity, they read public speaking manuals such as *Time to Speak Up: A Speaker's Handbook for Women,* by Jessie Haver Butler. Such manuals taught women how to captivate and persuade an audience.[7] At home behind closed doors, behind radio microphones, and in political and social groups, women public speakers learned how best to articulate their goals and shepherd their agenda forward.

But as they did so, they also experienced sexual discrimination in the workplace, at home, and in local and national political organizations. Women experienced themselves as confident, powerful political actors but many around them dismissed or trivialized their efforts. Deeply embedded gender definitions still relegated women to the "quiet," supportive backbench of American politics. Yet women's day-to-day political experience told them something different—that their gender need not preclude political efficacy. It was this frustrating juxtaposition of aspirations and inhibiting social and legal obstacles that created women's deeply felt sense of injustice which galvanized 1960s feminist protest.

PREVIEW

We set the speeches that follow in chronological order within four thematic time periods. Each section is preceded by a brief overview that sketches the historical and social context for the era, emphasizes key trends in women's public activism, and points to shifts in speech-making styles. Many of these speeches have not previously been published or are not widely accessible. Wherever possible, we included the entire, unedited speech. Thus, we retained spelling, grammar, and typographical errors, along with the speakers' revisions, in the texts printed in this volume. From the substantial number of speeches we gathered, we identified those that most clearly represented issues that captured the attention and imagination of women over this time period, and, as much as possible, we selected speeches that raised national issues and were given before national organizations or audiences. We attempted to strike a balance between speeches given by notable women and those given by less well-known women. Although we faced certain constraints in our efforts to include women of diverse race, class, and ethnic backgrounds, we made considerable progress. The volume includes speeches given by working, middle-class, and elite women as well as African American, Native American, and Latina women.

Part I, "What Next? 1920–1931," covers the period immediately following the passage of the nineteenth amendment when women stepped forward as fully enfranchised citizens, modern workers, and consumers. Part II, "Whose New Deal? 1932–1940" moves into the tumultuous years of the Great Depression, which was a time when activist women wielded power as governmental appointees within the expanding federal government. The causes they once championed from "the outside" became institutionalized within New Deal programs. African American women, female trade unionists, and advocates for birth control gained greater national attention as well. Part III, "Speaking of War! 1940–1945" highlights women's statements regarding US war policy as well as the specific duties each speaker believed women should fulfill during the war, both on the home front and abroad. Part IV, "Is That All There Is? 1945–1960" reflects women's response to a wide range of political and social issues in aftermath of the war, particularly the growing fear of nuclear weapons, the cold war, and environmental devastation, as well as women's expanding role in the nation's economy as activists, workers, entrepreneurs, and professionals. It counters the common view that the 1950s were a time of stable domesticity by revealing a growing level of anxiety and discontent among many politically active women.

In the speeches that follow, you will find a first-hand account of women's avid, wide-ranging, and rather noisy activism during this frequently overlooked period in their history. The words of the women who fill this volume reflect their thoughts about the place of women in public life but perhaps more centrally, in their speeches we find their dreams and demands for the nation. We hope and expect that readers and scholars will add their voices—quiet and noisy—to the vital questions that face them and all Americans at the start of the twenty-first century.

NOTES

1. See, for example, Ronald F. Reid, *American Rhetorical Discourse*, 2nd ed. (Prospect Heights, IL: Waveland, 1995); Karlyn Kohrs Campbell, *Man Cannot Speak for Her*, 2 vols. (New York: Praeger, 1989).

2. During the nineteenth and early twentieth centuries, women referred to the right to vote as "woman suffrage" (singular). However, for most of the period of

this anthology to the present day, conventional usage is the plural, "women's suffrage." We follow contemporary usage unless directly quoting from someone who used the singular form.

3. Louise W. Knight, "An Authoritative Voice: Jane Addams and the Oratorical Tradition," *Gender and History* 10 (August 1998): 217–251; *Public Speaking of American Women, 1800–1925: A Biocritical Sourcebook*, Karlyn Kohrs Campbell, ed. (Westport, CT: Greenwood Press, 1993); *Public Speaking of American Women, 1925–1993: A Biocritical Sourcebook*, Karlyn Kohrs Campbell, ed. (Westport, CT: Greenwood Press, 1994).

4. Kathleen Hall Jamieson, *Eloquence in an Electronic Age: The Transformation of Political Speech Making* (New York: Oxford University Press, 1988); and Kathleen Hall Jamieson, *Beyond the Double Bind: Women and Leadership* (New York: Oxford University Press, 1997).

5. Jerry N. Hess, Oral History Interview with India Edwards, January 16, 1969," *Truman Presidential Museum and Library* (website and database) June 22, 2001: 3 (www.trumanlibrary.org/oralhist/edwards1.htm).

6. Historians have tended to downplay "gender gaps" in voting patterns prior to the 1980s but recent work by Jo Freeman suggests that earlier gaps existed, particularly in women's support of Herbert Hoover and Dwight D. Eisenhower. Jo Freeman, *A Room at a Time: How Women Entered Party Politics* (Lanham, MD: Rowman & Littlefield, 2000).

7. Jessie Haver Butler, *Time to Speak Up: A Speaker's Handbook for Women* (New York: Harper's, 1946, 1952, 1957).

PART I

What Next? 1920–1931

With the passage of the Nineteenth Amendment, women had at last secured one of the most basic and sacred of democratic rights—the right to vote. In 1920, full political citizenship beckoned American women. Yet, the vote, an abstract legal instrument, offered only the promise, not the reality, of full political participation or true gender equality. The meaning, effect, and preservation of women's new status would be determined in the decades to come. Would the vote improve women's political or economic position in American life? Would politicians and unions court female workers? How would women reconfigure their vocational and work choices? Would women and men create more equitable personal and family relationships? Would all women have the right to vote, or would literacy tests, poll taxes, and anti-immigration laws bar minority and working-class women from the voting booth? What issues might women champion? Would or should women engage in bitter partisan struggles? In the wake of their victory, women of all backgrounds and political persuasions began to grapple with these and other questions as they redefined notions of modern womanhood. Their answers were complex, contested, and ever changing.

After decades of conducting their politics as unwelcome interlopers knocking on "male-only" political doors, women now had the opportunity and the obligation to operate as political insiders. Although not new to politics, women were new to full-fledged electoral participation. Denied suffrage prior to 1920, activist women of all races and classes had developed sophisticated political skills in the campaign for the vote as well as in their numerous efforts for Progressive Era reform. They were so successful that by the 1920s much of what had been considered the women's reform agenda (maternal and child health, urban reform, and education) had been taken up by what historians such as Paula Baker and Theda Skocpol have termed the domestic or maternalist state.[1] Following women's lead, the federal government passed national legislation and built social programs to soften the harsh realities of industrial capitalism. By the 1920s, women and their reformist agenda were knitted firmly into the fabric of mainstream American political life.

Many expected that once granted suffrage, women would vote together as a bloc. To their surprise, women never voted as one. This was apparent in the mix of ideas and goals generated by women who operated within new, existing, and reconfigured national political organizations as well as in the younger generations' "new style" feminism. The National American Woman Suffrage Association dismantled and reformed into the League of Women Voters while the National Woman's Party continued their militant activism by demanding an Equal Rights Amendment. Other government and non-government associations such as the Woman's Bureau created by Woodrow Wilson during World War I, and the Women's Joint Congressional Commission lobbied for an array of legal and social reforms. Women continued as idealists and pragmatists to move in both partisan and non-partisan circles.[2] Though a gender gap between male and female voters emerged in certain elections and regarding specific issues, women's vote, like men's, tended to splinter according to socioeconomic background, political philosophy, and personal interests.[3]

Still, in the 1920s, women redefined what it meant to be political and feminist and to speak in public. Sometimes these categories merged, but often they did not. In a decade bursting with contradictions (it was both radical and conservative, prosperous and corrupt, liberal and repressive), a flurry of new female public personas and images crystallized. Young working and middle-class women wore flapper attire on city streets; professional women testified before government agencies; and typists, factory workers, and department store clerks populated work spaces and city parks. African American entrepreneurs owned and operated businesses such as urban beauty shops, more white women than ever entered the labor force (continuing to work even after marriage), and Mexican American women labored, protested, and marketed their wares throughout the southwest. Waves of African Americans migrated to northern cities, and Mexican migration surged in California and Texas. In vivid sound and color, new mass-produced magazines, national radio programs, Hollywood movies, and popular songs disseminated the new styles from coast to coast.

In this mix, in both image and reality, American women—modern youth, former suffragists, African American domestics, Harlem Renaissance poets, social reformers, radical birth controllers, and home economists—redefined what it meant for women to take up public space. The speeches collected in this section reveal some of the parameters of this gendered terrain. As women took the public podium in the 1920s, they negotiated (challenged or reaffirmed) gender definitions via their topics, presentation, and ideological persuasion. They might place themselves within a variety of categories: party pol, lady reformer, youthful radical, concerned mother, or autonomous professional. Their choices would reflect their specific political concerns as well as oratorical training, forum, and audience. Women crafted their speeches to persuade specific audiences to support their cause; they spoke before single- and mixed-sex audiences, to the like-minded chorus, and to hostile opponents. They delivered their speeches in outdoor tents, on city streets, in formal convention halls, and before radio microphones.

Thus, these speeches reflect the state of women's political self-definition during the 1920s and early 1930s as they mapped and defined the nature of women's place in public life. As they did so, women of widely diverse backgrounds and political persuasions engaged in all manner of social and political issues, local and national. They did not speak in a single voice but instead provoked and engaged in the pressing debates of the day. Some speakers directly addressed "women's issues" and articulated clear feminist positions, while others only hinted at their views on such topics. For many, their political philosophy lay embedded within their statements about specific causes. And women's causes were many. Women addressed their new status as citizens as well as issues of war and peace, consumerism, conservation, and education. Thus, the careful reader will examine the exact lines women spoke *and* read between those lines to discover each speaker's expectations for the modern, public, enfranchised American woman.

In the speeches that follow, we find newcomers to the public sphere as well as savvy veterans. African Americans Mary Church Terrell and Nannie Burroughs, as well as Native Americans Ruth Muskrat Bronson and Gertrude Simmons Bonnin (Zitkala-Sa, Red Bird) challenged the United States to live up to its promise of "liberty and equality for all." Young lawyer Florence Ellinwood Allen made a splash as an orator with her rationale for outlawing war, and middle-class women affiliated with the General Federation of Women's Clubs addressed concerns ranging from forestry to immigration at their national conventions. We also note the appearance of radio as a medium for public discourse, one that reflected the rise of mass media and consumerism, and one that women such as Elizabeth Sippel and Florence Harriman used to their advantage. It provided an intimate link between female political activists and women listening at home. Now, speakers could champion their causes before a national audience—speaking to the rural farm wife as well as the urban working girl—all at once. We begin the volume with Jane Addams. Although her most profound political achievements occurred prior to 1920, her life, career, and speaking style set the stage for the next generation.

NOTES

1. Paula Baker, "The Domestication of Politics: Women and American Political Society, 1780–1920," *American Historical Review* 89 (June 1984): 620–647; Theda Skocpol, *Protecting Soldiers and Mothers: The Political Origins of Social Policy in the United States* (Cambridge, MA: Harvard University Press, 1992).

2. Sheila Rowbotham, *A Century of Women: The History of Women in Britain and the United States in the Twentieth Century* (New York: Penguin, 1997); and Nancy Woloch, *Women and the American Experience*, 3rd ed. (Boston: McGraw-Hill, 2000): 388–395.

3. Nancy Cott, *The Grounding of Modern Feminism* (New Haven: Yale University Press, 1987); Jo Freeman, *A Room at a Time: How Women Entered Party Politics* (Lanham, MD: Rowman & Littlefield, 2000); Melanie Gustafson, Kristie Miller, and Elisabeth I. Perry, eds., *We Have Come to Stay: American Women and Political Parties, 1880–1960* (Albuquerque: University of New Mexico Press, 1999). Freeman points out that though women did not vote as a uniform bloc, they voted in higher numbers for Herbert Hoover and Dwight D. Eisenhower.

Jane Addams (1860–1935)

Over the course of her lifetime, Jane Addams witnessed a social transformation that provided girls and women, mostly those with privileged backgrounds like hers, with opportunities for higher education. Higher education, in turn, helped them to participate in the creation of professional opportunities, constitutional rights, and advocacy organizations. Each of these creative innovations subsequently empowered women to participate more actively in public discourse.

Addams was born on September 6, 1860, in Cedarville, Illinois, just before the Civil War. Her father was an Illinois state senator and friend of Abraham Lincoln, who won the presidential election that same year. Addams developed a strong identification with Lincoln, apparent in her homage to Lincoln in the speech that follows.[1] In 1882, as women were beginning to benefit from higher education, Addams earned one of the first bachelor's degrees at Rockford Women's Seminary (now Rockford College), intending to pursue a career in medicine. However, she abandoned that goal because of what has been characterized as "ill health" and, following doctors' advice, traveled in Europe for two years.[2] A second trip to Europe, in 1887–1888, served as a catalyst for her life's work. Addams's solution to the problem of the limited career opportunities open to her and other educated women was to bring the settlement house movement, started in England, to America.

In "The Subjective Necessity for Social Settlements" (1893) Addams noted, "We have in America a fast-growing number of cultivated young people who have no recognized outlet for their active facilities" and who experience "a want of harmony between their theory and their lives, a lack

Jane Addams (right) and Mary McDowell campaigning for world peace, ca. 1926–30.

Jane Addams Memorial Collection (JAMC neg. 64), The University Library, University of Illinois at Chicago.

of coordination between thought and action."[3] And so, in 1889, she and a school friend, Ellen Starr, founded Hull House for the mutual benefit of the Hull House staff and their neighbors. Addams wrote: "It is an effort to add the social function to democracy. It was opened on the theory that the dependence of classes on each other is reciprocal."[4] It has been suggested that Addams's vision of how reciprocal class cooperation could be accomplished was essentially communicative, in that "Addams urged face-to-face (or arbitrated) debate, even confrontation, so that each side could see and hear each other."[5]

Opportunities for interaction abounded in the facilities and activities of Hull House. Among the firsts at Hull House were Chicago's first kindergarten and day-care facilities for children of working mothers. Addams and her colleagues also launched an employment bureau, art gallery, libraries, and various clubs. One such club was the Working Peoples' Social Science Club. It was "social, educational and civic in nature, the latter chiefly because it connected the House with the labor problems in their social and political aspects."[6] Addams's access to the civic podium and legislative lobbies led her to advocate for laws to protect women and children, the nineteenth amendment, and world peace. She worked for peace largely under the auspices of the Women's International League for Peace and Freedom, of which she was a founder.[7]

During her lifetime, Addams saw many social changes, including ratification of the Nineteenth Amendment, which instituted women's suffrage nationwide. By August 26, 1920, when the nineteenth amendment took effect, however, many who had devoted their lives to the women's suffrage movement were no longer alive to celebrate the victory. To honor their contribution, the National Woman's Party granted sculptor Adelaide Johnson a commission to create a marble monument featuring busts of three women's suffrage movement leaders, Susan B. Anthony, Elizabeth Cady Stanton, and Lucretia Coffin Mott.[8] This "Portrait Monument" was given to the nation on February 15, 1921, Susan B. Anthony's birthday.[9] On that occasion, Addams, who had supported women's suffrage because of the help she thought it would provide in solving city problems and securing world peace, gave the dedication address. Notably, the reception for sculptor Adelaide Johnson at the Capitol that day was the first reception for a woman ever held there.

By that point in her life Addams was a controversial figure. Long an outspoken supporter of trade unionism, she supported constitutional rights for all during the red scare, and she maintained her long-standing pacifist stance throughout World War I. Addams was a founder of a number of advocacy organizations, including in 1909, the National Association for the Advancement of Colored People (NAACP) and, in 1920, the American Civil Liberties Union (ACLU). After giving this address, she remained active in the Women's International League for Peace and Freedom, serving as the organization's president until 1929, when she resigned from the post and was elected honorary president for life. In 1931, she was corecipient of the Nobel Peace Prize—the first American woman to be so honored.

In the address, Addams depicts women's suffrage as an event in human progress, not just American political history, because, from her perspective, it was won through "effort" and even "struggle" but "free from the stain of blood." She does not disparage Lincoln for emancipating "another group" through the bloody Civil War of her early childhood, but honors both his achievement and the next evolutionary step, saying: "It is fitting that they [suffragists] stand next to the great emancipator of another group...."

NOTES

1. Jean Bethke Elshtain, *Power Trips and Other Journeys: Essays in Feminism as Civic Discourse* (Madison: University of Wisconsin Press, 1960), 6.

2. Addams's health problems included chronic spinal ailments as well as emotional aspects relating to her father's death a few weeks after she graduated from college. Her mother had died when Addams was two. See, for example, William L. Neumann, "A Prefatory Note on Jane Addams's Life," in *Jane Addams, A Centennial Reader* (New York: Macmillan 1960), ix; and Christopher Lasch, "Introduction," in *The Social Thought of Jane Addams* (Indianapolis: Bobbs-Merrill, 1965), xvi–xvii.

3. Jane Addams, "The Subjective Necessity for Social Settlements," in *Philanthropy and Social Progress* (New York: Thomas Y. Crowell, 1893), 1–26. Addams quoted her earlier essay in *Twenty Years at Hull House* (New York: Macmillan, 1920), 113–115, in *Jane Addams, A Centennial Reader*, 12.

4. *Jane Addams, A Centennial Reader*, 10.

5. Elshtain, 11.

6. Addams, "The Objective Value of a Social Settlement," in *Philanthropy and Social Progress*, 27–56, cited in *Jane Addams, A Centennial Reader*, 20.

7. National Association of Social Workers, "Professional Social Work Centennial: 1898–1998. Addams Work Laid the Foundation," *NASW News*, January 1998, available from www.socialworkers.org. Neumann observed that after Addams's name had become well known in Chicago, she "began speaking to many civic groups and reaching out to a larger audience by rewriting these talks and publishing them in the popular magazines of her time." See "A Prefatory Note," 10.

8. Controversially, a bust of Sojourner Truth, a black woman and former slave, is not included. See Janice K. Bryant, "Unfinished Business," *On the Issues* 6 (Fall 1997) [journal online] May 27, 2003 (www.echonyc.com/~onissues/f97bryant.html).

9. See Karlyn Kohrs Campbell, *Man Cannot Speak for Her*, Vol. I (Westport, CT: Greenwood Press, 1989), 182; Roger N. Baldwin, "Civil Liberties," in *Jane Addams, A Centennial Reader*, 220–222.

ADDRESS AT "PORTRAIT MONUMENT" DEDICATION (FEBRUARY 15, 1921)[1]

We are solemnly gathered here to place a significant milestone on the long road of self-government, which has slowly widened to include one enfranchised group after another. There are many such milestones behind us. A thousand years ago, the English barons erected one when they secured their first political power, and centuries later merchants and traders placed theirs, to be followed by working men slowly and painfully building in one country after another.

Now at last the women are coming into their own. In victorious and defeated nations alike, they are fast receiving long withheld political power.

But as we all know, the extension of the franchise, however normal and evolutionary it may seem in retrospect, did not come without effort and struggle on the part of those demanding it. None have worked more eagerly than women, and their victorious banner alone is free from the stain of blood.

The placing of this marble commemorates therefore much more than a grand achievement in the history of the United States, although as such it deserves an honored place in this rotunda, because these pioneer suffragists whom we are met to commemorate, all Americans as they are, were the first women in any country to form a definite organization for the sole purpose of securing rights for women, including "the sacred right of the elective franchise." They, therefore, became the pioneers of an historic movement not only of their own countrywomen, but also for the forward-looking women of the world. It is fitting that they should stand next to the great emancipator of another group, who has long since transcended national boundaries.

NOTE

1. Single page typescript (copy). Jane Addams Papers, Manuscript Division, Library of Congress, Washington, D.C.

Mary Church Terrell (1863–1954)

Mary Church Terrell was born in Memphis, Tennessee, in 1863 to former slaves. Her life spanned the years from the Emancipation Proclamation to the groundbreaking *Brown v. Board of Education* Supreme Court decision in 1954. In these decades of both heartbreak and enormous progress for African Americans, Terrell was instrumental in persuading the United States to grant greater equality to African Americans and to women. A lecturer, writer, educator, and suffrage advocate, she was also the first President of the National Association for Colored Women (NACW) and a founding member of the National Association for the Advancement of Colored People (NAACP).

Raised among the black upper class (her father was the first African American millionaire), Terrell received an outstanding education. Unusual for women of any race, she took the gentleman's rather than the lady's course at Oberlin College, where she received her B.A. in 1884 and M.A. in 1888. Though her father would have preferred she live a life of genteel domesticity, Terrell chose to combine marriage and family with committed public service. She taught school for several years in the District of Columbia, before being the first African American appointed to the District's Board of Education. In 1891, she married Robert Terrell, a promising young lawyer who became the first African American to serve as a judge in Washington, DC (1902–1925). Mary gave birth to one daughter and she and Robert adopted another (Terrell's brother's child).

Devastated by the lynching in Memphis of her friend Thomas Moss in 1892, Terrell channeled her sorrow and anger into a long career as an activist writer and national speaker. The Slayton Lyceum Bureau appointed Terrell

Mary Church Terrell, ca. 1920s.

Library of Congress, Prints & Photographs Division, [reproduction number, LC-USZ62-54726].

as a lecturer in 1892, and she quickly demonstrated her unusual abilities. A persuasive speaker, she appeared at a variety of forums, including local high schools, YMCAs, and churches, as well as national venues such as annual NACW meetings and congressional hearings. Terrell impressed her contemporaries with her commanding presence and her ability to address a wide array of complex social issues, including suffrage, lynching, Jim Crow, African American literature, 1920s morality, the ERA, party politics, international relations, educational policy, World War II, the Cold War, and 1950s desegregation.

Yet, surely one of Terrell's greatest contributions was her daring effort to coherently address the twin themes of sexual and racial politics within American culture and within the African American community. She continually articulated the complicated notion that African American women were both women and black, not one category or the other, reminding her audiences that African American women had two heavy loads to carry through an unfriendly world, race as well as sex.

At the same time, Terrell—wedded to the prescribed gender and class notions of her generation—perceived women like herself (educated, mannered, and cultured) as models of middle-class femininity. As such, she felt that her class was responsible for uplifting the race, especially women, by whom, as she stated, "the world will always judge the womanhood of the race."[1] Yet, as one historian has argued, by embracing such standards, Terrell and her cohorts adopted the "politics of respectability," a claim to the rights, respect, and personal safety granted to virtuous white women.[2]

The following speeches provide a survey of Terrell's range, her politics, speaking style, and devotion to racial and sexual progress. They also illustrate the various forums and audiences she addressed. In the first speech, "The Black Mammy Monument," (1921) Terrell rejects a proposal to erect a Black Mammy Monument in the Capital. She destroys the sentimental version of Mammy, creating instead for her audience of local DC politicians and community members, a vivid portrait of the dreadful reality female African American slaves endured.[3]

The second speech, "Talk to Young Men of Howard University," delivered to the men of Howard University in 1925, examines the impact of 1920s morality on personal and sexual relationships between black men and women. Though issues of sexuality, especially black male sexuality, were rarely directly addressed, Terrell waded in with full force. Fearing that holding black men accountable for mistreating black women or for enjoying the benefits of the double standard would fuel powerful stereotypes (often used to justify segregation and violence) which portrayed African American men as sexual brutes, most African Americans avoided the topic. Nevertheless, Terrell demanded that African American men improve their conduct, for the sake of women and their race. One of the historic black colleges, by 1925 Howard University was a prestigious, well established, coeducational, liberal arts college. Thus her audience, especially those taking the academic track, were most probably young men of the black middle class.

NOTES

1. Mary Church Terrell, "The Duty of the National Association of Colored Women," *A.M.E. Church Review* (January 1900); also, Mary Church Terrell, "Being a Colored Woman in the United States," Mary Church Terrell Papers, Manuscript Division, Moorland-Spingarn Research Center (MSRC), Howard University, Washington, D.C.

2. Evelyn Brooks-Higginbotham, *Righteous Discontent: The Women's Movement and the Black Baptist Church, 1880–1920* (Cambridge: Harvard University Press, 1993). See also Karlyn Kohrs Campbell, "Mary Church Terrell," in *Women Public Speakers in the United States, 1925–1993*, Karlyn Kohrs Campbell, ed. (Westport, CT: Greenwood, 1994), 108–119; Paula Giddings, *When and Where I Enter: The Impact of Black Women on Race and Sex in America* (New York: Bantam, 1984); *In Search of Sisterhood* (New York: Quill, 1988); and Darlene Hine Clark et al., eds., *We Specialize in the Wholly Impossible: A Reader in Black Women's History* (New York: Carlson Publishing, 1995).

3. For background on the controversial statue and the Mammy image, see Cynthia Neverdon Morton, "Afro-American Women of the South, and the Advancement of the Race, 1895–1925," and Deborah G. White, "Aren't I a Woman?" in *Female Slaves in the Plantation South* (New York: Norton, 1985).

THE BLACK MAMMY MONUMENT (1923)[1]

The women all over the United States stand aghast at the idea of erecting a Black Mammy Monument in the Capital of the United States. The condition of the slave woman was so pitiably, hopelessly helpless that it is difficult to see how any woman, whether white or black, would take any pleasure in a marble statue to perpetuate her memory.

The Black Mammy had no home life. In the very nature of the case she could have none. Legal marriage was impossible for her. If she went through a...ceremony with a slave man, he could be sold away from her at any time, or she might be sold from him and be taken as a concubine by her master, his son, the overseer or any other white man on the place who might desire her....No colored woman could look upon a statue of a Black Mammy with a dry eye, when she remembered how often the slave woman's heart was torn with anguish because the children either of her master or their slave father were ruthlessly torn from her in infancy or in youth to be sold "down the country," where in all human probability she would never see them again.

The Black Mammy was often faithful in the services of her mistress's children while her own heart bled over her own little babes, deprived of their mother's ministrations and tender care which the white children received. One cannot help but marvel at the desire to perpetuate in bronze or marble a figure which represents so much that really is and should be abhorrent to the womanhood of the whole civilized world.

Then when one considers the extent to which the Black Mammy was the victim of the passion and power of her master...it is hard to understand how for nearly three hundred years, the wives, mothers and sisters of slave owners could have stood by without frequent and vigorous protests to such degradation of the womanhood of my race. And it is harder to understand why their descendants should want to behold a perpetual reminder of the heart rending conditions under which Black Mammies were obliged to live.

We have all heard touching stories of the affectionate relationship existing between some Black Mammies and their little white charges whom they nursed with such tender care. The lot of some slave women was no doubt better than that of others. They were all slaves nevertheless.... And the amount suffered by one Black Mammy whose children were snatched from her embrace and sold away from her forever outweighed in the balance all the kindness bestowed upon all the slave women fortunate enough to receive it for two hundred and fifty years.

Surely in their zeal to pay tribute to the faithful services rendered by the Black Mammy the descendants of slaveholding ancestors have forgotten the atrocities and cruelties incident to the institution of slavery itself.

If the Black Mammy statue is ever erected, which the dear Lord [should prevent?], there are thousands of colored men and women who will fervently pray that on some stormy night the lightning will strike it and ... send it crashing to the ground so that the descendants of Black Mammy will not be reminded of the anguish of heart and the physical suffering which their mothers and grandmothers of the race endured for nearly three hundred years.

NOTE

1. Typescript with handwritten revisions. Mary Church Terrell Papers, Manuscript Division, Library of Congress, Washington, DC. Terrell dedicated the copyright of her unpublished papers held at the Library of Congress to the public.

TALK TO YOUNG MEN OF HOWARD UNIVERSITY (MARCH 20, 1925[1])

Reprinted by Permission of Howard University

I regard it as a privilege and an opportunity to meet with the young men in the Academic Department of Howard University, so that we may have a heart to heart talk about one of the most important subjects which we could possibly consider. Dean Parks asked me to talk about conditions which vitally affect your lives, the lives of young women with whom you come into contact and which, therefore, vitally affect the whole race.

I am well aware that we are living in a time when some of the old moorings of morality seem in imminent danger of being swept away. The World War is undoubtedly responsible for some of the unfortunate conditions which confront us in certain countries today. After the World War in 1919, I went abroad to deliver an address in Switzerland and I was shocked at the looseness and laxity of morals which prevailed in some parts of Europe at that time.

And now I want to call your attention to what some close observers fear is a growing tendency on the part of some of our young men to treat the young women of the race with scant courtesy and indifferent respect.

Some of the older men of the race insist that the young men of the present generation treat the young women with much less courtesy and respect than colored men did thirty and even twenty years ago. There is also a settled conviction in the minds of some colored women that they are not treated with the same courtesy and respect that the women of other groups receive from their men. I have also heard at least six or eight white men whose interest in the race could be neither doubted nor denied deplore the lack of courtesy which colored men show the women of their group.

I realize that this is a very delicate subject to discuss. For no matter how careful or tactful in expressing her opinions a woman may be, there is always a danger that she may be misquoted or misunderstood....I have come here this morning to appeal to the young gentlemen of this department to give the young women of the race a square deal. I have come to ask you to give our girls a chance, so far as in you lies, to be the kind of women whom I know each and every one of you admires, women who are refined and cultured in manner and whose characters are above reproach....

I am sure there is not a young man in this room who would wittingly, willfully take advantage of another young man....And yet, the very men who claim to be guided by such high standards with their dealings with their own sex show both by word and deed that they utterly disregard them when they deal with women. I mean by this that in associating with young women some young men seem to have no compunctions whatsoever. They do not hesitate to deport themselves...in a manner to which they...themselves would take offense, if any man treated their mother, their sister or any other women in whom they were especially interested in the same way.

These young men conduct themselves in a free familiar way with young women. They sometimes jerk a girl toward them roughly, or push her away from them crudely. They pat her on the cheek, tap her on the head, put [a] hand on her shoulder or around her waist and indulge in other familiarities which cause people to think lightly of the girl and perhaps give her a bad name. Many a young woman whose home training has been excellent and whose intentions have been the best,...has completely lost her reputation...not because she transgressed the moral law, but because some young man habitually conducted himself toward her in a familiar manner.

I hope you will not misunderstand me,...I am sorry we think and talk so much about sex[.] It is a great pity that young men and women cannot associate together in terms of absolute equality and forget all about their sex. To my mind that would be an ideal condition,...But unfortunately, we must take the world as we find it and not as we should like it to be.

There is altogether too much talk about sex. Sex is the most natural thing in the world. It was ordained by God. But we talk about it the wrong way....If the average young man realized to what extent he is responsible for the well-being and the happiness of the young women with whom he comes into daily contact, his attitude toward them would be far different toward them in many respects.

For years the world insisted that if a woman went astray, no matter what were the circumstances she had nobody to blame but herself....For hundreds of years even good women sanctioned that double standard of morals which teaches that a man may do anything he pleases, may commit any indiscretion he likes and not be held accountable for his lecherous conduct, but if a woman strays from the straight and narrow path, she must be banished from good society forever....Of course this double standard of morals is the result of opinions, created by men, broadcasted by men, for the benefit of men.

In his association with the average woman the average man has every advantage on earth. In 99 cases out of one hundred he knows much more about the ways of the world than she does....He knows how to present his case in a pleasing, plausible manner. He knows just what arguments to use which appeal most strongly to her emotions when he is trying to lower the bars erected by Society and the State to protect her. A man who does not practice self-control and is guided by no standards has the greatest possible advantage over a young woman...no matter how high the ideals of the girl herself may be.

To speak frankly with you, young men, for hundreds of years little or no effort was made to teach the boys in a family the daily necessity of self-control. The lesson of self-control was taught to nobody but girls. More than that, young men were impressed with the fact that if they practiced self-control it would endanger their health. They were simply warned, therefore, not to molest the girls who belonged in their particular class,...but they were given to understand that any girl beneath them was lawful prey. For hundreds of years, by tradition and custom, by precept and example, men were led to do many terrible things which made it exceedingly difficult for good women to preserve a high moral tone. For hundreds of years little effort was made to teach men how cruel and wicked it was for them to go through the world tempting women to break the laws made to protect the home and the State, and then holding these same women up to public obloquy, scorn and contempt after they had been induced to yield.

There are evil and designing women in the world whose chief aim in life seems to be to ensnare men. All women are not perfect, I am sorry to say....But even then it is far easier for a man to escape from the foils of such a woman than it is for a woman to escape from the foils of a man who is intent upon her ruin....No matter how much a young man might declare that he loves his race and wants to advance its interests, if by his word, deed, or influence, he did anything to blight the prospects of a single woman in the race in any way, shape or form, I would not believe a word he said.

Did it ever occur to you, young men, that a colored woman is the victim, not only of the evil men of her own race, but of the designing men of all the other races? In a large section of this land a man of the dominant race may misuse or abuse a colored woman in any way he sees fit without fear of being molested by the law. Personally I have never known a southern white man to be punished for committing any misdemeanor or crime against a colored girl he chose. Thousands upon thousands of colored women and girls have been the helpless victims of the southern white man's lust. If, therefore, the colored man has any sense of justice in his heart and cares anything about the welfare of his group, he will not only treat the women of his race with the respect which they deserve, but will protect and shield them in every way he can....In spite of the fateful heritage of slavery, in spite of the pitfalls laid not only by men of her own race, but of all the other races as well,...statistics compiled by men who would certainly not falsify in favor of our race show that immorality among colored women is not so large as among women similarly situated in at least five foreign lands.

The road which the average colored woman travels on her way to success and self-support is rough and thorny at best. The colored woman has a double burden to carry—the burden of race in addition to sex. White women all over the civilized world showed how heavy they thought was the burden of sex by the desperate efforts they made to secure suffrage. In spite of the obstacles to his progress, which the colored man has to surmount, after all the colored man has only one obstacle to impede his progress—the obstacle of race. Since the colored woman has two such heavy loads to carry...it behooves her brother to help her attain it in every way they can. And the best way for the young colored collegian to help the women of his race carry their heavy burdens and fulfill their destiny as wives, mothers, teachers and home keepers of his group is to treat the young women with whom he comes into daily contact with the respect which they undoubtedly deserve and which every gentleman shows a woman.

NOTE

1. Typescript with handwritten revisions. Mary Church Terrell Papers, Manuscript Division, Library of Congress, Washington, DC.

General Federation of Women's Clubs—Early 1920s, Various Convention Speeches

In the wake of winning the right to vote, club women inaugurated the process that redefined their place in American life. No longer excluded from voting, female volunteers and community activists crafted a new relationship with governing structures at the local, state, and federal levels—one rooted in their recently acquired right to act as enfranchised political citizens. The following speeches given in the early 1920s by members of the General Federation of Women's Clubs (GFWC) provide a glimpse into this transition. Formed in 1892, the GFWC served as an umbrella organization, which coordinated the thousands of women's clubs that sprang up in local communities throughout the country during the Progressive Era. The club movement attracted a wide array of women who addressed all sorts of issues in their communities and states.

Journalist Jane Cunningham Croly started the very first one, the Sorosis Club for Women in 1868, after she was denied entry to an all-male dinner in honor of Charles Dickens. In the following two decades, women's clubs proliferated. Club women campaigned for everything from better playgrounds for children to women's suffrage. When the GFWC was first established, it listed 500 clubs with over 100,000 members. By World War I, it had over one million.[1] More than a single-issue organization, the GFWC created six departments: Arts, Conservation, Education, Home Life, International Affairs, and Public Affairs.

The women who gave the following speeches did not gain national fame and did not leave much in the way of biographical records. The GFWC's own convention minutes listed many of their members by first initials and married surname only. Surely, additional research would yield more information, but in a sense the lack of such detail highlights one of the central aspects of women's public speech-making during the 1920s and much of the century. All sorts of "ordinary" women actively spoke in public to champion political causes without ever achieving notoriety. The speeches they left behind document the perhaps more typical account of women's public speech-giving: ever present and effective but not necessarily well known. Club women gave speeches that shaped public policy and galvanized constituents but did not make headlines or engender much controversy.

Primarily white, educated, middle- and upper-class women, GFWC members tended to marry and to enjoy economic privilege. Not required to support themselves, they were free to devote their skills and talents to volunteer activities. The GFWC, consistent with the worldview held by most of its members at the time, enacted racist and class-biased policies. For example, in 1900, Mary Church Terrell, "representing the National Association of Colored Women, was denied seating at a GFWC convention."[2] Prior to women's suffrage, the GFWC wielded powerful political weight, but as a pressure group rather than as, beginning in the 1920s, a body of individual, citizen voters. In the 1920s, the GFWC, never particularly radical, continued to define women's political role as distinct from men's and clearly linked to issues of home and hearth. It fell squarely into the "difference" camp within feminist ideology and it remained the largest women's organization in the country.

The five speeches included here illustrate the range of women's political concerns, the GWFC's efforts to redefine itself, and its quest to promote female involvement in the political process. Though expected to engage with the political process as women (mothers and wives with particular concerns and responsibilities), GFWC members did not retreat from the public stage. Rather, they continued to actively define and debate the critical issues of the day. The first speech addresses the topic of conservation; the second, home economics; the third, Pan-Americanism; the fourth, immigration; and the fifth, female citizenship. All of these speeches were given before members attending the Biennial Conventions of the GFWC between 1920 and 1926.

NOTES

1. Nancy Wolloch, *Women and the American Experience, A Concise History* (New York: McGraw-Hill, 1996), 187.
   2. Ibid., 189.

GENERAL FEDERATION OF WOMEN'S CLUB SPEECHES

Reprinted by Permission of the General Federation of Women's Clubs, Washington, DC

MRS. JOHN P. GOODING, CHAIRMAN FORESTRY DIVISION THE CONSERVATION DEPARTMENT'S FORESTRY PROGRAM (JUNE 22, 1920)[1]

Never has the need for the conservation of our forest resources been greater than now. Only one-fourth of our original forest area now remains in virgin timber and this is being cut and destroyed by fires and disease three times faster than it is being reproduced. Our forests are not being renewed. Each year there are thousands of acres of land made unproductive wastes, through destructive processes, adding to the many millions of acres already devastated.

The vitally essential conservation of our forests can be brought about by the adoption of a national forest policy providing for fire protection of national, state and privately owned forests, and for reforestation by national and state governments and also by private owners. The hopeful feature of the situation is the waking of the country to an understanding of it.

Tree Planting

If each club woman will take a personal interest in the conservation of the roadside shade trees and the planting of trees where it is necessary, the grand total of interest and effort would in a few years make of state highways beautiful avenues and enduring "roads of remembrance," as memorials to our soldiers and sailors.

"And this honor should not be confined to those who paid the supreme sacrifice. It should include, as far as possible, all those who entered the service of their country and who stood ready to back to the limit the cause of the United States and its allies."

We must study the condition and nature of our own localities. Almost every place has some need in forestry and can do something toward fulfilling that need to better the general conditions. Please join in this great forward movement for your state, so that it may be said of each one of us club women: "She has left the world more beautiful than she found it." Recommendations:

"Rally to the Cause of Forestry."

Work for a greater observance of Arbor Day and the care of trees after planting, national forestry policy and better fire protection; state, town and municipal forests as memorials and investment.

Urge reforestation of waste lands.

Plant memorial trees for "Roads of Remembrance."

Plant black walnut trees.

Aid the National Honor Roll, Memorial Trees.

"Stop feeding the waste basket."

"Stop paper waste; aid in saving our forests."

Urge the maintenance and extension of the Forest Service and forest purchases for preservation.

ADELAIDE STEELE BAYLOR
HOME ECONOMICS EDUCATION (JUNE 22, 1920)[2]

In the brief time following my arrival at this convention, I have listened with eagerness and conviction to the women of this country on a program that points unfalteringly and unquestionably to one institution as the saving grace, the power behind the throne, for the solution of problems of thrift, the welfare of children, the salvation of the adult. That institution is the American Home!

This query was once put to two children: "What is the beginning of a home?" The little girl quickly replied, "Furniture"; but the little boy studied a moment and then said gravely, "I think a mother is the beginning of a home." It sounds a little old and prosaic, doesn't it, and the modern woman is saying, and properly too: "A home is made through the right cooperation of all its factors"; but must we not still grant that the member of the family on whom we bestow the title of "home maker" is so vital to the development of the American Home, as it is now organized, that there is a great background of truth in the boy's reply?

What steps, then, are you taking to see that a functional program of education that trains for the work of home making is being set up and carried out in your communities?

True, home economics education has been a part of the school program for lo! these many years, and much splendid work has been accomplished, but a phase of education that is found in only one high school out of four, as was home economics in 1915, and has only one girl out of six enrolled in its classes, reaches so few people that a perceptible impression in the betterment of the 20,000,000 homes in this country would scarcely be in evidence.

Some of this work, to be sure, has been done in the elementary schools, but much of the work there has been disorganized, with little plant and equipment outside the large cities, untrained teachers, and rarely more than one to two hours per week allotted to it.

The past few years have demonstrated, as never before, the responsibility of home makers in national life, and in the scheme of reconstruction that is at hand their place will be second to none, as they establish the feeding, clothing, recreation, health, and thrift habits of the American people.

Such a tremendously important piece of work demands every facility for its development, and these are the pertinent questions for which every woman of the country should today be seeking a definite answer:

(1) Is there provision in the school program of my community that will bring to every girl training for home making?

(2) Does such training occupy a place on the school program that makes it stand to the pupil and the community as education, to the same degree as higher mathematics and foreign language?

(3) Is the subject matter based on an analysis of the home maker's job, so far as that can be determined at the present time, and thus made to include not only cooking, but all the term "foods" implies, not only sewing, but all the term "clothing" implies, as well as care of the health of the family, care of children, care of the sick, budgeting the income and the many other elements that must be brought to light by a careful analysis of what the home maker actually does?

(4) Is the subject really being taught as a vocation, and vocational contacts made through such avenues as the "home project"; and are the mothers in this community cooperating with the home economics teacher by allowing their homes to be used as laboratories in carrying out these projects?

(5) Are the wage-earning girls of my community,—part of that vast army of workers that constitute two-fifths of all the girls in the country between the years of 16 and 20,—having an opportunity to study home making in part-time classes, from four to eight hours a week?

(6) Are home-making evening classes open for girls and women who can, at no other time and in no other way, enlarge their fields of usefulness and add to their stature as home makers?

(7) Are all the agencies in the community that are available for training for home making being utilized, and are these agencies cooperating so there is no unnecessary duplication of work but the minimum of wasted time and energy?

If "Yes" is the answer to these questions, your community is contributing its largest share to the preservation of national life. If "No" is the answer to these questions, then it behooves you, as women and leaders in your community, to set about to modify conditions that the girls and women there may have, through your public schools, the kind of training that will best fit them for the great vocation of home making that will sooner or later come to from 80 to 90 per cent of their number, and is fundamental in begetting the citizenship essential to the life of a great democracy like America.

MRS. E. O. LEATHERWOOD
DEVELOPING BETTER UNDERSTANDING
AND FRIENDSHIP BETWEEN THE
PAN-AMERICANS (1924)[3]

Pan-America consists of the twenty-one American Republics. The territory extends from Canada to the southern-most point of South America. It includes one-sixth of the earth's land surface and 200,000,000 of its population. All types, races and classes are found among the people.

The great problem of each of these Republics is the molding of this heterogeneous population into a unified citizenship governed by and through representative democratic institutions. The success of this development depends upon the maintenance of peace among the Americas. The past stupendous development of the Americas has been due to the friendly relation of the governments of these Republics.

The time has arrived when there must be friendship between the citizens to insure lasting friendship between the governments. This friendship must be built on mutual understanding, respect and confidence. This can only come through acquaintance and knowledge.

One great means of developing such a friendship is through Exchange Pan-American Scholarships.

This is a field of peace service which the General Federation can well enter. It will be the lay women of the Americans clasping hands in friendship for where a mother sends her child there her heart goes, and those who are her child's friends become her friends. This organization could take up no work for peace that would be more far reaching in its influence. Shall not this Biennial direct the incoming board to organize a committee to develop this great work for maintaining peace and friendship among the citizens of Pan-America?

MRS. W. R. ALVORD
REPORT OF DEPARTMENT OF AMERICAN
CITIZENSHIP (1926)[4]

Madam President: I know of nothing that would induce the Department of Citizenship to give way for thirty minutes, excepting the desire to have the General Federation Maintenance Fund raised, or, at least, materially increased. It has been a pleasure, I assure you, to sit on the platform and listen to the funds come in.

No project in citizenship is so important at the present time as the arousing of men and women to an active participation in government affairs. Citizenship must begin in the home—it will when father and mother cease to be indifferent to their own citizenship obligations; citizenship must be taught in the public schools—no problem at all when teachers and school officials assume their citizenship responsibilities. An aroused citizenry will make "Get-Out-The-Vote" campaigns unnecessary, and will even solve the problem of law enforcement.

Church women must be made to understand that civic righteousness and religion go hand in hand. Business women must learn that success is easiest in those communities where local officials are honest and municipal affairs are on a business basis. College women must be taught that no courses in the foundation and history of free government can take the place of an active, conscientious interest in voting. Housekeeping women must learn that cleaning, cooking—all the mechanics of a home—are dependent upon the good citizenship which cleans streets, collects garbage, protects food sold in public places.

And men must come to realize the machinery of government is as important as the mechanism of their automobiles. "The average man," remarks Jesse Lee Bennett, "takes more interest in the brand of tire he puts on his car than in the caliber of the man he sends to high office." But developing better citizenship among women is our problem, though it may be our example is needed to make men better citizens.

The printed reports will convince you that notwithstanding the appalling statistics about the percentage voting at the last presidential election, club women do vote, are informing themselves on public questions, are developing a citizenship consciousness.

However, because of their knowledge of organization, and their experience in cooperating for community welfare, club women have a tremendous responsibility for the creating of a public opinion which will bring, not only the church, business, college and housekeeping women in a broader understanding of citizenship, but also to the foreign-born women and to women outside of organizations an understanding of citizenship facts and the relation of those facts to their own well-being.

Important as is the work among the foreign-born, club women must not fall into the error of thinking, as has happened in some states, that their whole citizenship duty is done if active Americanization work is being carried on. Native-born need instruction as well. Would you dare risk asking the members of the Ladies' Aid or the Bridge Club the same questions asked a class of alien women preparing to take out citizenship papers? When we are concerning ourselves with legislation having for its object the deportation of the foreign-born who, after a certain number of years, have not yet declared their intention of becoming citizens, ought we not to think out some punishment for those native-born who fail, year after year, to exercise the right of suffrage?

The truth is, the citizenship of the indifferent native-born and of the foreign-born must be the equal concern of club women. And what can be done to arouse these groups?

First, there should be established in every community a center or headquarters where citizenship facts are easily accessible, where any man or woman, native or foreign-born may learn, for instance, the method of marking a ballot; where impartial information relative to local issues may be given out; where there may be found lists of candidates with their qualifications.

So often it is assumed one knows countless details which he does not know at all; for example, where to pay taxes, what taxes pay for, where to complain about an ill-kept alley, where to register for voting. This center of information should not be just a club affair, but the League of Women Voters, the church societies, Rotary and Kiwanis clubs, the lodges should be invited to help. They are all patriotic, they mean to be good citizens and desire the best for the community. All that is needed is leadership to point the way. This is the club woman's opportunity and obligation.

These groups, once interested in the disseminating of citizenship facts, it will be but a step to the organization of a state Citizenship Council made up of representatives from a state organization having citizenship programs—a plan successfully tried in a few states.

The program of such a Council might include a state-wide Americanization program, plans for get-out-the-vote campaigns and community citizenship days. It might also devise some simple ceremony for welcoming into citizenship the foreign-born and the native sons and daughters as they attain the age of citizenship.

Next, we must face the fact that this government is a government by parties and much as we women prefer the nonpartisan aloof attitude, we shall not get far politically; we shall never enter into the inner councils of the politically elect where we can make our influence count for cleaner politics, unless we enter whole-heartedly into the parties.

A recent editorial commenting on the indifference toward the vote declares there is little enthusiasm because "the people are no longer invited to be players in the game. A cold duty is pointed out to them, and there is no fun in it." It used to be different, for, goes on the editorial, then "each Pooh-bah felt that it was he on whose sole arm hung victory, and he proceeded to work for it with all his might. He organized meetings and saw to it there were plenty of orators and still greater amounts of red fire. There were barbecues and other feasts. There were torchlight processions. Immense efforts were made to get the people to the polls. The result was that every voter felt he was part of the game, the tremendous game of capturing Congress and the White House for four years, a game well worth playing."

We may not desire to revive the past enthusiasms and floods of oratory, but surely we can call press meetings, have parades with bands and red fire if necessary and even hot coffee and sandwiches on occasion. In other words, we can try to evolve methods of putting new life into the parties and of rediscovering the personal touch.

Is it an indictment that red fire and music and food are needed to create an interest in citizenship! Not necessarily. It simply means that we are all friendly human beings and what is citizenship, if not making each one feel he is responsible for the welfare of the community? Once taking an active part in the community he will, in time, realize it is as important to him who sits in the White House and in the congressional seats, as who is mayor or commissioner of his home town.

The time has come when right-minded men will welcome women into the parties and we have only ourselves to blame that women who do not represent women and their interests have, in many instances, attained prominence politically.

Then when the campaigns are over and the tumult and shouting have died, the next job of club women is to follow up pre-election promises, and see to it that those officials who fail to keep those promises are made to pay the price at the next election. It must be made clear that a party platform is something to stand on after, as well as before, election.

Come then, Club Women of America, arouse yourselves. Concern yourselves less with Red in America and more with the "smug" indifference of the good people on your own street. Face yourself—are you the citizen you ought to be? Citizenship in America is so wonderful a thing. As Herman Hagedorn says, "American Citizenship means this: The opportunity to share in the most splendid adventure upon which any segment of mankind has ever set forth, upon a continent rich in beauty and abundant in resources; to take unto itself men of every land and every creed, every race and every social stratum and with them and of them build a nation and to create a people; drawn onward by a dream of government in which all shall share and under which all shall benefit, according to their gifts, their wisdom and their courage; a nation strong, just, and chivalrous; a people clean, generous, alert, granting to each the privilege of making his own life or marring it; of bearing high responsibilities, and, therefore, of growing; of developing within himself for the benefit of mankind that which differentiates him from all other creatures and which is, therefore, his holiest possession, his individuality; a people hating shams, loving beauty and true worth, knowing God and counting friendship as the corner stone of its national life. To have a part, to have even the smallest part in such an adventure is to hold a birthright such as no prince has ever possessed and no child of man shall outdream except at the gates of Heaven."

NOTES

1. Mrs. John P. Gooding, "The Conservation Department's Forestry Program," June 22, 1920, Fifteenth Biennial Convention, Convention Records 03-20401/4 1918–1924, Folder 0301-4-2, 336–337.

2. Adelaide Steele Baylor, "Home Economics Education," June 22, 1920, Fifteenth Biennial Convention, Convention Records 03-20401/4 1918–1924, Folder 0301-4-2, 336–337.

3. Mrs. E. O. Leatherwood, "Developing Better Understanding and Friendship Between the Pan-Americans," Seventeenth Biennial Convention, 1924, Los Angeles, Convention Records 03-20401/4 1918–1924, Folder 0304-4-4, 497.

4. Mrs. W. R. Alvord, "Report of the Department of American Citizenship," Eighteenth Biennial Convention, 1926, Atlantic City, NJ, Convention Records 03-20401/4 1918–1924, Folder 0304-4-4, 162–164.

Florence Ellinwood Allen
(1884–1966)

Florence Ellinwood Allen was the first woman to serve on the Ohio Supreme Court and the first woman appointed to the U.S. Court of Appeals. From 1934 until her 1959 retirement, and long after, Florence E. Allen was the highest-ranking female jurist in the United States.

Allen began her public life after receiving her BA and MA from Western Reserve University in Cleveland, Ohio.[1] Then, while a student at NYU law school, she worked as assistant secretary to Maud Wood Park, Executive Director of the College Equal Suffrage League. Allen delivered speeches on women's suffrage throughout the northeast, learning valuable lessons from her mentor. After graduating from law school, Allen returned to Cleveland and set up her own legal practice. In 1920, as soon as suffrage was official, Allen ran for and was elected judge for the Cuyahoga County Court of Common Pleas. She followed that with two more successful campaigns, in 1922 and 1928, for Associate Justice of the Ohio Supreme Court. Allen's 1928 campaign was notable for the breadth of its non-partisan support ranging from the Daughters of the American Revolution and the Women's Christian Temperance Union to the National Association for the Advancement of Colored People and organized labor. She also ran two unsuccessful campaigns for Congress in 1926 and 1932.

In addition to her political career, Allen was active in the international peace movement. One of her favorite speeches, delivered several times and reprinted here, advocated outlawing war. In 1925 she delivered the speech at the Conference on Causes and Cure of War, where she impressed Carrie Chapman Catt, who, though she disagreed with the concept of outlawing war, acknowledged Allen's influence and speaking ability.

Allen's biggest achievement, though, was still ahead. On March 23, 1934, her fiftieth birthday, Franklin Roosevelt appointed Allen to the U.S. Circuit Court of Appeals. This appointment is regarded by many as the second most significant achievement for women of the New Deal era after Francis Perkins's appointment to the President's cabinet. Molly Dewson and Eleanor Roosevelt lobbied aggressively for Allen's appointment. As a jurist, Allen's most noteworthy accomplishment was her 1937 landmark decision validating the Tennessee Valley Authority (TVA). Over the next twenty years her name was suggested for appointment to the U.S. Supreme Court twelve times, to three different Presidents—Roosevelt, Truman, and Eisenhower. Although she was a strong candidate, the barriers against women were even stronger, and her candidacy never materialized.[2]

Throughout her life, Allen had a reputation as a forceful and effective speaker, earning numerous invitations to speak at colleges and conferences and for women's organizations. Edward R. Murrow included her comments in his radio series, *This I Believe*. A number of Allen's speeches were published as speech texts or revised as journal articles or essays.[3] Perhaps her strongest speeches were those meant to inspire action, or commitment to a cause. These were the types of speeches Allen delivered as a young woman on behalf of women's suffrage. In a tribute to Allen, Emily Newell Blair made a case for Allen's credibility and authority as a woman. She described Allen's presence as calm and poised; warm but firm; passionate, but not emotional in the sense of being irrational. Allen's arguments were clear and consistent, not strategically adapted to various audiences; and she was always above partisan politics, working for the best interests of all citizens. In sum, said Blair, Allen "would do to serve as a model for a statue of the Motherhood of the Race."[4]

The following speech on outlawing war illustrates Allen's strength as a motivational speaker. Frances Parkinson Keyes praised Allen's effort in *Good Housekeeping* magazine, writing: "The final speaker of the afternoon was Judge Florence Allen....She possesses the 'gift of tongues' to an extraordinary degree, and held her audience spellbound from her first to her last word."[5] Powerful and emotional, this speech stands the test of time. Allen called for women's action to develop international laws making acts of war illegal, urging her largely female audience not to fall back into just a "cheer leading" role. She reminded her audience that emotions must be set aside so that the facts could be collected and understood. Allen argued that, although law itself would not stop war, "the first step in law enforcement is to declare the law." She ended with a story of two parents, a French mother and a German father, who lost sons in war. The example affirmed Allen's belief in the power of parental love for their children, and the power of women to do what is "everlastingly, eternally right." Clearly, this was the central rule by which Florence Ellinwood Allen tried to live her life.

NOTES

1. Biographical information and primary source material include, Florence Ellinwood Allen Papers, Manuscript Division, Library of Congress, Washington, DC; Florence Ellinwood Allen, *To Do Justly* (Cleveland: The Press of Case Western Reserve University, 1965); Jeanette E. Tuve, *First Lady of the Law: Florence Ellinwood Allen* (Lanham, MD: University Press of America, 1984); Beverly Blair Cook, "Florence Ellinwood Allen," in *Notable American Women*, Barbara Sicherman, et al. eds (Cambridge, MA: Belknap/Harvard University Press, 1980), 11–13.

2. See Tuve, *First Lady of the Law*; also Jerry N. Hess, "Oral History Interview with India Edwards, January 16, 1969" *Truman Presidential Museum and Library* (website and database) June 22, 2001: (www.trumanlibrary.org/oralhist/edwards1.htm)

3. See, for example, Judge Florence E. Allen, "Because Wars Unleash Demoralizing," in *Why Wars Must Cease*, Rose Young, ed. (New York: Macmillan, 1935), 99–118; Florence E. Allen, "Participation of Women in Government," *American Academy of Political and Social Science, Annals* (May 1947): 94–103; Florence E. Allen, "Human Rights and the International Court: The Need for a Juridical World Order," *American Bar Association Journal* 35 (September 1949); Florence E. Allen, "Nietzsche Stands Condemned," in *This I Believe*, Raymond Swing, ed. (New York: Simon and Schuster, 1954), 2–3.

4. Emily Newell Blair, "Americans We Like: Florence E. Allen," *The Nation* 125 (7 December 1927): 629.

5. Cited in Allen, *To Do Justly*, 76.

SPEECH ON THE OUTLAWRY OF WAR DELIVERED AT THE CONFERENCE ON CAUSES AND CURE OF WAR (JANUARY 18, 1925)

Reprinted by Permission of the Kelvin Smith Library, Cleveland, Ohio

Somewhat Condensed
[Introduction by the chairman, Mrs. Carrie Chapman Catt.][1]

Members of the participating organizations and friends: While I listened to the splendid expositions by the distinguished military officers, I have been wishing that I had the force and eloquence to take advantage of this opportunity to address delegates from such groups, from the American Association of University Women, those women who have had the training that a hundred years ago was denied to women the world over; from the Council of Women for Home Missions and the Federation of Women's Boards of Foreign Missions of North America, the women who believe that the ethics and philosophy of Christ ought to be put into practice in our daily life; from the General Federation of Women's Clubs, that splendid group which links together so many organizations with such a vast field of cultural and civic activity; from

the National Board of the Young Women's Christian Association, which benef-
icently directs the activity of the young womanhood of the entire nation; from
the national Council of Jewish Women, with such a heritage of law-making
behind them that they well may be proud and we may be well proud to have
them affiliated with us in this gathering; from the National League of Women
Voters, a league which includes in its membership many men, a league which
believes that every vote must be intelligently cast and that every woman and
thereby every man must be made an intelligent voter; from the National
Woman's Christian Temperance Union, that fighting group which first said
that the evil of the open saloon must go in America; and last but not least, the
National Women's Trade Union League, the group of women who do work
with their hands so well competing with labor in the open market that they
force the world to give them an honest living.

When we think of the ramifications of these organizations, their territorial
extent, the numbers which they represent, can we underestimate the power
which resides in this particular group? And, more than that, it is significant
that this is a group of women; but not because the war problem is primarily
a woman's problem; women suffer hideously in war and so do men; every
boy who lost his life in the World War had the greatest human right denied
him. We find these truths to be self-evident—that all men are endowed by
their Creator with certain inalienable rights, rights that cannot be taken
away, rights that cannot be given away—the right to *life*, liberty and the pursuit of happiness.

And we are here as a group to make a new Declaration of Independence,
to say that henceforth we will be independent of the curse of war; that we
hereby demand that the tyranny of the most colossal evil that the world has
ever seen shall cease. And, my friends, it is significant that this is a woman's
gathering because while men suffer with women in war and while men work
magnanimously with women to do away with war, as the presence of these
distinguished speakers evidences, the fact does remain that woman's task is
peculiar with regard to the abolition of war. We have to teach the human race
that ethical standards can be set up and maintained between nations as well
as between individuals. Women have to teach the coming generations that
the rules of right and wrong can be applied to every group, that there is no
situation in which the law of justice cannot and does not function if applied.
Women have to teach the coming race that this thing is not impossible; that
law can be substituted for the use of armed force in the settlement of international difficulties. In the long run, my friends, over and above and behind
and underneath all the plans which will be urged here for the cures of war,
and I probably am in accord with them all, the fact remains that you and the
women of the world who believe that this evil can and must be abolished,
have to go forth to change the conviction in men's minds that war is legal and
sanctioned and necessary; and that is primarily a task for women.

And then, too, women have another peculiar responsibility in this matter.
Women have within them that thing that Benjamin Kidd calls the power of
developing the emotion of the ideal, that power of working for something
which they see not, something which they only hope and dream will come
to pass. Thousands and thousands of women in this country joined the

ranks of those who demanded that liberty should be given to women as well as to men and died before we ever had the vote. That kind of spirit within women reaching out over the long years comes perhaps partly from our physical nature and partly from the long, sad training of the ages which has compelled us to achieve a masterly self-control. That power makes it possible for us to sacrifice and renounce and work for something which will not, immediately, be accomplished. And of course, my friends, in spite of advances which have been made in our lifetime in the peace movement, you and I know that it will be a long, hard process and that years and centuries will go by before the peace structure will finally reach the completion which we hope for it.

Now, this emotion of the ideal present in women makes us perhaps see with clearness certain fundamental facts, because we are looking forward not to a temporary advance but final consummation. We look forward to a great thing. Because of that perhaps we see more clearly certain practical aspects of the situation, and we wonder, as women, how it comes about that government spends so little money and such little effort for making peace and so much money and so much effort for making war. We say to ourselves that if centuries ago the finest minds had been gathered together to erect peace instead of to keep war machinery well oiled, perhaps by now the peace structure would have been built. We say to ourselves that if in 1500 A.D. the energies of the ages had been poured into substituting law for war the World War would never have been fought. And we say too that we demand substantial steps toward peace. We care little just how it is done. Women are not particular as to who does it; they are not particular as to who gets the honor of the achievement. They are not particular as to the name by which implementation of the peace movement is called, but women want war branded and made disreputable; they want its use made criminal; they want the sanction taken away from war, and they want the orderly, peaceful processes of enactment and adjudication substituted for war. They want, in a word, law, not war.

And just because we have within ourselves this mighty power, the emotion of the ideal, this power which is essential for winning causes as colossal even as this, we confront particular dangers. It has been said here in America since the women got the vote that we ought to be used mainly as a channel for engendering enthusiasm. And, my friends, creating enthusiasm is worthy for certain objects, but let us scrutinize the object. Let not these groups, let not these fine groups act as cheer leaders in a huge game in which they do nothing but the cheering.

And we face other pitfalls. I shall speak particularly of one this afternoon. It presents correlative dangers. We face the danger of thinking that we can help to do away with war without actual knowledge, and we face the correlative danger of thinking that we can be of no use in eliminating war unless we are experts. I shall first speak of the need of actual knowledge. We must not emotionalize. Every step we take; every measure we demand must be based upon our *knowledge of actual facts*.

Let me illustrate very simply with regard to the subject which is to be considered by you in the Conference, the codification of International Law.

Now, there are some people who think that the codification of International Law would have great weight in doing away with war, because they think that if law could be gathered together governing the conduct of nations, then, we would have laid the ground work for orderly adjudication of international disputes. If codify means to enact, then I agree that the codification of international law is very necessary; but codification in its usual sense, in the sense in which lawyers use it, does not mean to enact law. It means to make a compilation, to make an orderly, systematic assemblage of laws already existing. However, there is practically no important substantive international law existing and enforced by the courts with regard to the conduct of nations. Take the latest books on international law—Scott or Stowell or Munro, and look through those text books as to how courts have enforced international law, and you will look in vain for any case which has held any nation guilty of the crime of making deliberate, premeditated, aggressive war. You will look in vain for any case which finds any nation guilty of stealing, guilty of extortion, or guilty of oppressive acts to other nations. I may perhaps see the lack of such decisions more than some other people because of my legal experience. I have presided in a number of murder trials, and sometimes I ask myself how, when I was sitting in a trial court, I could ever have impaneled a jury, or how the jury could have convicted the accused, or how the accused could have been sentenced by the court, if there had been no law making murder a crime.

I wish to explain here very simply what to me the phrase, outlawry of war, means. It does not mean that the enactment of law making war a crime will of itself prevent war. I believe in securing peace by all means, and I do not pin my faith to one method only, but, my friends, how can we enforce a law before we declare the law? The first step in law enforcement is the declaration of the law. You lay down a moral basis upon which you begin to enforce moral law. And, my friends, I repeat that I do not believe that the mere enactment of law making war a crime would, of itself, stop war; but I am at a loss to understand how the world court or the Hague court or any tribunal which is constituted can brand the making of war illegal and disreputable so long as we recognize and tolerate and sanction the making of war. In other words, what the world needs in addition to machinery for enforcement, in addition to the world court, in addition to some kind of permanent continuously-operating international organization, is to declare moral law as applicable between the nations. The world needs to lay down a ten commandments between the nations: "Thou shalt not war; thou shalt not steal; thou shalt not oppress."

And by whom can this law be laid down? It can be laid down by treaty. It can be laid down by conference; it can be laid down by the League of Nations.

Other laws must follow, the law defining crimes between nations just as those crimes are defined between individuals. Suppose you were to cut out of the law of New York State, or Ohio, or California, the laws making murder and arson, rape and burglary crimes; as a result the whole bottom would drop out of the moral fabric of the state; you would lose the very basis upon which all law is built. The first step in law enforcement is to declare the law.

This law could be declared by the League Court or the world court, if they could lay down the law.

Now, in an arbitration legal or ethical principle is not laid down. Arbitration simply decides the case. It decides who wins, but not who is right or wrong. The League Court is bound by a similar provision in the statute creating it. Article 59 of the statute states, "The decision of the court has no binding force except between the parties and in respect to that particular case."

And so, my friends, the League Court cannot lay down law. I believe in adhering to the League Court because it can interpret law; because it can adjudicate cases which come within its jurisdiction, but we shall have to have law, not codified but enacted, declaring the primary crimes between nations before we can properly go forward to enforce that law. Sometimes when I think of the task which has been demanded, the thing that we have asked of the World Court, and the Hague Court, and the League of Nations—to ask them to prevent war, when up to this time in the history of the whole so-called Christian world, the whole civilized world has tolerated and sanctioned war,—it seems to me that we have been asking an impossible thing. The sanction must be taken away from war before we can enforce provisions against war.

And now, the women of this country demand that this be done; they demand that war shall no longer be sanctioned; they demand that the use of war as a means of settling international disputes be abolished; they demand that other methods of settling international controversies be adopted. Some people say this is impossible. Why, my friends, human history shows that this is the next step in our social development. There was such a thing as war between individuals. There was private warfare between individuals; private warfare has been abolished. There was warfare to determine legal questions. Men used to go out and fight to determine the titles of land in what was called the "wager of battle." That has been abolished. The duel which clung so long and so persistently has gone with the advance of civilization. Shall we say that men, men who swim beneath the sea in boats and who climb the sky in airplanes, are incapable of applying to themselves in groups the same law which they applied to themselves as individuals?

Now, I want just a second before I close to speak to you of the other danger which we face, the danger that we shall think we know too little to assist in solving this problem. I was interested to read the other day the account of a speech made by a distinguished officer for whom I have the highest regard. He said that pacifism in the United States was rampant because of the "women's insatiable desire to mix in things which they do not understand." He said that we do not understand war because war is a question of mathematics and of science. Of course, I do not know whether this distinguished officer said what is ascribed to him, but the fact remains that that view exists. It is true that science does go into the making of war. I could not calculate the trigonometric formulae which are said to be necessary to the direction of the shots from one of our great modern guns; I think very few men could. Science, of course, governs all of the laws of chemical specifications; science governs military tactics; science must always come into play when war is made, but the question of keeping out of war, the question of maintaining peace, the question of establishing peace is not a question of science and mathematics; it is a question of establishing moral principles between nations as law, enforceable as law, and that is a thing which is not a question of the parabola or the momentum or the velocity of a gun shot.

And then, on the other hand, there are some people who think we cannot help to establish peace because there is so much to know about the peace question. If we are to understand everything with regard to the workings of the League of Nations, to the treaty relations considered and acted on by the Senate; with regard to the World Court, and the workings of the Pan-American Union, we shall have to have some expert knowledge; we must have much more expert knowledge than we have. No woman's club or organization in this country ought to go further without having one member, a committee of one, to read the substantial proceedings of the League of Nations documents, to keep in touch with things that are going on in the Senate, to be posted upon our relations, particularly with South America and Central America and the Caribbean, and to report back to her own club. But after all, the basic policies which underlie the making of peace are not difficult of comprehension. Any ordinarily intelligent person can understand them. In fact, never until the ordinary person, the non-expert voter is taken into the confidence of the peace expert, never until that time can America take her place among the leaders in the peace movement of the world.

I remember there was a great meeting held once at the Masonic Hall in Cleveland at which Mrs. Catt spoke. Will Erwin had told us what would happen to the world in the next world war; that war would be directed against the whole civilian population; that the advance of chemical warfare would make the next war something undreamed of. Mrs. Catt had some scholarly address to make, and instead of making it she threw down her manuscript and came down into the center of the stage and called upon the women of the United States to end war. That call we are still hearing. I suppose I have quoted one hundred times something which she said that night. We don't always have Mrs. Catt with us in Ohio so we have to quote her. She said, "The women in this room can do this thing; the women in this room can do this thing." And when she said that she said something truer than she knew. For Mrs. Catt had seen just such a movement grow from a meeting in a little room; she had seen the woman suffrage movement start when women had no training, no education, no money, nothing but the inherent rightness of their cause; she had seen it sweep over the whole civilized world in her lifetime. The women in this room can do this thing; the women in this room can do anything which is right and just, my friends. Think of the colossal absurdity that we should have lived to this year of our Lord, 1925, and the slogan for nations during all this time until very recently has been, "The State can do no wrong." We have to change that slogan; we have to write new laws; we have to say, "The State shall do no wrong." And that thing can be done for America by the women in this room. We have mighty odds against us; we have mighty interests and mighty powers against us; we have something, on the other hand, to inspire us. The boys, you know, went out and met six times their number in the day of the first advance, six times their number of the crack troops of Europe, and sent them reeling back in their tracks. They fought for a number of things, but they fought principally because they thought that war would end war. If we have any conception of their sacrifice we will never let that standard fail; we will make this war the war which did end war.

All over the world the forces of human affection are working with us. Sometimes I get upset over the international situation, but I heard something this summer which I intend to keep before me as a symbol of the hope we have. A friend of mine did war work in Italy and France and Germany, and has all the decorations that it is possible to have. This summer she visited all her little villages and she personally investigated and proved that the incident occurred which I am about to tell. At Mont Faucon in France, which was so shelled that nothing but a remnant was left of the town when the Armistice was signed, a man came and knocked at the door of a little cottage. A woman came to the door and he asked if she was the woman of the house. He spoke a queer kind of French but she understood him. She said, "Yes," and he said, "Perhaps you won't want to talk to me because I am German." She said, "Go on, Monsieur." He said, "I had a son who was killed in the war. He was killed near here and buried somewhere near here; I came over as early as I could to hunt for his grave and I could not find it. I thought perhaps I could find some cottage where I could stay all night and go on in the search, but probably because I am a German you won't want me to stay."

And then she answered, "Monsieur, I had a son who was killed in the war, killed fighting for France; your son was killed fighting under orders, and I suppose he was killed doing what he thought was right; shall anyone say that as between a father who lost his son in battle, and a mother who lost her son in battle there is a gap that cannot be bridged? Come in Monsieur, and stay this night." I do not know how many of us could rise to that height. The great forces of human affection, the great love of fathers and mothers for their children the world over and fighting this battle. The women in this room can do this thing; they can do it because it is everlastingly, eternally right. There is no situation in the world in which the rules of right and wrong cannot function. There is no group in the world to which the laws of right should not apply, and you and I have to face this problem in the Conference and go out to teach the race that we will have law, not war.

NOTE

1. Florence Ellinwood Allen, *To Do Justly* (Cleveland: Case Western Reserve University, 1965), 153–162.

Ruth Muskrat Bronson
(ca. 1897–1982)

Ruth Muskrat Bronson was a Cherokee born in Indian Territory. In her youth she was active in the YWCA and represented North American Indians at the 1922 International Volunteer Conference in Peking (Beijing). She attended the Carlisle Indian School in Pennsylvania and the University of Oklahoma, then graduated from Mt. Holyoke College, and later pursued graduate studies at George Washington University in Washington, DC.[1]

After college, she worked for the Bureau of Indian Affairs. Much of her work there involved developing higher educational opportunities for Indian students. In 1944, she published *Indians Are People, Too*. Her main theme in the book is the need for Indian youth to gain positive role models—models of Indian leadership—through access to accurate depictions of traditional Indian culture and historical Indian leaders. She wrote:

Washakie, Crazy Horse, Sequoyah, Pope, Sacajawea, Chief Joseph, Samson Occum—these are names that belong in the building of Indian history, these and many more. Through those heartbreaking years of defeat and war, and back beyond, they gleam like priceless jewels in a diadem of many jewels.[2]

Bronson participated in Indian social movements such as the opposition to termination of federal trusteeship in the 1950s, serving as executive secretary of the National Congress of American Indians. She feared indigenous cultures would be lost through assimilation, and published on that topic in the 1950s.[3]

Her career as a writer began, however, in the 1920s. The essay "What Is Happening to the Indians" was published in 1929. In that article Bronson

Ruth Muskrat Bronson presents President Coolidge with a copy of *The Red Man in the United States*.

Library of Congress, Prints & Photographs Division, [reproduction number, LC-USZ62-107775].

spoke of the pressure placed on Indian peoples within the United States and communicated a sympathetic vision of Indian character in the face of that pressure. She wrote, "We are expected to revolutionize completely our civilization within the space of a few decades—a process which has taken other peoples centuries to effect." But, she claimed, "somehow the Indian character has remained essentially the same, adjusting itself to changing conditions with calm and dignity whenever possible, and raising up a new leadership to face each strange and bewildering era."[4]

The speech excerpted here was given in 1927. In it, the roots of her anti-termination, anti-assimilation stance are apparent in her admiration for Sequoyah, the originator of the Cherokee alphabet. Bronson viewed Sequoyah as an exemplar of the patience, courage, calm, and dignity that surviving as a culture would continue to require of her people and other indigenous peoples in North America.

NOTES

1. Bronson is the subject of at least one doctoral dissertation, and her work is commonly included in the syllabi of courses on American Indians/Native Americans. See Gretchen Grace Harvey, *Cherokee and American: Ruth Muskrat Bronson* (Ph.D. dissertation, Arizona State University, 1996).

2. Ruth Muskrat Bronson, *Indians Are People, Too* (New York: Friendship Press, 1944).

3. See, for example, "Ruth Muskrat Bronson Criticizes the Proposed Termination of Federal Trusteeship, 1955," in *Major Problems in American Indian History*, Albert L. Hurtado and Peter Iverson, eds. (New York: D.C. Heath, 1994), 492–494.

4. Ruth Muskrat Bronson, "What Is Happening to the Indians," *The Woman's Press* 23 (June 1929): 3991.

EXCERPT FROM "MISS MUSKRAT'S ADDRESS ON THE NORTH AMERICAN INDIAN" IN *THE AMERICAN INDIAN* (FEBRUARY 1927)[1]

Another kind of hero, but no less a great one, is Sequoyah, who dared to accomplish the task he set for himself in spite of the jeers of the very people who should have been the first to encourage him.

He was a comparatively young man when he first conceived his dream of a Cherokee alphabet. He had been a very skillful warrior and a very popular youth among his tribesmen. But when he left off these lesser things to follow the path of his great dream he lost his popularity. Oftentimes that is the price a dreamer has to pay if he would make his dreams come true.

Sequoyah's friends jeered at him and called him a fool. Even his wife declared him to be crazy or possessed by a devil. Then one day, at the end of those ten years, his wife in a rage of impatience with this husband whom she could not understand, burned all of his manuscripts and his records, the fruits of ten hard years of patient labor. In the face of even this devastating calamity, Sequoyah did not give up.

He started all over again, and this time with such earnestness that at the end of three years he had his alphabet completed much more perfectly than it had ever been before. It is said that no alphabet in all the history of mankind is more perfect than this invented by one Indian man, and that any

Cherokee who speaks this language may learn to read and write it in four or five hours of hard study.

Sequoyah's struggles were not ended with the completion of his alphabet. The first thing he did was to teach his little daughter to read; and then the whole tribe began to cry out that he had bewitched his own child and that both of them must be burned at the stake. There was a long trial by the members of the council, and at last it was decided to call in some of the younger warriors from a neighboring town to sit in judgement of this man who had just offered such a priceless gift to his people. "For," said the old chief, "it may be that he is inspired by the Great Spirit and not by the evil ones."

The young men sat in judgement. They proposed as a test that Sequoyah should teach his jurors to read and write his alphabet. He had only a few hours allowed him for this great task but he succeeded, and in this way the Cherokee alphabet was given to the world. What a heritage of perseverance his life is for all of us Indians who belong to this generation! What a vision for us to follow! What an example of patience and courage.

NOTE

1. *The American Indian* 1 (February 1927): 2–3, 15; an excerpt is posted at (www.anpa.ualr.edu/f_sequoyah.htm).

Nannie Helen Burroughs
(1879–1961)

Nannie Helen Burroughs, standard-bearer for the African American working class, especially women, was a powerful advocate for racial equality, and an effective leader in organizing institutions for self-help in the black community. A renowned orator, tall with a strong voice, Burroughs was able to move her largely black audiences to act, through arguments built on hard evidence, combined with passionate appeals to justice and moral rectitude.

In 1896 Burroughs graduated with honors from the M Street, or Colored High School in Washington, DC. Her speech, "How the Sisters Are Hindered From Helping," delivered at the organizational meeting of the Women's Convention Auxiliary to the National Baptist Convention in 1900, marked her as a leader. She was corresponding secretary for that group from 1900 to 1947. In 1918 she was elected president and served until her death in 1961.[1]

Meanwhile, after working as a bookkeeper, stenographer, and secretary to various organizations, in 1909 Burroughs founded and was named president of the National Training School for Women and Girls, later renamed the National Training and Professional School for Women and Girls. The purpose of this school was to provide educational opportunities for black women regardless of their social class or political affiliation. The curriculum focused on preparation for office or domestic work. Burroughs founded the National Association of Wage Earners (NAWE) in 1920, a somewhat short-lived reformist organization also devoted to helping train people for service related jobs.[2]

From the early 1920s to around 1932, the year of Roosevelt's election, Burroughs was an active member of the Republican Party, sought out

Nannie Helen Burroughs, President, National League of Republican Colored Women.

Library of Congress, Prints & Photographs Division, Nannie Helen Burroughs Collection, [reproduction number, LC-USZ62-99117].

especially for her effectiveness as a speaker. In 1924, the National League of Republican Colored Women (NLRCW) was formed, and Burroughs was named president. A strong supporter of women's suffrage, Burroughs was concerned that white women were not taking African American women seriously. Thus, in 1926, the executive committee of the NLRCW developed a resolution stating its goals, which they sent to Sallie Hert, Vice-Chair of the Republican National Committee (RNC) and head of its Women's Division. Hert responded by inviting Burroughs to speak at the first national meeting of Republican women in 1927.[3] This was an important achievement for Burroughs, who fought to gain the respect of her white Republican counterparts.

Initially elated at Hoover's 1927 victory, Burroughs's optimism was dispelled when she learned that the Republicans planned segregated inaugural celebrations for Hoover. She continued to be an active speaker for civil rights and racial pride, however. In 1933, her fiery speech in which she condemned "Uncle Toms" as worse than white bigots, and exhorted black men to work harder and black women to maintain their moral rectitude, was reprinted in a number of black newspapers.[4] After World War II, as the civil rights movement was developing, Burroughs argued that citizens of color needed to keep pressuring "the Anglo-Saxon" for dignity and justice.[5]

The speech that follows is Burroughs's celebration of Hoover's victory over Democrat Al Smith in the 1927 presidential election. Burroughs had been active in the campaign as one of the most sought after speakers appointed by the RNC to their National Speaker's Bureau.[6] Thus, it is not surprising that the speech began on a partisan note. She argued that blacks voted Republican because the platform, the candidate, and the campaign were superior to the Democrats. However, as the speech continued, Burroughs offered specific suggestions for change that were overtly nonpartisan, and ultimately asserted that the "only hope for a semblance of even handed justice for the Southern Negro is in a two-party government." In the end, though, Burroughs returned to her opening point that, for African Americans in 1927, Republicans offered the strongest platform and the most qualified presidential candidate. Throughout the speech, her language is characteristically bold and colorful as she celebrated victory, and called on the "Negro" to keep fighting for racial equality.

NOTES

1. Nannie Helen Burroughs Papers, Manuscript Division, Library of Congress, Washington, DC; Juanita Fletcher, "Burroughs, Nannie Helen," *Notable American Women*, Barbara Sicherman, Carol Hurd Green, eds. (Cambridge, MA: Belknap Press, 1980), 125–127.

2. Sharon Harley, "Nannie Helen Burroughs: 'the black goddess of liberty,'" *The Journal of Negro History* 81 (1996): 62–72; Lolita C. Perkins, "Nannie Helen Burroughs: A Progressive Example for Modern Times," *Affilia* 12 (1997): 233–4.

3. Evelyn Brooks Higginbotham, "In Politics to Stay: Black Women Leaders and Party Politics in the 1920s," in *Women, Politics, and Change*, Louise A. Tilly and Patricia Gurin, eds. (New York: Russell Sage Foundation, 1990), 210–11.

4. *The Black Dispatch*, Oklahoma City, OK, 23 December 1933, a copy is included in the Nannie Helen Burroughs Papers, Manuscript Division, LOC; *The Louisiana Weekly*, 23 December 1933, an abridged version is printed in *Black Women in White America: A Documentary History*, Gerda Lerner, ed. (New York: Pantheon Books, 1972), 551–553.

5. See Higginbotham, *Righteous Discontent: The Women's Movement in the Black Baptist Church, 1880–1920* (Cambridge: Harvard University Press, 1992); and L. H. Hammond, *In the Vanguard of a Race* (New York: Council of Women for Home Missions and Missionary Education Movement of the United States and Canada, 1922).

6. Higginbotham, "In Politics to Stay," 211.

WHAT THE NEGRO WANTS POLITICALLY (1928)[1]
You Heard about the Election

The Democratic Party is pretty well banged up! The Republican Party is all set up. It was a landslide! It was a political miracle! It is a waste of time trying to explain how it happened. It got started and nobody could stop it.

Now that a grand and glorious victory has been achieved in the name of Righteousness, let no group or race try to hog the victory. We cannot say that this great victory is attributable to any one source. "Take your share."

Of course the "Wiseacres" will say, "I told you so," and then proceed to tell how it all happened. The job-seekers will say, "I did it. With my bow and arrow, I killed 'Cock Smith.'" So over against what they put down as the "How and the Why," please do not allow them to overlook the real factors that gave to the Republican Party an unprecedented victory.

1st   The strength of the platform

2nd   The superior fitness and sanity of the candidates

3rd   The efficiency of the Hoover organization

4th   The perfection of the radio

5th   The power of the press

6th   The service of the "Spell-Binders"

7th   The horse sense of the electorate

8th   The Democratic Party that unwittingly ran a showman instead of a statesman. He woke them up and brought them out.

9th.   And above all, millions of women who talked Herbert Hoover up and talked Al Smith out.

Despite the fact that the campaign was begun on an elevated platform from which the American people were to discuss their ideals, hopes, and dreams in terms and promises of prosperity, projects, protection and peace, it ended in a fight on the sidewalks of New York, over rum, race, and religion.

The injection of the race issue into the campaign raised two questions—

First—Did many Negroes bolt the Republican Party? No. It is true that a larger number of colored people voted the Democratic ticket this year than at any time since they have had the franchise. There were two reasons:

(a) The race is actually chafing under national injustice and the Republican Party is justly charged with some "sins of omission" and dereliction of a patriotic duty.

(b) Tammany Hall helped finance the Democratic Party, and Tammany Hall bids for Negro votes because it needs them and it knew that in order to help the Democratic Party win, they would have to have a large defection of Negro votes. They did not get the large defection and Tammany Hall was kicked from the side walk into the sewer and the Democratic Party, which is the "solid South" was smashed to pieces and "all the king's horses and all the king's men" will never put the "solid South" together again.

The Republican Party cannot sweep this country without the Negro's vote. Oh, yes, it is said, they can but try it—"It can't be did."

Secondly—What does the Negro want politically? He wants his rights as an American citizen and not simply jobs for a few politicians. That's what he wants.

Thirdly—He wants general relief from demoralizing evils, rather than personal rewards for party fealty. He, will therefore, calls upon the Republican Party to—

1. Enforce the Constitution and all of its amendments.

2. Compel the Interstate Commission to make the railroads operating in "Jim Crow" states provide equal accommodations for the races on the trains and in the waiting rooms. The railroads are guilty of highway robbery. They charge Negroes first-class fares and give them cattle accommodations.

3. Break up segregation in the Departments at Washington.

4. Appoint a National, Non-partisan, Bi-racial Welfare Commission whose duty it will be to make unbiased investigations and practical suggestions that will give relief from:

    (a) Disfranchisement.

    (b) Unequal accommodations in travel.

    (c) Segregation in Federal Departments.

    (d) Race discrimination in Civil Service appointments.

    (e) Discrimination in relief work in times of floods and disasters.

    (f) Unequal opportunity, in times of peace, to learn the arts of war in army, navy, and aerial service.

5. Appoint two colored women, specialists, to work in the Children's Bureau and the Woman's Bureau, the former for child welfare and the latter for industrial and economic welfare among women. Both positions would require highly trained women and their work among colored women and children would parallel the work that is being done by the heads of these two bureaus, primarily for white children and women and incidentally, for colored children and women. Conditions and needs among the children and women of the Negro race justify these appointments.

Politicians need not try to further deceive the Republican Party by trying to make them believe that a recordership, registership, ministership, assistantship, or any of the usual "sop" appointments will ever be accepted by the Negro race as substitutes for simple justice and equal opportunity. At the proper time and in the proper way the men and women who are seeking relief for the masses from the injustices herein listed, will prepare their case, secure the backing of every Negro organization, political and non-political, and lay their petition before Congress and the Chief Executive and seek and work for redress.

In preparation for more effective action, the Negroes throughout the country should keep all of their clubs intact, hold regular meetings, carry on a campaign of education and enlightenment and thereby build up a vigorous morale and be ready for the "fire-works" four years from now.

The best advice to give our people, politically, is organize and keep organized, study men and measures, put down every "sin of omission, or commission," get every congressman's number—know what he is saying and how he is voting, and "meet him at Philippi." At the same time do not forget to repudiate all of the Negro political leaders who drag around begging for jobs for themselves and never contending for justice and opportunities for the race. They are more responsible for our political undoing than the whites. Do not let them out.

There is one thing that we do not want to see again—"Jim Crow" National Republican Headquarters. We had three. Ye gods, what next?—a duplication of machinery, a place for Negroes to disagree on everything from the personnel and the modus operandi to the postage stamp and sheet of paper, which they cannot get without an order.

We are calling upon the Republican Party to break up segregation in the Departments in the same breath we ask the National Republican Committee—the machine which puts the Party in power—to give us three "Jim Crow" headquarters.

Four years are not too long to work and wait. The smashing victory in Kentucky was due to the Negro vote. The breaking up of the "solid South," regardless of whether we believe it now or not, and the building up of a two-party government in the South is a move in the right direction. As long as the South remains a government of white men, by white men, and for white men instead of a government of the people, by the people, and for the people, the Negro will never enjoy his rights as an American citizen nor receive anything like just consideration in the distribution of funds from the taxes which he pays for public education, protection and general welfare.

With the ballot in his hand he has a weapon of defense, protection, and expression. Both parties will need his vote and he will learn to use it wisely.

Regardless of the cost to the Negro race of a few offices which we have held in the South as political rewards for party fealty, the gain to the race and to the Negroes of the South in a two-party government will be worth transcendently more than all the jobs which are given a few Negro politicians who have not been able and who would never be able to build up a Republican Party in the South and thereby deliver their race from political bondage. Only one Negro, Bob Church has really been able to build up a fighting organization.

The only hope for a semblance of even handed justice for the Southern Negro is in a two-party government. It is an American ideal and without two parties this country is not a democracy. It is half democracy and half oligarchy. On with the two-party government in the South or out with some of the representatives in Congress who ride into office on the backs of Negroes whom they use as political ponies.

Since the Negro vote helped the Republican Party win the 1928 victory, the question has been asked again and again, what does it profit the Negro to give his vote to keep the Republican Party in power? Here is the answer. With all its faults it is the better party. In this campaign the Negro voted against Democratic ideals for his race, against tampering with the Constitution, against an increase of the emigration quota, against tinkering with the tariff, against a man who is not qualified to be President of the United States. The Negro simply voted for the strongest platform and the better qualified man.

The Negro gave his vote to Herbert Hoover, because Mr. Hoover stood foursquare on the strong platform of the Republican Party and pledged equal opportunities to all, regardless of faith or race. The American Negro asks nothing more and will be satisfied with nothing less.

NOTE

1. Typescript with handwritten revisions. Nannie Helen Burroughs Papers, Manuscript Division, Library of Congress, Washington, DC.

Gertrude Simmons Bonnin (Zitkala-Sa, Red Bird) (1876–1938)

Gertrude Simmons Bonnin's life began on the Yankton Sioux Agency, a Native American reservation in South Dakota. Like many children, she attended a Quaker missionary school in her youth, but as an adult after completing college, she returned to reservation life as an activist for Indian rights (1902–1938). Though at age eight, she begged her mother to let her "ride on the iron horse...to see the wonderful land of the East" promised by the Quaker missionaries who came to recruit children for the school in Wabash, Indiana, she found the acculturation process quite painful and soon longed to return home.[1] But she no longer fit so neatly into her "old world." She decided to continue her education at Wabash, and then, after graduating from Earlham College, she became a teacher herself at Pennsylvania's Carlisle Indian School (1897–1899). From there, she pursued her love of the violin at the New England Conservatory in Boston. Though she enjoyed her studies, she felt moved to return to the reservation. She hoped to reconcile her two worlds and to find some way to improve the lives of those she had left behind.

Upon her marriage to Raymond Bonnin in 1902, she relocated to the Unitah and Ouray Reservation in Utah. A few years later, while still teaching, she joined the Society of American Indians, commencing her career as a reformer from which she never turned back. From the 1910s on, Bonnin acquired increasing responsibility as well as leadership positions in some of the most powerful national Indian organizations. Her election as secretary of the Society for Indian Affairs in 1916 brought her to Washington, DC, where she spent the rest of her life. An ardent advocate for Indian rights, she labored ceaselessly in the halls of Congress to dismantle the

Gertrude Simmons Bonnin, 1921.

Library of Congress, Prints & Photographs Division, [reproduction number, LC-USZ62-119349].

corrupt power of the Bureau of Indian Affairs and to create more just federal policies. In her travels to the reservations to survey Native American life, she could barely stand witnessing the daily poverty and oppression she encountered. With vivid language, hard data, and passionate persistence, she testified over and over before Congress to demand social justice and economic reform. Her greatest success was the passage of the Indian Citizenship Bill in 1924. When the Society for American Indians disbanded in 1926, she founded the National Council of American Indians

(NCAI) and served as its president. A strong advocate for self-governance, she allowed only Indians to be members of the NCAI. Throughout the 1930s, she continued to agitate for Native American rights as a lobbyist, investigator, spokesperson, and writer.[2]

Speaking before the Indian Rights Association in 1928, Bonnin detailed her response to the Meriam Report, a report she had instigated. Though not completely satisfactory to Bonnin, this report, unlike many government documents, portrayed Native Americans in a sympathetic light and provided empirical data to document their ill treatment and the dire economic conditions they faced. In her summation and response to the report, Bonnin placed the blame for these conditions squarely at the feet of the Bureau of Indian Affairs. Whereas the Meriam Report faulted the federal government for not supplying enough funds to the BIA, Bonnin held the agency directly responsible for both shaping policy and for its poor administration. She was especially outraged at the BIA's campaign to discredit the Meriam Report and to label critics of the Bureau disloyal to the United States. The Meriam Report and Bonnin's speech reflect the shape of the national debate taking place in the 1920s regarding Native American policy. Most Americans and federal officials supported policies of assimilation, but some early advocates had begun to argue for self-rule and the preservation of Native American ways of life.

NOTES

1. Zitkala-Sa, "The School Days of an Indian Girl," *Atlantic Monthly* 85 (February 1900): 186.

2. For biographical information, see Gertrude Simmons Bonnin, "An Indian Teacher Among Indians," *Atlantic Monthly* 85 (March 1900): 386; Linda K. Kerber and Jane Sherron De Hart, *Women's America*, 4th ed. (New York: Oxford University Press, 1995), 265; and *New York Times*, 27 January 1938, 21.

SPEECH BEFORE THE INDIAN RIGHTS ASSOCIATION, ATLANTIC CITY (1928)[1]

The opportunity to speak today in a conference discussing the report of the Indian survey made by the institute for Government Research is appreciated by this Indian speaker.

At the outset, permit me to explain that I did not learn English in the government Indian schools. I attended Earlham College, Richmond, Indiana. A brief sketch of my activities is given in *Who's Who in the Nation's Capital*, 1927.

I have the honor to be president of the National Council of American Indians, an all-Indian organization based upon citizenship rights granted by Congress June 2, 1924.

Before that, Indians were jailed if they held meetings without permission from a superintendent.

The National Council of American Indians was created by the Indians themselves and I was elected to office, which carries no pay whatsoever. I devote my whole time to its work and never have I sought any personal benefit.

The Indian's American citizenship has been dearly bought by repeated self sacrifices, until his unsurpassed loyalty and volunteer service in the World War won this recognition from Congress.

Many times, standing by the grave of the Unknown Soldier, I have felt that it may be an Indian boy, who bravely fought and heroically died for the principles of democracy, who lies there now.

Positively, no one on earth can honestly challenge the American Indian's loyalty to the government of the United States, though this government has waged more wars upon its Indian wards than any other nation against its own subordinate peoples.

There is a distinction between "government" and "servants of the government." Whenever an Indian complains of unfaithful servants of the government and the maladministration of his affairs, he is heralded as "disloyal to the government" from certain quarters. This is untrue.

This preliminary is made necessary today in refutation of false charges uttered on the floor of the House by Congressman Crampton of Michigan on December 11, 1928, against the National Council of American Indians. Mr. Crampton inserted in the *Congressional Record* a portion of a letter, which he misquoted as follows:

According to an Indian's statement and from my own personal observations, the Indians are very poor and hungry. They have no voice in their affairs. They are neglected. Whether sick or well, whether young or old, most of them or nearly all of them live in bad houses, wearing rags, and with little or no food. Their complaints to government officials go unheeded. Agents' offices are locked against the Indians most of the time.

And so forth ad nauseam.

Mr. Crampton described it as the "character of propaganda used to poison the judgment of the country against their own government." Yet before Mr. Crampton concludes his speech defending the Indian Bureau and the Budget Bureau for lack of adequate appropriations, and denying the disgraceful condition of Indian affairs, he contradicts himself. He agrees with me and with the report of the Institute for Government Research in their first sentence, which says: "An overwhelming majority of the Indians are poor, even extremely poor." Mr. Crampton falls into this agreement unwittingly in trying to refute the report that children in government schools are underfed. He said:

I have never seen any evidence of the children suffering from lack of food or from an undesirable character of food. Quite the contrary. It is true that oftentimes children will be seen in these schools who give evidence of lack of proper nutrition, but you must remember where these children have come from—the primitive sort of homes they come from to the schools.

The "primitive sort of homes"—that is exactly what I had in mind. The congressman admits these homes are bad and that food is lacking, and therefore, Indians young and old are hungry and sick.

The subcommittee of the Senate Indian Affairs Committee is holding hearings right now, and sworn testimony reveals horrible conditions—rotten meat, full of maggots, and spoiled flour which mice and cats had defiled, are fed to children in government schools. Sworn statements amply show that the report of the Institute for Government Research could all be transformed into the superlative degree and not begin to tell the whole story of Indian exploitation.

Had it been possible, these hearings of the Senate investigating committee should have been printed and read at this conference, together with this discussion of the report of the Institute for Government Research. We would all be convinced beyond any doubt as to the accuracy of this survey report under discussion. Printed reports of these hearings should be made available to the public—the American people. They have a right to know the facts if, as Mr. Crampton said, in justifying the Budget Bureau's cuts in Indian appropriations, increased appropriations would mean higher taxes upon the American people. Let the people know the facts, if this is a government "of the people, for the people, by the people."

As an Indian, speaking earnestly for the very life of my race, I must say that this report by the Institute for Government Research, *The Problem of Indian Administration*, is all too true, although I do not always concur in their conclusions, which tend to minimize the responsibility of the Bureau. On pages 11–12 the report says:

The survey staff finds itself obliged to say frankly and unequivocally that the provisions for the care of the Indian children in boarding schools are grossly inadequate.

The outstanding deficiency is in the diet furnished the Indian children, many of whom are below normal health. The diet is deficient in quantity, quality and variety. The effort has been made to feed the children on a per capita of eleven cents a day, plus what can be produced on the school farm, including the dairy. At a few, very few schools, the farm and dairy are sufficiently productive to be a highly important factor in raising the standard of the diet, but even at the best schools these sources do not fully meet the requirements for the health and development of the children. At the worst schools the situation is serious in the extreme. The major diseases of the Indians are tuberculosis and trachoma. Tuberculosis unquestionably can best be combated by a preventive, curative diet and proper living conditions, and a considerable amount of evidence suggests that the same may prove true of trachoma. The great protective foods are milk and fruit and vegetables, particularly fresh green vegetables. The diet of Indian children in boarding schools is generally notably lacking in these preventive foods. Although the Indian Service has established a quart of milk a day per pupil as the standard, it has been able to achieve this standard in very few schools. At the special school for children suffering from trachoma, now in operation in Fort Defiance, Arizona milk is not a part of the normal diet. The little produced is mainly consumed in the hospital where children acutely ill are sent. It may be

seriously questioned whether the Indian service could do very much better than
it does without more adequate appropriations.

I do not agree with this concluding sentence which minimizes the
Bureau's responsibility by blaming Congress for inadequate appropriations.

For more than eleven years I have lived in Washington, D.C., and I have
learned through attending congressional committee hearings and pending
Indian legislation that it is the Indian Bureau that drafts these appropriations bills. In fact, all other bills affecting Indians are also referred to the
Indian Bureau for its approval or disapproval. The American Congress is
dependent for its information upon the Indian Bureau. What "compromises" are made in congressional committees behind closed doors is
another chapter. In the printed hearings on Indian appropriations by the
House Indian Affairs Committee, Volume 1, page 806, year 1919, the assistant commissioner, Mr. Meritt, is quoted as follows:

After the next year (i.e., beginning 1921) I think there should be a gradual
decrease of the appropriations carried in the Indian Bill, and the only sure way for
bringing about that decrease would be for Congress to arbitrarily direct that there
be a decrease of appropriations for, say, a period of four years, of five percent per
year...I do not believe that the Indian Service would be very materially hurt and
it would result in saving the government approximately $750,000 a year.

Bear in mind, this was before President Coolidge's economy program.
There was no Budget Bureau in existence in 1919.

During the three last consecutive summers I have visited many Indian
reservations, keeping my information on Indian conditions up to date. This
past summer I went with Captain Bonnin, who was doing field investigation
work for the Senate Indian Affairs Committee, authorized by the King Resolution No. 79. Incidentally, the Indian Bureau opposed the passage of this
resolution. I will here tell you an observation of my own.

The Indian Bureau superintendents in the field have been holding meetings this summer discussing this same report of the Institute for Government Research before us now. Their purpose was to refute and disprove the
things contained in it! Subordinate employees have been approached and
told they should be "loyal" to the government when asked to refute statements in the report. At peril of losing their jobs, some of them refused to
deny the facts.

I repeat, "There is a distinction to be made between the government and
the government's servants." On Indian reservations, subordinate employees
as well as the Indians are called "disloyal" to the government by their superintendents when one of them dares to report existing evils. On the contrary,
any American citizen who can help to bring efficiency into the federal
machinery is "loyal to the government," though it may mean the dismissal
of inefficient employees—a real housecleaning in the Indian Service.

In addition to this pernicious activity among Indian Bureau superintendents trying to refute things told in the report of the Institute for Government
Research, there are circulated misleading articles emanating from the Bureau.

Recently I casually picked up from the reading table of a hotel a current magazine—the November 1928 issue of the *National Republic*. On page 34 is the caption "Education of the Indians"; the subhead states "Graduates of Government Indian Schools Are Doing Successful Work in All Walks of Life."

The pictures used are from the government Indian school, Haskell Institute. This is considered one of the best schools. But the article is upon the entire Indian field. The article, therefore, is entirely misleading. To show you the Bureau's own attitude toward its Indian schools, I quote from it:

Health promoting activities are given a prominent place in the conduct of the schools. The health of the pupil is the first purpose, and daily routine of the boarding school as to diet, bathing, exercise, sleep, periodical weighing and examination of pupils, and supervised nursing supplied by Indian girls, furnishes an organized system throughout the year for the protection of health and the formation of health habits. The value of a sufficient supply of milk daily is emphasized and an endeavor made to provide plenty for the schools....

It does not tell the American public, as a matter of fact, how miserably this endeavor fails to actually supply the necessary milk. This kind of a presentation of Indian matters is not conducive to having Congress make larger appropriations. Congress as a whole is dependent upon the Indian Bureau for its information, just as the American public is. Both Congress and the American people are willfully misled about the actual conditions of Indian want and hopeless destitution. The stubborn fact remains, just as told in the report of the Institute for Government Research made to the Secretary of the Interior about a year ago, particularly on pages 11 and 12, and supported by sworn testimony before the Senate Indian Committee and the Red Cross report.

The diet is deficient in quantity, quality and variety. The effort has been made to feed the children on a per capita of eleven cents a day, plus what can be produced on the school farm, including the dairy. At a few, very few schools, the farm and dairy are sufficiently productive to be a highly important factor in raising the standard of the diet, but even at the best schools these sources do not fully meet the requirements for the health and development of the children. At the worst schools the situation is serious in the extreme.

A superintendent who questioned the accuracy of the report on the eleven cents per child per day spent for food in government schools was invited to figure it out, which he did while I looked on. Much to his own surprise, he had to admit the survey staff of the Institute for Government Research knew their business and their report was correct.

The tabulations of Assistant Commissioner, Mr. Meritt, which Mr. Crampton put in the *Congressional Record* (December 11, 1928), denying the 11-cents-a-day-for-food-per-child report and showing it to be 20.4 cents instead, is only paper-talk, just like the menus placarded in the schools showing what the children ought to have, but in actual fact do not get because of lack of the materials.

In the printed hearings of the House Appropriations Committee in 1922, on page 328, Mr. Meritt said: "We favor keeping subsistence down to the lowest possible point." He was speaking of rations to old and indigent Indians and orphans. I have visited Indian homes during my three summer visits. They are extremely poor. They have scarcely any food in their hovels. They complain to me of starving.

This summer I went to see a proud Indian chief who was sick. Before I reached the hut I heard men and women crying aloud. I stepped into the open door. The Indian was dead. They were washing the body, ready for burial. The corpse was only skin and bones. These grief-stricken Indians, with tears streaming down their faces, came to shake hands with me. Utterly hopeless, they cried as only heartbroken humans cry, until I, too, wept with them.

The government doctor arrived. I asked him what disease caused the death of the old Indian. He replied that he had no disease, but simply starved to death.

There was a time, long ago, when Indians shared their food with the hungry, but that day is past. Now all Indians are too poor. They have nothing to divide. This is starvation.

On page 262 of the report of the Institute for Government Research, referring to the Red Cross survey of 1924, there appears the following: "It may be said in passing that the findings of the Red Cross report correspond very closely to those of the present survey as they relate to the same reservations."

This Red Cross survey of 1924 had been kept in the secret archives of the Indian Bureau these four years and has been refused to members of Congress who asked to see it. The evil conditions reported in the Red Cross survey remain unchanged, four years later.

Withholding reported facts of bad conditions in Indian affairs, the Bureau is broadcasting through the American press, and congressman Crampton through the *Congressional Record*, about *how much* the Indians have been helped and benefited; how the Indian population has increased; how well they are fed and housed!

In the *Native American* of December 1, 1928, published at the Leupp Indian School, Arizona, Assistant Commissioner Meritt has an article which he addressed to the Navajos, telling them about their "increase in population" and "their wealth derived from oil leases" under the administration of Commissioner Burke; but nowhere did Mr. Meritt tell, as a matter of fact, that under the same policy of the Bureau, the whole Navajo Indians are today suffering fast-approaching blindness! Nor does he mention the heated battles fought by true friends of the Navajos which defeated the Bureau policy and its endorsement of bills H.R. 9133 and S. 3159, under former Secretary Fall.

Those Bureau bills, had they passed, would have had the following effects:

(1)   To deprive the "Executive Order" reservation Indians of 37 ½% of their oil revenue, giving it to the states;

(2)   To exempt the oil companies from the production tax;

(3)   To provide a congressional declaration against the Indian claim of vested rights in 22,500,000 acres—two-thirds of the undivided reservation area.

These atrocious misuses of huge federal machinery against the Indian wards of the government are sugar-coated to fool the American public. The National Council of American Indians was one of the organizations that dared to defend the rights of the Navajo people and all of her Indian tribes who occupied "Executive Order" reservations.

If the high officials of the Indian Bureau continually fail to insist upon adequate congressional appropriations, are they ignorant of the actual suffering on the reservations? If not, they must be incompetent. If, on the other hand, these officials of the government prove unfaithful to their charge in "compromises" that would legislate away the wards' interests, knowing it means the ultimate destruction of helpless human beings—young and old—then they are criminals. In either case, a housecleaning is imperative.

I am desperately concerned for the life of my race while these countless investigations, revealing un-Christian exploitation of government wards, are made from time to time, only to lodge under lock and key in the Indian Bureau. How long—oh, how long!—shall this cruel practice continue?

The Indian race is starving—not only physically, but mentally and morally. It is a dire tragedy. The government Indian schools are not on a par with the American schools of today. The so-called "Indian graduates from Government Schools" cannot show any credentials that would be accepted by any business house. They are unable to pass the Civil Service examinations. The proviso in Indian treaties that educated Indians, wherever qualified, be given preference in Indian Service employment is rendered meaningless. Indians are kept ignorant and "incompetent" to cope with the world's trained workers, because they are not sufficiently educated in the government schools.

Secretary Work, in his annual report, 1928, page 13, states: "There is not an Indian school in the United States that is strictly a high school."

I quote this in refutation of the glowing propaganda in the November, 1928 issue of the *National Republic* and Mr. Crampton's speech in the *Congressional Record*, previously mentioned.

The topic of Indian education has already been discussed by others, but I am obliged to make a passing comment upon it.

The Secretary of the Interior in his report on education of Indians says in part (on page 13) as follows:

No complete high-school courses were taught for them until 1921 and then only at one school. In 1925, three such courses were added; one was added in 1926 and a fifth in 1927. The increase during the last three years in the number of pupils—junior and senior grades—has been by 1,178 in the former and by 526 in the latter. There are only six institutions maintained by the federal government where Indians may receive a high school education. Elementary and junior high-school courses are also taught in these institutions, the senior high-school grades constitute only one department. There is not an Indian school in the United States that is strictly a high school. Contrast these conditions with the educational advantages offered the white population.

Then he gives facts and figures. On page 15 of his report he says:

As the inadequacy of the educational system for the Indians was one of the reasons for the department's request for the survey and report, the following summary of the findings of the investigators on this subject is of especial interest:

The survey staff finds itself obliged to say frankly and unequivocally that the provisions for the care of the Indian children in boarding schools are grossly inadequate.

The diet is deficient in quality, quantity and variety.

The great protective foods are milk and fruit and vegetables, particularly fresh green vegetables. The diet of Indian children is generally notably lacking in these foods.

The boarding schools are overcrowded materially beyond their capacities.

The medical attention rendered the boarding school children is not up to a reasonable standard.

The medical attention given children in day schools maintained by the government is also below a reasonable standard.

The boarding schools are supported in part by the labor of students.

The service is notably weak in personnel trained and experienced in educational work with families and communities.

Now these are some of the things of which I have complained in the past, and as a result I am referred to by Indian Bureau officials and congressmen as being an agitator and disloyal to the government; they even infer that I am dishonest and living off of the Indians. Such statements are grossly untrue and unjust. The sole purpose in making any criticism has been with a view that the evils pointed out by me might be corrected.

The Secretary of the Interior's report contained these statements. It is evident that he regards them as of sufficient importance to incorporate them in his report. He further states that "this subject is of especial interest."

In this same report, on page 34 he deals with "Negro Education" and states as follows:

One of the more important activities of the department has been a comprehensive study of Negro colleges and universities throughout the United States. This study was conducted by the Bureau of Education. Its purpose was to ascertain the present status of Negro higher education and to recommend means for its improvement and development.

The results show marked progress and an extraordinary demand among the Negro people of the country for college and university education. Of the 79 institutions included in the Bureau's survey, 77 were doing college work as compared with 31 institutions ten years ago. The enrollment of Negro students in those institutions totaled 13,860 as compared with 2,132 in 1917, a gain of 550 percent. For every 10,000 Negroes in the United States 15 are attending college, as against 90 for every 10,000 whites.

With five exceptions, the colleges included in the study were located in Southern states, indicating a widespread sentiment in the South in favor of Negro higher education. Twenty-two of the institutions were operated by states and supported through public taxation. The Bureau's study also shows that the Negroes, themselves, have not been remiss in providing higher education, 17 of their colleges being owned, administered, and financed entirely by members of their race.

It will be noted that 17 of their colleges are owned and financed by members of the Negro race.

Indian funds might have been better used for higher education and colleges for Indians instead of building steel bridges, highways and expensive but worthless irrigation systems under Indian Bureau management.

Attention is also directed to the statement that "One of the more important activities of the department has been a comprehensive study of Negro colleges and universities throughout the United States. This study was conducted by the Bureau of Education. Its purpose was to ascertain the present status of Negro higher education and to recommend means for its improvement and development."

The Negroes are not wards of the government. Neither have they any treaty agreements with the United States for their education, as the Indians have. Yet means for educational development are sought for them. Why not extend such activities to the Indians?

In conclusion, I quote Major Frank Knox, who said at the close of his investigation of three reservations in Colorado and Utah in 1925: "The reform which good business methods, efficient administration and an adequate protection of Indian rights requires cannot come from within the Bureau. It must come from without."

Too often employees in the Indian Service are Indian-haters and they are discourteous to Indians in their daily routine.

Above all things let there be this proviso written large in the government's new Indian policy—"That no expert or subordinate shall be employed who has racial prejudice against the Indian people."

The problem of Indian administration cannot be solved by mere increased appropriations unless coincidentally a new personnel is had in the Indian Service, and a new Indian policy which will provide court review of the guardian's handling of Indian funds and property including natural resources estimated at a billion and a half.

NOTE

1. Gertrude Simmons Bonnin Collection, Harold B. Lee Library, Brigham Young University, Provo, UT.

Elizabeth Manroe Sippel
(ca. 1870–1940)

In some ways, Elizabeth Manroe Sippel represents the prototypical, white, middle-class clubwoman. Born into one of the oldest Baltimore families (both maternal and paternal ancestors arrived in the seventeenth century), she married a prosperous banker in 1890 and had one daughter. She moved through her life with economic and social surety. Yet, like many reform-minded women of her class and era, she believed that "those who have had the privileges of this country through several generations have a greater responsibility toward it than those who have not had such a heritage."[1] A Presbyterian and member of the Daughters of the American Revolution, Sippel's entry into the public realm began when she joined the Baltimore Sorosis Club. Foreshadowing the pattern she would sustain throughout her life, she became its president in 1912.

A steadfast Democrat, Sippel filled her adult life with service to political, national, and community organizations that included several governmental appointments. While holding the presidency of the Maryland Federation of Women's Clubs (1922–1926), she made her mark at the national level of the General Federation as Chairman of Resolutions and Chairman of Finance. This post led to her election as president of the entire General Federation of Women's Clubs (GFWC) in 1928. In the 1920s, she was appointed by President Hoover to the White House Conference on Child Health and the Conference on Home Building and Home Ownership as well as the President's Emergency Committee for Employment.

During the economic crisis of the Great Depression, Sippel emphasized the political philosophy that guided her entire public career. She believed it was up to women to keep "up the morale of the family [and]...to hold fast to the fine, the beautiful, the enriching influences of life." But she also promoted a less well-known cause—the need to improve services to rural women. As president of the GFWC, she encouraged "greater cooperation between urban and rural groups, and work[ed] to bring into the Federation a far greater number of rural women."[2]

In this radio talk, given when President of the GFWC, Sippel raises some of the most complex and interesting questions for historians.[3] On the one hand, the speech seems a conservative salute to the consumerism and female domesticity that some historians have labeled a "backlash" against the radical politics of the 1910s and the campaign for women's suffrage. Sippel clearly states her belief that women ought to take responsibility for the domestic realm. On the other hand, Sippel interprets the shift from home manufacturing of the nineteenth century to women's new role as scientific homemaker and expert consumer by the 1920s as a social development that granted women important new powers. Because women "do almost nine-tenths of all the buying," Sippel argued their economic clout ought to be taken into account in local and national policies. She also used this rationale to campaign for greater educational and vocational access for women in the "masculine" fields of money management, banking, and investment. Sippel demanded that women educate themselves about money matters, and she petitioned for government action in response to the rise of the consumer economy. But she also continued to maintain that women ought to devote their economic expertise to their proper sphere—the home.

Sippel's use of the radio reflects its growing importance to women speakers and to once isolated populations. Women speakers took advantage of this shift, plying their status as the nation's consumers into advertising revenues and product endorsements. At the same time, they, like Sippel, learned to craft speeches and modulate their voices to best convey their messages to a radio audience.

NOTES

1. GFWC, "Sippel, Elizabeth Manroe," Biographical Material, GFWC Archives, Washington, DC; and *American Women: The Standard Biographical Dictionary of Notable Women*, Darward Howes (Teaneck, NJ: Zephyrus Press, 1974).

2. Ibid.

3. See Dorothy Brown, *Setting a Course: Women in the 1920s* (Boston: Twayne, 1927); Ruth Schwartz Cowan, *More Work for Mother: The Ironies of Household Technology from Open Hearth to the Microwave* (New York: Basic Books, 1983); and Phyllis Palmer, *Domesticity and Dirt: Housewives and Domestic Servants in the United States, 1920–1945* (Philadelphia: Temple University Press, 1989).

WOMAN'S IMPORTANCE AS AN INVESTOR OF MONEY, TIME AND LEISURE (RADIO TALK, JANUARY 17, 1929)[1]

Reprinted by Permission of General Federation of Women's Clubs, Washington, DC

Did it ever occur to you, that we, the women of the United States are rapidly becoming the investors of this country? Time was that any investment of moneys in supplies, equipment, in property of any sort was mainly a man's affair while woman was the manufacturer of the family. We are all familiar with the kitchen and its "wide mouthed" fireplace, in which our great grandmothers and their daughters gathered not only to dry and preserve meats and fruits and vegetables, but to make candles and soap, to make cards for combing wool; to card wool and cotton and hatchet the flax; to spin and weave and knit cloth and clothing for all household uses and for almost all personal needs. But the great moving force of the nineteenth century, the Steam Engine, followed by the still more compelling force, Electrical Energy, wrested many manufacturing activities from the Housewife and turned her into an investor of family income.

It is estimated that women do almost nine-tenths of all buying, that they spend or invest fifty-two billion dollars annually. Obviously a large part of our country's wealth is handled by us. And upon the handling of that wealth depends not only individual wealth, health and effectiveness, but the very life of our nation.

Did you ever try to inventory or make a list of all things in your home, from screws to bedsteads? If you have, you too, must have been appalled by the vast number of *things* with which we humans live in well ordered households. The task of buying all those things—or almost all those things for probably friend husband has bought the screws and the coal shovel—falls to women. It is humanly impossible for her to obtain expert knowledge concerning real values of any large number of items she must purchase. How then, is she to know when she is making a good investment until after the purchase has been tested? Fortunately, the United States Department of Commerce is coming to her aid. It is working with manufacturers to establish minimum standards of quality; articles meeting such standards will be labeled, so that the retail consumer can determine from the label whether Government minimum standards have been met. Through its Division of Simplified Practice, the Department of Commerce is urging producers to eliminate the wide and useless varieties in sizes that now exist. For example, if you ask for a two-pound package of salt today, you will be sure you are buying two pounds of salt and be able to compare prices of different makes of salt, whereas until manufacturers agreed recently to standardize salt packages you had to look on each package before you knew whether you were getting 28, 30, or 32 ounces of salt for your money.

This work on articles in which the housewife is interested has only begun. The General Federation of Women's Clubs cooperating with the Government will attempt to keep women informed concerning the articles that have labels of quality or that are marketed in standard packages or sizes. But the success of the activity will depend on the housewife, for only when she makes a point of asking for standardized materials will the retailer be encouraged to carry goods of manufacturers who have agreed to standardize. The Federation has already issued booklets bringing together in picture and terse statement the scientific facts about different types of labor-saving household equipment for use of the housewife when considering purchase of such equipment.

We hope the day will come when women purchasers will be able to know with certainty what values they are getting for their money. But even then, buying things that are essential for health, which eliminate wasteful use of human energy and which contribute to the real joy of living, while putting aside a part of the income in interest-bearing investments so that such moneys will be available for the fulfillment of the needs or desires of tomorrow, will tax the intelligence of all women as long as we continue to be the investors of the family income.

Hitherto, married women have not been held responsible for the investment of funds—using investments in its more restricted meaning. Such investment has been the concern of the men of the family. How often, I wonder, have women who have been widowed regretted the fact that they paid no attention to the financial dealings of their husbands, that they were uninformed when fate shifted the responsibility of investment to their shoulders?

For some mysterious reason, the belief has widely prevailed in the past—and still persists to some extent today—that women are fundamentally less competent to handle money matters than men. Women themselves have been rather too ready to accept this opinion. Today over a million women make separate income tax returns to the United States Treasury. Almost four million make joint returns with husbands. Approximately one-half the stock of various leading American corporations is owned by women. It is stated that one-third or more of the stock in some of our leading metropolitan banks is held by women. While there is no very reliable way to determine the percentage of women bondholders, there is every reason to believe that this more conservative type of investment is even more extensively held by women. It is a matter of common knowledge that a very large percentage of all insurance policies name women as the beneficiaries.

Regardless of whether a woman is the homemaker for a small-income family or a large-income family, it is essential that she understand the principles of money investment so that she may place a true valuation when planning her family budget, on putting some money aside to earn money for her family. A regular investment of $25.00 a month in bonds averaging a return of only 5%, with interest promptly reinvested as it is earned, will at the end of thirty years produce a total of $20,696. Of this amount only a little over two-fifths will actually have been money saved while over a half will represent compound interest. These calculations, of course, do not take into consideration the possibility of loss during the period of investment. But if bonds are well selected, losses should be minor and the final result should not be materially affected.

And this brings me to the question of whether the modern woman can invest with safety and success. By careful study—and the Finance Division of our American Home Department is planning such a study—and by consultation with thoroughly reliable investment houses which not only confine their offerings to solid investment but which extend assistance to the investor so that he or she may adapt his or her selections to the purposes they are expected to serve, there is every reason why women should bear jointly with men this responsibility.

Alert investment bankers today fully realize the growing importance of women as investors. The services they provide are a great safeguard to women as well as to men in the accumulation and conservation of money. It is no longer necessary for women to seek the service of relatives or friends about investment.

NOTE

1. Presidential Papers, Speeches 1929–32, Folder 02 1102-1-2, GFWC, Washington, DC.

Florence Jaffray Harriman
(1870–1967)

In the pattern of many white, prosperous urban women, Florence Jaffray Harriman moved from society matron to social reformer during the Progressive Era, to government official in the 1930s and 1940s.[1] Though the advancement of women remained slow in the State Department, Franklin Delano Roosevelt appointed her U.S. Minister to Norway in 1937. Harriman's first forays into public life took the form of civic leadership. She was a founder of the Colony Club, serving as its President from 1903 to 1916, and was active in the National Civic League. By the 1910s, though, she began to operate in reform circles, first as manager of the New York State Reformatory at Bedford and then as the only female member of the Federal Industrial Relations Committee. She married her husband J. Borden Harriman in 1889. After his death in 1914, she moved to Washington, DC, and became a dedicated member of the Democratic Party. Though Republicans controlled the presidency throughout the 1920s, Harriman's "Washington home was a bastion of Democratic power." Upon FDR's election, he rewarded her devotion with the diplomatic appointment to Norway.

The speech below, as well as the two included in Part III, provide an overview of her political career, an introduction to her political convictions, and an account of some of her activities. Harriman's papers, collected at the Library of Congress, also demonstrate the complex nature of speeches as historical artifacts. Harriman wrote and rewrote her speeches, reworking her ideas in multiple drafts, notes, and line editing. It is easy to imagine that when she actually presented the speech, her language and perhaps even themes shifted once again. Without a voice recording, we lack the "actual" speech. On the other hand, the layers of documentation that do exist illustrate that she painstakingly and self-consciously crafted each speech so that it might best express her ideas before particular audiences. In each arena, her mentors emphasized the power of nuanced, formal language and a pragmatic but assertive oratorical eloquence. The way in which Harriman wrote and delivered her speeches reflected her privileged background as well as her stalwart activism.

The first speech, a short 1931 address sponsored by Pond's Cold Cream, shows her early concern with international issues as well as her skillful use of the most powerful form of national communication at her disposal, the radio. In the speech, she pays homage to her advertiser, but points out that the "Pond's method" did not circumscribe women to ornamental status, but rather the product's reasonably priced and efficient beauty regimen enabled them to participate in politics amidst their busy lives, while remaining feminine and attractive. Harriman challenged the still prevalent stereotypical image of political women as "stodgy" old maids. In her radio-friendly style, Harriman endorsed prevailing gender codes, which emphasized women's appearance and their expected role as the nation's consumers, but also advocated that women must use their "natural" pacifism to promote international peace. She effectively blended several key notions of modern life: mass consumerism, radio communication, and a stylish, feminine, but still activist role for women.

NOTE

1. Florence Jaffray Harriman, Papers Manuscript Division, Library of Congress, Washington, DC; Nancy Woloch, *Women and the American Experience*, 3rd ed. (Boston: McGraw-Hill, 2000). "Harriman, Florence Jaffray," *Encyclopedia Britannica* from Encyclopaedia Premium Service, May 27, 2003 〈http://www.britannica.com/eb/article?eu = 138074〉.

POND'S RADIO: MRS. J. BORDEN HARRIMAN (FEBRUARY 2, 1931)[1]

For February 10.

Good afternoon. I am so glad to be able to be at this Pond's tea, because it gives me this opportunity to tell you something about a subject that is, I am sure, of very close interest to every woman. I have lately come from Washington, D.C., where I attended an important conference on the cause and cure of war. The subject of International Peace is one on which every woman must feel strongly. The horrors of the recent war are still touching our lives— still wringing our hearts. If war is to be stopped, we women must help to stop it. We must see that today's children are brought up with a clear idea of the waste of war. If every mother will implant the seeds of peace in the minds of her sons and daughters, we may end war.

The child who grows up in an atmosphere of kindness and courtesy, who sees tolerance, fairness and self-control dominating the lives of those he loves and trusts, will be in no danger of love of conflict. He will not grow up with the habit of mind that makes nations rush to settle disputes by the sword instead of the council table. We women must lose no opportunity of impressing our children with the ghastly futility of wars and the glory of peace on earth. It is the only way we can protect our children and the world.

Many women attend all manner of conferences in Washington—busy women of all ages—of all incomes—and I am often impressed by the clear vital well-groomed complexions most of them have. I am sure that many of them are, as I am, grateful to Pond's for providing such excellent complexion safeguards so inexpensively. Personally I have used the Pond's method for years. It is so simple and so sure. The Cold Cream is the best cleansing cream I know, and I have never found Cleansing Tissues as soft as Pond's. The Skin Freshener tones your skin and the Vanishing Cream protects it—and that is all that is necessary. And all of these products are moderate in price. I am glad to have this opportunity to thank Pond's for these four excellent and comprehensive aids in looking one's best. Thank you and good afternoon.

NOTE

1. Typed manuscript for radio broadcast. Florence Jaffray Hurst Harriman Papers, Manuscript Division, Library of Congress, Washington, DC. Florence Harriman dedicated the copyright of her unpublished papers to the public.

Suggested Readings, 1920–1932

Anderson, Karen. *Changing Woman: A History of Racial Ethnic Women in Modern America* (New York: Oxford University Press, 1996).

Anderson, Kristi. *After Suffrage: Women in Partisan and Electoral Politics Before the New Deal* (Chicago: University of Chicago Press, 1996).

Baker, Paula. "The Domestication of Politics: Women and American Political Society, 1780–1920," *American Historical Review* 89 (June 1984): 620–647.

Brown, Dorothy. *Setting a Course: American Women in the 1920s* (Boston: Macmillan Publishing Company, 1987).

Chafe, William. *The Paradox of Change: American Women in the Twentieth Century* (New York: Oxford University Press, 1991).

Cott, Nancy. *The Grounding of Modern Feminism.* (New Haven: Yale University Press, 1987).

Daniels, Roger. *Coming to America: A History of Immigration and Ethnicity in American Life* (New York: HarperCollins Publishers, 1990).

Gordon, Linda. "Black and White Visions of Welfare: Women's Welfare Activism, 1890–1945," *Journal of American History* 78 (1991): 559–590.

Gordon, Ann and Bettye Collier Thomas, eds. *American Women and the Vote, 1835–1965* (Amherst, MA: University of Massachusetts Press, 1997).

Gustafson, Melanie, "Claiming Victory, 1918–1924," *Women and the Republican Party, 1854–1924* (Urbana, IL: University of Illinois Press, 2001): 173–195.

Higginbotham, Evelyn Brooks. "Clubwomen and Electoral Politics in the 1920s," *African American Women and the Vote, 1837–1965*, Ann D. Gordon et al. eds. (Amherst, MA: University of Massachusetts Press, 1997), 134–155.

Hoff-Wilson, Joan, ed. *Rights of Passage: The Past and Future of the ERA* (Bloomington, IN: Indiana University Press, 1986).

Koven, Seth, and Sonya Michel, eds. *Mothers of a New World: Maternalist Politics and the Origins of Welfare States* (New York: Routledge, 1993).

Kraditor, Aileen. *The Ideas of the Woman Suffrage Movement 1890–1920* (New York: W. W. Norton and Co, 1965).

Scanlon, Jennifer. *Inarticulate Longings: The Ladies Home Journal, Gender, and the Promises of Consumer Culture* (New York: Routledge, 1995).

Schott, Linda K. *Reconstructing Women's Thoughts: The Women's International League for Peace and Freedom Before World War II* (Stanford, CA: Stanford University Press, 1997).

Scott, Anne Firor. *Natural Allies: Women's Associations in American History* (Urbana, IL: University of Illinois Press, 1992).

Skocpol, Theda. *Protecting Soldiers and Mothers: Political Origins of Social Policy in the United States* (Cambridge, MA: Harvard University Press, 1992).

Thomas, Sue and Clyde Wilcox. eds. *Women and Elective Office: Past Present and Future.* (New York: Oxford University Press, 1998).

Tilly, Louise A. and Patricia Gurin eds. *Women, Politics, and Change.* (New York: Russell Sage Foundation, 1990).

PART II

Whose New Deal? 1932–1940

As the 1920s came to a close, individual and collective groups of women continued to navigate the ever-shifting tides of female public activism in deed and word. Their first decade as enfranchised citizens demonstrated that they did not compose a single-minded interest group; color, race, class, and age divided them, and their individual and organizational goals varied considerably.

In the 1930s, women public speakers confronted a host of new political issues—most significantly, how they might best respond to the worst economic catastrophe the nation had ever witnessed, the Great Depression. Because of the exigencies of the crisis, traditional gender definitions waned. Men lost their place as primary breadwinners, and women shouldered additional "masculine" responsibilities when necessary, such as head of the family, WPA field worker, union striker, or entrepreneur. Though in some ways the emergency created new opportunities for women, most women, as well as the nation itself, perceived their efforts as heroic and temporary. They were cast as exemplary women willing to sacrifice their own self-interest for the good of the nation rather than as reformers or feminists who wanted to challenge gender conventions.

The Great Depression also tended to intensify women's traditional domestic role (e.g., home canning, stretching the budget, taking in boarders, sewing their children's clothes, and living with in-laws); photographers and journalists rarely highlighted women on the streets or in public spaces. In contrast, images of lost and downtrodden men standing in breadlines and holding picket signs filled magazines and newspapers. New Deal programs, primarily designed to restore white, male workers to their socially ascribed breadwinner status, created race- and sex-specific benefits rather than programs that aided all "citizen-workers." While dire economic circumstances blurred gender boundaries, most Americans hoped and expected a return to "normalcy" once the crisis passed. Still, during the decade-long ordeal, women made an enormous impact on the public domain. They labored to sustain their families and communities; won social, artistic, and intellectual prominence; and thoroughly engaged with New Deal politics, as policy advocates, administrators, critics, and government appointees.[1]

In the 1930s, women speakers drew upon their prior activist experience and the rhetorical traditions and political advances made by preceding generations while spawning two new trends of their own. First, having won numerous government appointments, more women gave speeches as representatives of the state. New Deal women, including Eleanor Roosevelt, groundbreaking First Lady; Frances Perkins, Secretary of Labor and the first woman to serve in the President's cabinet; and Mary McLeod Bethune, Director of Negro Affairs, the first black woman presidential adviser, spoke as public servants on behalf of national programs. Perkins drafted and helped secure passage of the landmark Social Security Act, assisted by her two key aides in the Children's Bureau, Martha Eliot and Katharine Lenroot. Similarly, Florence Ellinwood Allen, the first woman appointed as a judge to the U.S. Circuit Court of Appeals, championed her cause from within the most formal of political structures. Once established as representatives of the state, speaking opportunities for many of these women expanded into new and varied venues.

Women's workplace experiences generated a second trend in their speech-making. In the 1920s, white, educated, professional women made the most substantial gains in the workplace, but women's employment numbers rose in all categories. Once in the workforce, whether for personal fulfillment or because of dire economic circumstances, women often encountered harsh conditions, including sexual harassment, racial discrimination, low pay, nonexistent child care, and union indifference. In response, they delivered hard-hitting, pragmatic speeches that directly challenged men and male bosses—employers, union leaders, and government officials. Ruth Morgan, an early leader in the League of Women Voters, encouraged women to stay active in party politics to make sure both Republican and Democratic leaders did not forget women's concerns in the midst of the crisis. Long-time union activist Luisa Moreno challenged the national labor unions as well as all "Spanish-speaking citizens and non-citizens" to organize and agitate for social change, and Ella Reeve "Mother" Bloor, from the far left, rejected capitalism altogether to champion socialist solutions.

At the same time, women continued to debate the merits of the Equal Rights Amendment. The General Federation of Women's Clubs held regular forums that presented both sides of the issue, while the National

Woman's Party's commitment never abated. Attacking all inequities, including those established to "protect women," NWP President Anna Kelton Wiley warned New Dealers not to embed sex-specific regulations into entitlement programs or social policy. New Deal appointees, in contrast, took their lead from Women's Bureau Director, Mary Anderson, who opposed the ERA, or what she termed "the blanket amendment." Most New Deal reformers feared that the ERA would undo hard-won, gender-specific legislative protections that provided what they considered only minimal benefits to vulnerable women, such as maternal health care, widows' pensions, and the ten-hour day.

In the 1920s and 1930s, as more liberal sexual mores along with the economic downturn made birth control less taboo, speakers such as Blanche Ames Ames and Margaret Sanger championed the issue in myriad public arenas. Unfortunately, they often relied upon class, race, and eugenics-based arguments to make their case rather than promoting the more radical rationale espoused by advocates in the 1910s who had championed birth control as essential to women's social and economic independence.

Radio dominated the country's parlors during the New Deal. The ever-present radio connected women, especially rural farm wives, to the public square. Local programs debated the application of national farm policies, advertised mass-produced consumer products, and spun the latest jazz records. FDR had "Fireside Chats," and ER had a weekly show. Preacher Aimee Semple McPherson took to the airwaves as the first woman evangelist on radio. Another technological advance was the addition of sound to motion pictures. Now, women on screen had voices, and, as one scholar observed, this "gave to the American woman, as performer and heroine, a chance to speak her mind, to have a real, not just a presumptive, say in her own destiny. It was a chance that women of the silent screen...were effectively denied."[2] Big screen images of fast-talking, independent women reinforced the public actions of real-life women during the 1930s as they asserted power in the New Deal government, political parties, and the workplace.

In the selections that follow, women public speakers addressed the critical issues that concerned the nation and, in so doing, did much to shape the meaning of local, state, and national discourses during a decade of tremendous government change as well as dire economic and social uncertainty.

NOTES

1. Elaine Tyler May, *Homeward Bound: American Families in the Cold War* (New York: Basic Books 1988); and Susan Ware, *Holding Their Own: American Women in the 1930s* (Boston: Twayne 1982).

2. Maria DiBattista, *Fast-Talking Dames* (New Haven: Yale University Press, 2001), 6.

Ruth Morgan (ca. 1880–1934)

In 1922 Ruth Morgan, "a neighbor and friend of the Franklin Roosevelts,...posses[ing] an internationalistic background, substantial means, and wide contacts," made the perfect Chair for the National League of Women Voters' first committee devoted to international peace: the Department of International Cooperation.[1] Coming of age in the early twentieth century as a New Woman, Morgan devoted her life to political causes and public activism. She subscribed to the precepts of what historians have termed "political motherhood." Because of women's natural capacity as caretakers and their historic role as advocates, Morgan believed that "for every cause that promised a better world for their children," a woman must also play a critical role in securing world peace. In the tradition of the League, she tended to refrain from partisan politics while actively pursuing interest- or issue-oriented political goals. Yet in her life and words, she prompted women to engage in local and national politics with passion and with savvy.[2]

A descendant of George Washington, Morgan spent part of her youth in France and then settled into upper-class New York society. Morgan championed an array of political and charitable causes and served as a member of the Board of Managers of Bellevue Hospital, but it was her war service that shaped her campaign for international peace. During World War I, she headed the Women's National Defense Committee in New York City and directed the Red Cross Nurses Bureau in France. Her witness to the horrors of war motivated Morgan to join the newly formed League of Women Voters, where she orchestrated campaigns to support Philippine independence, the League of Nations, the Kellogg–Briand Pact, and the World

Executive Committee of the National League of Women Voters, 1924. Left to right: Elizabeth Huser, Katherine Ludington, Ruth Morgan, Belle Sherwin, and Maud Wood Park.

Library of Congress, Prints & Photographs Division, [reproduction number, LC-USZ62-122140]. Used with the permission of the League of Women Voters.

Court. She attended the 1927 Geneva Conference and the World Disarmament Conference in 1932 and opposed interventionist policies such as President Coolidge's decision to send U.S. Marines into Nicaragua. Working in concert with Carrie Chapman Catt's "Committee on the Causes and Cure of War," she conducted study groups and participated in Catt's annual meetings and "Marathon Round Tables." Elected as the third vice president of the League of Nations, she remained devoted to the cause of world peace and was a committed public activist until her death.

As the third vice president of the League of Women Voters, Morgan delivered the following speech on April 27, 1932 to League members who had gathered for a general public meeting in Washington, DC. In this speech, Morgan paints a broad picture of her political philosophy, an introduction to the causes she championed throughout her life, and her agenda for the League in the immediate historical moment. It is also an "insider" speech—one prepared and given to like-minded, affiliated individuals. Morgan would want to provoke discussion and would expect to encounter difference of opinion as well as intra-organizational debate, but in this genre of speeches, women would also expect ready comprehension and general support.

In the midst of the economic devastation wrought by the Great Depression, Morgan challenged members to make sure that as the Democratic and Republican Parties met to map out their party platforms for the 1932 campaign, they would incorporate "women's idealistic" vision as well as practical strategies to remedy the suffering economy. She feared that women's reform agenda, which included child labor reform, maternity and infant health care, and world peace, would be dismissed as too fanciful because of the economic crisis. Morgan encouraged her audience to make sure that League members continued to play an active role in shaping the nature of the national political agenda. Morgan incorporated standard 1930s gender definitions into her thinking and speeches. She defined women as the more idealistic of the two sexes and therefore as the ones who must now blend that idealism with practical political action. Only in this way would the nation continue to move forward with progressive reform.

NOTES

1. Louise Young, *In the Public Interest: The League of Women Voters 1920–1970* (New York: Greenwood Press, 1989), 121.

2. Barbara Stuhler, *For the Public Record: A Documentary History of the League of Women Voters* (Westport, CT: Greenwood Press, 2000).

PRESS DEPARTMENT RELEASE
WEDNESDAY MORNING
NATIONAL LEAGUE OF WOMEN VOTERS
APRIL 27, 1932

CAMPAIGN ISSUES CHALLENGING POLITICAL PARTIES "CHALLENGE OF THE WOMAN VOTER"[1]

By Miss Ruth Morgan, Vice-President of the
National League of Women Voters
at the Public Meeting of that organization,
April 26th at 8:15 P.M.

Reprinted by Permission of the League of Women Voters

Picking the Issues

My great concern with the platform of the national parties is that they shall include adequate planks. The matter must be approached with some delicacy because I well recall a great preacher in New York who reminded us that the good were always right but they were never successful until they were joined by a few of the bad, by which I suppose, I should mean, that women must be joined by some of the realists in all the parties.

We are perfectly honest when we say that women care for men and children as they do for themselves, and we challenge all the parties and the government, itself, as these speakers have done tonight—women to face the fact that our very lives are bound up in the question of employment and prosperity—but—and it is a tremendous *but*—the best women have always desired to be idealistic and practical at the same time. It is no accident that all the female saints—from Joan of Arc to she who was the backbone of the Methodist Church where you and I were brought up—were strong in the church, and equally strong for every cause outside that promised a better world for their children. Therefore, woman challenges the parties in Child Labor and on the care of maternity and infancy—and demands that children not be exploited as cheap labor so that some greedy employer can make more money; nor that the maternity and infancy death rate shall be so high that the U.S. shall be a more dangerous place for mothers to have children in than other quarters of the globe. We don't want a Public Health like the man—we ask specifically for a Child Labor Amendment, and for the continuance of Maternity care, and we are bolder yet—like the old gentleman who forbade conjecture as form of conversation in his family and got no talk at all. We want some one or more experiments tried by Public ownership and control of Public Utilities—not to commit ourselves to principle, but why keep on guessing? Women say: Try some comparative experiment—it may prove we should have lower rates; certainly recent failures seem to prove we are asked to pay too much interest on somebody's capital. So we challenge the parties to recommend such an experiment.

We are concerned for the part that Americans shall play in the international world. We recognize the alarming, the terrific rapidity with which the international scene is changing. Now we appreciate that the economic depression from which the United States has suffered so deeply is *worldwide*, and not *national*. We recognize that for this reason, in every international question, the economic motive is of paramount importance, and also of international importance, and that this motive has forced prompt consideration in many fields in which delay had become chronic.

The independence of the Philippines, the control and direction of international finance, the attempt to stop war between China and Japan, co-operation instead of isolation with all countries, have become actual facts, where we, the voters, have thought that our grandchildren might be still considering these questions. It seems to me that only yesterday, people used to debate between the merits of isolation as advised by George Washington and joining the League of Nations, yet the irritation which we all feel is caused by the facts of the case. We have lost a great deal of money invested in Europe. Our international banking advisors have often seemed to give us very bad advice. We do not pause to consider that our national bankers have given us advise [sic] just as poor. In fact, that foresight in the economic world was, and is, sadly lacking. Nevertheless, a large part of this irritation lies in the fact they know we must go forward and cannot go back. We are on the eve of an international conference in Lausanne which is to discuss how we can possibly cure the economic ills of the world, together. We might findly [sic] wish that American economic ills could be cured without any reference to Europe, but I really can see no evidence that this is possible. In the same way, even the blindest advocate of the League of Nations must begin to see that when and if the United States plays its part in world affairs, it will find division of opinion right in the very heart of unity at Geneva. I believe that "Uncle Sam" (a somewhat weary old gentleman) has permanently taken the place of that very young girl "Miss Columbia." I am convinced that America must play a responsible part and that while she must take progress slowly, it must be progress. We are all obliged to "put away childish things." We must create a new citizenship responsible for United States interests and for those of the world together. To create this citizenship, if [sic] your task and mine. If we determine to ignore realities and seek isolation, we shall still find isolation impossible. Do I mean by that in view of practical considerations, the ideal must be overlooked? As some other countries are accused of doing, shall the U.S. profess one thing and do another? I have attended a good many national party conventions and it is certain that the perfervid oratory which adorns the rostrum and which is written into the platform sounds idealistic and is not, but what of it? We cannot abandon idealism nor can we pretend it. But what is the ideal? Out of the discussion of what we shall do there emerges some plain facts. Our ideal is to get rid of war, both as an ideal and as a practical measure. As an institution for settling difficulties, war is a complete failure and very expensive, and the biggest issue of the coming campaign is how far the government of the United States is determined to be rid of war and what steps shall it take about it. If we keep the ultimate goal in sight, the methods taken to build a peace machine are all important, but none infinitely more important than the other. The ideal point of view has never been overlooked. In the United States from the very dawn of our history when we built the land of the free, when we cleaned up the Barbary pirates and when we got rid of slavery—and when we finally sent two million men abroad to help in the Europe struggle, we have never hesitated to stand for idealism of standard in conduct. Nevertheless, it must also be admitted that a tendency to go home and think better of the matter—perhaps—sometimes to change our minds about it, is always part of our technique. Like perfidious Albion, who went home to her fog-bound Island, forgetting Europe so nearby. Well, now the difference in plain words is that we can no longer go home. What happens to the boy with college and school behind him, has happened to us and it is up to us to talk as men and women in a continuous international world in which there is no going home. We know that this new citizenship has got to be informed as to the doings, hopes and conditions of the rest of the world. We know that we can no longer use the double-headed phrase of President Wilson, "we want nothing for ourselves." We want a great deal for ourselves when we want a better world to live in and the idea which American [sic] encouraged that they would be ideal while other nations were practical, must be forgotten. Our ideal is a practical one. To find an international way to settle difficulties without going to war about them. To this end, the issues both for parties and governments in this country are, the ideal of no more war to be achieved by

1. Cooperation with the rest of the world that they may know not what the United States intends to do but that she may be depended upon to cooperate with them.

2. The entrance of the United States into the World Court to provide a legal method of settling difficulties in the international world.

3. The support of the present international disarmament conference so that an effective reduction of arms, in material, and in cost will be secured.

The conclusion, however, is that we shall have to fight like General Grant along this line if it takes all summer for the ultimate goal of a gradual disestablishment of the institution of war and settled international determination not to have recourse to it when international difficulties arise. The issue is drawn and we do not believe that might makes right in the international world!

Woman is studying out a challenge to the Political Parties deeper and wider than these—she asks for *the abolishment of child labor*, for the *care of maternity and infancy*, and for a *warless world*, for an *organized international world*. These are facts with which the parties must reckon—but above all, in this moment of economic sorrow, she asks the Political parties to reckon with her—she wants to be connected with man as the practical idealist, asking for a world of spirit and Beauty—she is the co-guardian—not only of the present, but of the future. She believes that all are entitled to the good life, or as Thomas Edison said, "A great fundamental law of science is that all forces must be kept in balance. We shall never get ahead materially until we advance spiritually."

NOTE

1. Records of the League of Women Voters, Bienna Series, 1930–2, Manuscript Division, Library of Congress, Washington, DC.

Ella Reeve Bloor (1862–1951)

Throughout her life, Ella Reeve Bloor, a deeply committed radical activist, consistently lay the blame for social injustice at the feet of industrial capitalism. On behalf of women, workers, political prisoners, and farmers, Bloor attacked the fundamental economic policies of the United States, which she argued favored business and the wealthy at the expense of workers and the poor. She began her political career in the fairly mainstream politics of Progressive Era reform, first as a member of the Women's Christian Temperance Union, and then as an advocate for women's suffrage. Unlike many of her fellow reformers, however, Bloor took the leap from reform politics to radical activism. She joined the Socialist Party in 1901, where, for the next seventeen years, she became a tireless advocate for "the worker" whether he or she labored in textiles, mining, or farming, she ran for Secretary of State in 1908 on the Socialist Party ticket. The first woman to run for statewide office in Connecticut. In 1918, she ran for Lieutenant Governor of New York.

As one of the leaders of the more radical faction of the Socialist Party, Bloor split from the Party in 1919 to help found the Communist Labor Party. She remained devoted to the Communist Party for the rest of her life. Her peers admired and recognized her political acumen and elected her delegate to represent the American Communist Party at the Communist International of Labor Union Conventions in Moscow 1921 and 1922. She also served as head of the Women's Commission. Not afraid to put her body on the line, Bloor was arrested and jailed, according to her own count, "hundreds" of times. Somehow she still found the time to publish numerous political tracts and articles in a variety of periodicals and wrote several books, including *Three Little Lovers of Nature* (1895), *Talks about Authors and Their Work* (1899), *Women of the Soviet Union* (1930), and her autobiography, *We Are Many* (1940).

Bloor never bowed to convention. She was married three times: to Lucien Ware, with whom she had six children (1881–1896); then to Louis Cohen (1896–c. 1902), with whom she had two children; and finally to Andrew Omholt in 1930. Bloor retired to her farm in Pennsylvania in 1937 and died in 1951. From her home base in Connecticut, Bloor traveled throughout the country, giving speeches, raising money, and organizing strikes.[1]

In the following speech, Bloor demonstrates her direct, rousing style as well as her belief that all workers, including farmers, shared common ground—ground that stood in direct opposition to that of the politically and economically powerful. To break the hold of the capitalist powers aligned against them (the "bosses," government officials, insurance agents, and bankers), she argued that labor would have to organize across trades, ethnicities, and genders. Once assembled, this mass power—"the mass power of the farmer backed up by the mass power of the worker"— would be unstoppable.

In 1933, when this speech was given, farmers faced severe price cuts and foreclosures due to overproduction, which made them more willing to forgo "rural individualism" in favor of organized protest and farmer's alliances. Although Bloor's confrontational politics and fearless rhetoric—as expressed here and in most of her speeches—suggests that she refuted all social conventions, including those of gender, she did not. Most directly, union activists gave her the affectionate nickname "Mother Bloor" (she had taken her colleague Richard Bloor's name, though she did not marry him during the late 1910s when organizing in Chicago). As "mother" of the movement, she could cast even the most radical and defiant speech-making as an aspect of women's "natural" moral superiority and inherent desire to nurture and care for the vulnerable. Nevertheless, this speech illustrates that in the 1930s Bloor and other radical women gave highly confrontational public speeches that expressed their deepest convictions without reservation. In part this was due to the politics and dire exigencies of the Great Depression. In the wake of what many considered the collapse of capitalism, many Americans began to consider radical solutions to the economic crisis. Leftist political organizations, including the Communist Party, made tremendous gains throughout the decade. Yet, if we consider women's public speech-giving styles as ranging along a continuum from the most conservative and courteous at one end to the most militant at the other, Bloor's "Milk Shed" speech offers an introduction into the politics of women speaking from the most radical edge.

NOTE

1. Alice Kessler Harris, *Out to work: A History of Wage-Earning Women in the United States* (New York: Oxford University Press, 1990); "Bloor, Ella Reeve," *Encyclopedia Britannica*. From Encyclopaedia Premium Service, May 27, 2003 (www.search.eb.com/woman/articles/Bloor_Ella_Reeve); "Biographical Note: Bloor, Ella Reeve," Sophia Smith Collection, Smith College, Northampton, MA.

SPEECH TO MILK SHED CONFERENCE, PHILADELPHIA (1933)[1]

Reprinted by Permission of Sophia Smith Collection, Smith College

IV. Ella Reeve Bloor, from the Iowa Regional Committee for Action, was introduced by the Chairman.

Fellow farmers and workers. There are some farmers who do not know me quite as well as the workers, and especially the miners; I used to work with the miners and the miners are especially interested in Pennsylvania and Illinois, in the welfare of the farmers. And they have helped in all their struggles; they have backed them up in many of their struggles. But I have a right to be here as a farmer, because I am the wife of a dispossessed farmer, and the mother of a dispossessed farmer.

As you may know, I have come to this section from Iowa. I am the secretary of the Iowa Regional Committee for Action which is composed of the states of Montana, North and South Dakota, Nebraska, and Iowa. We find many farmers all over the country, and the workers, too, are interested in our struggles in Iowa. And we have learned many lessons from those struggles. We have learned that the big fellows who are very few in numbers, but who still have the power of the police, the power of the sheriffs and the courts to attack farmers when they organize in great numbers. We have learned there is one thing that the insurance companies and the bankers, the organized milk trusts and others, fear more than anything else, and that is the mass power of the farmer backed up by the mass power of the worker. Of course, we have other things to fear—many ignorant farmers who thought they must not struggle very much, thought they still were sole and prime owner of their lands.

At a meeting of farmers in a schoolhouse out in Iowa, a young farmer got up and said—I am an independent farmer, I own my farm, and you said in your speech that the farmers today were slaves of the insurance companies and bankers. I am not a slave, I am an independent farmer. So I got up and asked him—do you own your farm? Yes. Have you got a mortgage on your land? He said yes. Have you got a second mortgage? Yes. Well, by any chance you haven't a mortgage on your crops? Yes. Have you a mortgage on your cattle? Yes. Have you a mortgage on your machinery? Yes. I said, what in the heck do you own, anyway? He didn't own anything. We had to break the illusion that the farmers owned the farms and land.

So the farmers have got their eyes opened, and if they strike they are going to strike not only for the cost of production, but for more than the cost of production, and they are going to strike as they have been striking all winter—for their homes, for their wives and children. We believe that the wives and children have the first mortgage on all our farms and we are going to strike for them. When they strike in Iowa they strike in the say [sic] way as they demonstrated—to keep the farmers from being evicted. They also believe in the picket lines; they should go on the highways. Some of the leaders said—strike in your own back yards. You do not want to strike against the poor cows—they did the best they could. Do the farmers carry the milk to market? No, they hire racketeers...so you see the importance of having regional committees of action, having all the states together and meeting as you are today. And they have the power of numbers to protect those picketers from going to prison. In the last strike they took 65 farmer strikers to a jail 200 miles away. What did we do to get those farmers out? We went up to the jail and we went around and around until we got that old sheriff dizzy, and then we went in there and said—you give us those 65 farmers, and they did. There they demonstrated the power of numbers.

And so we are growing. Last fall we struck for cost of production. Now we are striking for more than cost of production. The consumers of milk and cream are terribly afraid that we are going to raise the price of their milk and cream. We want to raise what we get to something like what the big fellows get—we get 96 cents a cwt. out in Iowa. If we demand together, as we might do—we could organize and march like one mass. We do not even have to strike if we are organized strongly enough. The farmers cannot sell and the workers cannot buy—we must all work together.

If you see an old farmer who tells you, you cannot do anything, you have got to get together with the big fellows, the leaders. Just listen to them, and they will tell you—of course a lawyer knows more than a poor farmer. And the poor judge—just think how the farmers spoiled the dignity of that old judge. Shedding crocodile tears for that old judge when thousands of children are starving.

I want to end up with this story. An old fogy was walking, and he had to pass a cemetery. And he was afraid that the ghosts would start walking around; that the dead men would walk around. Sure enough the graves began to open and the dead men began to walk around. The funniest thing is that they thought they were alive—they laughed and talked with one another, and pointed a finger of scorn at the one live man. Well, that is the way with the old man there. Those big fellows...We are the national, county and township committees of action—and those big fellows are walking around like ghosts and they don't know it.

NOTE

1. Typescript, "Minutes of the Milk Shed Conference," Sophia Smith Collection, Smith College, Northampton, MA.

Blanche Ames Ames (1878–1969)

Blanche Ames Ames filled her life with eclectic interests and constant political activity. She came of age as a late nineteenth century New Woman but adopted the mantle of modernity in the 1920s and 1930s. A suffragist, inventor, and birth control advocate, Ames was also an accomplished artist who became the sole illustrator for the many horticultural books written by her husband, the Harvard botanist Oakes Ames, including his "seven-volume treatise on orchids."[1] She also collaborated with her brother, Adelbert Ames II. Together, they explored "perspective and other aspects of pictorial art in the hope of using scientific findings to enhance the realism of their paintings."[2]

A lifelong Massachusetts resident, Ames was born in Lowell in 1878. Her upper-class origins were sustained by her marriage in 1900 to Oakes Ames, whose grandfather and father acquired great wealth in the shovel industry in the late nineteenth century. Though her husband's father, a key figure in the Crédit Mobilier scandal, faced personal and political reverses, Blanche and Oakes Ames enjoyed a life of financial privilege. She attended Smith College, relishing its intellectual rigor and lively social life. The Ameses had five children and together designed a stone mansion in North Easton that included a richly appointed art studio and over 1400 acres of gardens. Ames lived and worked there from 1911 until her death at age 91 in 1969.[3]

Ames began her political career at Smith College by joining the Massachusetts Suffrage Association. Her artistic talent led her to become art editor for *The Woman's Journal*. Her suffrage cartoons were published in the Boston *Transcript* as a well as pro-suffrage petitions and journals. Yet her politics were complicated. Like others of her time, Ames was prone to class and race bias. Furthermore, as with other suffragists, she believed that women ought to have the vote because of their biologically rooted, superior moral sensibilities. Nevertheless, she became a stalwart advocate for birth control, cofounding the Birth Control League of Massachusetts. As the speech that follows reflects, by the 1920s and 1930s, the birth control movement had shifted from its more radical origins to a "doctors only" policy. It was hoped that by granting doctors the singular right to disperse birth control, the movement would gain the legitimacy it needed to overcome religious and antifeminist attacks. Though birth control activists such as Margaret Sanger had once championed birth control as a fundamental right for women, after World War I, advocates tended to promote the more moderate but also more successful argument that women needed birth control for economic, medical, and eugenic reasons.[4] As Ames stated in her petition to the Massachusetts legislature, "we have a right to Birth Control service whenever we wish it to safeguard the lives of mothers and babies."[5]

In the following speech, Ames articulates this philosophy in the rationale she gave for her efforts to secure greater access to birth control for Massachusetts women. According to Ames and the Birth Control League, doctors ought to prescribe birth control to women because "wanted," well-spaced children, born to healthy women, who exhibited self-control and moral probity, would alleviate poverty and disease and thus strengthen the state and the nation. The speech reminds us that by the 1930s, women were sophisticated political strategists and, as Ames does here, testified before government bodies on a regular basis. It also shows how Ames's status as an upper-class, white woman shielded her. She could take controversial public positions, knowing that her economic and social status, even her reputation, risked little damage. In this standard stump speech, she marshals statistical evidence to promote her vision of social betterment through birth control. In her language and style, Ames employs some accepted gender and social codes (e.g., married vs. illicit sexuality; reproductive issues vs. sexual pleasure) to convince her audience of her position. She knew well that they feared that the "lowly" classes might out-populate native-born Americans. Yet, even while attempting to assuage her Catholic critics by pointing out the League's support of the rhythm method, she challenges the state to increase access to birth control as a humanitarian right.

NOTES

1. "Ames Mansion," *Places Where Women Made History*, [web site] NRHP Travel Itinerary May 27, 2003 (http://www.cr.nps.gov/NR/travel/pwwwmh/ma72.htm).

2. Roy R. Behrens, "The Artistic and Scientific Collaboration of Blanche Ames Ames and Adelbert Ames II," *Leonardo* On-Line 31 (February/March 1998): 47H54.

3. The estate, including the furnished mansion, was sold to the state in 1971 and became Borderland State Park. Ames's artwork remains on display.

4. See Linda Gordon, *Woman's Body, Woman's Right* (New York: Penguin, 1975); and John D'Emilio and Estelle Freedman, *Intimate Matters: A History of Sexuality in America* (New York: Harper & Row, 1988).

5. Blanche Ames, "An Address to the Governor and General Court of Massachusetts," c. 1930, Sophia Smith Collection, Northampton, MA.

STATEMENT BY THE PRESIDENT OF THE BIRTH CONTROL LEAGUE OF MASSACHUSETTS (JANUARY 1935)[1]

Reprinted by Permission of Sophia Smith Collection, Smith College

The Birth Control League of Massachusetts has always advocated dignified methods of publicity and the methods used have been made to conform with the wishes of our medical advisors and with the approval of our legal advisors.

The Birth Control League seeks to protect the rights of Parents to regulate conception and to acquire proper medical advice and materials by which to space conception of their children, in order to improve the chances for health and well being of these children-to-be-born and of the family.

It does not restrict the need for regulation to medical necessities only, but teaches wisdom of control for reasons of poverty, of insanity, of drunkenness, of malformation.

It asks the medical profession, both in private practice and in hospitals, to prescribe Birth Control, when parents want such information, whether they wish to regulate conception for economic reasons or for medical reasons or for personal reasons which have a worthy motive.

In urging the production of the finest and most vigorous children, and in safeguarding the health of mothers, the League strikes at the heart of the problems of eugenics, economics, and morals. And in ennobling the spirit, that is "the vital and conscious functions," in women and men, it seeks for harmony of married life in conformity with religion.

As a justification of the correctness of this policy and in answer to recent criticisms we would point to the achievements of the Mother's Health Office which confines the giving of contraceptive advice to married women whose physical or mental condition is such that it is believed that immediate pregnancy would be dangerous.

The success of this plan is proved by the fact that within two and one half years such information has been given to 650 women after careful physical examination had shown that there was a genuine reason for giving the advice. As further evidence of the confidence that the Mother's Health Office has inspired, patients have been sent there from 16 hospitals, 32 social agencies, and 53 private physicians.

This policy has been declared by our lawyers to be not within the prohi-
bitions of the Massachusetts statutes relating to the giving of contraceptive
advice.

Another recent activity of the League has been the circulation of the Parents' Petition which is a request to the Massachusetts Medical Society for an
investigation of the entire situation from the medical point of view. In this
petition the Medical Society is being asked to instruct the Parents of Massachusetts as to the relative value of modern contraceptive measures, including the so-called "safe period" as advocated in the book "The Rhythm"
which is published with the approval of the Archdiocese of Chicago (Roman
Catholic).

It has been felt by the officers of the League that a more substantial
advance could be made by following these lines of effort rather than by
methods involving greater publicity; that the sane and sound progress of the
movement depended to a great degree on the cooperation of the medical
profession and that this cooperation would be to a considerable degree
alienated by certain types of publicity.

NOTE

1. Typescript with handwritten revisions. Sophia Smith Collection, Smith
College, Northampton, MA.

Frances Perkins (1880–1965)

Frances Perkins was the first woman to hold a presidential cabinet position in the United States. Though it was a controversial appointment, Perkins served as Secretary of Labor from 1933–1945, throughout Franklin Roosevelt's entire presidency, longer than anyone else in that position. Perkins is acknowledged as the principal designer of the Social Security Act of 1935, but she also established the Labor Standards Bureau and, through the Wagner Act, supported workers' right to organize. The Department of Labor Headquarters in Washington, DC, is named for Perkins, and, in 1988, she was named to the Labor Hall of Fame.[1] During her long career she encountered, interacted with, influenced, and was influenced by a number of the women and organizations included in this anthology. For example, she worked at Jane Addams's Hull House, and received support from Eleanor Roosevelt when FDR nominated Perkins to become his Secretary of Labor.

After attending Worcester Classical High School in Massachusetts, Perkins entered Mount Holyoke College as a chemistry major. A speech by Florence Kelley, delivered at a meeting of the Mount Holyoke College chapter of the National Consumer's League, focused Perkins's attention on labor and industry issues.[2] She completed an MA in Political Science at Columbia University, then, like many young women of that era, exercised her rhetorical skills as a lobbyist and as a suffrage speaker. Further, in 1911, Perkins was deeply affected when she saw labor leader and industrial feminist Rose Schneiderman speak in outrage after the Triangle Shirtwaist Fire.

During the New Deal Era, Perkins was at the hub of a wheel of social influence, among the few most influential women throughout the period

Secretary of Labor Frances Perkins discussing the steel strike situation with reporters at a press conference, June 17, 1937.

Library of Congress, Prints & Photographs Division, [reproduction number, LC-USZ62-26653].

covered by this collection. She addressed women's groups and gave broadcast speeches and press conferences, developing rhetorical strategies to overcome gender bias toward female speakers. Perkins was skilled in adapting her message to various audiences. She built her credibility through careful selection of evidence, as well as straightforward language and clear logic. By August 1934, Perkins was acclaimed by the *New York Times* as one of the five best speakers in America.[3]

Frances Perkins's finest moments, however, were yet to come. First, as Chair of the Committee on Economic Security from 1934 to 1935, Perkins guided the creation and ratification of the Social Security Act, delivering over 100 speeches during this period. Second, perhaps an even stronger testament to her rhetorical prowess came after passage of the Social Security Act. A resolution of impeachment was brought against Perkins and two other government officials. She refused to deport labor leader Harry Bridges who had been accused of being a communist—accusations he denied. Perkins's voluntary statement before the House Judiciary Committee on February 8, 1939 not only stopped impeachment hearings, it also made an important argument on behalf of those suspected of being, but not proven to be, "undesirable."[4]

The speech included here was given on February 25, 1935, the last in a series of four radio speeches Perkins delivered, which justified and explained social security legislation. The first speech was presented August 13, 1934, just two months after Roosevelt created the Commission on Economic Security. She focused on building her credibility as committee chair, and presented a rationale for a new approach to economic recovery through government reform, as well as previewing the committee's task. The second and third speeches were both delivered in December 1935 before the recommendations were sent to the White House. Perkins announced completion of the committee's work and focused on building confidence in the concept of social insurance. The final speech, two months later, was delivered after White House approval and before the proposal was sent to Congress. In this final radio address, Perkins outlined the key recommendations and justified them as a sign of progress for American government. The outcome was the Social Security Act of 1935. Perkins's handling of the committee, the American public, and Congress in creating and securing support and passage of this momentous legislation is a landmark in American history.

NOTES

1. "Social Security Pioneers: Frances Perkins," Social Security Online: The Official Website of the Social Security Administration, May 27, 2003 (www.ssa.gov/history/perkins.html).

2. Jerry, E. Claire and Jennifer E. Christensen "Frances Perkins," *Women Public Speakers in the United States 1925–1993*, Karlyn Kohrs Campbell, ed. (Westport: Greenwood, 1994), 345–346.

3. Ann Atkinson, "Finding a Place at the Cabinet Table: Discovering the Rhetorical Disposition of Frances Perkins during the New Deal" (Ph.D. diss. University of Massachusetts, 1996), 116–117; Jerry and Christensen, 346, 348, 353–354.

4. Atkinson, 91–139.

SOCIAL INSURANCE FOR U.S.
BY HON. FRANCES PERKINS
NATIONAL RADIO ADDRESS DELIVERED
FEBRUARY 25, 1935[1]
10:30 P.M. NBC NETWORK

I have been asked to speak to you tonight on the administration's program for economic security which is now, as you know, before Congress. It seems to me that few legislative proposals have had as careful study, as thorough and conscientious deliberation as went into the preparation of these measures. The program now under consideration represents, I believe, a most significant step in our National development, a milestone in our progress toward the better-ordered society.

As I look back on the tragic years since 1929, it seems to me that we as a Nation, not unlike some individuals, have been able to pass through a bitter experience to emerge with a newfound insight and maturity. We have had the courage to face our problems and find a way out. The heedless optimism of the boom years is past. We now stand ready to build the future with sanity and wisdom.

The process of recovery is not a simple one. We cannot be satisfied merely with makeshift arrangements which will tide us over the present emergencies. We must devise plans that will not merely alleviate the ills of today, but will prevent, as far as it is humanly possible to do so, their recurrence in the future. The task of recovery is inseparable from the fundamental task of social reconstruction.

Among the objectives of that reconstruction, President Roosevelt in his message of June 8, 1934, to the Congress placed "the security of the men, women and children of the Nation first." He went on to suggest the social insurances with which European countries have had a long and favorable experience as one means of providing safeguards against "misfortunes which cannot be wholly eliminated in this man-made world of ours." Subsequent to this message he created the Committee on Economic Security, of which I have the honor to be the chairman, to make recommendations to him with regard to these problems. The recommendations of that committee are embodied in the Economic Security Bill, now pending in Congress. The measures we propose do not by any means provide a complete and permanent solution of our difficulties. If put into effect, however, they will provide a greater degree of security for the American citizen and his family than he has heretofore known. The bill is, I believe, a sound beginning on which we can build by degrees to our ultimate goal.

We cannot hope to accomplish all in one bold stroke. To begin too ambitiously in the program of social security might very well result in errors which would entirely discredit this very necessary type of legislation. It is not amiss to note here that social legislation in European countries, begun some 25 years ago, is still in a developmental state and has been subjected to numerous changes as experience and changing conditions dictated.

It may come as a surprise to many of us that we in this country should be so far behind Europe in providing our citizens with those safeguards which assure a decent standard of living in both good times and bad, but the reasons are not far to seek. We are much younger than our European neighbors. Our abundant pioneer days are not very far behind us. With unlimited opportunities, in those days, for the individual who wished to take advantage of them, dependency seemed a reflection on the individual himself, rather than the result of social or economic conditions. There seemed little need for any systematic organized plan, such as has now become necessary.

It has taken the rapid industrialization of the last few decades, with its mass-production methods, to teach us that a man might become a victim of circumstances far beyond his control, and finally it "took a depression to dramatize for us the appalling insecurity of the great mass of the population, and to stimulate interest in social insurance in the United States." We have come to learn that the large majority of our citizens must have protection against the loss of income due to unemployment, old age, death of the breadwinners and disabling accident and illness, not only on humanitarian grounds, but in the interest of our national welfare. If we are to maintain a healthy economy and thriving production, we need to maintain the standard of living of the lower income groups in our population who constitute 90 per cent of our purchasing power. England, with its earlier industrialization, learned this lesson earlier, as well. The world depression caught up with Great Britain sooner than it did with us. She has known the haunting fear of insecurity as well as we. The foresight of nearly three decades has, however, found her somewhat better prepared with the basic framework of a social insurance system. Social insurance in Great Britain has proceeded progressively since the first decade of the century. Championed by the liberal Lloyd George and beginning with the old age pension act of 1908, it has known many revisions and extensions. Since its inception, however, it has gradually overcome the opposition of its critics, and there has never been any thought of abandoning the system. It is today in a healthy state of growth. Practically all the other industrial countries of Europe have had similar experiences. In the trial and error procedure of Europe's quarter century of social legislation—in that concrete experience—is contained sound truths as well as mistakes from which we can learn much. But we cannot build solely on European experience. We, with our particular kind of state-federal government, our wide, expansive country, with its varying economic and social standards, have many needs different from those of the more closely knit, homogeneous European countries.

The American program for economic security now before our Congress follows no single pattern. It is broader than social insurance, and does not attempt merely to copy a European model. Where other measures seemed more appropriate to our background or present situation, we have not hesitated to deviate from strict social insurance principles. In doing so we feel that we have recommended the measures which at this time seemed best calculated under our American conditions to protect individuals in the years immediately ahead from the hazards which might otherwise plunge them into destitution and dependency.

Our program deals with safeguards against unemployment, with old-age security, with maternal aid and aid to crippled and dependent children and public health services. Another major subject—health insurance—is dealt with briefly in the report of the Committee on Economic Security, but without any definite recommendations. Fortunate in having secured the cooperation of the medical and other professions directly concerned, the committee is working on a plan for health insurance which will be reported later in the year. Our present program calls for the extension of existing public health services to meet conditions accentuated by the depression. Similarly, the provisions for maternal aid and aid to dependent and crippled children are not new departures, but rather the extension and amplification of safeguards which for a number of years have been a recognized part of public responsibility.

Let me briefly describe the other measures now under consideration which do represent something of a departure from our usual course.

Recognizing unemployment as the greatest of all hazards, the committee gave primary emphasis to provisions for unemployment—employment assurance. This measure is embodied in the $4,800,000,000 Public Works Resolution, which is separate from, but complementary to, the Economic Security Bill itself. Employment assurance, the stimulation of private employment and the provision of public employment for those able-bodied workers whom private industry cannot yet absorb is to be solely a responsibility of the Federal Government and its major contribution in providing safeguards against unemployment. It should be noted that this is the largest employment program ever considered in any country. As outlined by the President, it will furnish employment for able-bodied men now on relief, and enable them to earn their support in a decent and socially useful way. It will uphold morale, as well as purchasing power, and directly provide jobs for many in private industry who would otherwise have none. For the 80 per cent of our industrial workers who are employed, we propose a system of unemployment compensation, or insurance, as it is usually called. In our concern for the unemployed, we must not overlook this much larger group who also need protection. No one who is now employed can feel secure while so many of his fellows anxiously seek work. Unemployment compensation, while it has distinct limitations which are not always clearly understood, is particularly valuable for the ordinarily regularly employed industrial worker who is laid off for short periods because of seasonal demands or other minor industrial disturbances. He can, during this period when he has a reasonable expectation of returning to work within a short time, receive compensation for his loss of income for a limited period as a definite, contractual right. His standard of living need not be undermined, he is not forced on relief nor must he accept other work unsuited to his skill and training.

Unemployment insurance, wherever it has been tried, has demonstrated its value in maintaining purchasing power and stabilizing business conditions. It is very valuable at the onset of a depression, and even in the later stages will serve to carry a part of the burden of providing for the unemployed. For those who have exhausted their rights to unemployment benefits and for those who, in any case, must be excluded from its provisions, we suggest that they be given employment opportunities on public work projects. In these two measures, employment assurance and unemployment compensation, we have a first and second line of defense which together should form a better safeguard than either standing alone.

The unemployment compensation system has been designed to remove an obstacle which has long prevented progressive industrial states from enacting unemployment insurance laws—fear of interstate competition with states not having such laws. Having removed that obstacle, the law allows the states full latitude to develop the kind of unemployment compensation systems best suited to their individual needs. The bill provides for a Federal tax on pay rolls against which credit is allowed the employer for contributions to an approved state unemployment compensation fund. By this Federal tax every employer will be placed on the same competitive basis from a National standpoint, and at the same time, aside from compliance with a few minimum Federal standards, every State will be free to adopt the kind of law it wants. One of the most important of the Federal requirements is that all unemployment compensation funds shall be deposited with the Federal Treasury in Washington, so as to assure their availability when needed and make it possible to utilize the reserves which will accumulate in conformity with the credit policy of the Nation.

We feel that this is a most fortunate time for the government to take action on unemployment insurance. There has been a rapidly growing enthusiasm for it in the states for years. Many states have already prepared excellent legislation of this kind or are studying the subject, and they are but waiting word from Washington, so that they may proceed with the plans which have been so long under consideration.

I come now to the other major phase of our program. The plan for providing against need and dependency in old age is divided into three separate and distinct parts. We advocate, first, free federally aided pensions for those now old and in need; second, a system of compulsory contributory old-age insurance for workers in the lower income brackets; and third, a voluntary system of low-cost annuities purchasable by those who do not come under the compulsory system.

Enlightened opinion has long since discarded the old poor-house method of caring for the indigent aged, and 28 states already have old-age pension laws. Due to financial difficulties, many of these laws are now far less effective than they were intended to be. Public sentiment in this country is strongly in favor of providing these old people with a decent and dignified

subsistence in their declining years. Exploiting that very creditable sentiment, impossible, hare-brained schemes for providing for the aged have
sprung into existence and attracted misguided supporters. But the administration is confident that its plan for meeting the situation is both humane
and practical and will receive the enthusiastic support of the people.

We propose that the Federal Government shall come to the aid of the state
pension systems already in existence and stimulate the enactment of similar
legislation elsewhere by grants-in-aid equal to one-half the state expenditures for such purposes but not exceeding $15 per month. This does not nec-
essarily mean that state pensions would not anywhere exceed $30 per
month. Progressive states may find it possible to grant more than $15 per
month as their share. The size of the pension would, of course, be propor-
tionate to the need of the applicant and would quite likely vary with conditions in different states. A larger pension would, for example, be necessary
in certain industrial states than in communities where living conditions are
easier.

For those now young or even middle-aged, a system of compulsory old-
age insurance will enable them to build up, with matching contributions
from their employers, an annuity from which they can draw as a right upon
reaching old age. These workers will be able to care for themselves in their
old age, not merely on a subsistence basis, which is all that gratuitous pensions have anywhere provided, but with a modest comfort and security.
Such a system will greatly lessen the hazards of old age to the many workers who could not, unaided, provide for themselves and would greatly
lessen the enormous burden of caring for the aged of future generations
from public funds. The voluntary system of old-age annuities is designed to
cover the same income groups as does the compulsory system, but will
afford those who for many reasons cannot be included in a compulsory system an opportunity to provide for themselves.

Many of you will be interested to know that the two proposed annuity
systems in no way infringe on the commercial annuity markets. Officials of
insurance companies have themselves remarked that these measures would
touch a strata of our population for whom commercial annuities are prohib-
itively expensive. These officials feel that the measures we propose will
prove advantageous to their companies rather than the reverse, in so far as
they promote public interest in the insurance movement.

This, in broad outlines, is the program now before us. We feel that it is a
sound and reasonable plan and framed with due regard for the present state
of economic recovery. I can do no better than to pass on to you the words
with which President Roosevelt closed his letter submitting these recommendations to the Congress now in session: "The establishment of sound
means toward a greater future economic security of the American people is
dictated by a prudent consideration of the hazards involved in our national
life. No one can guarantee this country against the dangers of future depressions, but we can reduce these dangers. We can eliminate many of the factors
that cause economic depressions, and we can provide the means of mitigat-
ing their results. This plan for economic security is at once a measure of prevention and a method of alleviation.

"We pay now for the dreadful consequence of economic insecurity—and dearly. This plan presents a more equitable and infinitely less expensive means of meeting these costs. We cannot afford to neglect the plain duty before us. I strongly recommend action to attain the objectives sought in this report."

NOTE

1. "Social Security Pioneers: Frances Perkins," Social Security Online: The Official Website of the Social Security Administration, May 27, 2003 (www.ssa.gov/history/perkins.html).

Anna Kelton Wiley (1877–1964)

In Anna Kelton Wiley's long activist career, she never wavered from her commitment to equal rights feminism. An ardent supporter of the Equal Rights Amendment, she rejected all arguments, feminist and otherwise, that suggested women and men required different social parameters due to their distinct social or biological roles. In contrast to many reformers who came of age during the Progressive Era, Wiley opposed sex-differentiated political and legislative efforts designed to protect women, believing that such efforts perpetuated gender inequity. After women won the vote in 1920, Wiley threw her support to the radicals, particularly the National Woman's Party. In opposition to the League of Women Voters who supported protective legislation for women, Wiley campaigned for the Party's main objective, the passage of an Equal Rights Amendment to the United States Constitution, for her entire life. Introduced in 1923 by Alice Paul, the President of the National Woman's Party, the ERA was never passed, facing legislative defeat in 1982.[1]

In some aspects, Wiley's biographical portrait mirrors the path taken by so many New Women. She was born in Oakland, California, into an accomplished family (her father was Brigadier General John C. Kelton), moved to Washington, DC, when she was just eight, earned a Bachelor of Science degree from Columbian College (now George Washington University) in 1897, and then jumped full force into lifelong activist reform. Her hand stirred all pots, from helping to pass the Food and Drug Act in 1906, to picketing the White House for suffrage in 1917, to serving as Chairman of Indian Welfare for the General Federation of Women's Clubs from 1938 to 1940, to conducting a GFWC-sponsored Good Will Tour of Mexico in 1942. She seemed never to stop—constantly speaking, agitating, and traveling on behalf of liberal causes. The biographical note that accompanies her papers at the Library of Congress is broken into three twenty-five-year sections, followed by a last list of accomplishments, titled "The Awarding Years." George Washington University, the GFWC, the Women's City Club (DC), and the DAR all bestowed honors on her.

In other ways her life was a bit less conventional. She did not marry until she was thirty-three and chose to marry Dr. Harvey W. Wiley, who was sixty-six at the time. She also participated in some of the most traditional reform organizations (e.g., President of Housekeeper's Alliance, DC, and the DAR) while holding one of the more radical ideological positions on equality, as her steadfast support of the National Woman's Party and the ERA illustrates.

Wiley traveled and spoke on behalf of the Woman's Party, the GFWC, and numerous other organizations for over forty years. Her speeches are notable for the way in which she consistently advocated for passage of the ERA while addressing a variety of "women's issues." Though she incorporated clever and humorous language, she was not one to soften her positions. She knew how to translate the meaning of abstract judicial principles into heart-felt pragmatic realities that would galvanize her audiences. Whether a woman wanted to marry, "operate a beauty shop or a real estate office," she needed the ERA. As the following speech illustrates, even in the midst of the Great Depression, she attacked gender discrimination in the workplace and recommended the ERA as the solution. Wiley demanded that her upper-middle-class audience—those who "lived in sheltered homes with kind thoughtly husbands and fathers"—consider the impact of legal and economic discrimination on those women who needed to work to "earn a supplementary sum to care for the family." This speech, given before the Philadelphia Branch of the National Woman's Party in 1935, provides a clear and thorough exposition of her feminist politics, her pro-ERA position, and her use of empirical, pragmatic appeals to make her case.

NOTE

1. "Biographical Note," Anna Kelton Wiley Papers, Manuscript Division, Library of Congress, Washington, DC.

PHILADELPHIA BRANCH OF THE NATIONAL WOMAN'S PARTY
PHILADELPHIA WOMEN'S CLUB (MONDAY, SEPTEMBER 9, 1935)[1]

Women are credited everywhere with an insatiable desire to talk. I hardly think it fair to ascribe the preponderance of talking in the world to women. We can easily think of many occupations practiced mostly by men in which

talking is the main business. Such for example as Congress, the state legislatures, the radio broadcasters, the newspaper fraternity and the various
propaganda bureaus. However that may be it seems as though a woman, an
elderly woman I may say, who has driven as I have today, 125 miles to speak
for 30 minutes, must consider that she has a message of sufficient importance to take all that trouble. And indeed I have.

The National Woman's Party, which I represent here tonight is the only
organization whose sole object of existence is to secure *justice* to women. You
look in surprise and think I am talking in riddles. "Justice to women" you
say! "I know of no injustices in my life". And probably that is true. St. Paul
said 1800 years ago that "The law is not made for the righteous man but for
the lawless and disobedient." And so it is that women who live in sheltered
homes with kind thoughtly husbands and fathers do not know that there is
not a single state in the union today where all the laws apply equally to men
and women. That married women in almost one-half of the states are under
legal disabilities limiting their power to contract or to carry on a business.
For instance before a woman marries she is in the eyes of the law able to look
out for herself. If she wants to operate a beauty shop or a real estate office,
no one will hold an inquiry as to her capacity to run it. But when she marries, the law in some states places her under a disability and requires her to
go through a complicated court procedure to satisfy the judge as to her
capacity and competency to engage in business. While the most ignorant
man, married or single, may carry on a business and no inquiry is conducted
as to his qualifications. In more than one-third of the states the rights of
mothers over their children are inferior to those of fathers in some respect.
The inheritance laws in some states discriminate against women. About one-
half of the states deny to married women the power over their property,
which is freely given to married men as regards their property. Some of the
states give the earnings and services of married women to their husbands. In
two-thirds of the states a double standard of morals is sanctioned by law.

Sheltered married woman who live happy normal lives do not come up
against these discriminatory laws. Moreover, married women whose husbands earn a sufficient competency to prevent their having to earn a supplementary sum to care for the family do not suffer from the operation of the
Economy Act of 1932 which provided that in any reduction of personnel in
any branch of the government services, married persons, if living with husband or wife, be the first to be dismissed—that is if the husband or wife was
also in the government service. The obvious intent of the clause, though
written in terms of sexual equality was the ousting of married women,
despite the fact that the Civil Service Act provides that married couples may
enter the classified service together.

The unfortunate example of the Economy Act has been followed in the
legislatures of 9 states where bills of a similar nature have been debated,
namely in California, Delaware, Maine, Nebraska, New Hampshire, North
Carolina, Maryland, Pennsylvania, and Wisconsin (House bill 785 intro. by
Rep. Schwartz). As far as I know they were all defeated. In Ohio a survey
was taken this spring to ascertain in how many instances husband and wife
appear on the state payroll with a view to introducing a similar bill. In Ore-

gon those married women whose "husbands earn enough" were threatened to be excluded from employment in the state government according to Carl Cover, asst. state budget director. This is one of the many reasons why I believe in the program of the National Women's Party, which is working for an amendment to the federal Constitution providing that men and women shall have equal rights. Because if the fundamental law of the land is grounded in justice then the laws of the states reflect and emulate this principle.

As the Bible says:—

"The light of the boy is the eye; therefore when thine eye is single thy whole body is full of light; but when thine eye is evil thy body also is full of darkness. Take heed therefore that the light which is in thee be not darkness."

Our constitution is the eye of the body politic. If it is full of light then justice and right thinking will prevail in the states. It is so with the pure food law which Dr. Wiley drafted 29 years ago. The states have passed state food laws modelled on that statute.

It is really difficult to believe that any member of Congress of the U.S. would actually vote to dismiss from the service of the Government any person on account of sex or marriage. The advocates of this measure contended that social and economic justice was secured thereby. But such an arbitrary basis resulting in dismissal without regard to individual effort, training and efficiency can never promote social and economic justice. This dismissal of public employees on such ground without regard to efficiency is an injustice to the taxpayer and an affront to those who strive for honest advancement. Moreover it puts our Government in a very wrong, a very strange position. In the event a husband and wife are living together and each working from the government, they are *penalized*. In a period when the marriage rate is declining and the divorce rate increasing, it is proposed that this government should penalize successful marriage and encourage divorces. The institution of marriage does not warrant such treatment at the hands of Congress. It is impossible to figure out the social and economic justice that would result by dismissing, on account of marriage, and without regard to individual qualifications, effort and efficiency, those who entered the service, of the Federal government, through the Civil Service. It is also difficult to figure out why successful marriage should be penalized and why those who live separate lives should be favored by Congress.

Representative Emanuel Celler of N.Y. introduced a bill into the 74th Congress S.5051, providing "that no person shall be discriminated against in any case because of *his* or *her marital* status in examination, appointment, reappointment, reinstatement, reemployment, promotion, transfer, retransfer, demotion, removal or retirement" but the bill has not passed as yet.

So far what I have had to say deals with married women, but let no unmarried woman think that similar injustices do not also apply to her, also both abroad and here in our own beloved country. In Oklahoma a woman is barred from public office and position; in 27 states women are barred from jury service; women are barred from some of the leading schools, colleges and universities in the land and under the guise of *"protection"*, 48-hour and other laws have been passed restricting the hours of women in industry but not of men, which handicap wage-earning women and prevent them from competing on equal terms with men in earning their livelihood.

In Ohio recently the men teachers of the city of Cincinnati issued a set of 29 questions each beginning "Do you know" which are almost unbelievable. A few of them are to the effect that "do you know that out of 1850 teachers in Cincinnati 250 are men? That Cincinnati pays its men and women teachers the same salaries? That men teachers in Cincinnati public schools are the lowest paid group of professional male workers, whereas the women teachers are the highest paid group of professional female workers in the city? That a differential in salary between men and women teachers will easily absorb the reduction of $450,000 in the school budget? And finally, That it is economically unsound to pay all teachers a salary that is necessary to attract only a part of them?

The women teachers countered with a set of 29 queries ending with the statement that they resented the suggestion that they absorb the $450,000 shortage in the salary budget, that they contributed services equal to those of the men and that their obligations are just as binding and their burdens in many cases are greater and also that a differential between the salaries of the men and women teachers in order to attract men from other professions would have to be so *great* that no school system could maintain it, and that men attracted to the teaching profession chiefly because of the amount of money to be gained from it, would be poor teaching material.

In the legislative year 1933–1934 seven states passed minimum wage laws for women only (New York, New Jersey, New Hampshire, Ohio, Connecticut, Utah and Illinois). Previous to that between 1912 and 1923, 17 states had enacted such laws. Massachusetts was the pioneer state passing her law in 1912. But when in 1923 the Supreme Court declared the minimum wage law in the District of Columbia unconstitutional, there was a lull in the passage of such statutes until 1933, ten years later when this crop of 7 states passed similar laws. This was due to the influence of the present Administration, which believes in protective legislation for *women and children only* in the states while standing for protective legislation in the federal leg. In the lull of 10 years between 1923 and 1933 only four states, California, North Dakota, Oregon and Massachusetts continued to actively enforce their minimum wage statutes. The other states either repealed their laws, declared them unconstitutional or being chary of the constitutional issue did not appropriate funds for their enforcement.

The right of women to support themselves is threatened by the enactment of minimum wage legislation. Forced out of their jobs and forced to depend upon men for their livelihood women will again become a slave class. Minimum wage laws for women only, through which the states are taking the control of their lives out of women's hands and legislating for them as for children, are part of a widespread movement to eliminate women as competitors of men in the present economic struggle. State laws prohibiting night work and restricting hours of work, and state and local laws and national administrative policies leading to the dismissal and exclusion of married women are all a part of the same general trend.

Women who have held well paid political or semi-political positions are now being dismissed in order that the jobs may go to men, as take for instance the forced retirement of Dr. Amy N. Stanard recently from the Federal Board of Parole, an efficient and well equipped psychiatrist, to make way for Ex-Judge T. Webber Wilson of the Virgin Islands. *The Nation* of August 7th 1935 says of this incident: "The moral of the story is that a women is not safe in the government service; not even if she has performed invaluable work of an expert nature, not supplied by the men with whom she is working."

According to a survey made in 1935, by the League of Women Voters, there is a loss of 5 women legislators in 1935 compared with 1933 and 1934. 1929 was the peak year when 149 women sat in the state legislatures. This past year the total number of women legislators was 130, in 34 states.

B. C. Forbes in a recent statement suggested that in filling jobs suitable for either young women or men that the preference be given to the men because they constitute the country's defense in its hours of peril; because young men cannot make relief money go as far [as] women and because the advent of women into industry has been relatively recent. Mrs. Walter Ferguson in replying to these arguments said: "If young men are the country's chief defense, who provides these young men for the trenches? And again, taking jobs from women because they know how to stretch relief money further than the boys do, seems rather a harsh punishment for thrift! The statement that men have always been the providers may be challenged also. Men it is true have been the *earners* but in every era of history women have helped to provide. They have made valuable contributions to the family maintenance and they did not go into industry until industry had first invaded their realm and taken from them all opportunity to create, invent and produce."

In Europe the same trend is evident, only slightly more advanced than here, enabling us to look a little ahead and see just what will happen in this country. In England married women have for some time been largely excluded from government positions. In Germany, where women had reached important power, their position has become so deplorable that it has called forth a protest from the women's organizations in Great Britain. Frau Maria Halberstadt, German feminist in exile, states that the discrimination against women in Germany is of much more vital importance than the discrimination against the Jewish people. She contends that millions of women are in practical slavery in Germany. Those intellectuals among women who were not forced out of the country, she states, meet in groups of two or three to devise small ways of helping to overthrow the government. A meeting of a larger number is suspicious. She paints a dark picture for women in Germany.

In Belgium a circular of the Prime Minister of Apr. 12, 1934, states that the government had decided, until further notice, to reserve for men all available positions in public administrative departments including stenographers and typists positions. A Royal Order of Dec. 8, 1934, authorizes the Minister of Labor and Social Welfare to fix a small quota for the number of married and unmarried women who will be permitted in each branch of industry.

In Italy a Legislative Decree of Nov. 28, 1933, authorizes the government Departments to limit the number of women who are allowed to compete for paid positions and to exclude them altogether from competing for such positions, if it thinks wise. In an order of Oct. 11, 1934, by the Fascist Corporation of Industry and the Fascist Confederation of Industrial Workers specifies that women shall be replaced by men in all work normally done by women, as far as possible.

In the Netherlands, a Circular of the Minister of the Interior Mar. 19, 1934 recommends to all local authorities that they replace women by men in positions not specifically requiring female labor.

And so we could go on with orders from Cuba, Irish Free State, Luxembourg and Yugoslavia similar to those stated. Miss Paul brought us this research when she returned from Europe in July. It shows the trend abroad, only more emphasized than here, but the same trend.

Senator Bratton of New Mexico stated to a delegation of women only a year ago that within ten years there would be no women employed under national, state or local governments. I myself heard at a Town Hall, in Washington last winter, Mr. Lawrence Dennis who spoke on the topic "Is Fascism in the U.S. inevitable?" say that Capitalism had failed, that communism was not desirable but that fascism was inevitable. When asked by Miss Dorothy Detzer what would become of the women he replied that women would be liquidated. That the "mediocre ones would go back to the kitchen." One wonders at what point their mediocracy would be determined. Mr. William Green remarked at another Town Hall that the keystone of a man's economic liberty was his right to contract for his labor. One wonders why the keystone of a woman's economic liberty is not the very same right. Miss Genevieve Parkhurst in an article "Is Feminism Dead?" in the April 1935 *Harper's* tells of a group of women who went in to see a congressman in regard to the Economy Act. When they went into his office a man was leaving. "Did you notice that man?" he asked them. "It is a coincidence that you should be coming in just now. He has been talking to me for an hour, trying to persuade me that women are to blame for the depression. He is one of an influential lobby which is starting a movement to repeal the Nineteenth Amendment. He did not get very far with me. I don't think there is much chance of his succeeding in getting such a bill through this Congress. Still you cannot tell in times like these. A few flakes of snow have been known to start an avalanche."

What are you going to do when an eminent editor, Mr. Arthur Brisband, in the *Wash. Herald* of May 23, 1935, says to 350 women engaged in creative and executive fashion work at the Ritz Carlton Hotel in Washington, "that young business women fail to realize that getting married is the greatest thing they can do," and he advised them "each to have at least six children." Germany has gone one better. Wilhelm Frick, minister of the interior announced new citizenship legislation would require every German woman to bear at least one child before full citizenship is conferred.

No, women have been too supine. They have failed to unite and coordinate their power as they should, not only for their own protection but in order that the principles for which women stand may be embodied in our civilization. What kind of a civilization is this when men and women are at each other's throats. In the article just referred to by Genevieve Parkhurst she says "we must work as the women in Norway did. They wanted the vote but only as a step to something higher. They wanted it as a means of securing security for the entire population. Because of the reactionaries the forward-looking men had to have the help of the women. The Norwegian women could not help until they were on a solid basis themselves. They did not want to waste time by removing one discrimination here and another there, so they educated their women and stood together in a solid voting mass and secured a sex-disqualification act. And now the Norwegian women act as citizens, not as women in the social welfare program of their country." That is the example we must follow.

As the pioneer women of three-quarters of a century ago resolved, so we must resolve to-day "That the women of the country ought to be enlightened in regard to the laws under which they live, that they may no longer publish their degradation by declaring themselves satisfied with their present condition nor their ignorance by asserting that they have all the rights they want."

And the best way to do this is to join the National Women's Party in its effort to secure an amendment to the federal Constitution stating "That men and women shall have equal rights throughout the U.S. and in every place subject to its jurisdiction." This fundamental truth should have been included with the first ten amendments and would have been if we had had a few more Abigail Adamses, or a few of the brilliant women lawyers who are battling for us today. But we did not have a woman lawyer until nearly 100 years after the Constitution was ratified.

Let us not forget that our ancestors crossed the ocean in small and inadequate vessels and settled in inhospitable and dangerous country to secure equal rights in religious matters! Let us not forget that a bloody war lasting four years had to come to grant equality of opportunity as far as race was concerned. Today we are seeking to secure equality of opportunity as far as sex is concerned.

It is the last inner cidital [sic] which is being stormed and perhaps the most difficult. Women are not by nature fighters. They are accustomed to sacrifice. But light comes from more to more. At first we see as through a glass darkly and then face to face. Light is coming. The dawn is breaking. The National Women's Lawyers Assn. has endorsed our program. The Natl. Women Osteopathic Assn. has endorsed. Business and Professional groups here and there have endorsed while the Natl. B. & P. are studying the matter. Four state Federations, namely Michigan, D.C., Maine and Arizona, of the General Federation family have endorsed, while the General Federation is studying the matter. Study pamphlets have been circulated throughout the country and I find wherever I go a receptive attitude among clubwomen.

The subject of equality has been in the thoughts of men for a very long time. In the prophecy of Isaiah, two thousand years before Christ, when he said "Unto us a Child is born, Unto us a son is given and the government shall be upon his shoulder and his name shall be called Wonderful Counsellor, The mighty God, the Everlasting Father, The Prince of Peace, Of the increase of his government and of peace there shall be no end *** and upon his kingdom to order it and to establish it with judgment and with justice from henceforth even for ever." Does anyone for a moment suppose that that justice prophysied [*sic*] by Isaiah shall not be for women also?

Plato in his *Republic* proposed for his ideal State a guardian class, in which there should be no sex barrier. He insists that division of labor must be by aptitude and ability and not by sex. His words are "In the administration of a state, neither a woman as a woman, nor a man as a man, has any special function, but the gifts of nature are equally diffused in both sexes."

Coming down to our own times. Abraham Lincoln said, "Let us have faith that *right* makes *might* and with that faith let us dare to do our duty as we see it." [one sentence insert not legible] I trust that the women here tonight see their duty to help the Woman's Party to give fundamental protection to women by placing this amendment to the Constitution to safeguard their life, their liberty and their happiness.

NOTE

1. Typescript with handwritten revisions. Anna Kelton Wiley Papers, Manuscript Division, Library of Congress, Washington, DC.

Eleanor Roosevelt (1884–1962)

The most central public woman of the period from 1920 to 1960 was, unquestionably, Eleanor Roosevelt. She affected most of the women included in this anthology in one way or another, and many owed much of their own public position to her influence. Although she was subjected to an array of vicious personal attacks, especially during her years in the White House, her consistent, committed advocacy of democracy for all citizens won far more supporters than detractors. Whether recounting her experiences visiting Americans suffering economic deprivation during the depression, defending wage-earning wives and mothers (including herself), or challenging the privileged to work harder for democracy, Eleanor Roosevelt gave voice and hope to ordinary citizens.[1]

Her public life began in 1920 when she joined the League of Women Voters, campaigned with Franklin Roosevelt for the vice presidency, and became friends with FDR advisor Louis Howe, who coached her in public speaking. After Franklin was paralyzed by polio in 1921, Eleanor became his surrogate speaker. She joined the Women's Trade Union League (WTUL) in 1922, as well as the Women's Division of the Democratic State Committee. In 1928, the year FDR was elected Governor of New York, the Democratic National Committee (DNC) named Eleanor director of the Bureau of Women's Activities. Through her work with the WTUL and the DNC, she built a strong political, social, and educational women's network that lasted throughout her life.

When Franklin was elected President in 1932, Eleanor took her place squarely in the public eye. She served the administration as an intermediary between citizens and the President or New Deal Agencies. Also significant was her advocacy for racial equality. In 1933 she began her famous, all-women press conferences. She spoke frequently on the radio, including on her own program, for which she was paid. And just before FDR's re-election in 1936, she began a daily, syndicated newspaper column, "My Day." In addition, she was a very popular speaker, though a controversial person for some. Twice a year she traveled around the country on behalf of the President, speaking extemporaneously on a variety of topics. She continued to play important public roles, especially for the Democratic Party and the United Nations, until her death from tuberculosis in 1962.

The speech that follows is characteristic of her rhetoric. It was later polished and revised for publication, but this is the text for the oral presentation. It ends abruptly, and we can assume that she added some impromptu concluding remarks at the time of the speech. The overall style is conversational, making it easier for her to insert impromptu remarks throughout the speech. Personal anecdotes and simulated dialogue reinforced her theme on the importance of books and reading in a way that was personal and engaging.[2] In addition, Eleanor often addressed her audiences as if she were a teacher, and this speech is no exception. In assuming this role, however, she did not talk down to her audience. Using inclusive pronouns, she placed herself on equal footing with her listeners, remarking, for example, "We have come a long way. We have done a great deal...and we still have a tremendous amount to do with our libraries. We have got to make our libraries the center of a new life in the mind...." Thus, at the same time she celebrated librarians, she urged them to do even more to help the nation by teaching others to love books.

NOTES

1. Biographical information on Eleanor Roosevelt for this period includes "The American Experience: Eleanor Roosevelt," PBS *online* [web site] WGBH 1999 May 27, 2003 (www.pbs.org/wgbh/amex/eleanor); Blanche Wiesen Cook, *Eleanor Roosevelt,* 2 vols. (New York: Penguin, 1992, 1999); Debra L. Petersen, "Anna Eleanor Roosevelt," in *Women Public Speakers in the U.S., 1925–1993,* Karlyn Kohrs Campbell, ed. (Westport, CT: Greenwood Press, 1994), 379–394; Susan Ware, *Beyond Suffrage: Women in the New Deal.* (Cambridge, MA: Harvard University Press, 1981), and Holding Their Own: American Women in the 1930s (Boston: Twayne, 1982).

2. For more development of these ideas, see Peterson, "Anna Eleanor Roosevelt," 383–91.

WHAT LIBRARIES MEAN TO THE NATION—(APRIL 1, 1936) D.C. LIBRARY ASSOCIATION DINNER[1]

It has been a great pleasure to be here this evening and to hear all the things that have been said about libraries in the District and the libraries in general, and the librarians, without whom the libraries would be of little use, I am afraid. But as I sat here I fear that I have thought a good deal about the fact that there are so many places in the United States that have no libraries and that have no way of getting books. What the libraries mean to the nation is fairly obvious to all of us, especially to those who are here this evening. We know that without libraries, without education, which is based largely on libraries, we cannot have an educated people who will carry on successfully our form of government, and it seems to me that what we really are interested in is how we can make this country more conscious of what it has not got, because we do pat ourselves on the back for the things that we have and that we do. I was looking over some maps which were sent to me and I longed to have these maps very much enlarged and put up in many, many places throughout this country, because I do not think that many people know how many cities do not spend more than ten cents per capita for library books a year, and how many states have large areas, particularly rural areas, where one cannot get books.

One of the things that I have been particularly grateful for in the years of the depression—and, of course, I think, sad as it has been, we have some things to be grateful for—is that we have discovered so many things that we had not known before. These facts have come to the knowledge of a great many people that have simply passed them by before, because they did not happen to think about them, and one of these things, that we used to be able to hide, is the areas of the country which are not served in any way by libraries. I have seen photographs, for instance, of girls going out on horseback with libraries strapped on behind them and taking books on horseback to children and grown people in places that have been without libraries. We know a good deal about Mrs. Breckinridge's nursing service in Kentucky, but we know very little about the libraries that go out in the same way that her nurses do, on horseback. I have lived a great deal in the country, in a state which prides itself in spending much money on education, and I am quite sure that some people think there is no lack of education and no lack of library facilities, and sometimes I long to take people and let them see some of the back country districts that I know, in New York State. I know one place in the northern part of the state where I camped for a while in the summer, and I went to the school and talked to the teachers. They are using school books which have been passed down from one child to another. They have practically no books outside of the text books. The children in the district were so poor and some of them so pathetic that I suppose the struggle to live was so great you could not think much about what you fed the mind, but I came away feeling that right there, in one of the biggest and richest states in the country, we had a big area that needed books and needed libraries to help these schools in the education of the children, and, even more, to help the whole community to learn to live through their minds. Now we are doing a tremendous amount through the Home Economics colleges to help people to learn how to live in their homes, to better their standards of material living. We have got to think in exactly the same way about helping them to live mentally and to attain better standards, and we can do it only through the children. We can do ground work with the children; we must begin with them; but we have got to do a tremendous amount with the older people. I had a letter the other day which was pathetic. It was from a man who said he was 74 years old. He wrote to ask me to see that the adult education classes in that particular community were not stopped, because it had meant so much to him to learn to read. He did not think that I could understand what it meant never to have been able to understand a word on the printed page. He said, "I am not the only one. My next door neighbor is 81 and he learned to read last winter, and it has just made life over for us." It gave you the feeling that there was a good deal of education that was not being done in this country, in spite of all that *is* done.

We have come a long way. We have done a great deal, but we still have a lot that can be done to improve our educational system and we still have a tremendous amount to do with our libraries. We have got to make our libraries the center of a new life in the mind, because people are hungry to use their minds.

I feel that the care of libraries and the use of books, and the knowledge of books, is a tremendously vital thing, and that we who deal with books and who love books have a great opportunity to bring about something in this country which is more vital here than anywhere else, because we have the chance to make a democracy that will be a real democracy, that will fulfill the vision that Senator King gave us. It will take on our part imagination and patience and constant interest in awakening interest in other people. But, if we do, I think we will find that our love of books will bring us a constantly widening audience and constantly more interesting contacts in whatever part of the country we may go.

We are facing a great change in civilization and the responsibility, I think, for what we do with our leisure time is a very great responsibility for all of us who have intellectual interests. Somebody said to me, "I would not be so worried and I would not mind facing the fact that we are working fewer hours, if I only knew what people would do with their free time. I would not know what to do myself if I had only to work six hours a day." I think that is a challenge. We, here in this country, ought to know what to do with our time, if we have it. I do not know whether we are going to have it, but if we are going to have more leisure time, it is the library, and people who live in the libraries and work in libraries, who are going to lead the way, who are going to give other people the curiosity and the vision of useful things, and pleasant things, and amusing things, which can be done in those hours in which we may not have to work in the ways in which we have worked before. It is a very great responsibility, but it is also a very great interest. Now, I think here in the city of Washington, and in nearly all big cities, the problem is a different one from the one I know so well in the country districts. I think that perhaps there are more facilities and, for that reason, there are more stimulating people engaged in solving the different problems that affect education in cities. But there is a great need, a very great need, in rural America. There is a great need for imagination in the ways used to stir the interest of old and young to use what library facilities they have, and to insist that they shall have more and to make them willing to pay for more, because, in the end, they will get something that they want out of it. The more I have thought about the problem, the more I have felt that we do not use all our opportunities to stimulate an interest in books. Everything today in which people are interested, the radio, the movies—all of these—should, if properly used, stimulate the use of books. For instance, if there is a remarkably good movie, like "The Life of Pasteur," it seems to me that should be used by people in our rural schools and rural libraries, to create an interest in the life of Pasteur, the things that Pasteur did, the people around him, and all the discoveries that have come from that time on. I am sure that if we put our minds on it, there are a great many ways in which we can use the things which are coming constantly into the lives of people throughout the country to stimulate an interest in the oldest and most interesting recreation there is. But you do have to learn to love books, you do have to learn how to read them, you do have to learn that a book is a companion, and this is done in a great many different ways. I think we can do a great deal by having more copies of the same book, perhaps less expensive books, in the libraries so that we can have a good many people reading the same books and coming together for discussion. I know, for instance, that even in a small group, like a family, we all want to read one book at the same time, and we all want to tear each other's hair out when we can't get a copy. It seems to me that here is something we should be thinking about, to stimulate the reading of books in families and larger groups of people. I think the C.C.C. has made me realize this. One boy said to me, "Do you know about that book? I am so glad to be able to talk about it. . . . You know, it takes such a long time to get a book around." Now, if there had been a dozen or more copies of that book, the group would have talked about that book and it would have been a valuable contribution. It would have stimulated their intellectual thought.

NOTE

1. Typescript. Speech and Article File of the Eleanor Roosevelt Papers, Franklin D. Roosevelt Library, Hyde Park, NY.

Margaret Sanger (1879–1966)

Margaret Higgins Sanger, political activist for various labor and health issues, is remembered most for the cause to which she devoted her life, advocacy for birth control. Sanger was the sixth of eleven children. Her mother died at 48, her father at 84. Sanger, herself, and those who have written about her, comment that the contrast in her parents' life spans made a tremendous impression on her.[1]

She became a nurse before marrying William Sanger (architect, artist, and radical activist) in 1902. They had three children before their divorce in 1920. In 1922, she married J. Noah Slee, a wealthy man who financed her work and "agreed to respect her autonomy."[2] Sanger's distribution of seven issues of her periodical, *The Woman Rebel*, through the mail resulted in a federal indictment in 1914.[3] She fled to England for a time, during which her pamphlet, *Family Limitation*, was released.[4] After her return home, Sanger opened the first birth control clinic in the United States. The clinic, located in the Brownsville section of Brooklyn, New York, opened on October 16, 1916. However, it was soon raided and closed. Sanger was jailed for 30 days.

She persisted with her work, though, creating and editing the *Birth Control Review* in 1917, and founding the American Birth Control League in 1921. Furthermore, Sanger opened the Clinical Research Bureau to dispense and study effects of contraceptives (1923), founded the National Committee on Federal Legislation for Birth Control (1929), and helped instigate *U.S. v. One Package*, a test case that established physicians' right to import contraceptives (1936). Even after that victory, Sanger stayed active in US and international birth control organizations and facilitated research

Margaret Sanger, leader of the birth control movement, February 8, 1922.

Library of Congress, Prints and Photographs Division, [reproduction number, LC-USZ62-29808].

and development of contraceptives—including the oral contraceptive ("the pill")—into the 1960s. She lived 87 years—long enough to see the 1965 Supreme Court decision in *Griswold v. Connecticut* establish the right for married couples throughout the United States to practice birth control.

Throughout her life, Sanger was a controversial figure, denounced on religious and political grounds. Opponents to birth control on religious grounds saw the practice as in conflict with God's will; political opponents decried Sanger's association with socialists, anarchists, and other radicals. Even now, both her "doctors only" stance on birth control (allowing physicians, most of them male, to control access to contraceptives) and her "statist" perspective on eugenics (willingness to permit the government or "state" to mandate sterilization of the "unfit" and to issue licenses for motherhood) undermine her reputation, even among other strong supporters of birth control. However, one scholar has argued that "both critics and apologists...neglect perhaps her greatest skill; the ability to give energy to and to organize people."[5]

A constant speaker, Sanger often relied upon a stock speech about birth control, but she adapted it carefully to the audience and occasion. The presentations that resulted used a wide range of strategies and tactics, including appeals to authority, argument by definition and analogy, anecdotal evidence from letters of poor women to Mrs. Sanger, and, upon occasion, especially early in her career, rude personal attacks upon adversaries. Correspondence related to the speech that follows shows how Sanger and her staff worked to adapt a stock address to make it acceptable to the sponsoring organization. For example, after one of her assistants sent a memo to the Washington office commenting that the Federation of Jewish Women's Organizations was "evidently very timid about the subject of birth control" and "did not want Mrs. Sanger to be too specific,"[6] she changed the planned title, "Birth Control—A Constructive Force in Civilization," to "Woman and the Future." Nevertheless, as the following text demonstrates, Sanger did not abandon her core objectives—to promote audience members' acceptance of the term "birth control" and to increase their appreciation for the advantages of the practice.

NOTES

1. For example, Margaret Sanger, "Women and Birth Control," *North America Review* (May 1929); Ellen Chesler, *Woman of Valor: Margaret Sanger and the Birth Control Movement in America* (New York: Simon & Schuster, 1992), 43; John M. Murphy, "Margaret Higgins Sanger," in *Women Public Speakers in the United States, 1925–1993*, Karlyn Kohrs Campbell, ed. (Westport, CT: Greenwood Press, 1994), 239.

2. Murphy, "Margaret Higgins Sanger," 244.

3. Several issues of *The Woman Rebel* were declared unmailable because of obscene content, such as birth control information and advocating assassination.

4. Linda Gordon, in *The Margaret Sanger Centennial Conference. Proceedings.* Dorothy Green and Mary-Elizabeth Murdock, eds. (Northampton, MA: Sophia Smith Collection), 67.

5. Ibid., 35.

6. Margaret Sanger to Mrs. A. J. Davidson, December 23, 1936; "Memo to Washington Office," signed "FR," January 13, 1937; both from Margaret Sanger Papers, Manuscript Division, Library of Congress, Washington, DC.

WOMAN AND THE FUTURE
FEDERATION OF JEWISH WOMEN'S
ORGANIZATIONS, 17TH ANNUAL CONVENTION
HOTEL ASTOR, NEW YORK.
(RADIO BROADCAST, STATION WMCA, JANUARY 25, 1937, 11:45 A.M.–12 NOON)[1]

Opening Announcement:

Margaret Sanger, who is recognized as the leader of the birth control movement both in America and abroad, will speak today on the subject "Woman and the Future." Mrs. Sanger has devoted her life to the cause of womanhood, and the success which she has won gives her the right to speak with authority on this subject. Mrs. Sanger.

Mrs. Sanger speaking:

Just four years ago the Federation of Jewish Women's Organizations at whose annual convention I am speaking today went on record in support of the legalization of birth control. It is in great measure due to the active help of this organization and other groups of courageous women, such as the National Council of Jewish Women, the General Federation of Women's Clubs, and the Y.W.C.A. that the birth control movement is today celebrating a glorious victory and looking forward to the inspiring and constructive work which lies ahead.

We can today with some measure of clarity and hope talk about Woman and the Future. It has been a good fight but a long one.

In 1873 Congress, urged on by Anthony Comstock, passed the so-called obscenity laws, prohibiting the use of the mails and common carriers for items which were considered lewd and obscene. The general aim of these laws was perhaps laudable enough. But unfortunately articles and information relating to the prevention of conception were also classed as obscene. It was made a crime, publishable by $500 fine or 5 years imprisonment or both, for anyone, even a physician, to send contraceptive information or supplies through the mails or by common carrier, that is by express. Importation was also forbidden.

The birth control movement has spent years of effort in rectifying this mistake. For with the law thus tangled and confused, many doctors hesitated to give birth control advice, hospitals and dispensaries which should have been telling women how to space their children and plan their families were afraid to do so.

For the past seven years the National Committee on Federal Legislation for Birth Control, of which I am the president, has been seeking to have this law amended. We have found men in Congress brave enough to introduce bills exempting physicians from the restrictions of the law in matters relating to contraception. It may be hard for you to realize it, but at first it took courage for a member of Congress to come out openly for birth control. Hearings were held; the press gave its support, more and more men in Congress came to see the right and justice of what we were asking; a hundred thousand individuals and a thousand organizations placed themselves on record approving of what we were trying to do, and pledging their help.

A wise and reasonable court decision in a test case on the importation of birth control materials sent to a doctor for research purposes, (*U.S. v. One Package*) has given the medical profession what we were seeking through Congress. The United States Court of Appeals for the second circuit, in unanimously upholding the decision of the lower court has interpreted the Comstock Laws, and has defined the rights of the American physician in regard to birth control.

A decision, handed down on November 30, 1936, comes as a result of an informed public opinion, as the result of the support of organizations such as this Federation. "We are satisfied," said the judges, "that this statute embraced only such articles as Congress would have denounced as immoral if it had understood all the conditions under which they were to be used." That is, birth control as we understand it today, would not have been included in the statute.

"Its design" the decision continued, "was not to prevent the importation, sale or carriage by mail of things which might intelligently be employed by conscientious and competent physicians for the purpose of saving life or promoting the well-being of their patients."

With the tangles and confusions of the past cleared away, we can now look ahead. We can envisage what birth control can do for the woman of today and tomorrow. For up to now, woman has been a victim of her own powers of reproduction. It has been the comparatively few and more fortunate who have known how to have only as many children as they could take care of. A small fraction of all women have known how to make motherhood a matter of conscious and joyful choice, not a thing of tragedy and chance.

I will not speak today of what needs to be done in far countries, in China and India, in Japan. Nor will I speak of the women of Italy and Germany, who are being prodded and cajoled to produce cannon fodder for future wars. Let us think first of America.

Here a new epoch in the birth control movement has begun. Scientific and reliable information can now be given to every woman in the land. Every hospital, and there are seven thousand of them, every health unit and welfare center, every place which cares for the health of women, can now have a physician give birth control advice.

Last month, several hundred physicians, scientists, and representatives from birth control clinics, met in a two day Conference of Contraceptive Research and Clinical Practice. It was no longer necessary to prove the case for birth control. It was no longer necessary to talk of belief or disbelief, or of legality, or to bandy arguments or opinions. The entire matter had passed from the realm of propaganda to the realm of science. These fine men and women came together to confer and interchange their knowledge and experiences, so that we might have better methods, better ways of teaching women, more knowledge in the field. There was discussion at one interesting session as to what a birth control center should be called. Many thought it might better be called a Mother's Health Center or a Race Betterment Center, and these terms well describe what such a center is.

But I confess that I am in favor of the simple phrase birth control. As you may know, I coined it more than twenty years ago, and it must have something good in it, for it stuck. You will find it in dictionaries and encyclopedias, in scientific journals and in newspaper columns. Wherever people speak of bettering the lives of women, of bring[ing] forth a better, stronger, happier and healthier race, they speak of birth control.

Emphasis should be placed on the word control. Controlling the size of the family does not mean that births should be limited to any arbitrary number. Birth control is not a program for a one or two child family. We control our automobiles; we control the heat that keeps us warm in winter, and before long, so they tell us, we shall be controlling the heat that makes us unhappy in summer. We control our time, our appetites, our incomes, our lives. It is simple common sense to control the number of children in a family, in order that they may be cherished and loved, cared for properly and raised to become useful and happy citizens.

Children should be wanted. They should be conceived in marital love, born of the parents' conscious desire and given the heritage of health[y] bodies and sound minds.

I believe that the bearing and nurture of children are not the aim and end of women's existence. I want to see the woman of the future liberated, spiritually free, conscious of her creative powers. I want to see her using them with vision and intelligence, for greater happiness, for security, for peace. To do this, woman must first liberate herself. Motherhood must be conscious and voluntary, before it can be creative. Then she can make the most of the greatest of all her gifts and responsibilities, the handling of the precious, mysterious gift of life.

Through birth control women will gain control not only of their bodies, but they will develop their souls. They will lead the race to heights we cannot yet see. Birth Control is one of the greatest movement[s] of today and of tomorrow, and what it will do for the children, for the women of the future, none of us can yet visualize.

But we can believe and push on.

NOTE

1. Typescript for radio broadcast. Margaret Higgins Sanger Papers, Manuscript Division, Library of Congress, Washington, DC. Copyright dedicated to the public.

Mary McLeod Bethune
(1875–1955)

The trajectory of Mary McLeod Bethune's life and her heroic efforts to improve the lot of African Americans throughout the first half of the twentieth century defies easy summary or comprehension. From the humblest of origins and in the midst of severe and violent racial discrimination, Bethune managed to attain tremendous personal and professional success at the same time that she battled to win greater racial and economic justice for all African Americans. One of sixteen children born to former slaves in Mayesville, Florida, she was so eager for education that she walked ten miles a day to attend school. Through her diligence, she graduated from Chicago's Moody Bible Institute in 1895. Having experienced the transformative power of education in her own life, she made access to quality education the cornerstone of her lifelong political agenda. Bethune founded the Daytona Normal and Industrial Institute for Negro Girls in 1905. Furnished with milk crates and started with no assets to speak of, it merged with Cookman Institute for Boys, and in 1929 became Bethune-Cookman College. Bethune served as its president for almost fifty years (1905–1942, 1946–1947) and orchestrated each step of its development. By 1947, it had enrolled over 1,000 students and had earned national accreditation.[1]

Bethune expanded her purview to become a savvy political actor who agitated for African American equality on all fronts. To achieve her goals, she worked within a variety of organizations—effectively and willingly crossing racial, class, and gender lines. Bethune-Cookman College stands as only one part of her legacy. Bethune must also be noted for two other major contributions: her founding of the National Council of Negro Women (NCNW) in 1935 and her appointment by President Franklin

Mary McLeod Bethune (left) and Eleanor Roosevelt at a National Youth Administration meeting.

Library of Congress, Prints & Photographs Division, [reproduction number, LC-USZ62-117627].

Delano Roosevelt as Director of Negro Affairs for the National Youth Administration (1936–1944). Bethune founded the NCNW to serve as an "organization of organizations," to coordinate the efforts of the many African American women's associations that had formed in the early decades of the twentieth century to promote economic and social reform. As its president (1935–1949), she created the organizational and philosophical foundation that continues to unite and direct African American women's political activism today.

Hemmed in by the Jim Crow south, Bethune began her career with little political power, but through her devotion and acumen eventually pursued her goals from within the highest echelons of the American political system. By the 1930s, she had the ear of both Eleanor and Franklin Delano Roosevelt and used her considerable powers of persuasion to limit racial discrimination in New Deal programs and in World War II policies. As Director of Negro Affairs (the first black, female presidential advisor), Bethune operated as a member of what became known as Roosevelt's "black cabinet." Bethune also served as vice president of the NAACP from 1940 to 1955—the crucial years that led to the *Brown v. Board of Education* decision.

In a sense, Bethune had been a public speaker her whole life, from her first calling as a teacher, to her years as a college president, and throughout her campaigns for racial equality. For Bethune, speaking in public meant one more chance to agitate for social change—to secure social justice for all Americans—whether she spoke before poor, rural blacks, liberal white lady reformers, or white male politicos. African American women had not enjoyed the luxury of "domesticity" or the private sphere. In most cases, their families needed them to work, to become educated, to live a public life, making their political activism a less controversial undertaking. Still, African American women faced the constraints of racialized gender conventions. Expected to defer to African American male political leadership, black women filled church pews, marched long miles, created and distributed pamphlets, and housed and fed activists while charismatic male leaders tended to give the speeches. Yet Bethune, like many others, never hesitated to take the podium and rarely censored her views.

In the following address presented before the Association for the Study of Negro Life and History, Bethune illustrates both her intellectual rendering of racial politics and her pragmatic approach to social change. In her direct and passionate voice, Bethune implores her all-black audience to instill racial pride in themselves and others by learning and teaching the history of black achievement (the "great story of our rise in America") and by promoting the tremendous economic and social contributions that African Americans had made to the nation. In Bethune's trademark style, she employs dramatic narrative as well as hard statistics, all with oratorical flourish.

NOTES

1. Paula Giddings *When and Where I Enter: The Impact of Black Women on Race and Sex in America* (New York: William Morrow and Co., 1984); "Mary McLeod Bethune Council House" ParkNet [web site] National Park Service, May 27, 2003 (www.nps.gov/mamc/index.htm).

CLARIFYING OUR VISION WITH THE FACTS
(OCTOBER 31, 1937)[1]

John Vandercook's *Black Majesty* tells the dramatic story of Jean Christophe, the black emperor of Haiti, and how he molded his empire with his hands out of the rugged cliffs and the unchained slaves of his native land. One night, in the midst of his Herculean struggles, Sir Home, his English adviser, accused him of building too fast and working his subjects like slaves until they were discontent. For a long moment Christophe was silent....When he spoke, his full rich voice seemed suddenly old.

"You do not understand...."

He stopped again, seemed to be struggling for words, then he went on:

"My race is as old as yours. In Africa, they tell me, there are as many blacks as there are white men in Europe. In Saint Domingue, before we drove the French out, there were a hundred Negroes to every master. But we were your slaves. Except in Haiti, nowhere in the world have we resisted you. We have suffered, we have grown dull, and, like cattle under a whip, we have obeyed. Why? Because we have no pride! And we have no pride because we have nothing to remember. Listen!"

He lifted his hand. From somewhere behind them was coming a faint sound of drumming, a monotonous, weird melody that seemed to be born of the heart of the dark, rearing hills, that rose and fell and ran in pallid echoes under the moon. The King went on.

"It is a drum, Sir Home. Somewhere my people are dancing. It is almost all we have. The drum, laughter, love for one another, and our share of courage. But we have nothing white men can understand. You despise our dreams and kill the snakes and break the little sticks you think are our gods. Perhaps if we had something we could show you, if we had something we could show ourselves, you would respect us and we might respect ourselves."

"If we had even the names of our great men! If we could lay our hands"— he thrust his out—"on things we've made, monuments and towers and palaces, we might find our strength, gentlemen. While I live I shall try to build that pride we need, and build in terms white men as well as black can understand! I am thinking of the future, not of now. I will teach pride if my teaching breaks every back in my kingdom."

Today I would salute in homage that wise old emperor. I bring you again his vibrant message. Our people cry out all around us like children lost in the wilderness. Hemmed in by a careless world, we are losing our homes and our farms and our jobs. We see vast numbers of us and the land sunk into the degradation of peonage and virtual slavery. In the cities, our workers are barred from the unions, forced to "scab" and often to fight with their very lives for work. About us cling the ever-tightening tentacles of poor wages, economic insecurity, sordid homes, labor by women and children, broken homes, ill health, delinquency and crime. Our children are choked by denied opportunity for health, for education, for work, for recreation, and thwarted with their ideals and ambitions still a-borning. We are scorned of men, they spit in our faces and laugh. We cry out in this awesome darkness. Like a clarion call, I invoke today again the booming voice of Jean Christophe:

"If we had something we could show you, if we had something we could show ourselves, you would respect us and we might respect ourselves. If we had even the names of our great men! If we could lay our hands on things we've made, monuments and towers and palaces, we might find our strength, gentlemen..."

If our people are to fight their way out of bondage we must arm them with the sword and the shield and the buckler of pride—belief in themselves and their possibilities, based upon a sure knowledge of the achievements of the past. That knowledge and that pride we must give them "if it breaks every back in the kingdom."

Through the scientific investigation and objective presentation of the facts of our history and our achievement to ourselves and to all men, our Association for the Study of Negro Life and History serves to tear the veil from our eyes and allow us to see clearly and in true perspective our rightful place among all men. Through accurate research and investigation, we serve so to supplement, correct, re-orient and annotate the story of world progress as to enhance the standing of our group in the eyes of all men. In the one hand, we bring pride to our own; in the other, we bear respect from the others.

We must tell the story with continually accruing detail from the cradle to the grave. From the mother's knee and the fireside of the home, through the nursery, the kindergarten and the grade school, high school, college and university, through the technical journals, studies and bulletins of the Association, through newspaper, storybook and pictures, we must tell the thrilling story. When they learn the fairy tales of mythical king and queen and princess, we must let them hear, too, of the pharaohs and African kings and the brilliant pageantry of the Valley of the Nile; where they learn of Caesar and his legions, we must teach them of Hannibal and his Africans; when they learn of Shakespeare and Goethe, we must teach them of Pushkin and Dumas. When they read of Columbus, we must introduce the Africans who touched the shores of America before Europeans emerged from savagery; when they are thrilled by Nathan Hale baring his breast and crying: "I have but one life to give for my country," we must make their hearts leap to see Crispus Attucks stand and fall for liberty on Boston Common with the red blood of freedom streaming down his breast. With the *Tragic Era* we give them *Black Reconstruction;* with Edison, we give them Jan Matzeliger; with John Dewey, we place Booker T. Washington; above the folk music of the cowboy and the hillbilly, we place the spiritual and the "blues"; when they boast of Maxfield Parrish, we show them E. Simms Campbell. Whatever [white] man has done, we have done—and often better. As we tell this story, as we present to the world the facts, our pride in racial achievement grows, and our respect in the eyes of all men heightens.

Certainly, too, it is our task to make plain to ourselves the great story of our rise in America from "less than the dust" to the heights of sound achievement. We must recount in accurate detail the story of how the Negro population has grown from a million in 1800 to almost 12 million in 1930. The Negro worker is today an indispensable part of American agriculture and industry. His labor has built the economic empires of cotton, sugar cane and tobacco; he furnishes nearly 12 percent of all American breadwinners, one-third of all servants, one-fifth of all farmers. In 1930, we operated 1,000,000 farms and owned 750,000 homes. Negroes operate today over 22,000 business establishments with over 27 million dollars in yearly receipts and payrolls of more than 5 million dollars. Negroes manufacture more than 60 different commodities. They spend annually for groceries over 2 billion dollars, a billion more for clothes, with total purchasing power in excess of 4 and one-half billion dollars. Negro churches have more than 5 million members in 42,500 organizations, owning 206 million dollars worth of property and spending 43 million dollars a year. Some 360,000 Negroes served in the World War, with 150,000 of them going to France. Negroes are members of legislatures in 12 states; 3 or more states have black judges on the bench and a federal judge has recently been appointed to the Virgin Islands. Twenty-three Negroes have sat in Congress, and there is one member of the House at present. Under the "New Deal" a number of well qualified Negroes hold administrative posts. Illiteracy has decreased from about 95 percent in 1865 to only 16.3 percent in 1930. In the very states that during the dark days of Reconstruction prohibited the education of Negroes by law, there are today over 2 million pupils in 25,000 elementary schools, 150,000 high school pupils in 2,000 high schools and 25,000 students in the more than 100 Negro colleges and universities. Some 116 Negroes have been elected to Phi Beta Kappa in white Northern colleges; over 60 have received the degree of Doctor of Philosophy from leading American universities and 97 Negroes are mentioned in *Who's Who in America*. It is the duty of our Association to tell the glorious story of our past and of our marvelous achievement in American life over almost insuperable obstacles.

From this history our youth will gain confidence, self-reliance and courage. We will thereby raise their mental horizon and give them a base from which to reach out higher and higher into the realm of achievement. And as we look about us today, we know that they must have this courage and self-reliance. We are beset on every side with heart-rending and fearsome difficulties.

Recently, in outlining to the president of the United States the Position of the Negro in America, I saw fit to put it this way: "The great masses of Negro workers are depressed and unprotected in the lowest levels of agriculture and domestic service while black workers in industry are generally barred from the unions and grossly discriminated against. The housing and conditions of the Negro masses are sordid and unhealthy; they live in constant terror of the mob, generally shorn of their constitutionally guaranteed right of suffrage, and humiliated by the denial of civil liberties. The great masses of Negro youth are offered only one-fifteenth the educational opportunity of the average American child."

These things also we must tell them, accurately, realistically and factually. The situation we face must be defined, reflected and evaluated. Then, armed with the pride and courage of his glorious tradition, conscious of his positive contribution to American life, and enabled to face clear-eyed and unabashed the actual situation before him, the Negro may gird his loins and go forth to battle to return "with their shields or on them." And so today I charge our Association for the Study of Negro Life and History to carry forward its great mission to arm us with the facts so that we may face the future with clear eyes and a sure vision. Our Association may say again with Emperor Jean Christophe: "While I live I shall try to build that pride we need, and build in terms white men as well as black can understand! I am thinking of the future, not of now. I will teach pride if my teaching breaks every back in my Kingdom."

NOTE

1. Mary McLeod Bethune delivered this speech in 1937. It was published the following year in the *Journal of Negro History* 23 (1938), 10–15.

Aimee Kennedy Semple McPherson (1890–1944)

Aimee Kennedy Semple McPherson is widely credited with being the first woman to preach a radio sermon and the first woman to receive a Federal Communications Commission license to operate a radio station. The sermon was delivered using the facilities of the Rockridge Radiotelephone Station at Oakland, California, but there is controversy over whether it aired in 1921 or 1922.[1] The radio station was KFSG in Los Angeles—the radio voice of the Foursquare Gospel Church, the denomination "Sister Aimee" founded in Los Angeles, California.

Aimee Kennedy reportedly experienced a conversion and received a call from God to be an evangelist soon after meeting her future husband, evangelist Robert Semple, in December of 1907. She traveled with her husband to China, where they became ill with malaria and dysentery. Aimee, then pregnant, recovered; however, Robert died one month before his wife gave birth to their daughter. Mother and child returned to the United States, where they lived for a time with Aimee's mother until Aimee married accountant Harold "Mack" McPherson, with whom she had a son, Rolf. After Rolf's birth, Aimee suffered from severe postpartum depression and general ill health, from which she reportedly recovered only upon promising God she would follow her calling as an evangelist.

McPherson took to the road, accompanied by family members, and held tent meetings. After one cross-country journey with many such stops, she arrived in Los Angeles, where she raised donations and built the Angelus Temple. In the Angelus Temple, Sister Aimee was an innovator of worship, incorporating contemporary music, such as jazz, and stage plays. By 1924, the radio station of her nascent denomination, the Foursquare Gospel Church (KFSG), broadcast weekly live services from the temple.

Aimee Semple McPherson at an evangelist meeting in London.
Library of Congress, Prints & Photographs Division, [reproduction number, LC-USZ62-92329].

Aimee Semple McPherson, seen from today's perspective, appears not so different from contemporary televangelists who have lived controversial lifestyles. She disappeared for a time in 1926 in what she insisted was a kidnapping. She died of a drug overdose some call accidental; others, suicide. Still, Sister Aimee remains an intriguing figure of her time, the "Golden Age of Radio," and in the history of women in U.S. religious rhetoric (homiletics).

Janice Schuetz has argued that McPherson's sermons are worthy of study because of the "creativity, and use of dramatic and emotional appeal" in her preaching. Theatrically as they were staged, however, Sister Aimee's Sermons were typically on a single, simple theme. These sermons, on average, were about one-hour long.[2] The sermon included here is typical. In it she describes her calling—her God-given "task"—and explains her listeners' role in helping her accomplish it. Her task, she says, is to spread the Gospel around the world; their role is to help her. She preached this message, incorporating scriptural passages, historical references, and various devices in which she attempted to reflect the perspective of her listeners. For example, she would ask and answer hypothetical audience questions, as in this illustration from the sermon that follows:

You say, "Sister, it seems to me that you've bitten off a pretty big task there. You and who else can do all this?" God and you and I.

NOTES

1. Four Square Gospel Church documents set the date as 1921. See (http://www.libertyharbor.org/aimee.htm). However, the KFSG website, among others, set the date a year later, 1922. See, for example (http://www.kfsg.com/history/history.htm).

2. Janice Schuetz, "Aimee Kennedy Semple McPherson," in *Women Public Speakers in the United States 1925–1993*, Karlyn Kohrs Campbell, ed. (Westport, CT: Greenwood Press, 1994), 279, 281.

THIS IS MY TASK
A SERMON BY AIMEE SEMPLE MCPHERSON
GIVEN AT ANGELUS TEMPLE, LOS ANGELES,
CALIFORNIA (MARCH 12, 1939)[1]

Reprinted by permission of the Heritage Department, International Church of the Foursquare Gospel

This morning, our subject: "This is my task." The song is familiar to most of us:

> To love someone more dearly every day
> To help a wandering child to find his way
> To ponder o'er a noble thought and pray
> And smile when evening falls
> This is my task
> To follow truth as blind men long for light
> To do my best from dawn of day till night
> To keep my heart fixed in His holy sight
> To answer when He calls
> This is my task
> And then my Savior, by and by, to meet
> When faith hath made her task on earth complete
> And lay my homage at the Master's feet
> Within the jasper walls
> This crowns my task

The song has become one of those dear, familiar ones to our heart. But I would like to call your attention to several Scriptures this morning and "stir up your pure mind by way of remembrance" that you may serve and glorify the Lord.

Luke, the second chapter, 49th verse: "And Jesus said unto them, How is it that you sought Me? Wist ye not that I must be about My Father's business?" Bless the Lord.

Also, John the 4th chapter, 34th verse: "Jesus said unto them, my meat, the thing I live on—my meat is to do the will of Him that sent Me, and to finish His work. Say not ye, there are four months and then cometh harvest. Behold, I say unto you, Lift up your eyes, and look upon the fields, for they are white already to harvest. He that reapeth receiveth wages, and gathereth fruit unto life eternal,"—you'll be paid!—"that both he and the sower, and the sower, and he that reapeth may rejoice together...I sent you to reap whereon ye bestowed no labor: other men labored and you will enter into their labors. 'My meat is to do the will of Him that sent Me, and to finish My work.'" This morning by no means do I feel that my work is finished. I feel it's just started. Never in my life have I felt stronger or clearer mind, keener vision, or filled with inspiration, with ten thousand and one things to do, than I am now!

In the world, you know, they use slang once in a while, and they say, "The world is my oyster." Well, I wouldn't put it that way. But the world is my little problem. "It just seems so big!" Some people say, "The world's a big place!" I never think of it that way—it sits in my hand, there—you could hold a ball. And my task, as I see it, is to interest you folks to help me, to help them, to join the line right around the whole world! Not only to help the heathen abroad, but to help the heathen in Los Angeles. In America, too. By God's grace, if we can see our task and join hands and get together, we can spread the gospel around the world.

It's for your good! You have no business being sick—everyone of you should get well and get up and go to work, huh? Get up and go to work and earn some money and help send the gospel out! Amen! If these dear students, bless their hearts, are called to struggle and strive and pinch pennies and make their way through school and go out and lay down their lives for Christ, then certainly it's no harder to ask us to get a good job and work at it, and not give a tenth, but give the whole business, except just what we need to keep ourselves alive. That's what they'll be doing out there—what's the difference? Am I right or wrong? I believe that I am! "Wist ye not I must be about my Father's business?!" THIS IS MY TASK!!

What is my task? To get the gospel around the world in the shortest possible time to every man and woman and boy and girl!

You say, "Well, Sister, you won't make much headway in Tibet, I'm afraid—that's kind of a closed country yet." Well, I don't know...by God's grace we're gonna back a short-wave radio station right up against their border and shoot her over—and get the men there to pick it up and to amplify it. I never saw any one of those people in those countries who didn't like to hear a phonograph, to play over and over and over and over and over, or like to hear a radio. You say, "Well, maybe the government won't let you!" Well, how 'bout letting the government broadcast the weather report and the things they want to do certain hours and then we have certain hours. I think there's a way that anything can be done. Oh—I just feel my task this morning!

Remember that funny little ol' song?

If you've any mountains to be clumb
If you've any oceans to be swum
Uh, count on me!

I feel that way this morning! With God, I can do all things! But with God and you, and the people who you can interest, by the grace of God, we're gonna cover the world!

You say, "Well, Sister dear, we're looking for Jesus to come." I know we are. "But how long is this going to take?" It shouldn't take long. These are days when you can go around the world in less than a week in an aeroplane. These are days when we listen by radio. Did you happen to be awake last night? I just couldn't sleep—I had to listen to, at least, an hour or so of that broadcast from Rome. I thought it was so interesting, when the new Pope was being put in office. That was this morning. It was certainly impressive. I have never been brought up a Catholic—I mean, a Roman Catholic—we're all Catholics, aren't we? We're Protestant Catholics, whether we're from Methodist or Baptist or what. But I couldn't help being impressed with that ceremony. Especially the part where they set him aside and put oil on his hands and anointed him. They gave him the communion. I said, "Well, my, from now on when I ordain my young people, I'd love to see their elders anoint their hands with oil, that they may go out and lay hands on others. I believe that many of the early Catholic traditions are handed down from apostolic days, don't you, before the days of Martin Luther. Take the Lord's Supper that they may go—give it to others. We do not agree that there's just one mediator between God and man, and that's the Pope. We don't agree with that at all. We believe that Jesus Christ is the Mediator of all. But we cannot help but admire, the respect that is paid to the Lord Jesus. Certainly in this day we're out to preach Christ. But to hear that coming over, and I thought, "My…!" They described how the people cheered, and they said the nuns even took their handkerchiefs and waved and cheered and clapped as the cardinals went by, leading the Pope.

I thought, "My, won't it be wonderful when our High Priest, Jesus Christ, comes back again." Oh, if we do our task! I'll tell you, even you stiff-folks might bend and wave our handkerchiefs that day, when the Lord comes back. Amen?! Glory be to God!

I was so interested (in this radio program). I awakened the young lady at our house and I said, "Listen to this!" When Joanne came, it came to the part about the nuns even waving their hands and the people all cheering, I told of an experience of mine in Illinois where we were in a Foursquare church that had just been opened and the power was falling. Right next door to us was a convent. The sisters became so interested in the shouting and people praising the Lord, that they came over to see what it was all about. They had such sweet faces—in these black and white headgear. People had been falling under the power of God! Just going down under God's power all around. Do you know, that God's power struck them and they went down just the same way! Under the power of God! By and by, the Mother Superior came in to see what had happened to their daughters, and the power of God struck her. Why, we're all the same! I mean, we all have a heart, we all have tears, we all have sins, we all need a Savior, we all need the blood, and every one of us can work for Jesus. Whether we go across the ocean or whether we stay at home, this is our task. Lord, make us soul-winners, every one of us.

Yes! Glory to God! Rise—do the will of Him that sent you. Sleep no longer. Quench not the Spirit, but let the love of God be spread abroad upon all the face of the earth. For the days are short and the work is so great. Let the Word of God be preached in simplicity and power and Christ be exalted. Everyone say Amen! Let's all lift our hands. All over the building—everybody—say, "Lord, send the Word around the world! Lord, send the Word around the world! That is the desire of our heart!"

What is my task? First of all, my task is to be pleasing to Christ. To be empty of self and be filled with Himself. To be filled with the Holy Spirit; to be led by the Holy Spirit. Perhaps, students, you could put into words for me, could you, "I'll be somewhere working, for my Lord." Will you do it? Will you sing it right now? For the radio audience and the recording.

(The congregation sang and clapped to the following song)

> I'll be somewhere working,
> I'll be somewhere working,
> I'll be somewhere working for my Lord! (repeat)
> When He calls me, I will answer,
> When He calls me, I will answer,
> When He calls me, I will answer,
> I'll be somewhere working for my Lord.... everybody singing:
> I'll be somewhere working,
> I'll be somewhere working,
> I'll be somewhere working for my Lord! (repeat)

Oh, to be filled with the Spirit means to be filled with a burning desire to see other men and women saved, and to carry the gospel around the whole world. There are so many people who could—but they won't.

I heard a story this week of a man who wanted a gardener. He advertised and his friend sent a beautiful recommendation concerning a certain man and he said, "He's just a wonderful gardener!" He said, "He's capable of planting a kitchen garden. He's capable of nursing bulbs and bringing them up to fruition. He has the infinite patience of a gardener. He's able to put in a formal garden, and old-fashioned garden." The man began to say, "My that's just the man I want!" He came to the end of the page, turned it over and there were just three words there: "But he won't."

This man could do it, but he wouldn't. My, how many people are here that could pray in that Prayer Tower, but they won't? They could fill the last row in the choir, but they won't! They'd rather sit out there and see. They could be in the illustrated sermons, but they won't. They could be an usher, but they won't. They could fill-up the orchestra, but they won't. They could join the new club I'm talking about, "I Am Sending," but they won't. You say, "What is that club?" It's to pay $35.00 every six months or even one semester; to pay the tuition of a student through school, but they won't. They could draw from the bank if they had to—a good many people could do that—and buy one short-wave radio station, and say, "Sister, go to it! If you have this, this desire in your heart, God bless you and, more power behind you and prayers." But they won't.

He's a wonderful gardener. He can plant a kitchen garden, he can plant a formal garden, he can plant an old-fashioned garden, but he won't. Let us be the different kind and say, "He will!" Maybe we can't do it as grand as that man would do, but we will, hallelujah! Maybe we're not as oratorical as some, but we will. Maybe we haven't as strong a body to out to the foreign land with gospel, but we will. Friends, it means a great deal to be willing, doesn't it? Glory to God!

You all remember, perhaps, the story of a little girl who some time ago discovered a broken rail on a certain railroad track. She had wits enough about her to run to a telephone and call the superintendent, or rather I should say, the man at the depot. And he said, "Little girl, the train's already passed the station...stop it some way!" She never thought to argue. She said, "I'm little, but I'll do my best." She ran so fast and she waved her apron so hard, that the train stopped, and every life was saved.

This is my task.

It isn't how important you are and what great knowledge you have—it's a willingness to do it. To let God fill your life. Amen!

In the old-fashioned day of the stagecoach, over the Blue Ridge Mountains, a man was very much amused when the cabby asked him whether he wished to ride 1st class, 2nd class, or 3rd class. And he said, "Well, I'll ride 1st class." He paid the money. And when he got in, he was rather interested. He looked around and he discovered that they all sat in the same place. He wondered, "Why the difference of a few pennies?" But he noticed when they came to the stiff climb that the cabby put on the brakes. He said: "All 1st class passengers, keep your seats. Second class passengers, get out and walk! Third class passengers, get out and push!"

Praise the Lord! We may not be all 1st class bankers and lawyers and millionaires; but we certainly can get out and push! Amen! Let's encourage each one that is here for the Lord Jesus Christ.

This is my task. Let us be workers, not shirkers. I must finish my task.

A certain judge sitting on the bench of the eastern states some time ago had brought before him a man who had been arrested for gambling. As most culprits, the man denied vociferously his guilt. He put up quite a good story. He said, "I'll have you know I'm a silk weaver from Patterson. And I've a good job, I'm a silk weaver." The judge simply said, "Show me your hands." The man showed his hands and the judge said, thumping his gavel, "Thirty days!"

Show me your hands. My brother, my sister, we sing: "If you live right, heaven belongs to you." But, I believe that if we're living right, that entails working for Jesus Christ. Either going with the gospel, or paying the way for someone else to go! Either preaching, or making it possible for someone else to preach! But we mustn't muzzle the ox, you know, that treadeth out the corn.

Jesus is coming soon! Jesus is so exquisitely glorious! Salvation is so real and so to be desired. It must be had. The whole success or failure of these last few days depends on you, and God help me, upon me.

Adam had a task: to dress a garden and keep it. I'm sorry to tell you, he failed. And the whole world has always heard a man who failed. It doesn't matter very much how rich one dies, or how poor. The big thing is what you did when you were here. Did you do your task?

Noah had a job. His task, do you remember? (It) was to build the ark. He built it. Men bless him to this day.

Moses had a task. Go now to Exodus 3:9 and 10. "Go therefore." He was going to bring out all these multitudes of the children of Israel. And he did it.

Nehemiah had a task. The second chapter (of the book of Nehemiah), 5th to the 18th verse. He was sent to rebuild the walls. He was just a little man. He had just a little donkey to ride on. And no one even believed him at first. But he was so in earnest about the whole business, he kept shouting, "This is my task!" People began to believe him. They pitched in and helped him.

Friends, I know—as God is my Judge, that I don't amount to anything in myself. I know I'm just a girl from the farm. But I know as sure as God ever called anyone, God's called me and God's put it on my soul, you're to see the Foursquare Gospel go around the world. Do you say, "Do you mean, you're a denomination?" Not especially. I mean: Savior, Baptizer, Healer and Coming King. The preaching of the whole Word of the Living God!

You say, "Well, I like to identify with Him, but I'm one of these freelancers, you know. I don't believe much in church organization." Well, I never did either and I don't blame you one bit. The only thing is, when you have a hundred and eight mission stations, such as we have, you have to have some organization or someone's going to go hungry. It's a necessity. The best thing to do is to have as little organization as possible, and let the Spirit have His way. And yet, send out the gospel quickly!

I notice those who don't believe in uniting with a church or organization. I notice y'all use electric lights—that's organized! If it wasn't, you'd be electrocuted. I know Dr. Knight's always warning me, "Don't put your hands on the microphone!" It does something or other to the people listening in, it spoils the reception. Now, just a few minutes ago I was reminded of it. I don't know whether he realized it. I took a hold of the microphone and of my electric light here at the same time. I felt a little shock! Not very strong, but a little one. And I haven't put my hands on it since. I think it's a good way to break me of it. My Lord, put our task on us so that we'll feel a shock of the Spirit of God going through us! I know God has called me to send His gospel out and He wants you to help me. And we're going to do it. Why, this world's a little bit of a place.

Nehemiah finished his task; they went all the way around that wall. Why can't I go all the way around the world? With your help, and the Foursquare Gospel?!

A very famous Salvation Army lady went to India when a loved one died. "I must go on with my task.... Booth Tucker?" Mrs. Booth Tucker, who when death had come in the family and they said, "Oh, but you must take your time of mourning!" She said, "I am mourning. We all do when loved ones die, but I must go out and go on with my task."

Friends, this thing's bigger than I am! It's bigger than my family! It's bigger than you are. It's the world for God! I don't belong to anybody. I belong to Him. And because I belong to Him, I belong to everybody. You belong to me because you belong to Him, and if we Christians would ever get organized and join hands here, and stop punching each other, saying, "Well, I don't like the way so-and-so does their hair, or I don't like the way they tie their shoelaces," we'd begin to preach Jesus Christ and Him crucified, and get out and go on with the work, Glory to God! We can win the world for the Lord Jesus!

Martin Luther and Gutenberg, the printer, had a task. To print the Bible. Hid it away in bales of tea and cotton and smuggled it into England. They did it. True, people were burned at the stake for it—that was their task. It was brought to the attention of the king—you don't matter! *Foxe's Book of Martyrs* is well worth reading. Oh, it always gives me the shivers though when I read it. How those men stood there and were burned at the stake. But that's why we have the Bible I'm using today, to the King James Version; this was their task.

Like the little girl with her apron on, "I'm awful little, but I'll do my best." If you'll just get out there and run fast enough and wave your apron hard enough, you can do the work. Everybody said, "Amen!"

Mark 16:15 (says), "Go into all the world and preach the gospel to every creature!" And if you're ushers, orderly, prayer tower, band, teachers, employees, members—get your uniforms on! Oh, let's all shine where we are!

This is my task! And by His grace, we'll get the gospel clear around the world!

You say, "Sister, it seems to me that you've bitten off a pretty big task there. You and who else can do all this?" God and you and I.

NOTE

1. *Liberty Harbor Foursquare Church* [web site] May 27, 2003 (www.liberty harbor.org/sermon.htm). Copyright Liberty Harbor Foursquare Church. Revised May 31, 1999.

General Federation of Women's Clubs

FORUM: LUCRETIA MOTT AMENDMENT

Milwaukee, WI, GFWC Council Meeting (1940)

From the first introduction of the Equal Rights Amendment in 1923 until its final defeat in 1982, the General Federation of Women's Clubs as well as many other political bodies held regular forums to debate its merits. In the two speeches below, we see the contours of this debate as set forth in 1940. Mrs. Helen Robbins Bitterman argued for the amendment; Mrs. Laura Hughes Lunde argued against. Both women asserted their belief in equality for women. They differed, however, in their belief in whether the amendment would aid that end.

Much of their dispute was rooted in divergent philosophies regarding the meaning of equality. Those in support of the amendment believed that all laws should apply equally to men and women, even if this meant protection for men, whereas those against believed that men and women were not "the same" and therefore legislation was needed to account for such "functional" differences as reproduction, size, and strength. Were men and women the same or different? Should the legal apparatus of the United States account for differences or define all Americans as citizens without reference to gender? These questions continued to animate the debate.

In this debate, both speakers highlight four common rationales given for protective legislation: maternity, alimony, health and morals, and types of work. The core difference between the two camps was rooted in their conflicting views of the impact of the ERA on protective legislation.

Those in favor of the amendment wanted to do away with such protections, believing they limited rather than promoted equality. Like Bitterman, they asserted that such protections "deprived women of their right to work" and in fact harmed women with specious arguments about women's frail health and moral vulnerability. On the other side, Lunde and her followers feared that the ERA would do away with such "essential laws—laws which had only been secured after years of hard, patient work and after proving over and over again in legislatures and courts that they were absolutely necessary to give women even a measure of equality."

Yet by the 1940s, debate about the ERA focused on other issues as well. It took into account new social developments such as the greater acceptance of birth control, which made motherhood a choice (and thus not all women were to be mothers), as well as the increasing numbers of married women in the wage-labor force. In 1940, the discourse also reflected the particular view of each camp regarding whether the effort toward equality should proceed state by state or via a federal amendment. Although this split had long existed in political circles, including the campaign for women's suffrage, it took on fresh meaning in the wake of a decade that heralded tremendous federal government expansion. Because of the Great Depression, massive national programs such as the Social Security Act and the Works Progress Administration granted the federal government ever greater powers and responsibilities to ensure the nation's well-being. Individual citizens expected national leaders and the programs they passed to correct injustice and to provide social supports in a far more personal and individual way than they had in previous decades. Still, those against the ERA believed that "unjust laws [could] be corrected very easily in legislatures of the states." Women would find better remedy from their state legislatures, not the federal government.[1]

We lack biographical information for the two speakers below, but nevertheless chose to include them because their speeches represent the status of the debate in 1940: the typical arguments made by women in all sorts of public forums, in venues across the country, two decades after the amendment was first introduced. Within this debate, note the impact of shifting social conditions on the dialogue, as well as the passion, political sophistication, and mastery of arcane legislative detail each speaker possessed.

NOTE

1. Nancy Wolloch, *Women and the American Experience, A Concise History* (New York: McGraw-Hill, 1996), 187.

GENERAL FEDERATION OF WOMEN'S CLUBS
FORUM: LUCRETIA MOTT AMENDMENT
1940 COUNCIL
MRS. HELEN ROBBINS BITTERMAN—
FOR THE AMENDMENT
HISTORIAN, AUTHOR, LECTURER,
COLUMBUS, OHIO[1]

Reprinted by Permission of the General Federation of Women's Clubs, Washington, D.C.

It is my pleasure today to urge upon you the addition to the United States Constitution of one more amendment affecting women, the so-called Equal Rights Amendment, which reads: "men and women shall have equal rights throughout the United States and every place subject to its jurisdiction."

A comparison of the status of women a hundred years ago and today leaves one breathless with admiration for the courage of our early pioneers who dared to protest that woman, like her brother, is a human being possessed of certain inalienable rights. The position of women is mirrored in the laws governing them. The law of the thirteen colonies was the English common law, handed down to us as the basis of our state laws and of our federal constitution. According to the common law, married women had no rights. For example, married women could not enter business for themselves. Any contract which a married woman made involving services or property was void. They had no rights over their children nor even to the very wedding ring placed on their finger.

These laws are on the statute books in many states today. Almost a thousand of them still stand as mute testimony of women's bondage under the old English common law. I do not wish to emphasize the importance of these old laws too much. We have many old laws which have lost their meaning, like the law in one of the western states which forbids people to shoot jack rabbits from moving street cars. When we have outgrown a law, we don't bother to repeal it: We just move on and forget it. Some of these laws probably do not cause great inconvenience to the women or they would have been changed. For example, while fathers in Georgia can still legally deprive mothers of their children, the probability is that few of them do so, or we should have heard more about it. However, the fact that these laws remain on the books is a tacit reminder that women are still not in full enjoyment of adult rights and privileges. They are legal precedent, and nothing is more dangerous. After suffrage was won in 1920, women's organizations banded together to remove the objectionable laws and substitute desirable ones. But in the last twenty years, less than 130 have been changed. With a thousand such laws in existence, at the rate we have been going, it will take us a hundred years to complete the job. But even when a law has been changed, there is no guarantee that it will stay changed. Any subsequent law can repeal an earlier one. For example, in 1916, the Virginia legislature gave mothers equal rights with fathers to the custody, services, and earnings of minor children. A few years later, that law was repealed and was not restored until 1930. By adding an amendment to the Constitution of the United States prescribing equal rights for men and women, these thousand laws could be made inactive, and we would be sure that the change would stick. To date, seventeen national organizations of women and about two hundred state groups are on record in favor of the amendment because of these reasons.

There is another reason for a federal amendment, and this is in the Constitution itself. Like the laws of the states, it was based on the old English common law. It was laid down early as a principle of American law that a law must be interpreted in terms of the intentions of the men who drafted it (*Smith vs. Alabama*). It is most improbable that the Founding Fathers ever had any idea that women would be taking the part in life which they do today. Consequently, when women have asked that they be granted, as citizens, rights or privileges which men take as a matter of course, the Supreme Court has refused. The earliest case, in 1869, was that of Myra Bradwell, who asked the Supreme Court to compel the State of Illinois to admit her to the practice of law. The Court refused, saying that the right to be recognized as an attorney was not one guaranteed to women by the Constitution (*Bradwell vs. Illinois*), although twelve years before it had guaranteed it to men (*Ex parte...*). Archaic as the reasoning in that case is, it is the interpretation which has been followed by the Supreme Court of the United States as recently as 1931. In that year, a Massachusetts woman was convicted of bootlegging. She asked to have a woman included on the jury in order to be tried by a jury of her peers, as guaranteed to citizens by the Constitution. The Supreme Court has frequently held that when a negro is tried, he may, and some states he must, have negroes on his jury in order to be tried by a jury of his peers. But in the case of this woman, the Supreme Court ruled that it was not necessary for her to have a woman on her jury in order to be tried by a jury of her peers (*Welosky vs. Massachusetts; Minor vs. Flappersett; Mackenzie vs. Hare*). The Supreme Courts of the various states have followed that line of reasoning. In an Illinois case, in 1926, a woman asked for a writ of mandamus to force the inclusion of her name on the jury panel on the ground that to serve on juries was a duty of a citizen. The Supreme Court has held that a state cannot bar negroes from jury service, because the disbarment would brand them as an inferior class of citizens and would deprive them of the equal protection of the law which is guaranteed to persons by the Fourteenth Amendment to the Constitution (*Virginia vs. Rives; ex parte Virginia; Neal vs. Delaware*). But the Illinois Supreme Court held that this woman possessed only the right of a citizen to vote and might not claim jury duty as a citizen (*People vs. Barnett*).

In other words, under the federal Constitution, women are not persons. The Constitution guarantees to women nothing considered fundamental by men except the right to vote, and will guarantee other rights only when an express amendment for the purpose is added. This is to me the first fundamental reason why another amendment affecting women must be added to our Constitution.

The second reason is the tidal wave of bills which have recently been deluging legislatures to deprive women of their right to work. Last year, in almost half of the states, women were told that their place was in the home.

Bills were introduced to prevent married women from working outside the home for pay—a revival of the old Anglo-Saxon idea. School boards have been offering more pay to men teachers than to women doing the same work. Bills have been introduced in state legislatures to forbid employment in certain trades to "females" in order to make jobs for men. Twenty years after the battle for suffrage was won, we are in actual danger of being swept back from the position we fought so hard to win. Take, for example, bills recently introduced in the Ohio legislature. Ohio has the longest list of occupations prohibited to women in the United States. The first—working on certain kinds of moving abrasives—was passed in 1900. All the others were added in 1919, ostensibly to protect women but actually to make jobs for the veterans returning from the war. There are few of these jobs which a woman would choose from preference, or which employers would care to hire a woman to do. On the other hand, some of the prohibited jobs are held by women regularly, in open violation of the law. But my point is this: In the very existence of that section of the Ohio law lies a constant temptation to add to the list of jobs prohibited to "females," as the law so scientifically describes us. In 1935 and again in 1937, a bill was introduced to amend that section to prohibit women from working on punch presses. This is light work, punching out small articles, like wheels and the tops of tin cans. There is nothing harmful to health or morals. But the women were paid less than the men for the same work, so the men wanted to get rid of the unfair competition. That was openly admitted in the hearing on the bill in 1937. In each legislature, the bill failed to come out of committee. But it will be reintroduced again, never fear. And then we have Pat Dunn. Pat is the spearhead in Ohio for the "Git home, maw" legislation. A bachelor, he deluges the papers with touching letters describing the bliss of marriage where the wife stays home and the hell where she contributes to family support. Three times he has introduced his bill to prohibit the employment of both spouses by the state. Each time the forces of reaction have been stirred to white heat by his oratory. Each time his bill has been defeated, for women all know that, equal though the law appears on the surface, it is aimed at the employment of wives and not of husbands. This last time, every state-wide organization of women was mobilized against the bill. It was a thrilling exhibition of how women can work together for a common cause. Yet for all that, the Dunn bill passed the House of Representatives four to one and was killed only in the Senate Labor Committee. This is the sort of legislation for which we need the Equal Rights Amendment—this, and the legislation to come.

How do I know that the amendment would cover such laws as the Dunn bill, or cases where state governors have issued directory orders forbidding employment of working wives? I know because of the experience of Wisconsin. In 1921, Wisconsin passed an equal rights bill. It permits protective labor legislation for women only, and it prohibits the employment of women by the state legislature. But in all other respects, it is an equal rights bill. And that bill has stood as a bulwark between the women of Wisconsin and forces which would push married women back into the middle ages. We are facing an onslaught against the right of married women to work. One would think that women had never contributed to the support of their families before the recent depression. Yet except in upper income groups, American men have never completely supported their wives from the day the first colonists landed. Wives have always made their contribution to family support. True, most of them did it in the home by fashioning goods with their hands. Yet even in colonial days, an uncounted number of women worked in the home and for what amounted to starvation wages and disposed of the product outside. For example, tailors merely cut the clothes for their customers and gave them final finish. Women piece-workers did the stitching. When we speak of the wage-earning wife in the modern sense, we mean, therefore, the woman who earns wages outside the home. However, it is clear that the right of working women to marry and continue as wage earners is being challenged.

What will the amendment mean in actual changes in the laws now on our statute books? Opponents of the amendment have conjured up dire pictures of the terrible results of the amendment for our present legal structure. Actually little, if anything, would happen right away. Our archaic laws would stay in print, but would lose their force. When a specific case would come up, it would be interpreted according to the amendment instead of according to the old law. But the amendment would stand like a flaming sword between women and new laws aimed at them. In all states where such bills were introduced the bills would die in committee. And there is the reason we must have the Equal Rights Amendment and have it soon—not because of the past so much as because of future threats to our security.

The most potent argument which opponents of the amendment have advanced is the claim that under it all protective legislation for women only would go by the boards. Protective laws for women only fall into four chief types: maternity laws, support or alimony laws, no night-work laws, and minimum wage and maximum hour laws.

Maternity legislation is of three kinds. There is the Maternity and Infancy Act, which provides only for the furnishing of information, available to men and women alike. This would not be affected by the amendment. There are the children's aid allowances, sometimes erroneously called "Mothers' Pensions." These have been provided for by the Social Security Act so that any person caring for an indigent child is eligible for the pension. These would not be affected. Six states have laws prohibiting women from working for a specified time before or after childbirth, but which make no provision for the mother's support in case she depends on her work for her living. The benefit which these laws confer on the women affected may be questioned. However, even the laws as they now exist are in no danger. Childbearing is a special function necessary for the preservation of the state. Until recently, it was a sex function participated in by almost all women; but with the spread of birth control, all women are not mothers. Child-bearing thus becomes a special function of some women. Not all men are soldiers. Yet the soldiers of the last war were paid a bonus for their special contribution to their country. Is it unreasonable to suppose that proponents of these laws would not point to the infinitely greater contribution which mothers make to the community, and provide for their protection not in terms of a female function, but of a service to the community on a par with that of taking lives? As to the support and alimony laws, today under the laws of many states, husbands and wives owe each other, mutually, support and assistance. The practice of making the wife and mother, as well as the husband and father, responsible for the support of spouse and children is far under way in this country. One-third of the states already have such laws. The majority of wives now contribute to the support of husbands and families through their labor and services in the home, although such support is not recognized as such by law. Under the amendment, the wife's actual contribution to her family's support would be recognized. In thirteen states the law already recognizes mutual support between husband and wife who have been divorced. Records show that a large percentage of divorced women are not only supporting themselves but their children as well. Alimony is decreed in only about 10 per cent of divorce cases. Under the amendment, if the husband were penniless and the wife had money, she would probably be ordered to pay him alimony, as was done not so long ago in a New York case.

We come now to the laws designed to protect women's health and morals. There is a double background for these laws which should be discussed, the factual one and the legal one. At the turn of the century, public opinion was roused by the shocking conditions in industry. To improve them, legislation of various kinds was introduced. Where men were affected, the laws were declared unconstitutional because limiting the number of hours which a man might work or fixing the wage he must receive were considered restrictions of his right freely to contract for the disposal of his labor, a right guaranteed to citizens by the Fourteenth Amendment to the Constitution. The only way in which such legislation could be upheld in the courts was through the legal fiction presented in 1908 by the decision in *Muller vs. Oregon*, which upheld the constitutionality of an hours law for women only: "...by abundant testimony of the medical fraternity continuance for a long time on her feet at work, repeating this from day to day, tends to injurious effects upon the body, and as healthy mothers are essential to vigorous offspring, the physical well being of women becomes an object of public interest and care in order to preserve the strength and vigor of the race. Still, again, history discloses the control at the outset by superior physical strength, and this control in various forms, with diminishing intensity, has continued to the present. As minors, though not to the same extent, she has been looked upon in the courts as needing especial care that her rights may be preserved."

There is subtle irony in the fact that when this decision was handed down, one in five of America's working women were farm hands. However, in fairness to the proponents of labor legislation for women only, not only was this the only way such legislation could have been introduced into this country, but until recently, women did constitute a special labor group. Before the last world war, women did only unskilled work, they worked for very low wages, and they worked only until they were married. They made up a group which was a constant threat to the wage levels of the men workers. That is no longer true. The machine has changed all that. Former trades which required real skill are now done by machine, and the machine is quite indifferent to the sex of the worker. The conditions of men and women in industry are becoming more and more similar. Women, like men, work after marriage. True, women's wages still lag behind men's. But where employers can be brought to pay in terms of the job rather than the sex of the worker, that discrepancy can be less-ened. The federal government has recognized that the old differences between men and women workers are no longer great. The federal wages-and-hour law covers both men and women employed in inter-state industries. The con-ditions of the job are the things that count and not the sex of the worker. Fol-lowing this policy of the government, the Consumers League last year introduced similar bills for men and women in thirty states. I see in the Equal Rights Amendment a means of putting labor legislation on a more wholesome basis that would never have been possible before. Yes, the laws for women only would go. But the federal wages-and-hours law for persons would remain. And since legislation for all workers has been the professed aim of all proponents of the laws for women only, there can be no real objection on this score to the Equal Rights Amendment.

This brings me finally to the question of no-night-work laws for women and laws prohibiting the employment of women in certain industries. These laws would probably be stricken from the books. At hearings on such bills, we hear much about women's biological handicap. This is another of the vestigial remains of our pre-war civilization where men's strength was required in industry and where women could not compete with that strength without serious injury. The effect of increasing mechanization of industry has been to remove that handicap. Not even men do the heavy work they did even ten years ago. I have no intention of claiming physical equality for men and women. That would be as absurd as claiming physical equality for all men or for all women. But I would like to call your attention to recent medical findings summarized by Prof. S.J. Holmes of the Depart-ment of Zoology of the University of California (*Human Genetics and Its Social Import*, University of California, 1938). These show that not only do women have more resistance to disease and fewer congenital deformities, but they also withstand starvation, loss of blood, and loss of sleep better than men. It is not desirable for industry to place unreasonable strain on the worker. But in case it does, women are better able to stand it than men. My only reason for pointing this out is that these no-night-work laws and laws prohibiting the employment of women in certain occupations are grounded not in fact but in fancy, in a misdirected chivalry instead of in justice. Take the case of the no-night-work laws, which are not on the statute books of six-teen states. Night work is better paid than day work. The no-night-work laws have thrown thousands of women out of well paid jobs: women reporters, linotype operators, copy readers, telephone and telegraph opera-tors, railroad employees, candy store clerks, elevator operators (the night shift is the easy one), waitresses (tips are higher and trays lighter at night than at noon). It is interesting to note that the New York Labor Law of 1913, which prohibited the employment of women printers at night, permitted women to do the heavy cleaning in printing offices at night. With the admis-sions of the men at the hearings of last year ringing in my ears, forgive me if I insist that women are quite as capable of working for pay at night as men, and that they should have the opportunity of doing so. Do not let the appearance of sentimental chivalry blind you to the fact that the fundamen-tal reason for these laws is to get the jobs for the men.

And so I rejoice that the Equal Rights Amendment may abolish these unfair discriminations once and for all and put women on the legal and industrial place of equality where they deserve to be. Back of every man in this country stands the Constitution of the United States. Back of every woman is the Anglo-Saxon common law. In fairness and justice to the women of our country, put the Constitution back of the women of the United States by passing the Equal Rights Amendment.

MRS. LAURA HUGHES LUNDE
AGAINST THE AMENDMENT SECRETARY, ILLINOIS WOMEN'S JOINT CONFERENCE ON LEGISLATION, CHICAGO, ILLINOIS

I have always believed that women should have equal rights, equal opportunity, equal everything else with men. I think it would be hard today to find any women in this country who does not, and I think most men do too. I must confess that once, long ago, I joined the National Women's Party and accepted the idea of the Equal Rights Amendment. That was when my children were very small and I was on duty nights, Sundays and holidays, and anything which even suggested a change sounded pretty good. So when I heard that women were to be completely freed from everything with a federal amendment I said "all right," but I did ask, "Will this affect the laws which we now have and which protect women in industry?" I was assured that the federal amendment was patterned after the Wisconsin Equal Rights law, which does not affect these very essential laws—laws which had only been secured after years of hard, patient work and after proving over and over again in legislatures and courts that they were absolutely necessary to give women even a measure of equality. After accepting the assurance that women were to be given further equality and at the same time not be deprived of these equalizing protective laws, I was amazed to find, when I received my first packet of literature from the National Women's Party, that their whole attack seemed to be not on laws which really discriminated unjustly against women, but against the laws made to protect women from unjust exploitation. I remembered one pamphlet raved because women in a certain state were not allowed to be employed where they carried trunks weighing over 100 pounds. They said this interfered with women's freedom. Another pamphlet told how awful it was that in one state women were forbidden to take jobs guarding lonely railway crossings at night, where they might be exposed to wandering tramps. I began to think and decided that no woman in her senses would want to carry a trunk of over 100 lbs. And I clearly saw that that there were certain dangers to a woman in a lonely railroad crossing but that would not be the same in the case of a man. So I sent for a copy of the Equal Rights Amendment and found that it was not like the Wisconsin law and that it did [not] provide the necessary protective safeguards to make women equal with men in the industrial world. That was enough—I sent in my resignation and started to find out how to give women real equality.

The first thing I discovered is that you cannot make women and men equal by legislative or constitutional action. We just aren't built that way. In those places where men and women function as persons, such as in our citizenship duties, one law will do for both sexes—we should all be equal in voting rights, etc. But where we function differently as men and women, one single law usually makes for inequality.

Take the question of alimony. No one knows whether the Equal Rights Amendment would be interpreted to provide that no man, however wicked he has been, should have to support his wife and family or whether, in order to be equal, the injured wife should have to pay alimony to her erring husband—and yet, if we have a single law governing men and women, one of those two things will occur. What are we going to do in the case of support for children? Shall mothers as well as fathers be forced by law to support their children, or shall neither parent be required to support the family? What sort of equal rights would this amendment give in the field of a property inheritance? No one can tell exactly and it would take years of litigation before the various phases of the question could be settled, for many states have different laws in regard to the rights of husband and wife in one another's real estate. It is also possible that all inheritance rights might be wiped out, which would certainly be much harder on women than on men, for women, because many of them are home-makers, have no estate of their own and if they have no right to inheritance in their husband's property, might be left utterly destitute if they were widowed, even though in many cases they had helped the husband accumulate the property by their thrifty housekeeping. If this should happen, the Equal Rights Amendment would put women in quite an unequal position.

What is the use of spending all the time and money that it takes to pass an amendment to our Federal Constitution, which, when it is passed, will probably do more harm than good to women, when in each state unjust laws can be corrected very easily in the legislatures of the states. We are pretty sure what the amendment would do. All the protective legislation which has been passed to give women in industry equal opportunity with men, would be wiped out. It is quite significant that the National Women's Party has consistently opposed all such legislation when it has been under consideration. They say that they do this because they want men to have the same protection. But do they? As far as I can find, they did nothing to help in the passage of the wages and hours law and in my state they even were conspicuously absent when the "Little Wagner Act" was in the legislature. If one is to judge by their actions, they are more anxious to handicap women in the industrial world than they are to give women equal rights.

It is claimed that laws setting minimum wages and limiting working hours for women discriminate against women. But do they? There have been some very careful studies made over a long period of years which show that this is not the case. In all the years since the Illinois 10-hour law was passed, they have never found a single case where a woman lost her job because of that hour limitation. These laws which protect women and which were passed to give women equality with men in industry, really have helped industry raise the standards for men. This is particularly true with the minimum wage and hours limitation legislation. Any low paid over-worked group drags down the standards of the whole industry affected. When I was quite a youngster, I was asked to go into certain factories as a worker to find out about the conditions under which women were working. I found conditions far worse than they had been described. In one of the mills girls were working from 7:00 A.M. to 6:00 P.M. six days a week and half of them were making less than $1.00 a day. The sanitary conditions were horrible, the place a fire trap. These mills were working on government jobs and my uncle was the government official who gave the contracts, and because of this we were able to make the mills put in a better wage and set hour limitation for the girls. Then the factory managers found out two things—that it paid them to have these better conditions for there was less bad work done, and the regular work was better for the girls were not so exhausted. Then, since it wasn't worth while keeping the mill running with-out the women, the men got shorter hours and the minimum wage boosted all wage rates. Thanks to the work of many devoted women who have given their lives to securing protective legislation for women workers, conditions are better today than they were, but no woman who has ever worked on the lower paid jobs in industry would ever say that protective wage and hours legislation discriminated against women, for they know it has been the one thing which has given women in the working world a chance for equality with men. Any amendment or law which would wipe out these protective measures will push women down into an inferior position.

As one thinks more about the effect of this equal rights amendment on laws, one is confronted with a lot of curious questions as to its results. Take the question of rape. Would anyone say that a woman suspect should be given as severe punishment as a man guilty of that offense? What about the cases like the law in my own city which requires teachers who are expecting babies to take a two years' leave of absence? Are all prospective fathers to be forced to take two years off from work too? That would be rather hard on the family.

Proponents of the amendment have dug up a lot of queer old obsolete laws which limit women's sphere in life, but do they ever cite cases where these laws are enforced? Take the case of the state where a silly old law says men may will away their children. How many men are there in that state that have willed away their children? If there were actual cases like that the women in that state would have risen up long ago, and using their power as voters, have made the legislature repeal the law. There are hundreds of silly laws in the various statutes of our states which are never enforced because it is either impossible or because they are completely out of date. Anyone who wants some fun can go over our law books and find lots and lots of these ridiculous laws, but we don't have a federal amendment to eliminate them.

Take the case of those laws which seem to hold women down. Nobody knows whether the proposed amendment will correct the situation or not. It will take years of litigation before we know where we are. Take jury service. Is it a right or a duty? If it is considered to be the latter, it's quite possible the proposed amendment won't have any effect on the state laws or give jury service to women; and the women in the states which do not provide for women on juries will have to go on and pass state laws providing for this anyway. After all, whether jury service is a right or a duty, it is much better for women in the several states to go out and make their own fight for it. Our state recently passed the Women-on-Jury law, and though it took us some time, every delay taught us something and we really were far better prepared to use our jury service wisely when we won it ourselves than if it had been handed to us without any effort on our part. Go back to the sad case of law which allows fathers to will away their children. Suppose the amendment should be passed. In all probability its effect would be to give mothers the same right—that is, to will away their children—but a will is not effective until after death so that in order to get any good from the amendment a woman would have to die, or commit suicide. And will you tell me why anyone would want to spend all the time and money needed to pass a federal amendment, to get a woman a right she has to die to use. The simplest way to settle that law would be to repeal the law in the state legislature.

A federal amendment is such an important thing and takes up so much more legislative effort in Congress than in the state governments that it should never be attempted unless it is absolutely necessary. We don't want to get the habit or we may find ourselves proposing all sorts of amendments to our United States Constitution. Federal amendments should not be treated lightly. There isn't anything which this amendment could do that cannot be done much more easily and more effectively by acts in the several legislatures. Then there would be no need for endless litigation to find out what the laws mean. Passing a federal amendment to get rid of these old laws is like using a pile-driver to drive in a tack. In these days when there are so many more important and more vital problems facing us it does seem foolish to waste time and money on something which may or may not accomplish the end sought. For every woman who suffers because of some old discrimination in the law there are thousands and thousands who suffer because of poverty, starvation, poor housing, etc., and millions who suffer because nations have not learned to live at peace. With juvenile crime on the increase and education being curtailed in many states, doesn't it seem sad that any women are willing to spend their time on something which will probably not accomplish its aim and would not do much good if it did? And there is the chance that women would be worse off if it were enforced than they are now. At least now we know where we are and if the amendment were passed we wouldn't know for years and years.

NOTE

1. Mrs. Gustav Ketterer, Chairman, General Federation of Women's Clubs, "Legislation," "Official Report of the Council Meeting," Milwaukee, GFWC, Washington, DC., 1940.

Luisa Moreno (1907–1992)

An ardent activist, Luisa Moreno stood at the forefront of the American labor movement between 1928, when she immigrated to the United States, and 1950, when she was deported during the McCarthy era. Rather than focusing on one group of Latin Americans or one category of workers, Moreno devoted her extraordinary political and organizational talents to the cause of all "Spanish-speaking citizens and non-citizens." Propelled by this vision and employing her considerable powers of persuasion in both English and Spanish, Moreno drew thousands of Latin Americans to the political causes and the progressive unions she helped lead and direct.

Moreno was born and educated in Guatemala before moving to Mexico City, where she worked as a newspaper correspondent. In 1928 she moved to New York, finding work in the garment district. Moreno quickly joined the International Ladies Garment Union and by the mid-1930s was an organizer for the American Federation of Labor. After joining the CIO in 1937, Moreno traveled extensively on behalf of its affiliate, the United Cannery, Agricultural, Packing and Allied Workers of America (UCAPAWA). In this capacity, she was a leader of the 1938 strike against the Southern Pecan Shelling Company in San Antonio, Texas. Protesting a wage reduction, the workers were eventually victorious but not before being gassed, arrested, and jailed. In the next decade, Moreno organized cotton workers in Texas, beet workers in Colorado and Michigan, and cannery workers in California.

Also in 1938, Moreno became a principal founder of El Congreso de los Pueblos de Habla Español (Spanish-Speaking People's Congress).

More radical and inclusive than most, the Congress recruited Latinos of all nationalities and ethnicities, without regard to citizenship status. It set an ambitious human rights agenda; one that would attack all forms of discrimination as well as improve working conditions. In the 1940s, Moreno continued her labor activism. She traveled and spoke extensively for UCAPAWA locals in California. She was elected vice president of the Los Angeles Industrial Council and the California CIO Executive Board and was international vice president of UCAPAWA.

Moreno also headed the infamous Sleepy Lagoon Defense Team, the group that defended Mexican-American youths in the aftermath of the zoot-suit riots. In the summer of 1943, simmering tensions about immigration and rumors of Mexican gangs erupted into the zoot-suit riots. About 200 American sailors attacked Mexican youths whose flamboyant, fashionable, long-coat, peg-bottom suits signaled cultural pride to Latinos but defiance to Anglos. Moreno and others mobilized to provide a legal and political defense of the arrested Latinos. Assigning the blame to patterns of discrimination within the Navy, she pointed out that "these Mexicans lived an extremely hard life. They were poorly educated and attempted to better themselves through menial jobs. They avoided trouble and refused to complain. When confronted with discrimination, they swallowed their anger and sorrows."[1]

As the Cold War heated up, California State Senator Tenney and other anti-Communist agitators began to label Moreno a communist and her activism on behalf of Mexican Americans un-American. Despite such attacks, Moreno persevered. In the late 1940s, she established a Mexican Civil Rights Committee chapter in San Diego to fight discrimination and police brutality and continued to organize and give speeches on behalf of workers. Nevertheless, on November 30, 1950, Moreno, a "dangerous alien," was deported under the McCarran–Walter Immigration Act. With her husband, she moved to Mexico, then to Cuba, where she participated in the Castro revolution, and then to Guatemala, but never again returned to the United States.

Moreno delivered the following address to the panel of Deportation and Right of Asylum of the Fourth Annual Conference of the American Committee for Protection of the Foreign Born, which met in Washington, DC, on March 3, 1940. The speech captures Moreno's direct, passionate, but eloquent speaking style. It also spells out her political philosophy. She condemned racial discrimination, attacked economic injustice, and demanded that Mexicans be recognized for their historic contributions to American life and that they be granted full citizenship rights. In accordance with her organizational vision, she championed the cause of all "Spanish-speaking citizens and non-citizens" alike.

NOTE

1. Moreno interview, April 20, 1971, quoted in Carlos M. Larralde and Richard Griswold del Castillo, "Luisa Moreno and the Beginnings of the Mexican American Civil Rights Movement in San Diego," *The Journal of San Diego History* (Summer 1997).

CARAVANS OF SORROW
ADDRESS AT THE PANEL OF DEPORTATION AND RIGHT OF ASYLUM OF THE FOURTH ANNUAL CONFERENCE OF THE AMERICAN COMMITTEE FOR PROTECTION OF THE FOREIGN BORN, WASHINGTON, DC (MARCH 3, 1940)[1]

One hears much today about hemisphere unity. The press sends special corespondents to Latin America, South of the Border songs are wailed by the radio, educational institutions and literary circles speak the language of cultural cooperation, and what is more important, labor unions are seeking the road of closer ties with the Latin American working people.

The stage is set. A curtain rises. May we ask you to see behind the scenery and visualize a forgotten character in this great theater of the Americas?

Long before the "grapes of wrath" had ripened in California's vineyards a people lived on highways, under trees or tents, in shacks or railroad sections, picking crops—cotton, fruits, vegetables—cultivating sugar beets, building railroads and dams, making a barren land fertile for new crops and greater riches.

The ancestors of some of these migrant and resident workers, whose home is this Southwest, were America's first settlers in New Mexico, Texas, and California, and the greater percentage was brought from Mexico by the fruit exchanges, railroad companies, and cotton interests in great need of underpaid labor during the early postwar period. They are the Spanish-speaking workers of the Southwest, citizens and noncitizens working and living under identical conditions, facing hardships and miseries while producing and building for agriculture and industry.

Their story lies unpublicized in university libraries, files of government, welfare and social agencies—a story grimly titled the "Caravans of Sorrow."

And when in 1930 unemployment brought a still greater flood of human distress, trainloads of Mexican families with children born and raised in this country departed voluntarily or were brutally deported. As a result of the repatriation drive of 1933, thousands of American-born youths returned to their homeland, the United States, to live on streets and highways, drifting unattached fragments of humanity. Let the annals of juvenile delinquency in Los Angeles show you the consequences.

Today the Latin Americans of the United States are seriously alarmed by the "antialien" drive fostered by certain un-American elements; for them, the Palmer days [referring to the mass arrests and expulsions of suspected Communist subversives conducted under the direction of Attorney General A. Mitchell Palmer during the height of the infamous "Red Scare" of 1919–1920] have never ended. In recent years while deportations in general have decreased, the number of persons deported to Mexico has constantly increased. During the period of 1933 to 1937, of a total of 55,087 deported, 25,135 were deportations of Mexicans. This is 45.5 percent of the total and does not include an almost equal number of so-called voluntary departures.

Commenting on these figures, the American Committee for Protection of Foreign Born wrote to the Spanish-Speaking Peoples' Congress in 1939: "One conclusion can be drawn, and that is, where there is such a highly organized set-up as to effect deportations of so many thousands, this set-up must be surrounded with a complete system of intimidation and discrimination of that section of the population victimized by the deportation drive."

Confirming the fact of a system of extensive discrimination are university studies by Paul S. Taylor, Emory Bogardus, and many other professors and social workers of the Southwest. Let me state the simple truth. The majority of the Spanish-speaking peoples of the United States are victims of a setup for discrimination, be they descendants of the first white settlers in America or noncitizens.

I will not go into the reasons for this undemocratic practice, but may we state categorically that it is the main reason for the reluctance of Mexicans and Latin Americans in general to become naturalized. For you must know, discrimination takes very definite forms in unequal wages, unequal opportunities, unequal schooling, and even through a denial of the use of public places in certain towns in Texas, California, Colorado, and other Southwestern states.

Only some 5 or 6 percent of Latin American immigrants have become naturalized. A number of years ago it was stated that in a California community with fifty thousand Mexicans only two hundred had become citizens. An average of one hundred Mexicans out of close to a million become citizens every year. These percentages have increased lately.

Another important factor concerning naturalization is the lack of documentary proof of entry, because entry was not recorded or because the immigrants were brought over en masse by large interests handling transportation from Mexico in their own peculiar way.

Arriving at logical conclusions, the Latin American noncitizens, rooted in this country, are increasingly seeing the importance and need for naturalization. But how will the thousands of migrants establish residence? What possibility have these people had, segregated in "Little Mexicos," to learn English and meet educational requirements? How can they, receiving hunger wages while enriching the stockholders of the Great Western Sugar Company, the Bank of America, and other large interests, pay high naturalization fees? A Mexican family living on relief in Colorado would have to stop eating for two and a half months to pay for the citizenship papers of one member of the family. Is this humanly possible?

But why have "aliens" on relief while taxpayers "bleed"? Let me ask those who would raise such a question: what would the Imperial Valley, the Rio Grande Valley, and other rich irrigated valleys in the Southwest be without the arduous, self-sacrificing labor of these noncitizen Americans? Read *Factories in the Fields*, by Carey McWilliams to obtain a picture of how important Mexican labor has been for the development of California's crop after the world war. Has anyone counted the miles of railroads built by these same noncitizens? One can hardly imagine how many bales of cotton have passed through the nimble fingers of Mexican men, women, and children. And what conditions have they had to endure to pick that cotton? Once, while holding a conference for a trade union paper in San Antonio, a cotton picker told me how necessary a Spanish paper was to inform the Spanish-speaking workers that FSA [Farm Security Administration] camps were to be established, for she remembered so many nights, under the trees in the rain, when she and her husband held gunny sacks over the shivering bodies of their sleeping children—young Americans. I've heard workers say that they left their shacks under heavy rains to find shelter under trees. You can well imagine in what condition those shacks were.

These people are not aliens. They have contributed their endurance, sacrifices, youth, and labor to the Southwest. Indirectly, they have paid more taxes than all the stockholders of California's industrialized agriculture, the sugar beet companies and the large cotton interests that operate or have operated with the labor of Mexican workers.

Surely the sugar beet growers have not been asked if they want to dispense with the skilled labor cultivating and harvesting their crops season after season. It is only the large interest, their stooges, and some badly misinformed people who claim that Mexicans are no longer wanted.

And let us assume that 1.4 million men, women, and children were no longer wanted, what could be done that would be different from the anti-Semitic persecutions in Europe? A people who have lived twenty and thirty years in this country, tied up by family relations with the early settlers, with American-born children, cannot be uprooted without the complete destruction of the faintest semblance of democracy and human liberties for the whole population.

Some speak of repatriation. Naturally there is interest in repatriation among thousands of Mexican families in Texas and, to a lesser degree, in other states. Organized repatriation has been going on, and the net results in one year has been the establishment of the Colonia "18 de Marzo" in Tamaulipas, Mexico, for two thousand families. There are 1.4 million Mexicans in the United States according to general estimates, probably including a portion of the first generation. Is it possible to move those many people at the present rate, when many of them do not want to be repatriated?

What then may the answer to this specific noncitizen problem be? The Spanish-Speaking Peoples' Congress of the United States proposes legislation that would encourage naturalization of Latin American, West Indian, and Canadian residents of the United States and that would nurture greater friendships among the peoples of the Western Hemisphere.

The question of hemispheric unity will remain an empty phrase while this problem at home remains ignored and is aggravated by the fierce "antialien" drive. Legislation to facilitate citizenship to all natural-born citizens from the countries of the Western Hemisphere, waiving excessive fees and educational and other requirements of a technical nature, is urgently needed.

A piece of legislation embodying this provision is timely and important. Undoubtedly it would rally the support of the many friends of true hemispheric unity.

You have seen the forgotten character in the present American scene—a scene of the Americas. Let me say that, in the face of greater hardships, the "Caravans of Sorrow" are becoming the "Caravans of Hope." They are organizing in trade unions with other workers in agriculture and industry. The unity of Spanish-speaking citizens and noncitizens is being furthered through the Spanish-Speaking Peoples' Congress of the United States, an organization embracing trade unions and fraternal, civic, and cultural organizations, mainly in California. The purpose of this movement is to seek an improvement of social, economic, and cultural conditions, and for the integration of Spanish-speaking citizens and noncitizens into the American nation. The United Cannery, Agricultural, Packing, and Allied Workers of America, with thousands of Spanish-speaking workers in its membership, and Liga Obrera of New Mexico, were the initiators of the Congress.

This Congress stands with all progressive forces against the badly labeled "antialien" legislation and asks the support of this Conference for democratic legislation to facilitate and encourage naturalization. We hope that this Conference will serve to express the sentiment of the people of this country in condemnation of undemocratic discrimination practiced against any person of foreign birth and that it will rally the American people, native and foreign born, for the defeat of un-American proposals. The Spanish-speaking peoples in the United States extend their fullest support and cooperation to your efforts.

NOTE

1. Carey McWilliams Collection, University Research Library, Department of Special Collections, University of California, Los Angeles. Printed in David G. Gutierrez, ed., *Between Two Worlds: Mexican Immigrants in the United States* (Wilmington, DE: Scholarly Resources, 1996), 119–122.

Suggested Readings, 1932–1940

Becker, Susan D. *The Origins of the Equal Rights Amendment: American Feminism Between the Wars* (Westport, CT: Greenwood Press, 1981).

Chesler, Ellen. *Women of Valor: Margaret Sanger and the History of the Birth Control Movement in America* (New York: Simon and Schuster, 1992).

Coll, Blanche D. *Safety Net: Welfare and Social Security, 1929–1979* (New Brunswick, NJ: Rutgers University Press, 1995).

Cook, Blanche Wiesen. *Eleanor Roosevelt, 1884–1933*, Vol. 1 (New York: Penguin, 1993).

Cook, Blanche Wiesen. *Eleanor Roosevelt, 1933–1938*, Vol. 2 (New York: Viking Penguin, 1999).

Freedman, Estelle. "Separatism as Strategy: Female Institution Building and American Feminism, 1870–1930," *Feminist Studies* 5 (Fall 1979): 512–529.

Giddings, Paula. *When and Where I Enter: The Impact of Black Women on Race and Sex in America* (New York: W. Morrow, 1984).

Goldin, Claudi. *Understanding the Gender Gap: An Economic History of American Women* (New York: Oxford University Press, 1990).

Gordon, Linda. *Woman's Body, Woman's Right: A Social History of Birth Control in America* (New York: Penguin, 1976).

Hoff-Wilson, Joan and Lightman, Marjorie, eds. *Without Precedent: The Life and Career of Eleanor Roosevelt* (Bloomington, IN: Indiana University Press, 1984).

Jones, Correa M. "Different Paths: Gender, Immigration and Political Participation," *International Migration Review* 32 (Summer 1998): 326–49.

Kessler-Harris, Alice. *Out to Work: A History of Wage-Earning Women in the United States* (New York: Oxford University Press, 1982).

Kevles, David. *In the Name of Eugenics: Genetics and the Uses of Human Heredity* (New York: Knopf, 1985).

Klein, Laura F. and Lillian A. Ackerman, eds. *Women and Power in Native North America* (Norman, OK: University of Oklahoma Press, 1995).

Orleck, Annelise, "'We Are that Mythic Thing Called the Public'" Militant House-wives during the Great Depression," *Feminist Studies* 19 (Spring 1993): 147–72.

Ruiz, Vicki L. *Cannery Women, Cannery Lives: Mexican Women, Unionization and the California Food Processing Industry, 1930–1950* (Albuquerque, NM: University of New Mexico Press, 1987).

Ruiz, Vicki L. *From Out of the Shadows: Mexican American Women in Twentieth-Century America* (New York: Oxford University Press, 1998).

Sanchez, George. *Becoming Mexican American: Ethnicity, Culture, and Identity in Chicano Los Angeles, 1900–1965* (New York: Oxford University Press, 1995).

Solomon, Barbara. *In the Company of Educated Women* (New Haven: Yale University Press, 1985).

Ware, Susan. *Beyond Suffrage: Women in the New Deal* (Cambridge, MA: Harvard University Press, 1981).

Ware, Susan. *Holding Their Own: American Women in the 1930s* (Boston, Twayne, 1982).

Ware, Susan. *Partner and I: Molly Dewson, Feminism, and New Deal Politics* (New Haven: Yale University Press, 1987).

PART III

Speaking of War! 1940–1945

In 1939, the Axis and Allied powers officially declared war. Finally, facing the reality that Germany would not be "appeased," Europe erupted into all-out war. Americans, absorbed in events taking place three thousand miles across the Atlantic Ocean, began a long, national debate about their country's appropriate response. The country increasingly felt the impact of the war on its economy, politics, and culture and on American policies at home and abroad. But in the aftermath of World War I and the Great Depression, the majority of Americans tended to support President Roosevelt's officially stated isolationist position. Until Pearl Harbor, most Americans thought the country ought to stand clear.

Like their compatriots, women expressed a wide range of opinions; but for women activists, issues of war and peace had long been central concerns. Both cultural stereotypes and women's own claims tended to label women—the mothers of the race—as naturally more pacifistic. Some of the most prominent twentieth-century feminists, such as Jane Addams and Eleanor Roosevelt, championed this position. But most women, even those long resistant to "war for any reason," could not avoid the horrific power of Hitler and Mussolini's fascism. As Clare Booth Luce asked in her 1942 speech collected here, "How do women fight a war when they have to?" Presented with unbelievable threats to human dignity and equality, many women employed their powers of persuasion to support the war effort and to shape the United States' policy.

An array of female voices commented on, described, and responded to the war. Jessie Haver Butler included a sampling of women's wartime rhetoric in the first edition of her speaker's handbook for women published in

1945.[1] Women spoke in every venue, from small public forums to national, prime-time events. Perhaps most prominent was the voice of journalist Dorothy Thompson. She had been warning Americans about the dangerous rise of European fascism in her newspaper column, in lecture tours, and on the radio in the early 1930s. During the final days before England declared war on Germany, NBC radio featured Thompson for fifteen consecutive days, making her the voice of the war for many Americans. As these women argued their cases, they employed common strategies of effective war rhetoric, including appeals to Americans' sense of territoriality, ethnocentrism, and optimism.[2] Furthermore, women took advantage of calls for national unity, which de-emphasized partisan politics, and played to the stereotypical definition of women as politically pure.

War did not stop politics, however, though it had a significant effect on campaign rhetoric. When Roosevelt decided to run for an unprecedented third term as president in 1940, delegates at the nominating convention went along, in part because of the wartime situation. But confusion reigned over the nomination for vice-president. In a move that revealed her stature and authority, Eleanor Roosevelt, in an unscheduled, impromptu speech spoke to the delegates on behalf of FDR's vice-presidential choice, bringing order back to an unruly assembly. Other women, including Republicans Clare Boothe Luce and Margaret Chase Smith, along with Democrats Helen Gahagan Douglas, and Hattie Caraway, campaigned for their own election to Congress during the war years. For Republican women the challenge was how to support the war effort without endorsing Roosevelt; for Democratic women the challenge was how to remain credible voices for administration policies.

The lone female Senator in Congress, Democrat Hattie Caraway, urged women and men to stop being emotional about war and pay attention to the facts before jumping on the bandwagon in support of one side or another. In 1942, Republican Clare Boothe Luce, campaigning for a seat in the House of Representatives, alerted businesswomen to get ready for unavoidable and righteous sacrifice and to support the war effort. Two years later she spoke at the Republican Presidential Nominating Convention, claiming that "G. I. Jim" would not vote for Roosevelt. The speech so incensed Democrat India Edwards that she prepared a counterattack, which was delivered at the 1944 Democratic convention.[3]

Extremists on both the right and the left argued the antiwar position. The "Mothers Movement" led by Elizabeth Dilling and involving radio personality Catherine Curtis, supported by virulent anti-Semite Father Coughlin, opposed American involvement in the war.[4] From the other end of the political spectrum, Catholic Dorothy Day spoke out against war generally and specifically, in a speech delivered the same day the United States and Britain declared war on Japan, December 8, 1941. Most women, however, supported the war. Many focused on particular aspects of

women's wartime mobilization: defense industry work, family disloca-
tion, war relief, civilian defense, nursing, and armed service. Women's
Bureau Director Mary Anderson, for example, proudly broadcast to
England the work being done by women in American factories—a personal success for Anderson and a culmination of her efforts to provide
women good working conditions in industry.

Though many socialists opposed World Wars I and II, Ella Reeve Bloor
championed solidarity among "men, women, colored, and white, Jew and
Gentile," in her call for American women to support what she termed "the
people's war." And Mary Beard, speaking of the special need for nurses,
recruited young women into the profession and encouraged those who
had stepped out, especially mothers and wives, to return to nursing. Serving in one of the most sensitive diplomatic posts, US Minister to Norway,
Florence Harriman gave speeches in 1941 and 1944 that trace America's
wartime odyssey. An early advocate for intervention, she first encouraged
women to get involved in politics, then in 1941 encouraged the United
States to enter the European fray, and in 1944 attempted to slow the quickly
deteriorating relationship between America and Russia. Her 1944 speech
foreshadowed the complex series of political and economic questions
Americans would face in the postwar years; questions that included suspicions about individual loyalties, patriotism, and true "Americanism."

In many ways World War II heightened women's sense of responsibility
as citizens at home. For example, African American Pauli Murray, then a
student at Howard University, organized the first successful lunch
counter sit-ins, integrating restaurants in Washington, DC. Her efforts
were motivated by the recognition that black men who might otherwise
be fighting for civil rights at home were fighting a war for the nation overseas, in segregated units. She felt an obligation to do her part on behalf of
civil rights.[5]

Cold War fears stood just outside the door. Throughout the late 1930s
and early 1940s, women gave thousands of speeches that expressed their
views on the war, their hopes and dreams for the nation, and, in particular, their hopes for American women. Holding a variety of official and
unofficial positions and diverse political perspectives, they spoke before
assorted audiences as they articulated their reactions to domestic unease
as well as the international crisis.

NOTES

1. Jessie Haver Butler, "Representative speeches Delivered by Nationally
Important Women During the War Years—1940–1946," in *Time to Speak Up!* (New
York: Harper, 1945), 211–254.

2. Ronald F. Reid, "New England Rhetoric and the French War, 1754–1760: A
Case Study in the Rhetoric of War," *Communication Monographs.* 43 (November
1976): 259–286.

3. Jerry N. Hess, Oral History Interview with India Edwards, January 16, 1969," *Truman Presidential Museum and Library* [web site and database] June 22, 2001: 3 (www.trumanlibrary.org/oralhist/edwards1.htm).

4. Glen Jeansonne, *Women of the Far Right: The Mother's Movement and World War II* (Chicago: University of Chicago Press, 1996).

5. Pauli Murray, *The Autobiography of a Black Activist, Feminist, Lawyer, Priest, and Poet* (Knoxville, TN: University of Tennessee Press, 1987).

Eleanor Roosevelt

In 1932, Eleanor Roosevelt supported FDR's New Deal policies through her own unflagging public advocacy in print, on the radio, and in person (see Part II). She also brought a team of women to federal government who headed up important agencies and made significant contributions to social welfare in this country. By the end of the 1930s, though, it was clear that the focus was shifting from domestic concerns to international crises. It was the fear of war that led many in 1940 to believe Roosevelt should seek a third term as President.[1]

FDR, though, was not willing to campaign actively for the nomination. According to one account, he sent a memo to the Democratic convention stating that the delegates should nominate whomever they wanted. Then, dramatically, as the memo was being read to the delegates, a voice broke in over the loudspeaker system exclaiming, "We want Roosevelt!" After that, Roosevelt won the nomination, but the delegates were not prepared to honor his vice presidential preference, Henry A. Wallace. So FDR sent Eleanor to get the convention back on track. In what may have been an impromptu speech, she addressed the convention, validating their nomination of FDR and calling for unity behind his platform in a time of international crisis. Her appeal was successful, and the delegates endorsed the President's wishes after that. Many argued that "her remarks were responsible for bringing order out of chaos so that the proceedings could go forward."[2] Here is the transcript of that precedent-breaking appearance by a First Lady at a national nominating convention.

NOTES

1. "The 1940 Democratic National Convention," *History Files—Parades, Protests and Politics* [web site and database] 30 November 2000 (www.chicagohistory.net/history/politics/1940.html).

2. Jessie Haver Butler, *Time to Speak Up!* (New York: Harper, 1945), 211. Our thanks to Rita Miller for this reference.

TO THE DEMOCRATIC NATIONAL CONVENTION, CHICAGO (JULY 18, 1940)[1]
MRS. FRANKLIN D. ROOSEVELT PRESENTED TO CONVENTION

The Permanent Chairman: The call of the States having been completed, the next order of business is the call of the States for the casting of the ballots of the States for the nomination for Vice President, but before proceeding to the balloting for the nomination for Vice President, the Chair desires to present to this convention the First Lady of this great land. (Applause and cheers.)

There are many virtues for which this charming lady is noted but one of the things through and by reason of which she has endeared herself to the American people is the fact that though she has all her life been active in every worthy enterprise for the advancement and development of the welfare of American men, women and children, she has not been willing to retard her efforts in that regard because she happened to be the wife of the President of the United States. (Applause.)

It gives me supreme pleasure at this time to present to you Mrs. Franklin Delano Roosevelt. (Applause and cheers.)

ADDRESS OF MRS. FRANKLIN DELANO ROOSEVELT

Mrs. Franklin Delano Roosevelt: Mr. Chairman, Delegates to the Convention, Visitors, Friends: It is a great pleasure for me to be here and to have an opportunity to say a word to you.

First of all, I think I want to say a word to our National Chairman, James A. Farley. (Applause.) For many years I have worked under Jim Farley and with Jim Farley, and I think nobody could appreciate more what he has done for the Party, what he has given in work and loyalty, and I want to give him here my thanks and devotion. (Applause.)

I think that I should say to you that I am conscious that I cannot possibly bring you a message from the President because he will give you his own message, but as I am here, I want you to know that no one could not be conscious of the confidence which you have expressed in him.

I know and you know that any man who is in an office of great responsibility today faces a heavier responsibility perhaps than any man has ever faced before in this country. Therefore, to be a candidate of either great political party is a very serious and a very solemn thing.

You cannot treat it as you would treat an ordinary nomination in an ordinary time.

We people in the United States have got to realize today that we face now a grave and serious situation. Therefore, this year the candidate who is the President of the United States cannot make a campaign in the usual sense of the word. He must be on his job. So each and every one of you who give him this responsibility in giving it to him assume for yourselves a very grave responsibility because you will make the campaign. You will have to rise above considerations which are narrow and partisan. You must know that this is the time when all good men and women give every bit of service and strength to their country that they have to give. This is a time when it is the United States that we fight for, the domestic policies that we have established as a party, that we must believe in, that we must carry forward, and in the world we have a position of great responsibility. We cannot tell from day to day what may come. This is no ordinary time, no time for thinking about anything except what we can best do for the country as a whole, and that responsibility is on each and every one of us as individuals. No man who is a candidate, or who is President, can carry this situation alone. This is only carried by a united people who love their country and who will live for it to the fullest of their ability with the highest ideals, with a determination that their party shall be absolutely devoted to the good of the nation as a whole, and to doing what this country can to bring the world to a safer and happier condition. (Applause and cheers.)

EXPRESSION OF APPRECIATION TO MRS. FRANKLIN D. ROOSEVELT BY PERMANENT CHAIRMAN

The Permanent Chairman: On behalf of this convention, I express to Mrs. Roosevelt our profound thanks not only for her presence here tonight but for these fine words she has uttered to us out of a heart we know to be sincere and devoted to the best interests of America. (Applause.)

NOTE

1. As recorded in the *Official Report of the Proceedings of the Democratic National Convention Held at Chicago, Illinois,* July 15 to July 18, inclusive, 1940, 238–239.

Dorothy Thompson (1894–1961)

Self-described journalist and lecturer Dorothy Thompson was a natural orator. She was physically blessed with a strong and responsive voice, as well as a striking appearance; emotionally passionate and committed; and intellectually gifted in linguistic style and force of argument.

Like many successful women during the 1930s and 1940s, Thompson began her public life campaigning for women's suffrage, making speeches throughout central and western New York state. After graduating from Syracuse University, Thompson traveled throughout Europe, learning German, finding employment as a foreign newspaper correspondent, and marrying two times. With her second husband, writer Sinclair Lewis, she returned to the United States. In 1936 Thompson began writing a weekly column for the *New York Herald Tribune*, and in 1938 she added a radio broadcast that aired on Monday evenings at 9:00 P.M. At the same time, she was a widely acclaimed lecturer, traveling all over the United States, speaking successfully to widely diverse audiences. Only Eleanor Roosevelt could lay claim to a similar range of audiences; and only Anne O'Hare McCormick of the *New York Times* commanded similar respect as a journalist.[1]

Zionists who happened to be traveling to Europe on the same ship as Thompson during the 1920s engaged Thompson's passion. While in Europe she encountered rising Fascism, which, combined with her support for Zionism, led her to begin issuing warnings to US citizens. Thompson accurately predicted Hitler's rise to power and the tragic events of 1935–1941. Her unprecedented fifteen days on NBC radio beginning Wednesday, August 23, 1939, from 7:45 to 8:00 P.M., until Wednesday September 6, announced the beginning of all-out war in Europe. There were no inter-

Dorothy Thompson seated at the NBC microphone.
Syracuse University Library, Dorothy Thompson Collection, Series IV, Box 7.
NBC Photo by Ray Lee Jackson.

views, advertisements, or "sound bites" during Thompson's fifteen-minute
broadcasts. Each was an oral essay, composed by Thompson, which combined incoming news with her own analysis. Fluent in German, and having
interviewed Hitler in 1931, she was able to translate and interpret his words
directly for her listeners. At the same time, however, Thompson opposed
Roosevelt's New Deal economic strategies. Like Republican politicians
Clare Boothe Luce and Margaret Chase Smith, Thompson was ultimately
confronted with the question of how to support the war effort while oppos-

ing FDR. Unlike her Republican colleagues, however, Thompson, initially appalled at the thought of a third term for Roosevelt, changed her mind in 1940. That year she abandoned her support for Republican presidential nominee Wendell Willkie. Her reasoning involved both disappointment at Wilkie's lukewarm support of US involvement in the European war and a belief that FDR was an important symbol of hope and democracy for Europeans fighting in resistance movements.

Thompson met with each candidate personally before publishing an explanation of her about-face in the *Herald Tribune*. This so distressed publishers and readers that she was fired. The more liberal *New York Post* quickly hired her, however. From that point on, Thompson was an enthusiastic supporter of Roosevelt, advising him and campaigning actively on his behalf in 1940 and again in 1944. After the war, Thompson never found another issue to arouse similar passion and intellect, although she continued to enjoy wide readership of her monthly column for the *Ladies Home Journal*.

The speech included here is a sample of how Thompson made the war a voting issue in 1940. Delivered at a *New York Herald Tribune* forum, a location of considerable controversy for Thompson, she appealed for unity in support of the war effort, over a year before Pearl Harbor. All of the features of effective war rhetoric are present in Thompson's speech: appeals to territoriality, ethnocentrism, optimism, and war aims.[2] One of the most interesting aspects of the speech is the way in which she introduces implicit appeals to territoriality while building feelings of American ethnocentrism. For example, after exhorting her audience, "If it is only geography you would defend, you will fail," Thompson described in vivid detail an American landscape from shore to shore. This landscape, she asserted, was home to Walt Whitman's "common man," the "Great Race of Races." One of the most effective speakers and writers of her time, Dorothy Thompson, perhaps more than any other American, was able to articulate a rationale for war that resonated from shore to shore, ensuring Franklin Roosevelt's reelection in the process.

NOTES

1. Lisa Sergio, "Introduction," *Dorothy Thompson: An Inventory of Her Papers In Syracuse University Library*, Manuscript Inventory Series (Syracuse, NY: Syracuse University Library, 1966); Peter Kurth, *American Cassandra: The Life of Dorothy Thompson* (Boston: Little, Brown, 1990); Marion K. Sanders, *Dorothy Thompson: A Legend in Her Time* (Boston: Houghton Mifflin, 1973).

2. Ronald F. Reid, "New England Rhetoric and the French War, 1754–1760: A Case Study in the Rhetoric of War," *Communication Monographs* 43 (November 1976): 259–286.

THE GREAT DEMOCRACY OF THE FREE
AN ADDRESS FOR THE NEW YORK HERALD
TRIBUNE FORUM SESSION OF THURSDAY, OCTOBER
24, 1940 (AFTERNOON)[1]

Reprinted by Permission of Syracuse University Library

Mrs. Reid, Honored Guests, and Members of the Herald Tribune Forum:
You and I meet again here, for the fifth time in one of the most critical periods in the history of the free, democratic and civilized world, and we meet in a moment when this country is sharply divided on the issue of the Presidency. This division has strained personal and group relations, and finds many old and tried friends in opposite camps. Should it not therefore be a source of great confidence and joy that in this forum and from this platform, where all political viewpoints have been represented, there should have arisen so little divergence of opinion on the great underlying issues of the time? Should it not be a reason for almost prayerful gratitude that I, who have taken one stand in the current election campaign, should find myself able to endorse every word uttered yesterday by others, whose stand in the election campaign is the opposite of mine? This easing of antagonisms, this constant search for the *common* ground, as contrasted with the divergent, seems to me the very essence of the democratic political method, which is of periodic and *limited* warfare, followed by acceptance of and reconciliation with the results.

Democracy cannot be saved by tanks and airplanes, by trucks and soldiers, by ships and anti-aircraft guns, by diplomatic and political moves alone. Democracy can only be saved by democratic men and women. The war against democracy begins by the destruction of the democratic temper, the democratic method and the democratic heart. If the democratic temper be exacerbated into wanton unreasonableness, which is an essence of the Evil, then a victory has been won for the Evil we despise, and prepare to defend ourselves against even though it is three thousand miles away and has never moved. If the democratic method can be goaded into grasping the weapons of deceit, half-truths, suppressions, overriding of honest opinion, unbridgeable differences, all of which are essential characteristics of totalitarianism, then the Evil has achieved a victory, at the hands of the democracies themselves. If the democratic heart is broken, by fear, whether of one's own compatriots, of one's employer or employees, or of members of racial groups who are our neighbors, then the Evil has won a bloodless victory.

Therefore, I speak to you today in the midst of this campaign, for the democratic temper, the democratic method, and the democratic heart.

Our first stand for democracy is with ourselves, that we be democrats. (I am spelling this word, Mrs. Reid, with the small "d," on which we are all agreed). I am remembering the great first inaugural of Thomas Jefferson, after the most heated campaign in American history—the campaign of 1800. That election also took place in the midst of a revolution, and a war, raging in Europe. It was said of Jefferson then that he had set class against class, that he was an atheist and would burn churches, that he planned the expropriation of private property, and that he was blood brother of Robespierre. People even packed up their trunks and prepared to flee the country into exile in England, if he were elected. There was an England then, to which conservatives could flee. And I am remembering the great words with which Jefferson calmed the raging fears that the campaign had produced. He said: "we are all Republicans. We are all Federalists." He referred to the titles of the parties in those days. And he said, "If there be those among us who would wish to dissolve our union, or to change its form, let them stand undisturbed as monuments to the safety with which error of opinion may be tolerated, where reason is left free to combat it. Sometimes it is said that man cannot be trusted with the government of himself. Can man, then, be trusted with the government of others? Or have we found angels in the form of kings to govern us? Let history answer the question."

History has answered the question in this country for 140 years since those calming words were spoken in a distraught moment. And we, if we can be trusted to govern ourselves, will give the same answer for the next one hundred and forty. Hitler's thousand year Reich is only seven years old. Ours has weathered a century and a half, a union of races, a union of states, a union of divergent minds, and a Reich, a realm, of democratic hearts.

Yet, though we speak in confidence, confidence born of our passionate Faith, we must not close our eyes to the voices external and inner that bid us beware. Man, democratic man, has not fallen to his present low estate, where his back is against a wall and his hand and heart tremble, except through his own sins. I bid you take your eyes away from the Beast, from the Mad Horseman. That may sound strange from me, who have watched him in horror, predicting his course, through all the years since first I stood upon this platform. If one perceives an approaching cyclone, it is natural and fit that one should seek to warn one's fellows, yes, even to warn them at the top of one's lungs. But the warning is no longer needed. It is another warning that must be uttered, and our airplanes pass swiftly and brightly off the benches of the factories, as we begin swiftly to build powder factories and gun factories, as young men step up to register for the draft. The warning is: Be sure you know what you prepare to defend. If it is only geography you would defend, you will fail. Man loves the landscape of his home, the taste of his native apples, the contours of his native hills. He loves the acrid scent of the New England fall, of burning leaves, and wilted marigolds, and night frosts melting in the morning sun. He loves the endless shimmering corn-fields of the plainlands, if he is a man of the plains. He loves the ever-changing mountains, and the moody sea, if his home is a mountain home, or built close to shore. Yet it is not geography that makes an American. Of all peoples, it is Americans alone, who have been forced in this generation, or a previous generation—hundreds and thousands and millions of them—to adapt themselves to other apples and other mountains and other seashores than the ones where they were born. The American is a man whose forbears, or himself, have overcome nativity, overcome what Walt Whitman in a phrase pregnant with insight called "the ignominy of nativity," considering origin itself something that the complete human being must *transcend* in order to reach a larger fellowship. Not geography holds Americans together, whose very tongue is a superimposing of the idioms of all of Europe upon the English speech. Americans are held in union by devotion to a common idea. In this we are unique amongst the peoples of the earth. Whoever rules in Germany—a German is still a German. Let Vichy go through its marionette motions in France, and a Frenchman is still French. But let the American idea perish on this soil, the idea expressed in immortal words by our immortal heroes: by Washington, and Jefferson, and Lincoln, and the great company who bring renewed inspiration to every public school child, whether that child's name be Czech, or Anglo-Saxon, or German, or Jewish, or French, or Slavonic—let that idea falter, grow weak, become contemptible, and mountains and rivers and roads will not hold us together as the great new world. Rather, we shall break up into our component racial elements, the outcast and illegitimate children of the Europe from which we all sprang.

The great faith of America is faith in the common man. In the words of Whitman, a bard who wrote prophetically for another era; an era unborn in his days, but approaching now in ours:

"Other states indicate themselves in their deputies. But the genius of the United States is not best or most in its executives or legislatures, nor in its ambassadors, or authors, or colleges, or churches or parlors, nor even in its newspapers or inventors, but always most in the common people. Their manners, speech, friendship, dress—the freshness and candor of their physiognomy—the picturesque looseness of their carriage—their deathless attachment to freedom—their aversion to anything soft or mean—the fierceness of their aroused resentment, their self-esteem and wonderful sympathy, their susceptibility to a slight—their curiosity and welcome of novelty—the air they have of persons who never knew how it felt to stand in the presence of superiors—the fluency of their speech, their manly tenderness and native elegance of soul, their good temper and open-handedness—these are the people of America."

My friends, the people of America were never like this. Never were we this good. But the future of all peoples lives first in the imagination of their greatest poets. *They* see what no other eye sees; *they* believe, when none other believe; *they* prophesy what is surely to come.

The Common people of Whitman, the Great Race of Races as he called his compatriots, were no common herd reduced to the dead level of mediocrity. This was not Whitman's idea of Democracy. Rather he saw the people, the common people, elevated to the qualities of mind and heart and behavior, which we call Kingly. For what is "Kingliness"? Is it not freshness and candor, aversion to softness and meanness, self-esteem and wonderful sympathy, manly tenderness and native elegance of soul? Is it not good temper and open-handedness and a deathless attachment to freedom?

These, the qualities of kingliness and nobility, are the qualities to be distributed throughout the common people in The Great Democracy. We had them once, in greater part than we have them today. What has rubbed them off, what has destroyed their full flowering? What has made American men and American women grudging, fearful, mush-mouthed, irascible with men beneath them and obsequious to those above them, bitterly partisan, snobbish toward the man in overalls who often performs a task requiring more skill and more heroism than the white-collar man performs, tattle-telling and gossip purveying, hostile to citizens of other racial origins, never looking a man in the eye, and measuring him for what he is in terms of heart and brain and soul?

I will tell you what it is. It is the tyranny of values based on money. It is the tyranny of economic view, that judges men according to income and judges prosperity according to annual turnover; that judges culture according to price and merit according to sales and decrees that it is nobler because more profitable to write ads for toothpaste or cigarettes at one hundred dollars a week than it is to plant trees in impoverished soil, as a rejected worker in the C.C.C.

The measure of the success of a democracy can only be taken in human terms. Other countries may produce roads and automobiles and suburban homes. A democracy, to justify its existence, must produce better *men*, and it shall be measured wholly in the terms of the character of its citizens. No one needs to be conquered by Hitler to become a Nazi. The reason why this struggle comes home to us so nearly is that most of us have a little Nazi or a Nazi fellow-traveler in our own hearts. The Nazi in our own hearts says, "Get on. It's tough, but this is a world in which you step on the other fellow or he steps on you." The fellow-traveler *always* comes, in one's own mind, with the same argument: "Think again. Does it pay? Why stick your neck out?"

I tell you that Hitler has ceased to be a personality and become only the symbolic incarnation of man's basest instincts, conquers us on the home soil of our own minds and hearts. He is the miasmic terror which erases our courage and self-possession. The democratic man is the *self-possessed* man. He is the courteous man. He is unbribable, unseducable [*sic*], the proud and happy man. He is the free man—free because he has ceased to be afraid of himself. When all over this world people—enough people, the masses of the people—have ceased to be afraid of anything, the apocalyptic beast will have been slain.

We live in a very great age. There is a scourge across the world. But that scourge will not, unless we are finished as human souls, obliterate civilization. Rather, it will prove, in the long run, to have been a hideously painful cauterization process, to burn away the cancerous tissue that eats at the very heart of our society.

We speak of the danger of revolution. My friends, the great revolution has not yet come. That revolution was predicted in another dreadful time, a century ago, after the collapse of Napoleon and predicted by Victor Hugo: "the revolution of the XX century will be the revolution of civilization and humanity." What peoples will make the great Revolution, the great conversion?

Do you really think that the real revolution, the world revolution, the great conversion, is to come out of Soviet Russia—that vast sprawling land only beginning to emerge from feudalism and illiteracy and vermin-ridden peasant poverty? The idea is idiotic. Do you think it is to come out of Germany—that land-locked promontory, that state which was created in the first place by an army—the Prussian Army—which still thinks, in social organization, almost wholly in terms of an army, with a general, officers, subalterns and a regimented mass of obedient soldiers?

The Society of the Future will take shape in the English-speaking world—the world society of the future. It will take form amongst that race of men who are not a race at all, but a vast world wide brotherhood of men who speak a common tongue and owe allegiance to a common God, and have of all men on this earth been the servants and the masters of the concept of freedom.

In the days of Elizabeth, the English-speaking world was twelve million people on a little island. That handful of people gave the world the great language of resistance, a tongue composed of all tongues—Teutonic and French and Latin, containing words from the Arabic of desert tribes and from the Roman forum and from the lists of the crusades. That is the English language—a glorious and imperial mongrel, spoken today by two hundred million free people in all parts of this little globe.

Disraeli's Empire is not the glory of Britain. The glory of Britain is the independence of the United States and the free Commonwealths of Canadians and New Zealanders and Australians and South Africans, who speak the English speech in their own way and whose free institutions are to be found in every ocean and every continent of the earth. And it will prove to be one of the great poetic justices of history that it is not those whom Britain has enslaved, but those who have freed themselves, who will save the English-speaking world and build the New Jerusalem that William Blake foresaw. Britain may lose India, may lose Egypt; she will lose exclusive sovereignty over the Caribbean Islands. She will lose herself. And having lost herself, she will find herself again—in all of us—in the whole, world-flung, commonwealth of free men.

Today, under the hail of bombs, in the debris of wreckage, amidst the moans of heroes who die a soldier's death in children's dresses and matrons' aprons and the sober garb of business men and the overalls of workers, the new British democracy is being born. And see, it is the Common People become kingly! It is the Common People who behave like Shakespeare's kings! And as surely as I stand here and talk to you, there will arise in the English-speaking world a poet to write the story of this kingly common people when this war is over. Some new Shakespeare will write the drama of Dunquerke where, from a burning port, under unremitting fire, from the narrow corridor into which it was penned, the fishermen and yachters, the little pleasure launches, the barges and the lorries, carried off the army of Britain, the flower of British youth, back to the soil of England, there to take the great stand.

A wounded R.A.F. man who went through Dunquerke and has been retired for wounds, wrote me a poem about Dunquerke. There is a line in it I cannot forget. He says, "Saved by the rabble of boats." And I thought of Washington's rabble army, and then of England's rabble navy at Dunquerke. And I think every day that I read the papers, every time I listen to a speech of Churchill, of Lincoln's unconquerable faith in the common man, who is no common creature at all but a child of God made in the image of His own ideals, making himself, through the ages, a face. And it is not going to be the face of a robot. It will be the face of the Human which history will reveal.

Whom the Gods love then set in oceans. The sea and the men of the sea saved England, though it was twenty miles of Channel. The oceans will save America, not for a selfish and stupid isolation but as the unchallengeable highways to the common man throughout the world.

No nation can conquer peoples who control the highways of the world. The English-speaking people, with air and naval bases throughout this planet, are invincible. The struggle, intense and glorious, it is as much inner as outer. When it is over, I believe that the United States of America, the home of all European races, the home of the Common Man, the cradle of democracy, will be the center of an English-speaking world that brings peace to the nations and fulfillment to the prophecies of its poets.

NOTE

1. Typescript with handwritten revisions. Dorothy Thompson Papers, Department of Special Collections, Syracuse University Library, Syracuse, NY.

Hattie Caraway (1878–1950)

From 1931 to 1944, Hattie Caraway was the second woman to serve as a U.S. Senator.[1] Like her female predecessor, Georgia's Rebecca Felton, Caraway was first appointed by the governor of her state to fill her husband's (Thaddeus Caraway) Senate seat. Unlike Felton, who served briefly and never stood for election, however, Caraway chose to participate in electoral politics. She first had to run in a special election in January, 1932, in order to remain in office to complete her husband's term. She successfully fought off a surprise challenger in the Democratic primary, as well as two more challengers who ran against her as Independents in the general election. Furthermore, there were no funds to support the special election. Local male politicians seemed to think it was up to the women of Arkansas to come up with the money, which they did. A group was formed called the Arkansas Women's Democratic Club. They raised money and got out the vote, leading to a landslide Caraway victory.

In an interesting turn of events, Caraway filed for reelection at the end of what would have been her husband's first term in the Senate. Lacking both funds and organization, she was not considered a serious candidate. However, late in the summer of 1932, Senator Huey P. Long of Louisiana campaigned with Caraway throughout Arkansas. She managed to win the Democratic primary as a result and went on to win the general election, thus establishing herself as the first woman elected to the Senate for a full term in her own right. She successfully ran for a second term in 1938 with FDR's endorsement. In 1944 she tried for a third term, but she was beaten in the Democratic primary.

As a Senator, Caraway generally supported labor and FDR's New Deal domestic policies. In contrast to Eleanor Roosevelt and other New Deal

Hattie Caraway, March 24, 1943.

Library of Congress, Prints & Photographs Division, [reproduction number, LC-USZ62-12694].

women like Mary Anderson, however, Caraway supported the Equal Rights Amendment. She was the first woman in Congress to cosponsor the ERA in 1943, earning praise from Alice Paul. Caraway also opposed isolationism, again in keeping with FDR's general foreign policy. Overall, she appears to have been a conscientious but quiet Senator, speaking so rarely she was nicknamed "Silent Hattie" and "the Sphinx." Caraway delivered only about fifteen speeches in thirteen years as a Senator.

During her first term in office, in the early to mid–1930s, Caraway received a great deal of media attention. The spotlight faded during her second term, however, as war issues assumed more and more prominence. Caraway opposed war in principle, but she supported military preparedness. When addressing women on this issue, Caraway frequently repeated her belief, confirmed by her endorsement of the ERA, that men and women legislators should not be differentiated on the basis of sex. In a statement titled "Is War a Woman's Business?" written around 1940, she expressed disapproval of emotional oratory and debate that she claimed often characterized women's rhetoric on war issues. Caraway observed that women were "more emotional about war than men are...women are a little unreasonable...they don't have all the facts." But, men sometimes talked too much, also leading to excessive emotion in Caraway's judgment.[2] Both women and men needed to be rational thinkers when it came to government.

Her own verbal style was simple and straightforward, reinforcing her stated preference for commonsense reasoning, and the no-frills "back-home, back-bone kind of women." The speech included here is a radio address justifying Caraway's support for the 1941 "lend-lease" bill. In the speech, she asserted her belief that the only hope of keeping Hitler away from American shores was military preparedness. In keeping with that view, Caraway ended the speech by mentioning that both her sons were already in military service, and that she would cast her vote in favor of the lend-lease bill. Solid, thoughtful, and plain spoken, Hattie Caraway probably spoke, as she herself believed, for the "great silent vote," the vote that put her husband in the Senate and "has since kept me there."[3]

NOTES

1. Biographical information is from, Diane D. Kincaid, ed. *Silent Hattie Speaks: The Personal Journal of Senator Hattie Caraway* (Westport; CT: Greenwood Press, 1979); Hope Chamberlin, *A Minority of Members: Women in the U.S. Congress* (New York: Praeger, 1973); Annabel Paxton, *Women in Congress* (Richmond, VA: Dietz Press, 1945); Louise M. Young, "Hattie Ophelia Wyatt Caraway," in *Notable American Women, 1607–1950,* Edward T. James, ed. (Cambridge, MA: Belknap Press, 1971).

2. Senator Hattie Caraway, "Is War a Woman's Business?" Typescript, Bess Furman papers, Box 73, File "Caraway, Hattie," Library of Congress.

3. Caraway, "Is War a Woman's Business?"

THE LEND-LEASE BILL
ADDRESS BY HON. HATTIE W. CARAWAY, OF ARKANSAS
RADIO ADDRESS DELIVERED ON FEBRUARY 27, 1941[1]

I wish to speak to you briefly on some phases of the lend-lease bill now before the United States Senate.

There have been three major issues considered by Congress having to do with our preparedness; the neutrality law, the Selective Service Act, and the pending bill.

The controversy going on over the lend-lease bill presents a familiar picture. We have much of the same old scenery that attended the consideration of the neutrality bill. Practically the same type of speech is being made against this bill as was made against the neutrality measure. At that time, the constant cry of those opposed to the neutrality legislation was that it would lead us into war. There are but few who do not realize now that the neutrality law has done more than any single thing to keep us out of the conflict.

The same gentlemen who are opposing the lend-lease bill in the Senate now said in 1939 that the neutrality bill would put us into war. The same gentlemen also said later on that if the Selective Service Act passed we would be in the war in 30 days. They were false prophets then. Is there any reason to believe that their present dire forecasts are more accurate than their other attempts at prophecy?

During the consideration of the Selective Service Act there was the same oft-repeated chant that that bill would bring us into the conflict immediately. The passage of that law was wise. If the United States is forced into war, that measure will help protect our boys by making them better prepared. Untrained troops stand no chance against trained ones in modern warfare. In addition, it has acted to prevent war being made on this country. No bully is apt to attack one who is prepared.

It is my firm belief that the passage of the pending lend-lease bill will have the same result as the other two major preparedness measures which I have mentioned, and that the wisdom of the bill will be proved. I believe that the enactment of this bill into law will do much to prevent our being drawn into the conflict.

I realize that the citizens of this country have had dinned into their ears day after day the continuous repetition of the statement that the enactment of the lend-lease bill will bring us into war. The adroit opponents of the measure realize that the vast majority of our citizens are opposed to war. In order to capitalize on that knowledge, they have never made a speech that did not contend as its main theme that this measure would bring us into war. They fear to do anything lest it bring Hitler's wrath down upon them.

Why all this cringing before Mr. Hitler? Why the fear that we may do something which would make the German dictator angry? There are those who have been so fearful of his ire that they would not have us prepare, and yet those people know that the only law which Mr. Hitler respects is that of force and are aware of the fate of nations which have not been in a position to meet force with force. I, for one, am weary of this attitude on the part of those who would cringe and make an attempt to appease the one man in the world who seeks to dominate it according to his own ideas.

Against the lend-lease bill we see the same old flood of familiar propaganda directed against it that poured onto Congress when the other two measures were being considered. The volume is greater. This is not true of the mail from my state. I believe 90 percent of my people favor the bill. I have never seen as much propaganda directed against any measure, with but one exception, since I have been a United States senator. Perhaps the majority of those writing against the bill are sincere. However, I am confident that the slimy hands of Nazi propagandists have been at work, and still are, as never before concerning any measure which has come before the congress. There are many people and a number of organizations opposed to the bill who are unwittingly being used as tools by the Hitler machine. We have seen the results of Nazi propaganda in other countries. It is definitely certain that Dictator Hitler and the subversive interests of this country not overlook a chance like this to spread their poison.

I am the only woman Member of the United States Senate. Because of that fact, I have received a great many communications against the bill that would not otherwise have come to me. They urge that because of my sex I should, in support of their views, vote against this proposed legislation. I stated when I entered the Senate that I saw no reason for differentiating between men and women who serve in legislative capacities. There should be equal responsibility among them with a view toward equal service to achieve identical goals.

Those opposing this measure are seeking to frighten the women of this country by their constant cry of "War." However, I do not believe they take into consideration the fact that the history of this country shows that the women of America are just as loyal, just as courageous, and just as self sacrificing as the men. I know that if war should come to us, the women would show equal courage with the men. In fact, I sometimes think they would have to show more, for long after war is over the women will still be fighting for American principles.

Let us view this matter without emotion. Let there be borne by all the desire alone to have what is best for the United States. The present war is one of ideas. The dictators, believing that might is right, are seeking to impose upon the world a system of moral, economic, and political control to which it has never before been subjected in history. These theories are opposed to our belief in freedom and democracy. They are opposed to the American doctrine of self government. They are against Christianity or any other form of religion except the worship of the state under the control of a dictator. It is opposed to the American theory of life, liberty, happiness, and the right to worship God according to the dictates of our own consciences.

If Hitler wins, we will face not only a hostile Germany but a hostile world. There can be no doubt but that Hitler desires to impose his system upon the whole world, including the United States. He has said so.

The opponents of this measure would seek to lull you into security, saying that there would be no possibility of Hitler's attempting an invasion of the United States. They have said that the German Dictator could not do many things of a comparable nature. He has done them. In fact, the fate of some of the destroyed nations is due in part to their belief that Hitler could not do those things which he has done. The opponents of the measure scoff at the idea of Hitler's being able to transport troops to this country. During the World War the United States transported millions of soldiers across 3,000 miles of water and supplied them. This was done because the allies commanded the seas. If England goes down and Hitler dominates the oceans, who is there among us who can say with any certainty that an invasion of the United States could not be attempted?

Many believe that Great Britain is fighting for us. I think that England is fighting for her life. However, I do believe that Great Britain and the other democracies are not bearing the brunt of the fighting for that which Americans believe is right.

One of the primary purposes of the lend-lease bill is to aid England and the democracies in that fight. That is not all of it, however. We, as a nation, have a selfish interest in this matter. Most of those who support this bill do so because, in part, they believe it is for our own preservation. If England wins, we know what to expect in the future. If Hitler were successful, God alone knows what the United States and the world would face.

In this fight I do not believe England needs or wants our men to go overseas. She does want materials and munitions of war in order to carry on her fight. If the aid which we are to extend to England and the democracies is to be helpful, we must hurry. It may be later than we think. Interminable time has been spent in debate, much of which is a constant repetition of what has been said before. Every day of delay may prove costly.

The press of the past week has shouted from its front pages that Hitler says the British will be doomed by April. Most military and naval experts believe that a supreme effort to destroy England will be made soon. Full speed ahead is necessary. If we fail to render prompt and effective aid to England and the democracies, it may be the most tragic mistake America has ever made.

I have never thought that we would be drawn into the conflict. I may be in error. Who knows but that regardless of what we do in a legislative way this conflict may be forced upon us? What Solomon is there among us who can assure what the future may hold? After all, I think that the decision of whether we will be forced into the war or not rests in the hands of one man—Adolph Hitler.

This is not a partisan issue. It is one which should not divide our people into antagonistic groups. Much ill feeling has been engendered because of the controversy over this bill. It has not helped national unity. After all, it is your country and mine. America, united, can withstand the force of an attack far greater than any the world has yet known. Divided, it might easier invite aggression. One of the principal methods of Hitler's war strategy is a division of popular opinion in the nation to be attacked. It has proved as potent as guns and ammunition.

In addition to the cry that this bill will lead us into war there has been a constant attack upon President Roosevelt. I think that a fair and unbiased study would reveal that the President has handled the foreign affairs of the Nation wisely. I devoutly believe that Franklin D. Roosevelt will continue to do all in his power to keep us out of the conflict. The pending bill does not delegate to the President any legislative power. We have had quite a battle in Congress about the delegation of lawmaking power. The President has none. What does this measure do? It enlarges the Chief Executive's administrative defense powers and provides for their simple and effective use.

I think that I have as much interest in keeping this nation out of war as anyone. I have two sons already in the military service. They entered the army because it was their wish to do so. I gave my consent. If they were civilians and there was a national emergency and they did not do their part, I would disown them.

I do not want war. I do not know of any senator favoring this bill who is for war. Many of them have sons as have I. These sons are either already in the military service or will be called sooner or later.

The overwhelming majority of the American people, regardless of race, color, religion, creed, politics, or origin, favor this measure as one of the greatest effectiveness in the national defense.

It is not so much a question of whether we will get into the war. It is rather one of whether the war will come to us. For my part I state to the mothers and fathers of America, and I repeat to the young men of my country, that it is my firm belief that the pending measure, if enacted into law, will do much to keep the war from our shores.

As a representative of a sovereign state, as an American mother, as one who has been a constant advocate of peace, as one who believes that humanity is at stake and that some measure must be taken to safeguard it, I will case my vote for the lend-lease bill.

NOTE

1. This speech was entered into *The Congressional Record*, 77th Cong., 1st Sess. 1941, 87, part 10, Appendix, A893–A894.

Dorothy Day (1897–1980)

Journalist, reformer, activist, pacifist, and committed Catholic, Dorothy Day lived her life to the full.[1] She was born in New York, but her family moved to San Francisco when she was a child. Her father was a journalist who moved his family east to Chicago after their short stay in California. While in Chicago, Dorothy became interested in the labor movement. After two years of college at the University of Illinois, the family moved back to New York City. In New York, Day joined in reform and radical movements of the early twentieth century. She was arrested with woman suffragists in Washington, DC, supported and practiced sexual freedom, and joined in labor movement activities. After publishing an autobiographical novel, *The Eleventh Virgin*, in 1924, she bought a small house on the shore of Staten Island, where she lived with Forster Batterham, biologist and anarchist, giving birth to their daughter, Tamar, in 1927.

During this period, Day was increasingly drawn to the Catholic Church. When her daughter was born, Day wanted her child baptized. Batterham, however, was opposed to religion, and said he would leave if Day joined the church. After a period of agonizing soul-searching, Day made a commitment to the church, knowing that her common-law marriage was over. Throughout this period, she supported herself and her daughter as a freelance journalist. After her conversion to Catholicism, Day began writing for the Catholic magazine *Commonweal*. In 1932 she met Peter Maurin, a French priest who was also writing for *Commonweal*. Together they founded the Catholic Worker movement in the United States. On May 1, 1933, they sold their first issue of the *Catholic Worker* newspaper for one cent. The newspaper has been published continuously ever since, still sold for one cent.

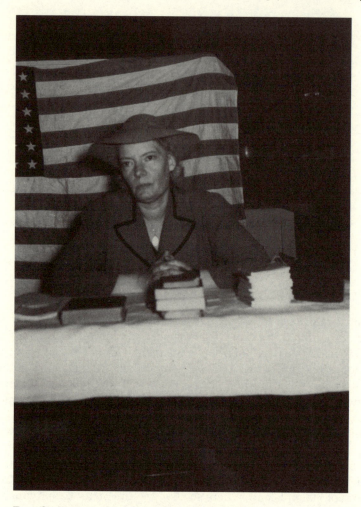

Dorothy Day speaking in Seattle, February 1940.
Courtesy of the Marquette University Archives.

Although Day always credited Maurin as co-founder of the Catholic Worker movement, it was really Day who was the organizational leader and "driving force" of the magazine and movement.[2] In addition to the paper, she wrote eight books, and traveled and lectured widely. Like many other women who were active in the women's suffrage movement, Day was drawn to an international, antiwar point of view. Consistent with this, the Catholic Worker movement was ardently pacifist, as well as anti-capitalist, and was dedicated to vows of poverty. Initially experiencing success with their movement, evidenced by the growing number of Catholic Worker hospitality houses throughout the United States, World War II made their pacifism difficult to defend. Many hospitality houses closed, and support decreased.

Nevertheless, true to form, Day argued against war the day after Pearl Harbor was bombed, in a speech to the Liberal–Socialist Alliance of New York City. On December 8, 1941, she asserted, "We must renounce war as an instrument of policy. We must affirm that there will be no more war." She continued, "Even as I speak to you I may be guilty of what some men call treason. But we must reject war;...I tell you that—within a decade— we will have weapons capable of ending this world as we have known it." After the war and the devastation of the atomic bombs dropped in Japan, Day's words proved prophetic, and she continued witnessing for peace to the end of her life.

NOTES

1. Biographical information from "Dorothy Day Library" on the Web *The Catholic Worker Movement* [web site] May 27, 2003 (http://www.catholicworker. org/dorothyday); Carol Jablonski, "Dorothy Day," in *Women Public Speakers in the United States, 1925–1993*, Karlyn Kohrs Campbell, ed. (Westport, CT: Greenwood Press, 1994), 161–174; and the Dorothy Day–Catholic Worker Collection, Marquette University Archives, Milwaukee, WI.

2. Jablonski, "Dorothy Day," 165.

TEXT OF DOROTHY DAY'S ADDRESS TO THE LIBERAL–SOCIALIST ALLIANCE IN NEW YORK CITY (DECEMBER 8, 1941)[1]

Reprinted by Permission of Marquette University Archives

There is now all this patriotic indignation about the Japanese attack on Pearl Harbor and Japanese expansionism in Asia. Yet not a word about American and European colonialism in this same area. We, the British, the French, and others set up spheres of influence in Asia, control national states—against the expressed will of these states—and represent imperialism in the Orient. We dictate to Japan as to where she can expand economically and politically and we declare what policy she must observe. From our nationalistic and imperialistic point of view we have every right to concentrate American military forces in the Philippines, confronting Japan at her front door. Were Japan to face us from Cuba what would be our reaction? If the United States insists upon a colonialist policy in Asia then this nation must be prepared for militaristic backlash....

I share my deepest sympathy with the parents, wives and friends of the American military forces that perished at Pearl Harbor. But I count these young men as victims, tragic victims, of a blindly mistaken American foreign policy...

Hitler is a madman; however, our American State Department is quite aware that—under treaty—Germany must declare war on any power which moves against the Empire of Japan. Need I remind you that the Fascists are allies of the Russian Communists? What action will Moscow take in support of Germany? Are we actually prepared to confront a German–Russian alliance? But let us suppose that the Soviet Union does nothing at the moment at least. Is it not probable that Hitler will observe his own dicta and move "to the East where expansionism can readily be accomplished"? How then can the United States justify a military alliance with Stalin whose blood baths have rivaled Hitler's purges? So we are faced with a dilemma: either we go to war against a German–Italian–Russian–Japanese alliance—a suicidal undertaking—or we become Russia's defender—an ideological crime.

But I waste rhetoric on international politics—the breeding grounds of war over the centuries. The balance of power and other empty slogans inspired by a false and flamboyant nationalism have bred conflict throughout "civilized" history.

And it has become too late in human history to tolerate wars which none can win. Nor dare we quibble about "just wars." Well did Pius X tell us that "in any conflict both sides claim moral justification. We find the term repugnant and impossible to define. All wars are, by the very nature, evil and destructive."

It has become too late for civilized people to accept this evil.

We must make a start. We must renounce war as an instrument of policy. We must affirm that there will be no more war. Never—but never—again.

Thoreau bid us to make a stand, Markand denounced war as insanity, Pius X could find no definition for a "just war." Evil enough when the finest of our youth perished in conflict and even the causes of these conflicts were soon lost to memory. Even more horrible today when cities can go up in flames and brilliant scientific minds are searching out ultimate weapons.

War must cease. There are no victories. The world can bear the burden no longer. Yes we must make a stand.

Even as I speak to you I may be guilty of what some men call treason. But we must reject war; yes we must now make a stand. War is murder, rape, ruin, death: war can end our civilization. I tell you that—within a decade—we will have weapons capable of ending this world as we have known it.

War is hunger, thirst, blindness, death. I call upon you to resist it. You young men should refuse to take up arms. Young women tear down the patriotic posters. And all of you—young and old—put away your flags.

It is too late for nationalism.
It is too late for war.
War is rapine, bloodshed, brutality, death.
It is too late for this.
It has always been too late.
Let us make an end of it.
War will be no more.

NOTE

1. Dorothy Day Catholic Worker Collection, Department of Special Collections and University Archives, Marquette University Libraries, Milwaukee, WI.

Clare Boothe Luce (1903–1987)

Clare Boothe Luce, over the course of her long life, was a journalist, playwright, member of Congress, and U.S. ambassador to Italy. She remained active in politics and public discourse well into the 1980s. The year before she died, the *Ladies Home Journal* included her in its list of the twenty-five most important women in U.S. history.[1]

After her first marriage ended in divorce, she married Henry R. Luce in 1935, owner of *Time* and *Fortune* magazines. Around this time she shifted her focus from magazine writing and editing to writing plays, the most successful of which was *The Women*. In a book, *Europe in the Spring*, (1939) based on her visits to several European countries as the Nazi movement was gaining momentum, Luce decried lack of preparation for war in Great Britain and France and warned against U.S. isolation. Politics was now her focus, and, although she had supported Democratic candidates in the past, the Republican Party was about to become her political home.

As a journalist, playwright, and politician, Luce spoke before many different types of audiences on a wide variety of occasions. Indeed, the Library of Congress holds more than 600 texts of her speeches. She campaigned for Wendell Willkie in his unsuccessful challenge to Roosevelt in 1940 and remained an active Republican speaker thereafter. In September 1942, Luce became the Republican Party nominee to run for the House of Representatives from the fourth district in Connecticut. She won the election by running a well-organized, politically astute but tradition-defying campaign in which she supported, in the context of the war effort, civil rights for "Negroes," women's rights, and workers' rights.

As a member of Congress, Luce was not only forthright in expressing her views and willing to marshal emotional arguments, but also unre-

Clare Boothe Luce during her congressional campaign in Fairfield County, Connecticut.

Library of Congress, Prints and Photographs Division, [reproduction number LC-USZ62-120335], in album: Tale of Politics starring Clare Boothe Luce, compiled by Tere C. Pascone, 1948, [p. 11].

strained and even vitriolic in her use of satire and other forms of wit. Her first speech in Congress, an attack on Vice President Henry Wallace in February 1943, characterized his international perspective as "globaloney." Additionally, Moya Ann Ball has noted that Luce often spoke with the voice of a prophet.[2] For example, on June 6, 1944, D-Day, Luce delivered a radio address from the House of Representatives, at 12:30 P.M., that began: "This is the hour that marks the beginning of the Battle for the World." That same month in Chicago, Clare Boothe Luce became the first woman to give the keynote speech at the convention of a major political party.[3] In her keynote, as in many others (including the speech that follows), Luce spoke as if she believed she could voice the sentiments of other women, and often directed remarks explicitly to women.

Also in 1944, she ran for and won reelection to the House, in spite of a campaign against her that brought top Democrats such as Franklin Roosevelt and Dorothy Thompson to Connecticut to campaign against her. However, after a conversion to Roman Catholicism in 1946, she retired from Congress and focused for a time on writing and speaking on Catholic themes and against communism. She campaigned against Truman in 1948 and for Eisenhower in 1952. In Eisenhower's administration, Luce became the first female US ambassador to a major European country, Italy. After she resigned her ambassadorship in 1956, her Cold War era speeches continued. These included several with topical titles, such as "Little Rock and the Muscovite Moon." After Henry Luce's death in 1967, she moved to Hawaii but remained active as an author and gave speeches throughout the nation well into the 1980s.

The speech included here is a testament to Luce's femininity, toughness, knowledge, political savvy, and audacity. It was given on September 25, 1942, to the Bridgeport, Connecticut, Women's Committee of the American Institute of Banking. Although she had just been nominated to run for the House of Representatives from that district, she was asked not to give a political speech. Luce responded by calling the speech "off the record" in her campaign. Still, she unabashedly used devices common to political campaign rhetoric, such as demonstrating her knowledge of major local industries. She also lauded women's volunteerism in the war effort and the roles that women in banking played in promoting free enterprise. But she reminded her audience of bankers that their lives remained relatively comfortable, despite the war, in contrast to the hardships being suffered by women in many other places in the world. She warned them that they would be soon called upon to sacrifice their current level of comfort in pursuit of victory.

NOTES

1. For biographical information, see Ralph G. Martin, *Henry and Clare* (New York: G. P. Putnam's Sons, 1991); Moya Ann Ball, "Clare Boothe Luce," in *Women Public Speakers in the United States, 1925–1993*, Karlyn Kohrs Campbell, ed. (Westport, CT: Greenwood Press, 1994), 50–57.

2. Ball, "Clare Boothe Luce," 52.

3. See *Vital Speeches of the Day* 10 (July 15, 1944): 586–588.

THE ROLE OF AMERICAN WOMEN IN WARTIME
7 P.M. STRATFIELD HOTEL, BRIDGEPORT,
CONNECTICUT (SEPTEMBER 24, 1942)[1]

With your kind invitation asking me to attend your meeting tonight, I received the request to speak on the subject of "The Role of American Women in Wartime." The chairlady said in short that this was not to be a political speech. So don't look now, anybody, I'm running for Congress. Nevertheless I hasten to reassure all of you, though, that it is my earnest wish that no one read any personal political implications into anything I say tonight. This, insofar as my campaign is concerned is completely off the record.

As we sit in this comfortable room, after so pleasant a dinner, it is easy to contemplate, calmly and impersonally, what lies ahead for us women in this wartime America of ours. For us this is not a subject that burst upon us suddenly on the day the Japs attacked Pearl Harbor. For we women of Connecticut long before that day had started to play an important part in the defense effort. Long before Pearl Harbor some of us were busy in the expanding munitions industries of our state; some of us were busy at our desks, more crowded with work than for many years; some of us were already beginning to tackle jobs being vacated by men as they left for military service.

Some of us were busy in the production rooms of our Red Cross chapters; we were taking courses in first aid, nutrition, home nursing and all the rest.

And women were busy at a lot of other, more familiar tasks, too, for in spite of the quickened pace of their daily lives, they could not stop being homemakers. They had homes to manage, children to rear, husbands to feed.

So, as I say, it did not take Pearl Harbor to make the women of Connecticut conscious of the fact that their daily lives were being changed by war. Long before Pearl Harbor the women of Connecticut were already making ready to serve their country, as they served their homes.

And certainly long before Pearl Harbor, you women were actively interested in the problems of banking. Banking, I sometimes think is one of the most natural spheres for women's activities. For banking is balancing the budget, a problem which housewives have handled for hundreds of generations, from the time when one bone equaled two pots of stew for three hungry cavemen until now, when inflation threatens, and women once again must call upon these age-old resources of their minds to cope with this new, grim, financial problem.

For you know and I that banking is not all dull statistics, and cute pie charts of output and climbing stair graphs of outgo; it is the blood and guts of American economy. Hitler, with his slave labor, need not worry—for the moment—about banking. He simply loots. But in our America we still believe in honesty and a fair day's pay for a job well done. Banking today has a tremendous job to do in seeing that our production lines keep rolling, that our boys in the armed forces are supplied, that the home front is vigorously maintained, that our form of Government survives.

Banks have also done a tremendous job in fighting the war directly selling billions of dollars of War Bonds (85% of total). They have financed the conversion and expansion of industry from peace-time to war-time production, and they have fought inflation by restrictions of consumer credit and unwise expenditures. And they have frozen foreign credits to prevent their falling into the hands of the enemy or his satellites.

Today it is up to us women to play our part in making sure that the free enterprise of which the banking system is an inherent part, endures. Incidentally it is because of my own belief in that system that I am campaigning as the Republican candidate for Congress from this district.

You all remember that President Henry W. Koeneke of the American Bankers Association wrote in the recent "Convention in Print" issue of Banking Magazine:

"War is an intolerant taskmaster. It requires that private institutions serve its needs as effectively as they serve the needs of the peacetime way of life. Otherwise it may not tolerate them. Therefore we have a dual obligation as private institutions. It is to see that these institutions serve as effectively as wartime mechanism as they do as a peacetime mechanism. As they help to win the war and to serve the war needs of the people will they assure their continued place in society."

President Koeneke has summed up the problem before us women here tonight in that memorable statement. We are gathered here, all of us, dedicated to the proposition that private enterprise and private institutions shall endure, not for their own sakes but because we believe that freedom of thought and ability is the best guarantee that we shall win this war and the peace that follows.... Freedom to think and to criticize constructively on war plans and post-war aims; ability to carry those plans into actual achievement....

Today, only those unfamiliar with our State could doubt that in Connecticut women have a very real place in that achievement. Tonight in Bridgeport thousands of women are working at Remington Arms Co., turning out the tools of war. More are building planes at Vought-Sikorsky in Stratford, while others are busily sewing the stout fabric of victory at Singer Sewing Machine Co. within a few miles of this meeting. The list is endless; Connecticut women are working for victory at the Auto Ordinance Corp. in Bridgeport...manufacturers of the all-important machine tools. And over in Stamford women work at the lathes in Yale and Towne, making locks of war that will one day bind Hitler into a strong-studded cell.

And you women here tonight, who are studying for new and ever more important duties in war-time banking; your job is not the least of these, for without the ready, controlled flow of capital and credit into these industries, jobs would stop, production would halt, the brave boys of America would be stranded on lonely, far-flung beaches for lack of the very tools of war.

It is your job to provide those tools. It is your job to keep the institutions of credit and finance alive and vigorous, able to do its job smoothly and well in these perilous times. The sombre shadow of inflation hangs heavy over the land tonight. In Washington a group of selfish men seek at this very moment to send food prices sky-rocketing so that their own favored groups may benefit.

It is your dual job, to paraphrase President Koeneke, to fight this war as women bankers and as women. As our own chancellors of the home excheq-uer we know what the high cost of living really means in terms of less food on the table, less milk for the children, fewer meals for our men. And as bankers you know what inflation can do to our economy. None knows bet-ter than you that inflation can blow our production lines powder-keg high, shatter our form of government, and blast us into a ruthless dictatorship, where the great steadying strength of finance is gone and only brutal force remains.

And now I am going to say something which I could only say among us girls. So far in this war we are still the luckiest women in the whole world. For instance we still have lipsticks, and even some silk stockings. And although many of us have gone into uniforms, they are still made of good cloth and are well cut. Sisters, for a lot of us, perhaps too many of us, impor-tant though the part we have played in it so far, it is still easy—and I almost said "glamorous" for us. But, believe me, for each of us these are the good old days now, my friends.

Now we have got to face a great, big fact. We have got to face the fact that the 'interesting' part of our participation in this war effort is just about over. There isn't going to be any glamour in what we have to do from here on in. I realize that for most women there is little that is glamorous in a war, any war. But we have to be frank enough with ourselves to admit that in our effort to help, we have still managed to do a lot of things that are both help-ful and, by a remarkable coincidence, attractive. We've been able, as we went about our wartime activities, to find time to wonder, as I say, a little about those uniforms. We've had time to be disturbed a bit about the freez-ing of fashion designs, about the lack of silk stockings. Yes, we've found time to look a little for the glamorous.

But, from here on in to victory, glamour is out and toughness is in. From here on in to victory, girls, the way is going to be hard. From here on in, women and men and children, too, for that matter, are going to have to take on the serious task of winning this war. Our president has called this the "toughest war in history" and whether you here tonight class yourself as a political follower of the president or one of his political opponents, you must accept that definition as completely accurate.

What, then, are we women going to do in the tough days that lie ahead? Well, we're going to do a lot of the things we are doing right now, but we are going to do them a lot more intensely and, if you will pardon me, a lot more *intelligently*.

With our men, we're going to work and fight for victory. We're going to submit, but we're going to understand why we submit to, rules and regula-tions; we're going to take, and manage with, more and more rationing. We're going to have colder homes, different foods, less clothing—we're going to accept the challenges imposed by these conditions. We're going to keep our homes and jobs going because we know, being women, what hap-pens if we don't keep them going.

The women of the next few years—and please believe that my use of the plural 'years' while pessimistic, is honest—the women of the next few crucial years are going to see that their children, those precious treasures for whom we fight, are kept healthy and warm and well fed and well schooled and as happy as possible under conditions which are bound to become less and less favorable and not at all glamorous for anyone from here on in.

Yes, ladies, the road ahead is going to be a bumpy one. It is going to be full of ruts and rocks, the ruts of endless, colorless effort, and the rocks of almost insurmountable obstacles. It takes no gifted prophet to foresee this road to victory. A soft war leads to a hard peace. A hard war leads to a happy peace. We must fight a hard war. I think we will not much long kid ourselves that this war can be won by an effort which, though extremely great, is still a comfortable one. I think we are coming to the grim realization that such dreams of comfort are insidious saboteurs of our war effort.

We have got to come to some grim conclusions in the days that lie ahead. We have got to come to the conclusion that this war will not be won until many thousands of men—perhaps your men and perhaps my stepsons and brother—have risked their lives, perhaps died to win it. And we have got to come to the conclusion that it will not be won until we all fight to win it, every minute of every hour of every day, *from here on in*. We dare not measure our effort by its drain on our comforts; we dare to measure it only by its contribution toward the victory for which we fight.

How do women fight a war when they have to? Certain pictures come to my mind. One is the picture of an old Chinese woman, dragging her tired body down the hot, dusty Burma road. No glamorous representative of her truly magnificent people, this old woman, and yet she fought. Haggard, ragged, hungry and tired, she fought. There is not much room in her weary mind for worries about fashion freezing, or a low sugar ration—or even a shampoo and wave once every two weeks, or a meatless day once a week. What was fashion or lipsticks to her who had worn one blue coolie coat for perhaps five years? What is a low ration to her who got no sugar or meat at all from one end of the week to the next? No there is nothing soft about this woman in my memory. She was merely a tired old woman, fighting her country's war, all-out.

And how did she fight? Did she knit, or sew, or work in a factory? No, my friends, her job is a little harder. She carried a factory. She carried a factory in her bare hands, piece by piece, wheel by wheel, belt by belt and shaft by shaft—over hundreds of miles of road, so that those factories, dismantled in an area which can be reached by Japanese bombs, may be set up again in the interior, to produce their brave materials, temporarily safe from attack. There is another alarming picture, a picture of a healthy young Russian girl. I have seen that one in the papers. What does she do to fight? She kills Nazis—over 300 of them. She hides in the corner of a bombed building and she snipes at Nazis as they advance toward her lines. Fashions, rationing, shortages? Do they trouble her?

And there is another picture, this time of a British Mother, as she gazed at the ruins of the house that once was hers, the house that held her every dream, her every hope—bombed to bits, blasted to a splintery oblivion. I saw her face lined with harsh wrinkles, it had a message: keep fighting, it said, keep fighting, keep fighting, all day and every day.

Those pictures, my friends, are alarming—not because we would flinch in the face of necessities as stern as those women face. Rich or poor, women in banking, or factories, or homes, we have the stuff that it takes to face them; make no mistake about that. I have gone about the world considerably of late and I have come to see and know its people, and if there is one thing I believe in it is that we Americans have whatever degree of courage or stamina or guts that this war will take. We lack only one thing—a little more knowledge of what odds we face and the way we are being coddled and cozened beyond our will. But that, I cannot mention for that would lead me into a campaign speech. Nevertheless, my friends, those pictures are alarming because they reveal that those women are displaying a determination we have not yet been told we may be yet forced to assume. Between the backbreaking work of the old Chinese woman and the comparatively comfortable effort women like ourselves are making, there is an alarming gap. If I were to be asked what is the chief job of the American women in the days that lie ahead, I would say that is the job of closing that gap, despite the soft confused war efforts still being made in Washington. It is the job of facing the fact that this is the toughest war in our history and of making every other American understand that great big fact. This is no easy job, and it will not be a pleasant one.

So let us women here tonight resolve that we will now, tonight, begin to assume it. Let us both do our jobs, as all women in this war will do their jobs, resolutely and well, whether they are making bombers at Las Vegas, sewing sailor suits in Brooklyn, or learning to fight the silent but vital battles of our national economy and well-being here in Bridgeport tonight. And help our country to do its job, which is to fight this war, so that we shall win it, without wrecking our country, throwing our economic system into hopeless disrepair, and wasting the blood of our sons needlessly.

NOTE

1. Typescript, Clare Boothe Luce Papers, Manuscript Division, Library of Congress, Washington, DC. Luce dedicated the copyright of her unpublished papers to the public.

Mary Anderson (1872–1964)

An active agent for social change all her life, Mary Anderson did not participate in the women's suffrage movement, but rather devoted her energy to trade unionism. Her tenure as director of the Women's Bureau of the U.S. Department of Labor from 1920 to 1944 was, in a sense, a culmination of the labor movement efforts begun in the nineteenth century.

Anderson came to the United States from Sweden when she was sixteen. After she secured steady work at Schwabs shoe factory in Chicago, a representative for the Boot and Shoe Workers union invited several young women to a union meeting. Anderson went and soon became the shop collector for the union, then was elected president, a position she held for fifteen years. During this period, she met other women involved in the Chicago Trade Union movement, including Jane Addams and leaders of the Women's Trade Union League (WTUL).

In 1911, Anderson became a paid organizer for the WTUL, playing an important role in the process of establishing arbitration as a means to settle labor disputes. Furthermore, Anderson was one of the first to articulate the point of view that was later labeled "social feminism."[1] In her eulogy to Jane Addams, Anderson approvingly asserted that Addams "was not one of those feminists who are for women alone. Her heart and brilliant mind recognized that as long as one group could be exploited, society as a whole must suffer."[2]

In 1918, Anderson was appointed assistant director of the Women in Industrial Service, becoming director in 1919 and remaining, after a name change to the Women's Bureau, until she retired in 1944. Thus, her work at the federal level began and ended during times of world war. Under

Mary Anderson, Washington, DC, June 1942.

Library of Congress, Prints and Photographs Division, [reproduction number, LC-USZ62-98833]. Photo by Marjory Collins.

Anderson's direction the Women's Bureau collected data and issued regular publications detailing women's status in the workforce, documenting both problem areas and achievements. She also supported educational programs for working women, most notably the Bryn Mawr summer schools organized in conjunction with the college's famous president, M. Carey Thomas. In addition, Anderson took on conservative groups, led by the DAR, which accused Anderson and the Women's Bureau, among others, of communist sympathies.

Central to Anderson's objectives, however, was gaining protective labor legislation for women. Thus, when the National Woman's Party head, Alice Paul, showed Anderson the "so-called Equal Rights Amendment," Anderson was concerned, ultimately concluding "the amendment could not be worded so as to safeguard labor legislation."[3] She worked hard, organizing plans and people, nationally and internationally, to quell support for "the blanket amendment" and maintain protective labor legislation for women.

In the 1940s, as World War II loomed and the need for women workers in factories became clear, Anderson focused on getting women into needed jobs, assuring adequate training and high workplace standards. However, while efforts to recruit, train, and maintain women in industry during World War II were noteworthy, Anderson acknowledged the need for labor and industry to be prepared for a tough transition after the war. She was not to be part of that, however. Changing attitudes, including increasing support for an ERA and her own strained relationship with Labor Secretary Frances Perkins, along with her advancing age, led Mary Anderson to retire in 1944.

The following speeches describing women's role in the American war effort were made in a radio broadcast to Britain on December 22, 1942. Although she retained traces of her Swedish accent in both inflection and grammar, Anderson's remarks were, nevertheless, clear and detailed. They reveal well the kind of work done by the Women's Bureau under her direction. The speeches also reveal Anderson's generally inclusive stance, the basis of her fundamental belief in arbitration rather than strikes as the most effective means for settling disputes. They illustrate further the culmination of Anderson's work for women in the industrial workplace.

NOTES

1. Mary Anderson and Mary Winslow, *Women at Work* (Minneapolis: University of Minnesota Press, 1951); Susan Ware, *Beyond Suffrage: Women in the New Deal* (Cambridge: Harvard University Press, 1981), 17.

2. Mary Anderson, "Tribute to Miss Jane Addams," June 19, 1935, in the Mary Anderson Papers, 1918–1960, Microfilm (M-64, Reels 71–74), Schlesinger Library, Harvard University, Cambridge, MA.

3. Anderson and Winslow, 162; and Susan Becker, "International Feminism Between the Wars: The National Woman's Party versus the League of Women Voters," *Decades of Discontent: The Women's Movement, 1920–1940*, Lois Scharf and Joan M. Jensen, eds. (Westport, CT: Greenwood Press, 1983), 223–242.

RADIO SPEECHES (FEBRUARY 22, 1942)[1]

Transcribed from audio recording by Sandra J. Sarkela

I welcome this opportunity to send you a heartfelt message from our women workers in the United States. We have been deeply impressed and inspired by the heroic efforts of women among our allies in this great fight for democracy. In our country also as in yours, we are having an industrial revolution to meet war needs. Here, too, we are adopting the British slogan: "Nothing that women can do or learn to do should be allowed to absolve a man of military age." American women are good soldiers in the labor front and are winning real victories. They are not afraid to tackle any task in the key war industries. Large numbers of women are supplanting the work of men on production lines. But women are doing more. To a growing extent they are replacing men inducted into military service or more skilled jobs.

The situation was quite different before the war. During our so-called defense program, from the days of Dunkirk to the attack on Pearl Harbor, women were ready and eager to work in our munition plants. But most of these plants did not want women. The management had a backlog of unemployed men to draw on. Also, many employers were skeptical as to women's mechanical ability. But immediately after our entrance into the conflict, opposition to women for war production began to collapse. Obviously, several million women would have to be recruited to meet President Roosevelt's blueprint for war material, particularly with millions of men required for the armed forces.

Also, resistance by organized labor to women in certain male dominions has given way to ready acceptance of women as co-workers in the plants and as co-members of the unions. But men want assurance that women will not be used to undercut labor standards. Today, men, both management and labor, express amazement at women's skill and speed. Countless employers now boast that women are as good as men in many operations and even better at some jobs. President Roosevelt, after his swing around the country some weeks ago to inspect war production, praised women for their unflagging attention to their jobs.

In our Women's Bureau investigation we find women here, as with you, able and eager to do any kinds of work. They are experts at processes requiring painstaking hand position. They are as good as men at hard jobs like welding or operating electric cranes. Many women can run a drilling machine as well as an eggbeater. Many take to riveting like a duck to water. We have, in this country, about four million women in war jobs, less than a fourth of all our women workers. But the number in war employment is steadily growing.

Most dramatic has been the influx of women into the aircraft factories. Just before we entered the war, less than four thousand women were in airplane production, chiefly in the fabric department. Today about a hundred and thirty-five thousand women are helping to make planes of all types from the Mustang and likely to the Flying Fortress and Liberator. Women are now doing more and more of the necessary operations for building aircraft.

Thousands of women are at work in arsenals on all kinds of ammunition, bullets, shells, and bombs. Thousands of women are making war instruments and electrical equipment. Thousands are helping to produce tanks,..., rubber rafts, lifeboats, and parachutes. Many women now work in ordinance plants, turning out guns and firearms. Only a few of our women were so employed a year ago. Women in these plants operate more different kinds of machines than any other industry.

Last summer women gained a foothold in the machine tool shop for the first time since the World War I, and women are on the increase in many of these plants. One factory, the largest manufacturer of lathes in the United States, now reports almost one thousand women employees. They constitute two-fifths of the force.

Our shipyards have begun to take on women, more and more of them. The government navy yards have led the way. One is employing women for the first time in its hundred and forty-one years of existence. The private yards have also begun to hire women for growing number of jobs. Of course, when the emergency is over women will cease to engage in many of the present occupations.

In the postwar period there will be a scaling down of munition industry. We shall have to readjust large groups of workers, both men and women. Many women will automatically withdraw from the labor force. But many of our women will still have to earn their living and support dependents. Women by the thousands will still have to replace men—the men who come back maimed or fail to return from the combat. Special postwar plans must be made to meet the needs of women, who as unknown heroes of the labor front have made their contributions and sacrifices, too, for victory and democracy.

It is a real privilege to greet you and tell you in this way about changing patterns for women workers in the United States. The women in your country and ours are drawn closer together by our common cause. The situation for American women does not parallel that of women who have endured and conquered the hardships during three years of hard warfare, brought to their very homes and workplaces. But even a year of war has led to social revolution here. The changes, though gradual, are quite apparent.

The trends in women's employment have been considerably altered. The attitudes of women as workers, the attitudes of employers towards a feminine work force, have been revamped. Many college graduates and girls from well-to-do homes turn willingly to work on the industrial front, because they feel they take a more vital part in war when they work on bombs, tanks, ships, and planes. Some girls are eager to help make planes for their brothers, husbands, or sweethearts to fly. And the wages are usually good in such plants. A young college woman doing research work for a firm in a big industrial center the other day told me all her girlfriends are in the war production. Most of them, she said, were on the swing shift, three to eleven p.m. Others worked on the graveyard shift through the night and they like their jobs. This situation can be duplicated in all parts of the country.

Service in war plants, as in the armed forces, is proving a great socializing influence. In the Women's Bureau we had occasion to check on the previous occupational experience in a large aircraft engine plant. Here's the list of the women's former jobs: hotel keepers, domestic workers, housewives, stenographers, sales girls, saxophone player, blues singers, cashier, candy store work, garment and jewelry factory workers, beauty operators, debutantes, waitresses, schoolteachers, college graduates in chemistry and physics, commercial artists, and so on. All those women with very different backgrounds were getting new and wholesome ideas from their contacts with women in other walks of life from their own.

Other encouraging trends have been a breakdown in discrimination against certain types of workers. Of course we've not reached the millennium. Prejudices still linger in various quarters, but progress is being made. Married women who during our years of depression were discriminated against by many employers are now in great demand. Older women in their forties, fifties, or even sixties, who a year ago were unable to secure any kind of a job, are at last finding themselves employable to an increasing degree. Negro women workers formerly barred from many occupational fields are beginning to have unusual opportunities open up to them. Such trends have been spurred by an executive order of President Roosevelt. This prohibits applicants for war jobs from being discriminated against on account of race, creed, color, or national origin.

In the Women's Bureau, we find that the national emergency and the global war have widened the horizon of American women. They have a greater pride as workers. They have a new feeling of unity. They have a much stronger sense of responsibility as citizens.

NOTE

1. Audio Recording. "Department of Labor Women's Bureau," Object 48-360, National Archives and Records Administration, Washington, DC.

Mary Beard (1876–1946)

Mary Beard was Director of Nursing Services for the American National Red Cross from 1938 to 1944, a crucial period in the history of recruiting nurses for wartime service. Born in Dover, New Hampshire, she graduated from New York Hospital School of Nursing in 1903 (which became the Cornell University Hospital School of Nursing in 1942).[1] In 1904, Beard began work as a visiting nurse in Waterbury, Connecticut. From 1912 to 1924 she worked in Boston, first as Director of the Instructive District Nursing Association and later as Director of the Community Health Association. In 1924, she returned to New York City and became Associate Director of the International Health Division of the Rockefeller Foundation. While she was with the Rockefeller Foundation, she published *The Nurse in Public Health* (1929).

World War II began during Beard's term as Director of Nursing for the American Red Cross. According to a history of American Red Cross nursing, World War II was a crucial moment for emergency medical services. The need for Army and Navy nurses was almost overwhelming. Thus, a network of 340 nurse recruitment committees was set up that included both nurses and lay members. In the first year, these committees, reportedly "recruited over 22,000 nurses for the armed forces—almost as many as served in World War I."[2]

The radio address that follows was part of that recruiting effort. As Beard told her audience, the American National Red Cross had been the official recruiting agency for military nurses since 1912. Beard began and ended this radio address with a tribute to "six heroines of Corregidor and Bataan," who had been decorated for their courageous service by Col.

Julia O. Flikke, Superintendent of the Army Nurse Corps.[3] She also referred to nurses who remained behind and continued to "care for the sick and wounded." Beard spoke of her own intense pride in the service of all these nurses, and, in so doing, she appealed to the compassion, patriotism, and pride of nurses, former nurses, future nurses, and even women without nurse's training—all of whom she asked to volunteer for service. She told the women in her radio audience that serving as a nurse was the noblest role available to women during World War II. She urged each of them to offer her service and, if necessary, her life as a wartime nurse.

NOTES

1. Mary Beard, the nurse, should not be confused with Mary Ritter Beard, a historian, born the same year. Biographical information, in the form of a time line, was provided by the Collection of Regional History and University Archives, John M. Olin Library, Cornell University, Ithaca, NY.

2. "The History and Organization of the Red Cross Nursing Service," American National Red Cross, 2000 [web site] May 27, 2003 (http://www.redcross.org/services/nursing/history/).

3. Flikke, Superintendent of the Army Nurse Corps, received a temporary commission as a colonel and her assistant, Capt. Florence A. Blanchfield, received a temporary commission as a lieutenant colonel. However, they were denied the pay of those grades because a decision of the Comptroller General stated that these women were not "persons" in the sense of the law under which they were promoted. However, in 1952, the 82d Congress (in Private Law 716) reversed the decision and they, then retired, received the pay that had been withheld for ten years. See SSG Carl Snyder, "100 Years of Red Cross Nursing Chronology," 1996 (http://www.armymedicine.army.mil/history/ANCWebsite/chrono.htm).

RADIO BROADCAST TO NURSES (JULY 1, 1942)[1]

Reprinted by Permission of Cornell University Library

MISS BEARD: I hope that you nurses listening in all over America were affected as I was as Colonel Flikke decorated those six heroines of Corregidor and Bataan. And I hope that your hearts went out as mine did to those others, heroines all, who remained behind to care for the sick and wounded when Corregidor fell.

For if you feel at this moment as I do...proud and choked with emotion...you will hesitate no longer in enrolling with your American Red Cross Nursing Reserve for war service. If you feel as I do at this moment, you will push aside all the barriers of your own and of others' making and rally now to your country's call. You will put aside personal thoughts and personal problems for the duration and give yourself, your very life if necessary, to the service of the men who are fighting for the liberty and the decency and the morality of all the world. In so doing, you will be giving yourself to the noblest cause available to your profession and indeed, to your sex.

The United States Army and the United States Navy need you right now more than they have ever needed you before. The Army has just called upon the Red Cross to recruit a minimum of 25 hundred nurses a month. That is exactly 250 per cent more than have ever been needed before, even since Pearl Harbor. And that number doubtless will increase as our forces on foreign soil grow and as more and more of our men go into battle.

The Navy's needs are correspondingly large. Its drain upon the Red Cross Nursing Reserve will also grow as ship after ship is placed in service and more and more men stand at their fighting guns. I am glad to report that this afternoon Congress has granted officers' rank to the nurses of the United States Navy.

Since 1912 Congress has designated the Red Cross as the official recruiting agency for both the Army and Navy Nurse Corps. It is our duty to enroll you for service and it is your duty to volunteer.

I am sure that after today, after the inspiration of these nurses just decorated, none will have to urge you further.

I would like to add one thing more. As the qualified nurses leave their civilian jobs to answer their country's call, there will be gaps to fill and it is the women of America who must fill them. So let me urge all of you women who qualified to enter schools of nursing to do so, and all of you who were nurses at one time but who, for one reason or another have left the profession, to re-enter it immediately. And to the others, those of you who have had no training at all, you can enlist as Volunteer Nurses' Aides. Your Red Cross will train you to serve in civilian hospitals, to help fill the gaps left by war nurses.

In closing, let me again pay tribute to our honored heroines. From the very bottom of my heart I am proud of you…each of you. And I know that when the names of brave and heroic women are called yours will be near the top of the list…

NOTE

1. Typescript for radio broadcast. Mary Beard Papers, 1926–1948, Collection 2641, Division of Rare and Manuscript Collection, Cornell University, Ithaca, NY.

Ella Reeve Bloor

Ella "Mother" Reeve Bloor published her autobiography, *We Are Many*, in 1940 (see Part I). Although she was seventy-eight years old, she did not see this as her final statement, and the title of the following speech gives some insight into her views. Speaking before several Ohio audiences in August 1942, Bloor avidly championed America's role in World War II because, as she stated, "The People's War is on." She especially championed women's war work but also saw the war as an opportunity to unify all Americans: "Men and Women, colored and white, Jew and Gentile, all creeds and nationalities" for a noble cause—the defeat of "Hitler's hoards." Union members, immigrants, the poor, minorities, the working classes, and women were all "American citizens." Bloor believed that as such, they ought to be granted all the rights and fulfill all the responsibilities citizenship entailed, including fighting for one's country. Women astounded her with their skill and commitment to defense work and to sustaining the home front, but she also emphasized the need to support budding efforts to provide collective day care. A committed socialist and member of the Communist Party, Bloor perceived her activism not as opposed to the American way of life but instead as an effort to strengthen it—to persuade the nation to fulfill its democratic promise.

A close reading of the organization of this speech, as well as Bloor's specific wording, reveals her continued socialist perspective, nuanced feminism, and her still passionate devotion to "the people." Bloor makes clever and evocative use of patriotic symbols to link her lifelong, radical views to mainstream American values.

RADIO BROADCAST
WOMEN'S ROLE IN WINNING THE WAR
COLUMBUS, AUGUST 25, 1942; YOUNGSTOWN,
AUGUST 26, 1942[1]

Reprinted by Permission of Sophia Smith Collection, Smith College

Fellow Americans:

Never before in this history of America have women faced such tremendous responsibilities. And they are ready. While they still have true, deep emotions—they are not hysterical.

Having just visited nearly all the large cities of the West Coast and the Midwest, I can truthfully say that it was a revelation to me to see the shining faces of women and girls—changing shifts—in war production shops. Skillfully and speedily promoting the aircraft and other industries, to such a degree that in many they even excel the men in speed and skill.

In actual War Relief, and emergency work of all kinds, they are marching together in a practical, organized manner. Young, strong mothers have found the way opened for them to enter industry—to take the places of the men who have gone to war—against the worst enemy of womanhood—Fascism.

On the West Coast, the Women's Auxiliaries of the Steel and Machinist Unions—with the help of Parent-Teacher Associations—have taken the lead in the organization of Day Nurseries, Kindergartens and Playgrounds for the Children of these Mothers, who must be released for Industry.

50,000 women have been called upon to register in Seattle for War Work. In the Boeing Air-Craft shop in Seattle, one woman was found who brought three children with her to work, and while she was in the shop, locked them in her automobile, releasing them at noon to eat their lunch.

This moved the owners of the shop to secure at once a suitable building near the shop for a Children's Day Nursery, and for Health Supervision and Child-Care generally.

The American Woman's Voluntary Service Corps has done wonderful work in their Child Care Department. In some cases, securing permission from the Board of Education to use large airy rooms in large school buildings for the summer.

The neighborhood and community work is carried on successfully in many cities. Women Air-Raid Wardens have gotten acquainted with every family in the Block—and helped in a closer bond of understanding of what this People's War Against Fascism, really means to all women. It is especially helpful—this Community work—to families whose sons have entered the war.

I have just heard of the inspiring example set by the girls at the barrage balloon plant of the General Tire & Rubber Co. in Akron. Only women are employed there and every one of them has assigned *at least* 10% of her wages for War Bonds.

I have also heard of the splendid work being done by tens of thousands of Akron women—in the big war factories and in Civilian Defense. I know that thousands of other mothers here would gladly enter the factories if they had Day Nurseries where their children would be cared for while they produce the necessary weapons to annihilate Hitler's axis.

No mother or wife today wastes any time in loneliness, or tears. As the Russian women said to us in the midst of their terrible suffering from the brutal attacks upon them, by the enemy: "This is no time for tears."

Women! Just think how our men and boys EVERYWHERE will be happy to know that their wives, mothers and sweethearts are busy and useful. They will respect all women more, because their own are busy and cheerful, and full of courage.

We all know how men hate to see weeping women. We are very glad to hear of the Stalin–Churchill–Harriman Conference in Moscow, which strengthens and develops this unity, the friendship, and the joint efforts of the United Nations. We are very glad to hear of the large Commando raid on the coast of France early last week. This is a good omen of the Second Front.—That men and machinery will pour into Europe to scare Hitler's hordes, will smash their brutal attacks upon Russia and those countries they have conquered and enslaved.

What a remarkable world crisis this is, today. To the Allies—the United Nations—will be given: Not only the responsibility, but also the honor, and glory of saving America: yes—civilization itself will be saved by a tremendous, powerful *Second Front*. The People's War is on. Whole-heartedly we march together—Men and Women, colored and white, Jew and Gentile, all creeds and nationalities.

All Unions! This is our country, Our America! We built it together by our labor. Many of our countrymen have speculated about what will happen *after* this people's war. We must not speculate about that at this time. There is one outstanding fact, however, that if Hitler's forces win in Europe—we shall fail. Not only in the Soviet Union—but also our country would be lost. Our culture, our democracy, our children—all would be lost.

Therefore we cannot—we must not lose.

NOTE

1. Typescript for radio broadcast. Sophia Smith Collection, Smith College, Northampton, MA.

Florence Jaffray Harriman

Just as World War II was about to erupt in Europe, Florence Harriman took her post as U.S. Minister to Norway (see Part I). She served from 1937 until she fled Europe in 1940 in fear for her life, just ahead of the Nazi invasion of Norway. Franklin Delano Roosevelt appointed Harriman, who became only the second woman to achieve ministerial status in the United States. Her appointment came at the apex of a long career devoted to public service and the Democratic Party.[1]

The following two speeches, the first just prior to the U.S. entry into the war (c. 1941); and the second near the end of it (1944), illustrate her patriotic zeal and her political prowess. But, as these speeches attest, Harriman was an ardent internationalist. A consistent critic of isolationism, she advocated early intervention by the United States and was a strong proponent of continued postwar diplomatic engagement with the Soviet Union. Harriman's speeches reveal her powerful intellect and her sophisticated renderings of international affairs. In clear, evocative language she dissects international conflicts and avidly articulates her recommendations for American foreign policy. Her direct and persuasive speeches are particularly noteworthy because she operated within the political spheres—military diplomacy and foreign policy—most hostile to women. Yet, she was also clearly comfortable relying upon the gendered political philosophy in which she came of age. Though perhaps less so than some other political women of the 1930s and 1940s, Harriman believed that women were naturally more pacifist than men and naturally more inclined to foment cooperative strategies on the international stage. This is particularly apparent in her attempt to humanize the Russian image by pointing to the common bonds that existed between Russian and American women.

According to Harriman, women's inherently more tolerant, peaceful, and nurturing persona could transcend cultural difference and international conflict. Harriman also published two books, *From Pinafores to Politics* (1923) and *Mission to the North* (1941).

NOTE

1. Florence Jaffray Harriman," *Encyclopedia Britannica* from Encyclopaedia Premium Service, May 27, 2003 (http://www.britannica.com/eb/article?eu=138074).

WOMAN AND WAR (1941)[1]

We women have our own special reasons for hating war. The glory and the glamor [sic] of war have not been for us. Ours has been the agony of suspense, the fear of danger to our loved ones which we could not share, and the duty to nurse the human wrecks which war leaves behind.

With their usual mastery of psychology the Nazis are now moving Heaven and earth to exploit this feeling of the women of America. They appeal above all to our women with their slogans "Stop Aid to Britain," "Keep America out of War." American women hate war, but there is one thing they hate worse than war, slavery. They want to keep their husbands and sons at home, but they want still more a world in which their children can develop freely and not be molded according to the wishes and purposes of a dictator.

Like our men we women of America are prepared for war if it is necessary to preserve a free America. But, if we act quickly to save England now, war may still be avoided here. Our only hope of keeping war away from America is to beat Hitler in Europe. At the same time we must make haste to arm the brave representatives of the countries of Europe, who are heroically defending the outposts of freedom.

What we Americans, men and women equally, need right now is more confidence in ourselves. Our resources are ample to accomplish the downfall of Hitler if we have the will to do it. In Britain we have an associate whose will nothing can break. We can rely upon the British to use our help with skill and undaunted courage. Let our confidence equal theirs.

Whoever doubts our success in our present effort doubts not only our material resources but our moral character. The great masses of our people, I am convinced, share no such doubts. They do not intend to give Britain limited aid. They intend to give Britain enough all-out aid to ensure all-out victory. The day will come when the planes out of American and British factories will drive the Nazi planes from the skies both over the Atlantic and over Europe. That day will be the end of Hitler and Hitlerism. There is no doubt that it will come. Our choice is only between making it come lingeringly and making it come speedily.

Let us settle every delaying domestic controversy, every delaying cowardly doubt, and let us drive this war off this earth with all the speed that our fearless and matchless energies command.

We are a Mighty Nation. Let us act as befits a Mighty Nation.

NOTE

1. Typescript. Florence Jaffray Hurst Harriman Papers, Manuscript Division, Library of Congress, Washington, DC. Harriman dedicated her unpublished papers to the public.

AMERICAN–SOVIET FRIENDSHIP
(DECEMBER 9, 1944)[1]

For three long years the United States of America has felt total war. And yet, despite the sacrifices we have had to make—each of which has assumed—in the face of the stress of war—greater significance than we like to admit to ourselves, we are compelled to acknowledge that our burden has been the lightest. We have not been bombed. Our lands have not been ravaged. Our homes have not been burned and plundered. Our cities stand undemolished. The New York skyline has known nothing worse than the normal ravages of weather. San Francisco has been as hospitable as ever to throngs of tourists. Washington, New Orleans, Boston, Chicago, Detroit and all the other cities have felt no more acute discomfort than overcrowded living conditions due to an increase in war production.

Above all, our civilian population has remained safe. Murder, pillage, rape are conditions the existence of which we recognize as accompanying war—but only *that* war which is occurring on the opposite sides of two vast expanses of ocean.

Of course, we have suffered in common with the other nations of the world, the agony of losing brothers, husbands and sons on the battlefield. Such grief is not relative—and no one can say that any individual or nation has suffered more than another that way, whether the loss has been of a single loved one or thousands of the male population. There are no infallible units of measurement for human emotion. The palpable comparison exists only in the material results—such as the effect which an enormous loss of manpower might eventually have upon an industrial country, or a nation whose livelihood depended on its commerce, or a nation whose farms and agricultural produce are its life force.

But when the two—war between soldiers, and war upon the population—are combined, and a nation can see not only the flower of its youth falling, but also the symbols of its future—its women and children, its helpless and ill, forced to conduct a war of equal savagery—*then* it would be both illogical and inhuman not to admit that there are some who have a fuller knowledge of what total war is than we.

The world has recognized, in this respect, the magnitude of the sacrifice of Soviet Russia. The words of a great leader in another country, suffering equally, have immortalized this sacrifice. The important thing is that we must not let our consciousness of the sacrifice flag. It is a human failing to forget the causes of war and thus to lose sight of what we have been fighting for. Our debt to Russia as an ally in wartime must not be forgotten when the peace is finally signed. Differences in political ideologies should be set aside in the face of the more important fact that we have been fighting side by side with the people of a country whose basic hopes and aspirations are no different than ours—we all want peace—and we want the kind of peace which will allow us not only to pursue our own ways of life, but will point toward knowledge and understanding of the other peoples of the world.

The strongest weapons we possess for the accomplishment of this worthy objective are the weapons of tolerance and understanding. The United States may have been able to remain untouched by the phase of the war which forced the civilian to shoulder arms, but there is no question that in the anticipated era of peace every single American will have to assume responsibility for a major portion of the burden of education which will preserve the peace.

It would be so easy for us to return to the way of bigotry and intolerance vis-à-vis Russia, that it is not pleasant to contemplate it long. We have had a bitter struggle against certain forces which saw in Russia only a threat to the democracies—and which preferred to disregard the people of Russia in favor of the particular symbol which represented them. The symbol is not important. More and more, as the war has progressed, Americans have come to recognize the complete insignificance of the symbol. That a bigotted [sic] minority still exists it is true, and a disheartening proof of it appeared in a recent publication. Much that various writers wrote was true but they used a weapon unworthy of the opponent whom they were trying to belittle.

Those men, two of whom are liberals, have allowed their personal prejudices to blind them to the picture as a whole. The third is married to the daughter of one of the late Czar's generals, and the indignities and cruelties that he suffered in the Revolution have made it impossible for his son-in-law to be just. I have talked with him myself and know how difficult it is for him to allow that there is any good to be found in the Soviet Union.

It is to the women perhaps more than to the men, I think, that we have to look for tolerance and the practice of the Golden Rule. Russian women, like the women of any country, were among the first to introduce the study of other nations in the schools something we should do here. The fact that women in Russia have been as much soldiers as the men—right in the front lines fighting—and have undergone such barbaric experiences in this war, has not made them inhuman creatures—as stories coming from the front lines can testify.

NOTE

1. Typescript with handwritten revisions. Florence Jaffray Hurst Harriman Papers, Manuscript Division. Library of Congress, Washington, DC. Harriman dedicated her unpublished papers to the public.

Suggested Readings, 1940–1945

Anderson, Karen. *Wartime Women: Sex Roles, Family Relations, and the Status of Women During World War II* (Westport, CT: Greenwood Press, 1981).

Campbell, D'Ann. *Woman at War with America: Private Lives in a Patriotic Era* (Cambridge, MA: Harvard University Press, 1984).

Coontz, Stephanie. *The Way We Never Were: American Families and the Nostalgia Trap* (New York: Basic Books, 1992).

Crapol, Edward P., ed. *Women and Foreign Policy: Lobbyists, Critics, and Insiders* (Westport, CT: Greenwood Press, 1987).

Gluck, Sherna B. *Rosie the Riveter Revisited: Women, the War, and Social Change* (Boston: Twayne, 1987).

Goossen, Rachel Waltner. *Women Against the Good War: Conscientious Objection and Gender on the American Home Front, 1941–1947* (Chapel Hill, NC: University of North Carolina Press, 1997).

Hartmann, Susan M. *The Home Front and Beyond: American Women in the 1940's* (Boston: Twayne, 1982).

Hegarty, Marilyn E. "Patriot or Prostitute? Sexual Discourses, Print Media, and American Women During World War II," *Journal of Women's History* 10 (Summer 1998): 112–137.

Higonnet, Margaret Randolph, et. al., eds. *Behind the Lines: Gender and the Two World Wars* (New Haven: Yale University Press, 1987).

Honey, Maureen, ed. *Bitter Fruit: African American Women in World War II* (Columbia, MO: University of Missouri Press, 1999).

Honey, Maureen. *Creating Rosie the Riveter: Class, Gender, and Propaganda During World War II* (Amherst, MA: University of Massachusetts Press, 1985).

Jeansonne, Glen. *Women of the Far Right: The Mothers' Movement and World War II* (Chicago: University of Chicago Press, 1996).

Kaminski, Theresa. *Prisoners in Paradise: American Women in Wartime South Pacific* (Lawrence, KS: University Press of Kansas, 2000).

Litoff, Judy Barrett and David C. Smith, eds. *American Women in a World at War: Contemporary Accounts from World War II.* (Wilmington, DE: Scholarly Resources, 1996).

Milkman, Ruth. *Gender at Work: The Dynamics of Job Segregation by Sex During World War II* (Urbana, IL: University of Illinois Press, 1987).

Rupp, Leila. *Mobilizing Women for War* (Princeton, NJ: Princeton University Press, 1976).

Ware, Susan. *Modern American Women: A Documentary History* (Belmont, CA: Wadsworth, 1989).

Weatherford, Doris. *American Women and World War II* (New York: Facts on File, 1990).

PART IV

Is That All There Is? 1945–1960

Americans entered the postwar years jubilant with victory but also awash with uncertainty. In contrast to the common understanding of this period, women remained active and vocal citizens. The speeches contained in this section reveal that women addressed the broad scope of complex and controversial issues that faced the nation. Popular literature of the period encouraged women to combine domestic responsibilities with work outside the home. In addition, study of primary materials shows many women were committed to civic activism. Finally, civil rights issues gained greater national attention as African American women continued to agitate for social change in all their capacities, including church members, workers, and street activists.[1] During the postwar period, as in the preceding three decades, women were not only active, but also actively organized.

Political women continued to travel across the country, speaking to public forums and through radio broadcasts. However, in the 1950s they also appeared on television. They gave live and taped speeches and held debates before national audiences on a variety of programs. During the 1956 presidential campaign, Senator Margaret Chase Smith and Eleanor Roosevelt were the first women to appear as guests on the CBS news program "Face the Nation." In a precursor to the televised presidential debates that would follow, Smith and Roosevelt argued the merits of Dwight D. Eisenhower versus Adlai Stevenson. Republican Smith cited a prosperous economy at home and the Party's commitment to the United Nations as the hallmarks of Eisenhower's administration, whereas Eleanor Roosevelt expressed concern about the draft and the atomic bomb, in support of Stevenson's candidacy.[2] Another partisan, Katie Louchheim, waged her campaign for the Democratic Party from her national leadership position as first director of women's activities of the National Democratic Party and then vice chair of the Democratic National Committee.

Several prominent women took an especially strong lead in issues of war and peace. During these years the United States fought the Korean War, bomb shelters appeared in backyards and basements, and emergency drills forced schoolchildren to "duck and cover" under their school desks. Marine Margaret M. Henderson argued that femininity and military service were not incompatible, as she crossed the country recruiting women for the armed forces. On the other hand, the devastation wrought by World War II, and particularly the atomic bomb, made warfare seem even more barbaric and outmoded to many activist women. Women used their status as "mothers of the race" to challenge the nation and the world to make sure this never happened again. Having moved from domestic to international politics, Eleanor Roosevelt became an ardent advocate for the United Nations and chaired its first Commission on Human Rights. Emily Greene Balch received the Nobel Peace Prize for her work on behalf of world peace and freedom.

One of the most radical activists of her time, Dorothy Day advocated and practiced civil disobedience as part of a pacifist antiwar philosophy and religious orientation. She joined in protests of nationally mandated air raid defense drills, supported young men who were debating whether or not to register for the draft, and asked fellow Catholics to accept and respect interracial marriage.[3] Day's activities during the 1950s in word and deed laid the basis for her growing credibility and central role in the civil rights and antiwar movements of the 1960s and 1970s.

Women also weighed in on the nation's response to real and imagined fears about the spread of communism. Democrat Helen Gahagan Douglas and Republican Margaret Chase Smith, in particular, were visible and forceful advocates for women's issues and opponents of Joseph McCarthy's anti-Communist attacks.[4] New York City judges Dorothy Kenyon and Justine Wise Polier also risked attack by standing against policies of oppression and fear. On the other hand, Dorothy Shaver promoted American designers and the "American look" on the basis that, since it embodied both function and beauty, it proved American superiority when contrasted with the boring functionalism of Soviet design.

World War II gave new impetus to campaigns for equal rights for women. Some New Deal administrators who had opposed the ERA, for example, Mary Anderson, left office, and others, such as Labor Secretary Frances Perkins and Eleanor Roosevelt, shifted their positions. Mary Church Terrell, who had been a member of FDR's "Black Cabinet," testified before the House Judiciary Committee in support of the ERA. Working and professional women also made their case before the nation. In contrast to the nostalgic view of women as homemakers in the 1950s, more and more women actually worked for wages outside the home. Along with Republican Senator Margaret Chase Smith, women in labor unions such as United Electric, in volunteer organizations such as the AAUW and BPW, and even journalists in popular women's magazines, including writers such as Dorothy Thompson, argued for comparable worth in pay scales.[5]

Furthermore, increasing numbers of women stepped up their protests of segregation and inequity in the military and discrimination throughout American institutions at home. Black female activists championed their causes via specifically feminist and civil rights organizations as well as a variety of other political forums and voluntary associations. Organizer Maida Springer-Kemp, for example, used her labor and union platform to begin to campaign more directly and aggressively for the Civil Rights movement. It was in these years that Rosa Parks declined to give up her seat, and landmark Supreme Court rulings, particularly the *Brown vs. Board of Education* decision, gave legal impetus to the modern civil rights movement. African Americans pressed their case in the North and the South, in the streets and at lunch counters, as well as the courts. JoAnn Robinson's memoir, *The Montgomery Bus Boycott and the Women Who Started It*, documents the important organizational role women played in the South.[6] And Ella Baker lent her experience and ethic of grassroots, nonhierarchical organization to the Southern Christian Leadership Conference and in 1960 was among the founders of the Student Nonviolent Coordinating Committee. Extant texts or recordings of speeches delivered by these women are difficult to find. Included here is a speech by Pauli Murray, who continued to challenge the government's failure to accord its black citizens equal status.

The speeches in this section, perhaps more than any other, highlight the distance between prescriptive ideals, inaccurate historical myths, and the real experiences of American women. In the 1950s, as in the decades preceding, women articulated their political ambitions and personal aspirations within numerous organizations and from a range of political perspectives. As these speeches illustrate, women from all walks of life expressed increasing concern and frustration over a variety of problems, issuing warnings and preparing the organizational and rhetorical foundations for the period of intense social activism just ahead.

NOTES

1. Susan Lynn, "Gender and Post–World War II Progressive Politics: A Bridge to Social Activism in the 1960s U.S.A.," *Gender and History* 4 (Summer 1992): 215–239.

2. For a transcript of this program, see *Face the Nation*, 1956, vol. 2 (New York: Holt Information Systems), 354–360; Margaret Chase Smith described this event in detail in her memoir *Declaration of Conscience*, (Garden City, NY: Doubleday, 1972), 201–211.

3. Dorothy Day, "C. W. Editors Arrested in Air Raid Drill," *The Catholic Worker* (July–August 1956): 1; Dorothy Day Library on the Web (www.catholicworker.org/dorothyday/).

4. Smith's "Declaration of Conscience" is reprinted in Margaret Chase Smith, *Declaration of Conscience*, 12–18; Marlene Boyd Vallin, *Margaret Chase Smith: Model Public Servant* (Westport, CT: Greenwood Press, 1998), 153–157; S. Michele Nix, *Women at the Podium* (New York: HarperCollins, 2000), 128–133.

5. Frances Freeman, "Speech–Richmond, Virginia, May 14, 1957," delivered before the national AAUW Status of Women Committee. A/F 85 Papers, Schlesinger Library, Harvard University, Cambridge, MA; Lisa Kannenberg, "The Impact of the Cold War on Women's Trade Union Activism: The UE Experience," *Labor History* 34 (Spring–Summer 1993): 309–323; Joanne Meyerowitz, "Beyond the Feminine Mystique: A Reassessment of Postwar Mass Culture, 1946–1958," *The Journal of American History* (March 1993): 1455–1482.

6. David J. Garrow, ed., *The Montgomery Bus Boycott and the Women Who Started It: the Memoir of JoAnn Gibson Robinson* (Knoxville, TN: University of Tennessee Press, 1987).

Helen Gahagan Douglas
(1900–1980)

Helen Gahagan Douglas named her autobiography *A Full Life,* an apt title, given her experiences as an actress, opera singer, wife, and mother—all before she embarked on a career of public service.[1] In 1938, she became politically active in California through the John Steinbeck Committee to Aid Migratory Workers. Soon thereafter, she rapidly rose to prominence in the Democratic Party, becoming Democratic National Committeewoman in 1940. First elected to the House of Representatives in 1944, she served for three consecutive terms, representing California's fourteenth district in downtown Los Angeles.

Her district was both commercial and residential; its residents, ranging from wealthy to indigent, were ethnically diverse, including 25% African American. In her autobiography, Douglas describes how, without passing legislation, she used her position as a member of Congress to advance the interests of her African American constituents, and, in the process, helped to integrate the congressional staff. She tells the story of hiring an African American secretary, constituent Juanita Terry, and then convincing the operators of the cafeteria and dining room for House staff to integrate those facilities so that Terry could eat her lunch with other congressional secretaries.

During her three terms in Congress, however, Douglas was unable to convince fellow members of Congress to enact into law the many bills she introduced. Still, labor lobbyists and liberal journalists valued her willingness to address their issues directly. Her wide-ranging legislative agenda included advocating for the Equal Pay and Equal Status bills for women (both of which died in committee), disabled veterans' rights, public

Helen Gahagan Douglas addressing the World Youth Rally in New York City,
March 21, 1945.

Library of Congress, Prints and Photographs Division, [reproduction number, LC-USZ62-
111664].

kindergartens, and migratory workers' rights. She also pressed for legislation to end employment discrimination based on race or religion, and to
stop lynching.[2]

In 1950, she ran for the Senate against Richard Nixon and was defeated
after a negative campaign in which Nixon characterized her as "pink right
down to her underwear."[3] In the Cold War context of that campaign, the
expression accused Douglas of being dangerously soft on communism
and implicitly invited voters to discount her through the latently obscene
metonymy. Douglas, though, commented that she never felt she "was
treated differently because of my sex.... Even Richard Nixon did not say I
was a lightweight because of my sex."[4]

After losing the Senate race, Douglas concentrated on family concerns,
but grew more and more convinced of the need for disarmament. Her
stance against the escalation of US involvement in Vietnam led to the
breakdown of her friendship with Lyndon Johnson. She refused to campaign for Hubert Humphrey in 1968, but, even after breast cancer surgery,
Douglas found it impossible not to campaign in 1972 for George McGov-

ern—who was campaigning for peace and against Nixon. As the Water-
gate scandal associated with that campaign gained momentum, Douglas's
schedule had taken on a new momentum of its own on behalf of the
Women's Liberation movement. *Ms.* magazine made her the subject of its
cover story in October 1973.

Although Douglas may be most often recalled as "the Pink Lady," she
should be remembered more for the liberal idealism voiced in her
speeches as a member of Congress. The speech featured here, "My Democratic Credo," was delivered on March 29, 1946. Douglas wrote it in
response to an incident on the House floor that brought her into conflict
with John Rankin, a Congressman from Mississippi. One writer labeled
Rankin "a segregationist and noted anti-Semite" who, in 1947, "called for
a purging of Communists in the film industry" thereby giving impetus to
actions that led to episodes such as the legal battles involving the so-called
Hollywood Ten.[5]

One day, during a House debate, Douglas noticed Rankin gesturing in
the direction of where she was sitting with other liberal Democrats and
referring to them as "these communists." She stood and objected, saying,
"I demand to know if the gentlemen from Mississippi is addressing me."
Eventually, Speaker Sam Rayburn compelled Rankin to respond and he
said, "I am not addressing the gentlewoman from California." In spite of
Rankin's denial, Rayburn granted Douglas permission to "set the record
straight on [her] commitment to democracy." "My Democratic Credo"
constituted her response.[6] Throughout the speech, Douglas depicted herself as a patriotic (and admittedly privileged) American who believed in
free enterprise. She argued that neither she nor most other Americans
would ever trade democracy for communism if democracy "fulfill[ed] its
promise." However, she also warned her audience: "[T]o attack each new
development in the progress of American Democracy as communism is to
dig the grave of government of the people, by the people, for the people."
Incidentally, if the "voice" seems to change abruptly in the final paragraph, it is because that paragraph was evidently written by Lyndon Johnson. Douglas and Lorena Hickok were editing the speech when Johnson
dropped by and decided to help them. Douglas explained that Johnson
"thought the speech needed more flourish at the end and proceeded to
write my final paragraph. I thought his language a little picturesque but I
accepted it rather than spurn the gift."[7]

NOTES

1. Helen Gahagan Douglas, *A Full Life* (Garden City: Doubleday, 1982).

2. Ingrid Winther Scobie, *Center Stage: Helen Gahagan Douglas, A Life* (New
Brunswick: Rutgers University Press, 1992) 169; also Jane Blankenship, "Helen
Gahagan Douglas," *Women Public Speakers in the United States, 1925–1993* (West-
port: Greenwood, 1994) 207–220.

3. Dan Rather and Paul Gates. *The Palace Guard* (New York: Harper & Row, 1974) 114.

4. Douglas, 329.

5. Greg Mitchell, *Tricky Dick and the Pink Lady* (New York: Random House, 1998), 60.

6. Douglas, *A Full Life,* 329.

7. Ibid., 230–231.

MY DEMOCRATIC CREDO
U.S. CONGRESS, HOUSE OF REPRESENTATIVES
(MARCH 29, 1946)[1]

Mrs. DOUGLAS of California. Mr. Speaker, I think we all know that communism is no real threat to the democratic institutions of our country.

But the irresponsible way the term "communism" is used to falsely label the things the majority of us believe in can be very dangerous.

I do not think communism in Russia need prevent international cooperation in building the peace, any more than it prevented international cooperation in winning the war.

I know that the road ahead is not without difficulty or without its vexing problems, but, if we could solve all the difficulties and the problems that arose during the war, surely we can solve them in peace.

We solved them in war because we had to. If we had not, we would all now be slaves of the Axis Nations.

We will solve them in peace if we fully realize the grim fact that if we do not, civilization has run its course.

We have reached a point where war can no longer be the final recourse. We have reached a point where we either grow up or blow up.

If it is blow up, the issues over which we struggle today are meaningless. I have asked to talk about communism. But I am also going to talk about democracy—democracy, which I strive daily to live—democracy which is the only form of society in which I believe—the principles of which were fed to me with my first spoon of cereal—democracy which my forefathers helped establish on this great continent.

I shall talk about democracy because it is democracy that we believe in and live by—or should live by. We are interested in communism as a system that challenges democracy. I am not afraid of that challenge.

I do not think we value democracy highly enough. The great mass of the American people will never exchange democracy for communism as long as democracy fulfills its promise. The best way to keep communism out of our country is to keep democracy in it—to keep constantly before our eyes and minds the achievements and the goals which we, a free people, have accomplished and intend to accomplish in the future under our own democratic system.

I am jealous for democracy. I do not like to see the things that democracy can accomplish credited to communism. Through the years democracy has given the people of the United States more freedom and a higher standard of living than any system that we know—and it has done so with less inequity, less persecution, less infringement on the rights of free thinking speech, and free action than under any other form of government anywhere in the world. I do not want the things that democracy has done ascribed to anything other than the democratic process.

I am jealous for the school system we have built under democracy, and I do not want its extension, including fair salaries for teachers, day nurseries, school-lunch programs, and Federal aid to education, called communism.

I am jealous for the reputation of our democratic institutions to achieve a high level of employment, and I do not want to see measures for increasing that employment attributed to communism.

I am jealous for my belief, and the belief of millions of other Americans, that in our democracy the Government is the servant of the people, and that, as the servant of the people, it will protect the people—all of us, Protestant, Catholic, Jew, or gentile: black, white, or yellow. I do not like to have that belief, the very cornerstone of our greatness, disavowed and called communistic.

I am jealous for that greatest of all our institutions, the American home. I pay my disrespect to those short-sighted individuals who called our housing program for our returning service men and women, the program which would have helped millions of them start their homes, communistic.

I believe now, and I shall always believe, that this Government of the people is capable of self-growth, is capable of making whatever adjustments are needed in a world that has changed so greatly since the days when my grandfather, the Reverend William Harrison Gahagan, helped found Dayton, Ohio.

I do not claim that democracy, as we know it, is perfect, but I know that it has the capacity to remedy its own imperfections, and I do not want to hear each remedy called communism.

I have a respect that amounts to reverence for our kind of Government and for this body of which I am privileged to be a Member.

As a child, the Congress of the United States was to me the symbol of freedom. It was the embodiment of all the great phrases and words that I had heard spoken in my home and at school, words I memorized in my heart and mind.

"Sweet land of liberty," "We, the people of the United States," "One Nation, indivisible, with liberty and justice for all," "A Government of the people, by the people, for the people," "the land of the free and the home of the brave," "From every mountainside let freedom ring!"

As a very little girl I stood holding my father's hand and looked upon the Members of this body. In my childish way I thought to myself how wonderful to be a Member of the Congress of the United States—to speak for the people—to be a part of the people's government.

In the years that followed, I, as many other Members of this House, earned in a few weeks what we are paid here in a year. But the privilege and satisfaction of becoming a Member of this House are greater than any I ever enjoyed outside. For I still feel now, as I felt as a child, that the confidence of people in their Representatives whom they have freely chosen, is in itself the greatest reward—and cannot be measured by any material standards.

That confidence demands that we give to our role our hearts, our minds, the whole of our talents. It is here, so long as we are permitted to serve as Members of this House, that the greatest of all possible rewards is found. For the greatest of all possible trust has been given to us, a trust to protect the liberties of the people and fulfill their hopes.

This is the role, as a representative of the people, which I cherish above all I have ever held, or could ever dream of holding.

It is as a representative of the people, a democratic people, who believe in the principles and future of democracy—that I now speak about communism.

There is no word in the world today more misused or misunderstood. I, for one, would not pretend to give a final definition of the word.

I have no special contribution to make on the subject. I am not a student of communism. I have not been to Russia.

That, however, does not mean that I have not thought about communism and tried to understand it and take an objective view toward it. One of the most important things today is for the American people to try to understand the Russian people and the Russian people to understand us.

I think we do a disservice to democracy when we dismiss communism as the devil's handiwork. Of course, there is competition between democracy and communism in the world today.

There is no doubt in my mind that the result will continue to be the triumph of democracy in the world if we spend our energy and genius in demonstrating to the world what democracy can do.

One-sixth of the globe today, an area as large as the United States, India and China combined, is inhabited by people who are living under a form of state socialism known as communism.

Primarily as a result of geographic isolation, these people since the Middle Ages have lived under the cruelest, most barbaric autocracy in world history. Under the czars, the nobility held huge estates. There was a relatively small trading class, and working class of artisans. In 1917, when the revolution began, there were only 10,000,000 industrial workers in the whole country. There were many more millions of peasants who worked the land with the most primitive tools and methods; mentally and physically debased, almost to the level of animals, and who until less than a hundred years ago were bought and sold like the animals on the land of the big estates on which they lived and worked.

When Lenin with the philosophy of Marx and Engels arrived in Petrograd in the midst of a revolt against the czars and the war, there was small wonder that the Russian people followed him who promised bread and freedom.

In other words, communism was born out of hunger, slavery, illiteracy, superstition, degradation.

But, communism has no place in our society. We have something better. We have democracy. Communist methods are foreign to ours. Their policies are superimposed from the top and you take it from the top whether you like it or not.

Under our democratic system, programs are proposed from many sources in the community. A candidate running for office stands for a certain program, and the people elect him or reject him on the basis of that program. In other words, the people themselves select or reject what is good for them. We do not believe that one man or a group of men can save the people. We believe that the people save themselves.

The Soviets have never developed certain rights which to us are fundamental—the civil rights we cherish, the political rights we so boisterously and vigorously enjoy. They have sacrificed the competitive free-enterprise system we believe in.

Since the war, I think we must all admit that some good things have been accomplished under communism for the Russian people.

But, communism is the receiver which takes over when bankruptcy takes place.

It is our job not only to see that bankruptcy never takes place here, but that through democratic processes the welfare and security of the people which are what make a society solvent increase day by day.

The fear of communism in this country is not rational. And that irrational fear of communism is being deliberately used in many quarters to blind us to our real problems. The spreading of this fear is in fact propaganda for communism.

I am nauseated and sick to death of the vicious and deliberate way the word Communist has been forged into a weapon and used against those who organize and raise their voices in defense of democratic ideals—of hearing the very program initiated by Franklin Roosevelt and which the majority of American people voted for in four successive national elections and to which President Truman has dedicated himself in his twenty-one point program called Communistic by those who seek to defeat the majority will of the American people.

Communism could successfully invade only a weakened democracy. A vigorous democracy—a democracy in which there are freedom from want, freedom from fear, freedom of religion and freedom of speech—would never succumb to communism or any other ism.

Our fight is not against the windmill of communism in America. Rather it is against those who would make a treadmill of democracy through special privilege, bigotry, and intolerance.

Those who serve democracy and the future of democracy best are those who believe that full employment and fair employment practices can be achieved under our free enterprise system and who fight for full employment and fair employment practices through the democratic process.

It is up to us, the people, to show that we can have full employment and full production and freedom at the same time. That is a test democracy faces.

Nobody believes in free enterprise or its future more than I do. I have had all the benefits of this free enterprise system. I was bred in a family that handed down its business from father to son, a family that believed and believes today that individual initiative is the source of our economic vitality. I have every advantage and every opportunity that a child born into that kind of family would have.

It is because I know what education and opportunity and the respect of the community mean in the development of human beings that I fight for them for everyone.

I have never been in a breadline. I have never had to live on a ditch bank. I am not one of the millions who have never known a doctor's care.

I was not one of those 200,000 women a year who gave birth to their children without medical attention. I do not belong to a minority—at least I think the Irish are not considered a minority in America any more.

But I have been in the slums of America. I have been to the ditch bank and have seen the people who came out of the cities because there was no place for them there. I have seen the people who were blown off, tractored off, or, because of lack of markets, were pushed off the land.

I have seen their miserable cars with all their worldly belongings strapped to them wending their weary way through State after State, millions in all, hunting for a job, hunting for somewhere beside the road to lay their heads.

I have seen shanty towns where the dust blinded and choked—where there was no water to relieve the thirst—no water to wash sick children, or when it rained rivers ran through the tents or the improvised shanties.

I have seen the children with sore eyes and swollen bellies. I have looked deep into the despairing eyes of fathers and mothers without jobs—or hope of jobs. I have seen minorities humiliated and denied full citizenship. And I tell you that we betray the basic principle upon which this Government of free people was founded unless this Government of the people finds a way by which all the people can live out their lives in dignity and decency.

Yes; I believe in free enterprise. I believe in it so much that the whole object of my participation in government as a representative of the people is to make it free, free for everybody.

It is a good thing to own your own business, to own your own farm. The problem that confronts this Congress is that not enough people own their own businesses and own their own farms. The test again and again is whether we side with the great monopolies or with the people. The great monopolies are suffocating free enterprise and, if not halted in their growth, will in the end destroy not only their own dynasties but democracy itself.

Only 10,000 persons own one-quarter and 75,000 persons own one-half of all the corporate stock in this country. Only 61,000 persons out of 130,000,000 collect half the dividends.

The war Franklin D. Roosevelt talked about in 1936 is still going on. It is, as he said, "a war for the survival of democracy," and the battle should not rage around the bogus issue of communism but around the real issue of monopoly and the exploitation of the people and their resources.

Monopolies did not build America. It was not monopoly that built our great industrial economy. It was competitive enterprises which later were too often strangled by the forces of monopoly. Typically, our plants, factories, mines, and mills, were built by enterprising businessmen, creating income for their respective communities. But after the facility was built, too often it was taken over by the large combine, the Wall Street group.

Not only did monopoly fail to contribute materially to the development of our industrial structure, it actually promoted illegal price fixing and the restriction of production, which resulted in underconsumption and under-employment.

Monopoly, through cartels, contributed seriously to our industrial unpreparedness for war by restricting the production and distribution of such vital materials as magnesium, synthetic rubber, aviation gasoline, and electrical equipment and many other products.

Monopoly deeply affects the spiritual and economic lives of those who live in communities which it dominates.

In a study prepared by the Smaller War Plants Corporation and printed as Senate Document 165, a comparison was made of the levels of civic welfare in what were termed "big business" as against "small business" cities. It was found that in the big-business cities—those in which most of the working population was employed by a few large plants or absentee-owned corporations—the level of civic welfare was lower than in small-business cities—those in which most of the workers were employed in many small, locally-owned businesses.

It was found that the chance that a baby would die within one year after birth was considerably greater in big- than small-business cities.

Slums were more prevalent in the big business cities.

The "big-business" cities had less home ownership; they spent less per capita on health, on public recreation, and on public libraries; and they had a lower degree of church membership than did comparable "small business" cities of the same size located in the same area, possessing the same type of population.

These are only a few manifestations of the lower level of civil welfare which were found to prevail in the "big business" cities.

The alternative to this concentration is its very opposite—more privately owned business, more employers competing for the respect of the community, more participation in ownership.

Democracy cannot long survive when the people permit their lives to be dominated—economically or politically—by a powerful few.

We must make democracy work. We must realize the greatness that is in America. We are proud of our past and proudest because of what we can build upon that past. We do not want to turn our eyes backward and to keep the dead hand of the past upon our growth. And above all we want to shake off the deadening hand of monopoly.

We must reverse the trend to monopoly. We must enlarge the opportunities for all, with our magnificent capacities for production and distribution. It is in this atmosphere of hope and freedom that we became great and shall go forward to new leadership in the world. It is in this setting that we can undertake to provide new security and well-being for all our people, rather than much for the few and little for the many.

To make democracy work, we must recognize its real enemies. And one of the most dangerous of its enemies is intolerance born of fear and loss of faith in America.

Intolerance which poisons the sweet air of liberty.

I do not agree with everything that is said. But I will fight with the last ounce of my strength for the right of people to say what they will.

One of the great privileges of democracy is the privilege to make mistakes—the privilege to say foolish things, the privilege to expound ideas with which others violently disagree, the privilege to say them without being tracked down and labeled as subversive, the privilege to criticize our Representatives mercilessly, whoever they may be, and, next to the secret ballot, the greatest privileges of all are the right to organize and defeat or elect candidates to public office. The whole history of American politics is the history of vigorous and often violent disagreements.

We believe and we have shown by experience that we can afford these luxuries—these luxuries which are a necessity of democracy—because in a people's government balance is found and kept in the final voice of the majority; the majority which at all times defends the minority. There is no danger in letting people have their say. We have proved that. There is only danger when you try to stop them from saying it.

This, the most powerful nation on earth, stands today as irrefutable proof that there is no danger in a conglomeration of peoples and ideas freely expressed. In fact, out of the very conglomeration a rich harvest, which is the growth of America, has been reaped.

There is danger in the hysteria that always follows war. That danger is suspicion—suspicion that breeds in ignorance, thrives on bigotry, reaches epidemic proportions on hysteria.

Tom Paine said:

Suspicion is the companion of mean souls and the bane of all good society.

This is true at home and abroad, as true in 1946 as it was in 1776. And former Secretary of State and War Henry L. Stimson wrote a few days ago:

The chief lesson I have learned in a long life is that the only way to make a man trustworthy is to trust him; and the surest way to make him untrustworthy is to distrust him and show your distrust.

Mr. Stimson said this in reference to the atomic bomb and our international relations, but what is true of international relations is also true here at home.

We, the Members of this body, will fail in our duty if we permit suspicion of another's purpose to divert us from our own purpose—that of making democracy function at full efficiency for our own people.

To be sure, there are Communists in America. There are a few people in America who believe the free enterprise system has run its course. As I have made clear, here today, I share no such belief. But to attack each new development in the progress of American Democracy as communism is to dig the grave of government of the people, by the people, for the people.

If we succeed in the practice of democracy, communism will never take over, as some faint-hearted but loud-mouthed have proclaimed.

We cannot fail if we carry forward into the future the principles which have made America great.

Mr. Speaker, this body must always be loyal to the principles of its founders and the teachings of its fathers.

It must never yield to the tyranny of bigotry.

It must never succumb to the rantings of the demagog.

It must always be the forum where justice is dispensed and intolerance is despised.

It must be the protector of free speech and the guardian of free worship.

It must never become an arena where class is arrayed against class—where race hatreds are bred and suspicions nourished.

We, the Members of this Congress—chosen by a free people to protect their rights and to bring reality to their hopes and faiths—are not bigots. We do not believe in name calling. We do not agree that everyone who disagrees with us should be hunted down like a criminal, denied his civil rights, and deprived of his ability to earn a living.

We, the Members of this House, do not believe that Capitol Hill is a hill on which to kindle a fiery cross but rather one on which to display the shining cross which since Calvary has been to all the world the symbol of the brotherhood of man.

NOTE

1. *Congressional Record*, 79th Cong., 2nd sess., 1946, 92, pt. 3.

Mary Church Terrell

In the next speech, Mary Church Terrell, now in her eighties, championed the Equal Rights Amendment (ERA) before the House Judiciary Committee (see Part I). Terrell, already a leading activist and prolific writer when the ERA was first introduced in Congress in 1923, had witnessed its decades-long neglect. Though the ERA was reintroduced in every session of Congress between 1923 and 1948, co-sponsored by one person in the House and one in the Senate, it had failed to gain widespread popular support or congressional approval. In the wake of World War II, it received yet another hearing. Terrell, who by this time, had given hundreds, if not thousands of public speeches, pulled no punches. As was her style, she used a somewhat deceiving eloquent tone as she chided the Committee members and demanded that they listen to their conscience in "the name of justice" and pass the amendment. Her effort, while not wholly successful, did help push the measure forward. In 1946, just two years prior to this speech, the ERA was narrowly defeated by the full Senate but in 1950, the Senate passed it, though unfortunately with a rider that nullified its equal protection aspects.[1]

In her testimony, Terrell did not address race explicitly, but she did argue that the ERA would alleviate some of the most pressing difficulties faced by African American women in postwar America. First, she asserted that women had little choice but to work, and without the ERA they faced severe wage inequities and workplace discrimination. In postwar American society, Terrell suggested, women could no longer depend on stable, financial male support (due to death and desertion). And second, women needed the ERA to fight the daily humiliations and injustices (political and personal) they encountered. Short and to the point, Terrell displayed her signature command of the language and her skillful ability to explicate the real issues at stake.

NOTE

1. See "Chronology of the Equal Rights Amendment," National Organization for Women [web site] May 27, 2003 (www.now.org/issues/economic/cea/history.html).

TESTIMONY BEFORE THE HOUSE JUDICIARY COMMITTEE ON THE EQUAL RIGHTS AMENDMENT (MARCH 10, 1948)[1]

...I am now appealing to each and every member of the House Judiciary Committee to take the time and the pains to consider carefully the many strong reasons why the Equal Rights Amendment deserves his support. It would be an unwarranted reflection upon the integrity and sense of justice of those Congressmen who have opposed it in the past to accuse them of deliberately and willfully withholding for a group of loyal citizens, simply because they happen to be women, that equality of right which is necessary to enable them to earn a living or in some cases to make a brilliant record for themselves along certain lines of human endeavor and at the same time to make valuable contributions to their country which it is now deprived.

I am sure the members of the House Judiciary Committee who have opposed the Equal Rights Amendment have not taken that stand simply because they want to be unjust or unkind to women, but because they have failed to realize that, owing to the conditions under which they are living today, it is absolutely necessary for women to secure the rights for which they are asking so that they will no longer be the victims of the cruel injustice which will continue to humiliate, handicap and harass them in the future as it has done for so many years in the past.

Many years ago it was customary for men in all walks of life to support their families...But today conditions are entirely changed. Today thousands of women are obliged to support themselves and their families...Today women sorely need the kind of help to discharge their duties and obligations to their families which the Equal Rights Amendment could so easily afford. It is hard to believe that the men in this country who have it in their power to deal justly in this particular will refuse any longer to enact this legislation which will redress a wrong and lighten the burdens which thousands of women now unnecessarily bear. As unbelievable as it may appear, it has actually come to pass that the Equal Rights provision in the Constitution of Japan enacted a few years ago, enables the Japanese women to enjoy advantages and opportunities which are denied the women of the United States.

Finally, Gentlemen of the Judiciary Committee, when you consider the Equal Rights Amendment this new year, I appeal to you in the name of Justice to make a favorable report.

NOTE

Typescript with handwritten revisions. Mary Church Terrell Papers, Manuscript Division, Library of Congress, Washington, DC.

Emily Greene Balch (1867–1961)

Emily Greene Balch was the second female U.S. citizen to be awarded the Nobel Peace Prize. Born on January 8, 1867, in Jamaica Plain, Massachusetts, to a prosperous family, she attended private schools for girls and went on to graduate with the first class of Bryn Mawr College in Pennsylvania. Bryn Mawr awarded her a fellowship for a year of postgraduate European study that took her to Paris to study public assistance in France. She also studied at the Harvard Annex (later Radcliffe College), the University of Chicago, and in Berlin.

There were essentially three phases to her career: settlement worker, professor of economics, and peace activist. Balch helped found and became first head worker at Denison House, a settlement house near Boston in the 1890s. During this time she joined the American Federation of Labor (AFL) and helped establish the Women's Trade Union League (WTUL). She had a twenty-one-year career on the faculty at Wellesley College before her peace work led to nonrenewal of her appointment by the trustees. Even after losing her faculty position, however, she continued to work for peace and, in 1946, she received the Nobel Peace Prize.

In several ways Balch's career parallels that of Jane Addams, whom she first encountered when Addams gave a lecture in Plymouth, Massachusetts, in 1892; whom she succeeded in the leadership of the Women's International League for Peace and Freedom (WILPF); and whom she followed in becoming a Nobel Laureate. Both women opposed our entry into World War I and were among the US women who sailed, in 1915, to the International Woman's Congress at The Hague.

As a delegate to the Congress at The Hague, and afterward as a delegate from that Congress to Scandinavia and Russia, Balch worked to end

World War I. Later, she campaigned against U.S. entry into the war.[1] The press condemned her antiwar activism. At least one editorial referred to her as "Emily Greene Balch of Wellesley College," asserting that she and fellow pacifists were "doing the work of sedition and treachery to the law of the land and the country whose citizenship they abuse."[2] Balch was on sabbatical at the time, but rather than further embarrassing Wellesley by returning to the college at the end of her sabbatical, she asked for and received an additional year's leave without pay. At the end of that year, the trustees decided not to renew her contract.

The coming of World War II created a crisis of conscience for Balch, by then a Quaker. In that era, a number of WILPF associates and Jewish friends suffered (and some died) in concentration camps or otherwise as a result of the war.[3] For a time, Balch's emphasis was on freedom without abandoning strategies for constructing a permanent peace. She ultimately supported the US war effort against Hitler. After the war, her efforts on behalf of peace and freedom continued. In 1956, frail and no longer able to afford her home in Wellesley, she moved to a nursing home in Cambridge. Still, she continued her work almost until the day she died, January 9, 1961, at age ninety-four.[4]

Part II of Balch's Nobel Address, "Toward Human Unity or Beyond Nationalism," follows. She was, by 1946, a fragile octogenarian but her perspective was optimistic, forward looking, and fresh. Balch's speech was a learned, carefully detailed, but youthful-sounding interpretation of the potential for human societies to evolve toward peace. In Part I of the address, Balch expressed the belief that humans are active agents who "need not only to study" events, "but to act." She also concluded that both the "unifying" and "divisive trends" she perceived in the world during the years directly following World War II were required for constructing a peaceful, harmonious world community.[5]

In Part II of the address, she employed imagery and devices from biology, economics, literature, and metaphysics. She cited concrete historical and contemporary examples to illustrate her contentions and gave credit for positive human action to individuals by name (printed in all capital letters in both manuscripts of the speech used for reference). Near the beginning of Part II, Balch compared temporally and spatially divergent contributions toward the goal of world peace to "springs" of groundwater and then delineated, as in a classroom lecture, two kinds of peace work, individual and collective. Next, she discussed possible forms of international organization that would differ from government. She associated government with armies and navies, policing and taxing subjects; but she expressed hope that new forms of functional organizing would emerge, involving "contact, consultation, cooperation." In the course of her remarks, she made several innovative proposals, including, "securing the general adoption of a universal auxiliary language." She also recommended international administration of aviation, atomic power, global waterways, and polar regions. Near the end of the address, Balch shared her vision that a "world community" developing in peace would "open up great untapped reservoirs in human nature," thus connecting her opening description of "many springs" to an image of potential confluence.

NOTES

1. Mercedes M. Randall, *Improper Bostonian: Emily Greene Balch* (New York: Twayne, 1964), 234–235; Lynne Derbyshire, "Emily Greene Balch," in *Women Public Speakers in the United States, 1925–1993*, Karlyn Kohrs Campbell, ed. (Westport, CT: Greenwood Press, 1994), 29.

2. *New York Evening Sun*, May 31, 1917:2, in Derbyshire, "Emily Greene Balch," 29–30.

3. Randall, *Improper Bostonian*, 410.

4. For example, she wrote "greetings" to the executive committee of WILPF in her 85th year and open letters "To the Chinese People" and "To the Jewish Women of Palestine." The first is reprinted in *Beyond Nationalism: The Social Thought of Emily Greene Balch*, Mercedes Randall, ed. (New York: Twayne, 1972), 156–157. The two open letters are reprinted in Randall, *Improper Bostonian*, 433–435.

5. Balch, *Toward Human Unity or Beyond Nationalism* (Stockholm: Kungl. Boktryckeriet P.A. Norstedt & Soner, 1949), 250, 252–257.

TOWARD HUMAN UNITY OR BEYOND NATIONALISM (SECOND PART) NOBEL LECTURE, OSLO (APRIL 7, 1948)[1]

Reprinted by Permission of Swarthmore College

The peace movement or the movement to end war has been fed by many springs and has taken many forms. It has been carried on mainly by private unofficial organizations, local, national and international. I would say that peace workers or pacifists have dealt mainly with two types of issue, the moral or individual, and the political or institutional.

As a type of the former we may take those who are generally known specifically as pacifists. Largely on religious or ethical grounds they repudiate violence and strive to put friendly and constructive activity in its place.

There has been personal refusal of war service on grounds of conscience on a large scale and at great personal cost by thousands of young men called up for military service. While many people fail to understand and certainly do not approve their position, I believe that it has been an invaluable witness to the supremacy of conscience over all other considerations and a very great service to a public too much affected by the conception that might makes right. It is interesting that at the Nuremberg war-guilt trials the court refused to accept the principle that a man is absolved from responsibility for an act by the fact that it was ordered by his superiors or his government.

This is a legal affirmation of a principle that conscientious objectors maintain in action.

It is to me surprising that the repudiation of the entire theory and practice of conscription has not found expression in a wider and more powerful movement drawing strength from the widespread concern for individual liberty. We are horrified at many slighter infringements of personal freedom far less terrible than this. But we are so accustomed to conscription that we take it for granted. A practical and political form of opposition to conscription is the proposal, first put forward, as far as I know, by an American woman, DOROTHY DETZER, long secretary of the United States Section of the Women's International League for Peace and Freedom. She urged something that suggests the Kellogg Pact but is quite specific, namely a multilateral treaty between governments to renounce the use of conscription. A bill to this effect is now in the United States Congress but attracts little attention.

I feel it rather surprising also that the refusal of war has never taken the form, on any large scale, of refusal to pay taxes for military use, a refusal which would have involved not only young men but (and mainly) older men and women holders of property.

Peace work of this first type depends mainly on education. The work done and now being done to educate men's minds against war and for peace is colossal and can only be referred to.

Perhaps it is under this head that the Nobel Foundation and the work of BERTHA VON SUTTNER should be listed, for this the world, and not alone the beneficiaries, must be grateful.

The other type of "peace" activity is political, specifically aiming to affect governmental or other action on concrete issues. For instance, peace organizations criticized the terms of the Peace Treaties made at Versailles and (in America at least) opposed the demand for unconditional surrender in the Second World War.

The Women's International League for Peace and Freedom (with which I have long been connected) has worked both as an international body and in its national sections from 1915 till now and I trust will long do so, in the political field of policies affecting peace, though not alone on the political level. Among its strongest supporters have always been Scandinavian women. I am presenting to the Nobel library, if I may, a brief history of this organization, "A Venture in Internationalism," a pamphlet now out of print and consequently rare.

The form of work for peace which has most obviously made history is the long continued effort to create some world organization which should both prevent wars and foster international co-operation.

The efforts to secure peace by creating a comprehensive organ have been many and varied. One of the most curious was the confederation of certain tribes of Iroquois Indians in America known as "the Six Nations." One of the earliest was the ancient Amphictyonic Council in Greece. There has been a long series of schemes, each more or less premature and Utopian, but each making its own contribution, from those of SULLY and WILLIAM PENN and KANT to WOODROW WILSON and his co-workers and successors. WILSON did not live to see the League of Nations established nor did his own country even join it. At present there is a tendency to underrate its importance. I, for one, would not for a great deal lose out of my life my years in Geneva during the first spring-time of the hopes and activities of the League of Nations.

As we know only too well, the League of Nations, lacking Russia and the United States, was not sufficiently inclusive. And when the pinch came, different governments proved unready to make the sacrifices or face the risks involved in effective opposition to imperialism in Japan, reaction in Spain, fascism in Italy or nazism in Germany.

The new institution, the United Nations, has some marked advantages over its predecessors. Its origin was the work, not of a small group of salesmen preoccupied with elaborating the treaties of Versailles and the rest, but was worked out in careful preliminary discussion first at Dumbarton Oaks, then at San Francisco, by a comprehensive group of countries which included, this time, the United States and Russia, though not the Axis powers, and which owes a great debt to President FRANKIN ROOSEVELT. It has the experience of the League of Nations to draw upon and the second world war offers it useful warnings. With less of a flush of idealism, hopefulness and confidence than the League of Nations enjoyed in its early days, it is soberer and Norway has given it in TRYGVE LIE, a Secretary General who inspires confidence and hope.

On the other hand, it suffers from handicaps that the League of Nations did not. Most serious of all, unlike the League of Nations, it is called upon to begin its active life before the peace treaties are complete. Germany and Austria and Japan are still occupied. A war settlement is a problem that, as has been said, "evokes all the appetites." The world is not even technically at peace; an agreement has not yet been reached on the absolutely crucial question of Germany. The United Nations are moreover faced with the necessity for immediate decision and action on several peculiarly poignant and complicated problems in Greece, in Palestine, in Korea and elsewhere. Still more, it operates in a world half wrecked by the destruction of war on an unimagined scale. We are more or less used to famine in India and China (though I suppose it is as painful there as nearer home). Now we see Europe herself hungry, collectively and separately, covered with masses of broken rubble, charred timber and vast fields that carry white crosses instead of grain. Production and trade are so deeply affected that their reconstruction presents problems which would be almost insuperable even if they were not complicated by political difficulties. At the same time there is extraordinarily bitter ideological and nationalistic opposition between the Soviet Union with its friends, and the Western Democracies, so that two great powers, or bloc of powers, face one another in mutual suspicion and fear.

That the new world organization has done as well as it has under such circumstances is surprising. Indeed the fact that it has actually been set up and is actually functioning is, if you think about it, a miracle.

But its testing time is not yet passed. In the crucial matter of national disarmament and organization of collective security forces, either as constabulary or as military, it has made no obvious progress. In regard to the throat-gripping problem of effectively controlling the use of atomic energy it is stalled by what seem on the surface like trivial differences as to how to proceed. The still uglier menaces of bacteriological warfare and other abusive uses of scientific knowledge are not, so far as I know, ever under discussion.

This failure to equip itself with force has led to a widespread impatience, and one of the most striking recent developments in the peace field is a widespread and eager demand for actual world government. One must feel great interest in this growing movement. It is doing important service in educating people to the need of limiting national sovereignty—of sacrificing national self-will and national self-determination, as far as may be necessary, for the sake of the will and purpose of the all-inclusive human group.

But this movement has also its very real dangers. In so far as it leads to depreciation of the United Nations and to the growth of a certain cynicism in regard to it, it must be deplored. My hesitations go further than this, however. I see governments as a peculiar historical kind of organization which is not necessarily the last word in human wisdom. We have, I believe, yet much to learn, possibly from China, Russia, India and from the Montesquieus of the future as to possible political forms. Do not let us force our young and still plastic world organization prematurely into old and rigid molds.

Governments seem to have a bad inheritance behind them. They are dangerous because we personify them and idealize them and because they are tainted with lust for power and with much too great concern for prestige. Above all, they are the final depository of the power of physical coercion which is everywhere more and more discarded. What is a Government? It is what owns and operates armies and navies, and polices and taxes subjects. (As for taxes they are all right as long as they are for right objects and in right measure, and people in general, I suspect, are not taxed enough quite as often as too much.)

Sometimes what is meant by "world government" is a body modeled more or less closely on the Swiss or American pattern with its executive and legislative branches and its judiciary. Sometimes the idea is a much more modest one and what is proposed is merely a delegation of strictly limited powers to a central authority with especial view to the control of aggression and the prevention of war. There is what seems to me a rather naïve hope that the dangerous possibility of having to discipline a nation which refuses to abide by international legislation can be circumvented by directing coercive action against individuals not governments. In 1939 what individual would have been singled out for discipline if not Hitler? And would an attempt to discipline Hitler not have meant fighting a great people in arms?

I admit the critical importance of organizing collective security against violence and aggression, and certainly a highly important function of the United Nations, as of the League of Nations, is to prevent situations out of which "shooting wars" develop, and finally, to control by collective action aggression by the ill disposed or wrongly led. Up to date no adequate solution has been achieved. Conceivably possible, conceivably adequate and effective are non-military controls, moral pressure, collective political pressure, collective economic pressure through so-called economic sanctions of many kinds and, finally, organized police methods and armed constabulary forces of a non-military type. Yet such methods are apparently being little studied.

Disarmament, so fundamental to a really peaceful world, certainly does not look near or even nearer than it was.

Yet, important as are the methods of preventing aggression, curbing violence and creating collective security, which are the special field of the Security Council, I regret that there is not more vivid public interest in the other aspects of world organization, especially in the growth of world co-operation in different fields. This functional approach to world unity seems to hold very great promise. The organization of such co-operation comes not as an expression of a theory but as an answer to felt needs. It is the direction in which the United Nations is making growth spontaneously in response to the pressure of realities and the call to get together on common business that needs to be attended to. The list of the special commissions and other agencies already at work is long and is destined to be longer. Besides those in the field of security, there are those dealing with Labor, Trade, Civil Aviation, Communications, International Law, Banking and Money, Human Rights, the Status of Women, Food and Agriculture, Health, Control of Epidemics, Refugees and Displaced Persons, Education, Science and Culture (with innumerable subdivisions), Trusteeship, the enormous question of Population, Statistics and so on.

Thomas Carlyle used to talk of "organic filaments" and in the co-operative organs of the United Nations we seem to see the time-spirit weaving a web of the peoples and creating, we hope, an unbreakable fabric binding all together by the habit of common work for common ends.

The administrative aspect of the United Nations also seems to have great possibilities for development, and international administration is in this context one form of co-operation.

The administrative function of the United Nations is up to now chiefly exerted in the form of trusteeships. This idea of political trusteeship is one of the relatively rare inventions in the political field. It is curious that while inventions in the technical field, in the arts of dealing with matter, are so numerous and effective men are so relatively poor in inventions for dealing with one another. The Greeks gave us public assemblies, the British their representative parliaments and parliamentary government. Switzerland and the United States created federal patterns of government combining centralization with decentralization. But on the whole the list is a meager one and one of the latest, modern propaganda, is a sinister and portentous development of legitimate education of public opinion.

The conception of the public trustee, whether an individual or a body, may prove a fruitful political idea. In the United States hospitals, colleges, all sorts of undertakings for the public welfare are largely carried on by Boards of Trustees entrusted with their administration, and they have an honorable record of devotion to their trust. The same man who, trading in Wall Street, prides himself on his skill in making money conceives himself, when he finds himself trusted to carry on a public service, as a public servant, and devotes his ability no longer to making money for himself but to the welfare of the park, or the research foundation or to other matter with which he now identifies himself.

But colonies are not the only field of possible international administration. It is greatly to be deplored that aviation, so international by its very nature, has thus far developed along lines of private and competing business. It is a thousand pities that it evolved too early, or world organization too late, for it to grow up from the start as a common business of the peoples of the world. This would have had an enormous influence on the character of the war and on its control as well as on international intercourse. Atomic power likewise demands international administration, and it is at least recognized that this is so.

The world of waters, the international waterways of the globe, are as yet unpreempted. Until yesterday Britannia ruled the waves, and her place has not yet been taken up in that regard. Why should not the United Nations now create a supreme authority over both the "ocean seas" and the channels and canals, artificial and natural, which are of peculiar importance and create peculiar public problems.

To suggest but one instance, the internationalization of the Dardanelles under properly equipped world authority would take the poison out of one of the "hottest" spots on the political map.

The uninhabited Polar areas are another area that seems peculiarly fitted for international administration under the United Nations. They are now largely unappropriated and the claimants and rivalries there are continually getting more numerous and more clamorous.

It is to be hoped that at the next General Assembly some Government will get these two matters put on the agenda and ask to have two special commissions appointed to study the Polar and Maritime problems and make recommendations.

World organization of a functional and not at a governmental level is also beginning on the cultural level. If UNESCO has not yet fully found itself that is because the potentialities that lie before it in the field(s) of science, music, art, religion and education are so vast and as yet so undefined. Here what is wanted is not so much administration as contact, consultation, co-operation.

If UNESCO succeeds, as it well may, in securing the general adoption of a universal auxiliary language, such as the International Language Association is now engaged in selecting and elaborating, it will be the dawn of a new day in literature such as the world has hardly dreamed of. None of the natural languages will be tampered with, reformed, or cut down to a restrictive base. But all men who can read and write may command an idiom universally understood. This will not only be an enormous benefit in business, in travel and in all sorts of practical ways. Far more important will be its service in the world of ideas. Poets and the great writers will have open to them a reading public including not only all European and American peoples but the Chinese, the Arabs, the island peoples and the people of Africa, who may yet make a great contribution. Music and Mathematics already command a universal notation not yet available for the expression of thought. Such a public for the printed and spoken word, comparable to that for music, would give an immense impetus to world literature.

In such a world all war would be civil war and we must hope that it will grow increasingly inconceivable. It has already become capable of such unlimited destruction and such fearful possibilities of uncontrollable and little understood "chain reactions" of all sorts that it would seem that no one not literally insane could decide to start an atomic war.

I have spoken against fear as a basis for peace. What we ought to fear, especially we Americans, is not that someone may drop atomic bombs on us but that we may allow a world situation to develop in which ordinarily reasonable and humane men, acting as our representatives, may use such weapons in our name. We ought to be resolved beforehand that no provocation, no temptation shall induce us to resort to the last dreadful alternative of war.

May no young man ever again be faced with the choice between violating his conscience by co-operating in competitive mass-slaughter or separating himself from those who, endeavoring to serve liberty, democracy, humanity can find no better way than to conscript young men to kill.

As the world community develops in peace, it will open up great untapped reservoirs in human nature. Like a spring released from pressure would be the response of a generation of young men and women growing up in an atmosphere of friendliness and security, in a world demanding their service, offering them comradeship, calling to all adventurous and forward-seeking natures.

We are not asked to subscribe to any Utopia or to believe in a perfect world just around the corner. We are asked to be patient with necessarily slow and groping advance on the road forward, and to be ready for each step ahead as it becomes practicable. We are asked to equip ourselves with courage, hope, readiness for hard work, and to cherish large and generous ideals.

NOTE

1. Emily Greene Balch Papers, Swarthmore College Peace Collection, Swarthmore College, Swarthmore, PA.

Margaret Chase Smith
(1898–1995)

Margaret Chase Smith, Republican of Maine, was the first woman elected to both houses of Congress, and the first woman to seek the Republican Party's nomination for president.[1] Born and raised in a working-class family in Skowhegan, Maine, and unable to afford college, Chase became a full-time working woman in the midst of World War I, four years before American women were allowed to vote. In 1930 Chase married liberal Republican State Representative Clyde Smith, who was elected to the U.S. House of Representatives in 1936. Working as his congressional secretary and campaigning actively for his reelection, Margaret Chase Smith was her husband's clear choice to complete his unexpired term when he died suddenly in 1940. She proved to be an able and effective campaigner, winning three more terms for herself in the House of Representatives. Smith was a quiet but active Representative, cosponsor of the ERA (which she also cosponsored as a Senator), and prime mover behind Public Law 625, the Women's Armed Services Integration Act, which gave women equal status in the military.

In 1947 Smith announced her decision to run for the U.S. Senate, winning a big victory. During her first term, she received national attention for her Senate speech attacking the tactics of fellow Republican Senator, Joseph McCarthy. McCarthy set up his supporter Robert Jones to run against Smith in her second Senate campaign in 1954. Riding high on waves of national popularity, however, Smith confidently campaigned throughout Maine on her trademark slogan, "Don't Trade a Record for a Promise." When Edward R. Murrow patched together a "debate" between Jones and Smith based on excerpts from each of their campaign speeches for his television program *See It Now*, Jones didn't have a chance. *Time*

Margaret Chase Smith, 1947.
Margaret Chase Smith Library Center, Photographs—1947, number 1,277.

magazine reported the primary results on July 5, 1954, noting, "The election did prove what every county chairman in the State knew: Maggie Smith is one of the most formidable vote getters Maine ever saw, as well as one of the most valuable Senators now in Washington."[2]

Smith's second term began with a world tour to meet with various heads of state. Her interviews were televised about fifteen times on Murrow's program *See It Now*, from 1954 to 1955. Television appearances continued in 1956 when Smith and Eleanor Roosevelt became the first women to appear on NBC's interview program *Face the Nation*. In 1960 Smith ran for reelection against a female opponent Lucia Cormier, former schoolteacher and Democratic floor leader in the Maine legislature. This was the first time two women had run against each other for a Senate seat. Magazines enjoyed the novelty, but Cormier was no match for the chic, experienced, and powerful incumbent. Smith won again with a substantial majority.

Republicans lost the presidential race nationally, however. Unhappy with Kennedy's foreign policy, Smith announced on January 27, 1964, her decision to run for the Republican presidential nomination. Although she did not fare well overall (her name was on the ballot in only three primaries), Smith was nominated for President of the United States at the 1964 Republican convention. This demonstration of tribute to Senator Margaret Chase Smith of Maine marked the beginning of the end of her political career.

Smith won her Senate seat again in 1966 and was instrumental in securing passage of Title VII of the Civil Rights Act of 1964, which prohibits discrimination on the basis of sex. She was also ranking Republican on the Senate Armed Services Committee during the Vietnam War. In 1972, after winning another tough primary election, Smith lost her Senate seat, continuing her life of public service as a private citizen.

The speech that follows is Smith's 1949 speech to a national meeting of the Business and Professional Women (BPW), the organization that Smith credited for teaching her many important political and administrative skills. Smith was typically a careful but effective speaker; the significance of her achievement in winning a Senate seat and the role of the BPW in making this possible are apparent in her opening words. Her international focus and interest in securing world peace through the United Nations would become themes for the rest of her Senate career. In addition, her concern for education, health care, minimum wage, and working conditions, as well as the Equal Rights Amendment, were never expressed more clearly than in this January 1949 speech to the BPW.[3]

NOTES

1. Margaret Chase Smith, *Declaration of Conscience* (New York: Doubleday, 1972); Janann Sherman, *No Place for a Woman: A Life of Senator Margaret Chase Smith* (New Brunswick, NJ: Rutgers University Press, 2000); Janann Sherman, "'They Either Need These Women or They Do Not': Margaret Chase Smith and the Fight for Regular Status for Women in the Military," *The Journal of Military History* (January 1990): 47–78; Sandra J. Sarkela, "Margaret Chase Smith," in *Women Public Speakers in the United States, 1925–1993*, Karlyn Kohrs Campbell, ed. (Westport, CT: Greenwood Press, 1994), 90–107.

2. *Time*, July 5, 1954: 9.

3. The Margaret Chase Smith Library Center (MCSLC) in Skowhegan, Maine, houses the Senator's personal and professional papers. A published *Guide to the Archives, Margaret Chase Smith Library*, is available.

BUSINESS AND PROFESSIONAL WOMEN'S CLUBS
STATLER HOTEL—LUNCHEON (JANUARY 3, 1949)[1]

Reprinted by Permission of the Margaret Chase Smith Library Center

I shall preface my remarks with what all of you know—that this is a great day for me. To be completely honest with you, I must confess that I'm nervous, I'm walking on air, and I'm choked up a little with my heart in my throat. What is happening to me today has never happened to another woman or man. Rarely has a woman taken a seat in the Senate and I doubt if the hundreds of men Senators have been showered with the generous friendship and honor that you have given me today.

I'm naive enough to admit to you that I can hardly realize that I am not in a wonderful dream. But if that is lack of Sophistication, it is because I know now, and I shall always remember, that these unprecedented honors are granted to me not because I am Margaret Chase Smith, but rather because I am merely a symbol of those who have granted me these honors. Any one of you could be in my place today had you been fortunate enough to have the good breaks and fervently sacrificing friends that I have had.

And I am not a United States Senator today simply because I am a woman. I was not elected just because I am a woman. To the contrary, I was elected in spite of the fact that I am a woman. And that in itself was victory for all women, for it smashed the unwritten tradition that the Senate is no place for a woman. The point that so many miss is that women do not blindly support some candidate just because they are women, we are not headed for an Amazonian world—rather that no one should be barred from public office just because she is a woman.

Perhaps the greatest significance of my victory is the growing realization that ability and proved performance, rather than sex, are the best standards for political selection just as much as they are for any other kind of selection. I like to think that I am a symbol of this growing realization.

I have been repeatedly warned that while officially I will be the junior Senator from Maine—officially, I will be the Senator-at-large for women all over the nation. While my first duty is to the people of Maine, I will gladly accept the unofficial responsibility of being Senator-at-large for America's women to the extent that the women desire. This would mean that I should hold myself in readiness to be a voice of America's women on the Floor of the Senate and in committees.

But are there any subjects in which women have exclusive interests that might come before the United States Senate? If I were to guess on the subjects of greatest interest to women, I would say (1) world peace and (2) domestic security. But men are just as interested in these subjects as women—men and women are no different on this point.

Through national polls and the great national women's organizations, such as the Federation of Business and Professional Women's Clubs, the great majority of women have gone on record as being convinced that the United Nations is the only hope for peace. The pace of the United Nations has been far too slow to satisfy most of us. But the United Nations has been laboring under the great handicap of the uncompromising attitude and obstructionist tactics of one of the largest nations.

The potency of the United Nations has been challenged first by the earlier Dutch–Indonesian War and second by the Palestinian War. In these two instances, it did not fail as it issued cease fire orders which were obeyed. True the deep differences between the warring sides have not as yet been reconciled—but the important thing is that the United Nations stopped warfare. For that it must be given credit—for that there is justification in our continued hopes that the United Nations will, in time, accomplish its principal objective of preventing and stopping all war and establishing permanent world peace.

But again, the potency of the United Nations is threatened by renewed fighting of the Dutch–Indonesian war. Holland has defied the United Nations by starting what it calls "police action" in Java. Whether it is formally declared as an "police action," people have been killed by the use of arms. If the United Nations fails to stop this war, then its own future is threatened.

But the United Nations can do no more than its "Big Four" will do. That puts the question directly up to the United States as one of the "Big Four." The question is what can se [sic] do? Since it is farily [sic] clear that Holland has started this war, the question is then how can we make Holland stop the war. The most obvious way is to cut off Marshall Plan aid to Holland if our persuasion fails.

Some say that this would be fatal as it is reported that Holland has said that if we do this then she will start courting Russia. This is a counterthreat to break up the alliance of the western nations of Europe against the sperad [sic] of communism and for a common defense front. If we succumb to this counterthreat, then the United Nations might as well fold up. The basic loss will be in the fact that we are not willing to take the necessary steps to stop war in its incipiency—and if we are not willing to do that, let us remember that incipient, regional wars almost inevitably become full-fledged world wars.

This is one time that a woman, or women, can do something to prevent war and to make peace. Repeatedly, I have said that there should be more women in the United Nations organizations and our other international peace organizations. Repeatedly, I have pointed out that the most peaceful nations of the world are those nations in which women are given greater opportunity to participate in public affairs and the government.

But now my past expressed faith in the desire and ability of women to achieve peace is definitely on trial. Not here at home in America, but rather across the ocean in Holland. Because the ruler of Holland is a woman. The ruler of Holland is Queen Juliana. It is within her power—within the power of a woman to stop war, to order that her Dutch soldiers silence their guns, and to refer the controversy to the United Nations for peaceful settlement.

In my first act as a United States Senator, I am prompted by what I know is in the hearts of American women to call upon the Queen of Holland to exercise the power that is here to stop the Dutch–Indonesian fighting. Women of the world are on trial. Queen Juliana by her individual decision can prove to the world the will and the power of women for peace. Here is an unprecedented opportunity for women.

At home there are growing signs that we are approaching a buyers' market—and gradually easing away from a sellers' market. Supply is catching up with demand. But that is not the whole story. Buyers are looking more closely at prices. They are hesitating. They are watching for bargains. They seek more quality for less money. The luch [sic] days when anything sold at any price are over. Merchants now fear intensive buyers' strikes.

This means that we are at last beginning to curb inflation. And the country can thank the women mostly for this happy turn of events, for it is the women who do most of the consumer buying. They are bringing prices down to fairer levels. They are erasing black markets. They are doing these things themselves which Congress could not do, with or without price control. And yet some people still underestimate the power of American women.

But while we are beginning to solve the very core of our problem of domestic security in the curbing of inflation by consumer restraint rather than government controls, we don't want the curbing of inflation to nosedive into drastic deflation. One need not elaborate on what drastic deflation means or what it is like. One need only remember the depression of the early thirties to realize that we must avoid drastic deflation.

What the women of America want is the highest possible standard of living at the lowest possible cost for the greatest number of all Americans first—and then the rest of the world. They want homes—homes at prices that they can afford. Or they want apartments at lower rental charges—apartments where babies and dogs are not barred—apartments where they can live a healthy, normal American life rather than subject to restrictions that don't make for normal living.

What the women of America want are reasonable prices for good food. They want to be able to go to the neighborhood grocery store and buy enough food for a family meal without draining their pocketbooks.

What the women of America want is a respectful salary scale for the teachers who shape the lives of their children. They want school houses that aren't crowded school houses, that aren't firetraps. They want school lunches that give real nutrition to their children. In short, they want their children to have the best food possible, whether it be for the head in what they are taught or for the stomach in what they are fed.

These are not unreasonable demands. They are not unnecessary drains on the taxpayers. They are sound investments in the future of America. And after all, these are the desires of the taxpayers themselves for the bulk of our taxpayers are mothers and fathers.

And as the only woman United States Senator, I pledge myself in full support of these objectives of the women—not just because they are objectives of the women, but because they are objectives upon which we must lay the foundation of America's future.

I am proud to have been a member of the BPW for more than 26 years. The BPW is largely responsible for putting me in the Senate. My work in the BPW taught me the very touchstones of political success. BPW work taught

me to develop cooperation. As an inclusive, rather than exclusive, organization, the BPW offered me greater variety of personal contacts than other
groups. It taught me efficiency in committee work and officership. It taught
me how to give and take in the participation of debates and discussions, in
the development of powers of expression, and the growth of ideas.

I know of no organization that has as much to offer business and professional women as the BPW. I know of no organization that can provide better
training in cooperation, tact and efficiency. I know of no better way of
increasing one's chances of success than participation in the BPW.

And the BPW shows its loyalty to its members when it really counts. I
know, because the Maine Federation of the BPW was the only women's
organization to endorse my candidacy for the United States Senate. I shall
never forget what the BPW did for me in my hour of need—and how the
BPW stood out far above the crowd, and significantly before victory.

NOTE

1. Typescript. *Statements and Speeches*, Vol. 6, 37–40, Margaret Chase Smith
Library Center, Skowhegan, Maine.

Maida Springer-Kemp (1910–)

Maida Springer-Kemp, through labor union activism, battled prejudices based on race, class, and gender in the United States, and, through her work with labor and government leaders in Africa, actively participated in nation building abroad. She worked alongside A. Philip Randolph (President of the Brotherhood of Sleeping Car Porters), her mentor and friend, and twentieth-century labor and civil rights leader.

Although she was born in Panama, Maida was raised and educated and worked in the New York City area. Arriving in New York during the 1920s Harlem Renaissance, her mother became a follower of Marcus Garvey who was a leader in the Universal Negro Improvement Association (UNIA) and the back-to-Africa movement. She took her daughter along with her to meetings and marches. Maida attended a Catholic school, then a private boarding school in New Jersey. This was not a "hoity-toity" school, she later commented, but a coed, industrial training school for Americans of color.[1] Thus, she was prepared to be an educated member of the workforce. While in high school, she worked in her first job in a garment factory operating a pinking machine.

After high school Maida worked as a receptionist, then married Owen Springer in 1927. Her son, Eric, was born in 1929, just as the depression hit. The need for additional family income led her back to work in a garment factory. In 1933 she joined Local 22 of the International Ladies Garment Workers Union (ILGWU) because she believed working conditions were unfair and dangerous. Her work with the American trade union movement continued, first as a member of the executive board and education committee of Local 22, then as education director of Local 132. She ran unsuccessfully for the New York State Assembly on the American Labor Party ticket

Maida Springer-Kemp (far right) as a union official for International Packing House Workers, ca. 1952.

Library of Congress, Prints and Photographs Division, A. Philip Randolph papers, [reproduction number, LC-USZ-104209].

in 1942. Throughout this period, she felt privileged to have, in addition to "Brother Randolph," female role models such as Pauline Newman and Fannia Cohn from her own union, the ILGWU, who were, in Springer-Kemp's words, "rambunctious, tenacious women who made themselves heard."[2]

During World War II, Springer-Kemp was appointed to a War Price and Rationing Board of the Office of Price Administration. She traveled to Britain as the first black woman representing the American Federation of Labor (AFL) abroad to observe wartime working conditions. Her international work continued after the war through involvement with the trade union movement in several African countries that were also seeking political independence. This led to her presence in 1955 as one of five non-African observers, and the only woman, at the first International Confederation of Free Trade Unions (ICFTU) conference in Accra, Gold Coast (now Ghana). The trip also apparently led to the final break in her marriage. She and Owen Springer divorced in 1955.

She was a close friend of Pauli Murray, and encouraged Murray to run for office and travel to Africa. In 1965 Maida Springer married James Kemp, who, although they eventually separated, supported her activism and remained a close friend until his death. Springer-Kemp's work with trade unions, civil rights, and the women's movement continued throughout her life. She currently resides in Pittsburgh, Pennsylvania.[3]

The following 1949 speech delivered at Freedom House shows how Springer-Kemp's fundamental commitment to the trade union movement became integrated with the emerging American Civil Rights movement. She opened by making an interesting distinction between civil liberties, those broad rights "which are not to be restricted by government" such as freedom of speech; and civil rights, "the rights due from one citizen to another" such as "the right to a home, the right to a job." Her speech deals with the second of the two terms. Springer-Kemp noted that labor and minorities faced a parallel struggle for civil rights. After explaining that federal laws, while significant, were inadequate, she urged continued support for the trade union movement as the key to protection of individual civil rights. In particular, she described the important contributions of the ILGWU, "my union," observing that it "ranks first in its broad social philosophy." Springer-Kemp concluded the speech by asserting the critical importance of trade unions not only in protecting the civil rights of minorities, but also in helping "the union worker" become "a total citizen."

NOTES

1. Brigid O'Farrell and Joyce L. Kornbluh, "We Did Change Some Attitudes: Maida Springer-Kemp, International Ladies' Garment Workers Union," *Rocking the Boat: Union Women's Voices, 1915–1975* (New Brunswick, NJ: Rutgers University Press, 1996), 84–109.

2. Ibid., 99.

3. "History Note," Maida Springer Kemp Papers, Schlesinger Library, Harvard University, Cambridge, MA; *Pauli Murray, The Autobiography of a Black Activist, Feminist, Lawyer, Priest, and Poet* (Knoxville, TN: University of Tennessee Press, 1987).

CIVIL RIGHTS AND LIBERTIES
FREEDOM HOUSE (MARCH 4, 1949)[1]

Reprinted by Permission of the Schlesinger Library

Civil Rights and Liberties

The American People have taken pride in the belief that ours is a government of laws and not of man. In view of the current widespread interest in laws to protect civil rights, it might be helpful if we define our terms at the outset. Civil rights and civil liberties are often used interchangeably. As I understand the terms, 'civil liberties' include those broad liberties of the members of society which are inalienable and the heritage of free men, liberties which are not to be restricted by government so long as they do not infringe upon the rights of other members of society. When we speak of civil liberties we usually refer to freedom of speech, press, religion and assembly, and the right to petition one's government for the redress of grievances. Our concern here is with the protection of these liberties from *governmental* invasion.

On the other hand 'civil rights' are the rights due from one citizen to another, such as the security of the person from violence and terror, the right to participate in the election of one's governmental representatives; the right to a home, the right to a job, the right to equal opportunity. Here our concern is with the protection of these rights from violation by private individuals as well as by government.

In attempting to destroy the fundamental rights of workers and minorities, certain groups found it necessary to develop a whole body of laws to insure inferiority. Labor and minorities have had a parallel struggle for status. It is no historical accident that the turn of the century saw the enactment of numerous segregation laws directed against Negroes while at the same time 'yellow dog' contracts and labor injunctions were being rigidly enforced.

Civil Rights Report

The President's Committee on Civil Rights declared in its report, "the aspirations and achievements of each member of our society are to be limited only by the skills and energies he brings to the opportunities equally offered to all Americans. We can tolerate no restrictions upon the individual which depend upon irrelevant factors as his race, his color, his religion or the social position to which he is born."

The right to job opportunity without arbitrary discrimination is as important as the right to life itself. Trade unionists know only too well the long and bitter struggle for the recognition of this principle—a struggle which is not yet won. Traditionally, an employer had the absolute right to hire and fire whom and when he pleased, and had the sole prerogative to determine rates of pay, hours and working conditions. The right of the worker to organize and bargain collectively for better conditions was neither recognized nor protected by law. It was not until 1935, with the enactment of the National Labor Relations Act, that we wrote into the basic law of the land the principle that workers have a right to employment without discrimination solely because of their union affiliation.

Today this principle has been extended to include the right to equal opportunity in employment without discrimination solely Because of race, color, creed, national origin, ancestry or sex.

FEPC

The right to opportunity in employment is so elementary it should seem unnecessary to focus attention upon it. However, during World War II when it was vitally necessary to organize our total human resources for the successful prosecution of the war, the denial of equal job opportunity (of which minorities had always been painfully aware) became a matter of national concern. The Committee on Fair Employment Practices, created by an emergency executive order, was the first organized national attempt by government to make the public aware that th [sic] job exclusion of any group adversely affected the nation's war effort and potentially threatened the survival of the nation itself.

Examination into the problem revealed that employer exclusion took many forms, including the refusal to hire or upgrade, opportunity for training, assignments of minorities to inferior jobs in which they were frozen; early and disproportionate discharge.

Unions, too, were found to be guilty of discriminatory policies. The Fair Employment Practices Committee found there were a number of craft unions who practiced outright exclusion or segregation of Negro workers.

Statute

It may be well to examine law and custom as an influence upon union racial policies before discussing what unions have done and can do to implement civil rights. For example, consider the following statute taken from the 1942 South Carolina Code: S 1272—(*Separation of employees; different races in cotton textile factories*)—It shall be unlawful for any person, firm or corporation engaged in the business of cotton textile manufacturing in this state to allow or permit operatives, help and labor of different races to labor and work together within the same room or to use the same doors of entrance and exit at the same time, or to use and occupy the same pay ticket windows or doors for paying its operatives and laborers at the same time, use the same stairway, windows, lavatories, toilets, drinking water, buckets, pails, etc. provided equal accommodations are supplied by said person, firm or corporation without distinction as to race, color or previous conditions.... (The statute provides a penalty of $100.00 fine for each violation or 30 days hard labor, or both at the discretion of the judge. 1932 Code sec. 1272.) Here we again have the myth of equal but separate accommodations. The implication is clear.

While the South Carolina statute is perhaps one of the most extreme, yet similar laws requiring segregated facilities of one type or another in certain fields of employment are found in Arkansas, North Carolina, Oklahoma, Tennessee and Texas. Furthermore, in 1945, the legislature of Alabama passed a joint resolution calling upon its representatives in Congress, and I quote from the resolution, "by every means within their power to oppose the enactment of such Federal Legislation as the so-called Permanent Fair Employment Practice Law, the welfare of Alabama, in our opinion, demanding that they do so." Among the reasons given for opposing such legislation, the Resolution declared, "That in Alabama there exists conditions with respect to the relationship between the races which are not general to the Country as a whole as, for instance, that in certain counties of this State the colored population very greatly exceeds the white population."

On the positive side of the ledger a number of states have considered the right to equal opportunity in employment so important, that they have enacted protective legislation to guarantee this right. 6 states have FEPC laws. 3 of these states—New York, Massachusetts, and Connecticut—have included strong enforcement provisions in their statutes. The other 3—New Jersey, Wisconsin and Indiana—have FEPC laws which are primarily educational and do not have strong enforcement procedures. Several other states have miscellaneous statutes directed against discrimination in various fields of employment such as civil service, public works, public school teaching and some of the professions.

Trade Unions

This summary shows how inadequately the law protects the individual seeking job opportunity and indicates the enormous responsibility which falls upon private groups and organizations. Trade unions, because of their nature and function, must be in the forefront. They have taken and must continue to take the initiative in securing job opportunity free from racial or religious restriction just as in the recent past they undertook to secure such opportunity without discrimination because of union membership.

Of the 2 large labor federations, the American Federation of Labor is the older, more craft-ridden and bound by tradition. Nevertheless, it too is rising to the challenge of civil rights. [handwritten marginalia: Matter of fact, many of the unions which previously had exclusionary clauses or rituals have eliminated them.] Its work, though not so spectacular, is moving steadily forward. It is obvious to the A. F. of L. leadership that the men who are the Poll Taxers and racial bigots and filibusterers are also proponents of the Taft–Hartley law which threatens virtually every guarantee of the wage earner.

CIO

The Congress of Industrial Organizations is the younger, more flexible group, dedicated to the mass organization of industrial workers, skilled and unskilled. As a matter of intelligent self-interest the inclusion of all workers in its ranks was necessary for the union's success. The national CIO has done yeoman service in the field of civil rights through its national Anti-Discrimination Committee and through its educational campaigns.

United Automobile Workers

The United Automobile Workers, largest of the CIO unions, is a notable example of the effectiveness of the principle of workers' solidarity without distinction because of race, color or creed. Situated in a state where migrant workers were recruited from areas where racial tension is chronic the union was confronted with the most acute of racial and religious antagonisms. The success of the teaching of the union's principles was demonstrated during the bloody Detroit riot of 1943 when black and white union members continued to work side by side in the plants. As a matter of self-regulation the UAW has set up its own anti-discrimination committee.

I.L.G.W.U.

My union, the International Ladies Garment Workers Union, is a family of some thirty-two national origins. With modesty I can say that the ILGWU ranks first in its broad social philosophy and its opportunities for the education, recreation and cultural development of all its members.

This union was organized by immigrant workers, most of whom themselves were the objects of discrimination, confined as they were by a language difficulty, relegated to living in virtual ghettoes and working in sweatshops under inhuman conditions. Those were the days when the worker carried his machine on his back, set it up in some dismal cellar or loft, worked twelve to fourteen hours a day for a pittance and suffered every conceivable indignity. The only demand not made upon him was that he pay the employer for the privilege of working in the sweatshop. Having lived through this period, the leadership of the union was acutely aware of the viciousness of discrimination in any form.

Long before the United States Employment Service discontinued its practice of accepting race and nationality tags on employer requests generally, the ILGWU pressured the Needle Trades branch of that agency to discontinue such designations when filling employment orders in the garment trades.

One of the problems of minority workers is the rule of seniority, particularly where they are the last to be hired and the first to be fired. In the dress industry, this problem does not obtain. After the trial period of 35 hours, a worker becomes a citizen of the shop and is entitled during the slack period to an equal share of work, whether he is a piece or week worker.

Until recently the percentage of skilled Negro workers in the dress trade was relatively low for a variety of reasons, two of which were (1) most of the operators in the past learned their skill from a relative or friend and worked on a cooperative basis until the learning period was over, and (2) not until the early 30's did any appreciable number of Negro workers attempt to enter the industry. During World War II there has been a noticeable increase of Negro workers on all levels.

Through cooperation with the Fashion Institute of Technology, talented young people from all over the country are granted scholarships for special study to which the union contributes. On the senior high school level the union has encouraged the system of student teams to work alternately in the shops while they are studying, receiving a minimum wage while they are doing so. These activities offer training and opportunities to young Negroes in common with others.

The union itself is a large employer with a huge staff of technicians, doctors, research personnel, secretarial and clerical workers, in which is represented almost as many national strains as the membership itself.

Furthermore, the wide variety of educational and cultural activities offered by the Union to all of its members enriches the life of the individual members with experiences formerly not available to working class people. The common experience of going to an art class, singing in a chorus, attending a theatre party, participating in a book discussion, competing for a scholarship, spending a weekend or vacation at Unity House, the union's summer house in the Poconos, is an irrefutable argument that racial or religious restrictions serve no purpose except to thwart the growth of a whole people.

Conclusion

Our union participates in all of the struggles to protect and extend the rights of all minorities on every front. Despite this record of which we are proud, we must go forward. The union's ultimate concern must be the union worker as a total citizen. Unions must increasingly provide leadership which stimulates political and civic awareness in the individual worker so that he translates his economic security and equal job opportunity into the life of his community.

NOTE

1. Typescript with handwritten revisions. Maida Springer Kemp papers, Schlesinger Library, Harvard University, Cambridge, MA.

Dorothy Kenyon (1888–1972)

Dorothy Kenyon, New York lawyer and judge, an active supporter of civil rights and free speech, was the first person to appear before the Senate Foreign Relations Subcommittee in 1950 to defend herself against charges of communist activities. Born into a family of lawyers, she graduated from Smith College and New York University Law School. She was admitted to the bar in 1917, but instead of joining the family firm that practiced patent law, Kenyon became a research specialist within a group of lawyers who were advising delegates to the Versailles Peace Conference.

Later, she joined the firm of Pitkin, Rosenson & Henderson. However, she left that firm in 1930 to found, with Dorothy Strauss, a firm of their own on Fifth Avenue. Kenyon and Strauss remained law partners until 1939. Throughout this period Kenyon supported labor rights and women's rights, especially the right to birth control. She actively opposed censorship. For example, in 1931 she delivered a radio address explaining "prior restraint" and how it operated through movie censorship; the categories of materials deleted by censors, and the outcomes of movie censorship in terms of "art" and "intellectual content." She used humor to spotlight how to apply legal definitions of obscenity, observing:

The difference between material that is indecent and material that is obscene is something that I don't understand, but the Boards of Review have no difficulty in distinguishing them. So many feet of film to a kiss, one foot or more makes the difference between decency and indecency, or obscenity, if that's what it is. I don't know, but the Boards know, always, and infallibly.[1]

Kenyon adopted various strategies and tactics to promote social reform and to defend civil liberties. Sometimes she acted through non-

Dorothy Kenyon testifying before the Senate Foreign Relations subcommittee, answering accusations of Joseph McCarthy that she lent her home to communist front organizations. (AP/Wide World Photos.)

Library of Congress, Prints and Photographs Division, NYWT&S Collection, Associated Press photograph [reproduction number, LC-USZ62-128430].

governmental social reform movements; other times she followed governmental avenues to social improvement. Kenyon acted both locally, in New York City, and internationally, first through the League of Nations and, later, the United Nations.[2]

Kenyon had a well-developed understanding of the art of speech making and once summarized her perspectives on content, organization, diction and delivery for a magazine article. She urged potential speakers first to be sure they had something important to say. Second, she counseled careful analysis and organization. Next, turning to diction, she recommended simple clarity, saying: "Never use five syllable words where a one syllable word will do instead. Above all, never use words nor talk about things you don't yourself fully understand." Her advice about delivery focused upon adequate vocal projection and incorporating just the right touches of informality and humor. And, in concluding this brief article, she said: "And last and most important, believe, if you can, in what you say. Your own sincerity and conviction are what lend weight and force to your words. Speak, in short, as though it were an extemporaneous exercise. But never, never speak extemporaneously."[3]

In 1950, Senator Joseph McCarthy charged that Kenyon was affiliated with communist front organizations both before and during her work for the United Nations. Her files include correspondence, research, and briefs related to her successful response to those charges. She also preserved her work for the American Civil Liberties Union (Kenyon served on the National Board of the ACLU from 1930 until her death), and briefs prepared for the NAACP's Legal Defense and Educational Fund in the 1960s. In addition they contain material related to a number of community projects in lower Manhattan, including the Mobilization for Youth (legal services for the poor), which she co-founded in 1968, at age eighty.

Although Kenyon advised speakers to cultivate humor, and did so herself in many speeches, there is little comic relief in the Senate testimony that follows. It represents a serious response to a serious threat to her reputation and career. Kenyon recounted a substantial part of her curriculum vitae in her testimony, before the Tydings Committee, that, in 1950, investigated whether the persons disloyal to the United States had been employed by the Department of State or other Government agencies. Before doing so, however, she offered something of an apology for "remarks in unparliamentary language" she had made when, only a week before, she had learned of the charges against her. However, she also told the subcommittee that she was still very angry "that such outrageous charges should be publicized before this subcommittee and broadcast over the entire nation without any notice or warning to me."

In the testimony that followed, she totally denied charges of disloyalty, either through being a communist or associating with communists. Instead, she characterized herself as "an independent liberal Rooseveltian democrat" who was devoted to improving the lives of working men and women and preserving civil liberties. She acknowledged that she probably had made enemies by championing those and other unpopular causes. However, she firmly denied ever advocating the overthrow of the US government and defiantly challenged anyone to prove that she had ever knowingly supported subversive activities.

NOTES

1. Dorothy Kenyon, "Motion Picture Censorship" Radio Address NY: W.O.V. (13 minutes), August 12, 1931.

2. See numerous examples in the Dorothy Kenyon papers at the Sophia Smith Collection, Smith College, Northampton, MA.

3. Dorothy Kenyon Papers. Typescript dated November 12, 1951, prepared for publication in *Junior League Magazine*.

TYDINGS COMMITTEE TESTIMONY (MARCH 14, 1950)[1]

Reprinted by Permission of the Sophia Smith Collection, Smith College

Senator Tydings, before Judge Kenyon began her testimony, read Senate Resolution 231, agreed to on February 22, 1950: "That the Senate Committee on Foreign Relations, or any duly authorized subcommittee thereof, is authorized and directed to conduct a full and complete study and investigation as to whether persons who are disloyal to the United States are or have been employed by the Department of State. The committee shall report to the Senate at the first practicable date and the results of its investigation, together with such recommendations as it may deem desirable, and if such recommendations are to include formal charges of disloyalty against any individual, then the committee, before making said recommendations, shall give said individual open hearings for the purpose of taking evidence or testimony on said charges. In the conduct of this study and investigation, the committee is directed to procure, by subpena [sic], and examine the complete loyalty and employment files and records of all government employees in the Department of State and such other agencies against whom charges have been heard."

Tydings continued, as follows: Senator McCarthy, on the first day he appeared before our committee in open hearing, made certain statements, Judge Kenyon, in which your name was drawn. You are now at liberty to proceed to answer them in such manner as you see fit.

Before you testify, will you stand and raise your right hand.

Do you solemnly promise that the testimony you shall give in this matter pending before the committee, in accordance with resolution 231, shall be the truth, the whole truth and nothing but the truth, so help you God?

Kenyon replied: "I do" and Tydings indicated that her testimony could proceed. Below is a substantial excerpt from that testimony:

My name is Dorothy Kenyon. I live at No. 433 West 21st Street, New York City. I am a practicing lawyer with offices located at No. 50 Broadway, New York City.

When I was informed of the accusations that were made against me before this subcommittee last week, I *did* explode. Doubtless my indignation led me to make some impulsive remarks in unparliamentary language. Reflection, and a recollection refreshed by such investigation as I could make in the interim, now permits a more dispassionate approach. However, nothing can diminish the deep resentment I feel that such outrageous charges should be publicized before this subcommittee and broadcast over the entire nation without any notice or warning to me.

My answer to these charges is short, simple and direct. I am not, and never have been disloyal. I am not and never have been, a communist. I am not, and never have been a fellow traveler. I am not, and never have been, a supporter of, a member of or a sympathizer with any organization known to me to be, or suspected of being, controlled or dominated by Communists. As emphatically and unreservedly as possible, I deny any connection of any kind or character with Communism or its adherents. If this leaves anything unsaid to indicate my total and complete detestation of that political philosophy, it is only because it is impossible for me to express my sentiments. I mean my denial to be all-inclusive.

So absolute a negation of the charges should be supplemented with an equally positive, but brief, affirmation of what I am and have been.

I received my A.B. degree from Smith College and my law degree—Doctor Juris—from New York University Law School. I am a member of Phi Beta Kappa and have been for several years a Senator of the United Chapters of Phi Beta Kappa.

I come from a family of lawyers, my father having been a patent lawyer in New York City where my brothers and a cousin now practice under the name Kenyon and Kenyon. My father's cousin, William S. Kenyon, was for many years a member of the United States Senate and later a federal Judge in Iowa.

I was admitted to the Bar in 1917 and have practiced law continually ever since except during certain periods when I held public office. Mine is a general practice. I am a member of the Bar Association of the City of New York, the New York County Lawyers' Association, the New York Bar Association, the American Bar Association, the National Women Lawyers' Association, the American Society of International Law, the American Branch of the International Law Association, and several others.

I have held public office three times, first from June 1, 1936, to December 31, 1937, 2 years, as Deputy Commissioner of Licenses by appointment of Mayor Fiorello LaGuardia; second from January 1, 1939, to December 31, 1939, 1 year, as Municipal Court Judge in New York City, also by appointment of Mayor LaGuardia; and third, from January 1, 1947, to December 31, 1949, as Delegate to the Commission on the Status of Women of the United Nations, by appointment of President Truman, ratified and confirmed by the Senate. I was also appointed in January, 1938, by the League of Nations as one of a Commission of seven jurists—of whom I was the only American—to study the legal status of women throughout the world. This commission continued to operate until the war made further communication between its members impossible. I also served on a number of governmentally appointed Commissions and committees dealing with such varied subjects as the regulation of employment agencies, minimum wage legislation, consumer cooperative corporations, problems growing out of the war-time employment of women, et cetera. I have also done a small amount of labor arbitration.

My interest in good government led me early into the ranks of the League of Women Voters, of which I have been a member for almost thirty years and which I have served in many capacities and offices. It also led me into the Citizens Union of New York, of whose Executive Committee I have been a member for almost twenty years. When the American Labor party was formed in New York I was one of the earliest members but I left it after our efforts to save it from communist domination failed....

I am now a registered Democrat. I am also a member of the Americans for Democratic Action. My interest in civil liberties led me equally early into the ranks of the American Civil Liberties Union, of which I have been a member of the board for almost twenty years. In that connection I have fought on many civil liberties issues and have participated in many briefs amicus in defense of the Bill of Rights.

My interest in education, in labor problems and in the problems of women made me an early member of the American Association of University Women, of which I am now second vice president. I am also a member of the board of the Young Women's Christian Association, a director of the Women's City Club of New York, the association for the aid of Crippled Children, and the Committee of Women in World Affairs. I was also for many years on the board of the Consumer's League of New York and was for a time its President. I am also a member of numerous other women's organizations.

I am, and always have been, an independent liberal Rooseveltian democrat, devoted to and actively working for such causes as the improvement of the living and working conditions of labor and the preservation of civil liberties. To the latter cause I have given much time and attention and have made speeches on that subject for many years in various parts of the country. At times, I have espoused unpopular causes in that connection and probably have made some enemies of those who disagreed with my views.

I am, and always have been, an ardent, outspoken American Citizen, yielding to no one in my admiration of the great privileges this country offers to all its sons and daughters and determined to do all I can to maintain the privileges inviolate forever. I am, and always have been, unalterably opposed to anyone who advocates the overthrow of our government by force or violence, or who otherwise engages in subversive activities or entertains subversive ideas. I am not content to rely on these general denials and observations, however, and I therefore proceed to deal more specifically with the charges against me. In substance, as I understand it, it is claimed that it can be established by documentary proof that I have been at some time a member of 28 or more Communist Front Organizations and therefore stand convicted under the doctrine of guilt by association.

Thus far I have not been confronted with this documentary proof and as I am totally unaware of the contents of most of the documents, I am in no position to make any categorical denials or assertions regarding such statements as they may contain. Here and now, however, I can and do state, with the absolute confidence borne of my personal and positive knowledge, that there does not exist and never has existed any genuine document that proves, or even tends to prove, that I have ever knowingly joined or sponsored or participated in the activities of any organization known to me to be even slightly subversive. Frankness and caution admonish me to avoid creating false impressions or otherwise putting myself in a position of the lady that protested too much. I cannot and do not deny that my name may have been used, even at times with my consent, in connection with organizations that later proved to be subversive but which, at the time, seemed to be engaged in activities or dedicated to objectives which I could and did approve. Nevertheless I challenge and defy anyone to prove that I even joined, or sponsored, or continued to identify myself with, any organizations or individuals I knew, or had reason to believe, were subversive.

I do not even know the names of all the 28 or more Communist Front Organizations I am supposed to have joined. I have taken the list of organizations from the published reports in the press. The names may not be quite accurate, and the list is apparently incomplete, or else my arithmetic is wrong. It is impossible for me to identify some of the names and events described in those charges. I have done the best I could, however, in the brief time since hearing of them and have searched my files, and my own memory in respect to each one. If any further organizations are alluded to today I shall ask the Committee's indulgence for time to investigate and make my replies thereon at a later date....

At that point, Senator Tydings stated, "That will be granted." After thanking Tydings, Kenyon proceeded to deny specific claims and account for specific associations, consistent with her claim never to have "knowingly joined or sponsored or participated in the activities of any organization known to me to be even slightly subversive."

NOTE

1. Dorothy Kenyon Papers, Sophia Smith Collection, Smith College, Northampton, MA.

Margaret M. Henderson (1911–)

Margaret M. Henderson served as Director of Women Marines from 1959 to 1964. Born in Cameron, Texas, on February 6, 1911, Henderson earned a degree in Business Administration from the University of Texas in 1932 and taught elementary school for eleven years in Lubbock, Texas, before enlisting in the Marines in 1943, the first year enlistment in the Marines was open to women. After completing Reserve Officer Training in Mt. Holyoke, Massachusetts, she was commissioned as a second lieutenant on June 30, 1943. She served as an instructor of Women Marines at Fort Lejeune, North Carolina, before becoming Officer in Charge of the business school at the Marine Corps Institute in Washington, DC. By 1945, she had been promoted to the rank of captain and returned to Fort Lejeune as Executive Officer of the women's reserve battalion.

Released from active duty on June 14, 1946, during the general demobilization of women marines after World War II, Henderson taught for two years at Texas Technological College (now Texas Tech University) before being offered and accepting a commission in the regular Marine Corps in 1948, the year Congress first authorized the enlistment of women into the regular Marines.[1] Between 1948 and 1959, when she was appointed Director of Women Marines, she served from coast to coast as a teacher and administrator. After finishing her term as Director in 1964, Henderson served until 1966 at the Marine Corps Recruit Depot in San Diego. She retired effective March 2, 1966.

Margaret M. Henderson's papers include a number of speeches given between 1952 and 1987.[2] Most of the speeches were given at Marine Corps functions, such as graduation or commissioning ceremonies for women marines. One 1952 speech summarized the past year's activities of women marines for the Defense Advisory Committee on Women in the Service (DACOWITS). The 1952 speech excerpted here was titled "Women Share Service for Freedom." It was delivered on February 16, 1952, at the Hotel Sherman in Chicago at the 5th Annual Patriotic Conference of the ladies auxiliary of a national veterans' organization.

Listed on the program as Major Margaret E. Henderson, Deputy Director of Women Marines, Henderson outlined a recruiting effort that was attempting to enlist 72,000 new servicewomen during the Korean War. She sought the listeners' help in achieving that goal. After discussing recruiting goals, she explained standards for enlistment and commissioning, training procedures, and the policies established for utilization of women personnel. The speech also included a composite portrait of the typical servicewoman of 1952, useful for the insights it provides into value-based expectations for young women in that time period. These expectations included marriage (whether or not it meant giving up one's career) and a preference for feminine attire, as well as being motivated to show men that women can do whatever society asks of them.

NOTES

1. The U.S. Representative from Maine, Margaret Chase Smith, was largely responsible for this legislation. See Janann Sherman, 'They Either Need These Women or They Do Not,' Margaret Chase Smith and the Fight for Regular Status for Women in the Military," *Journal of Military History* (January 1990): 47–78.

2. Margaret M. Henderson Papers, Southwest Collection, Texas Tech University, Lubbock, TX.

WOMEN SHARE SERVICE FOR FREEDOM (EXCERPT) HOTEL SHERMAN, CHICAGO (FEBRUARY 16, 1952)[1]

Reprinted by Permission of Margaret M. Henderson

Ladies, I sincerely appreciate this opportunity which you have given me to participate in your 5th Annual Patriotic Conference. May I offer my congratulations to you for your active interest in helping the women of our country to better understand today's national security problems.

When thinking and talking about the foundations of our national security, most of us tend to stress America's natural resources and production know-how. We point to our minerals and forests, our success with mass production, our far-flung and high speed systems of transportation, and all our other material advantages. Too often we tend to neglect our greatest strength—the healthy men and women who make up our human resources.

When the Korean military action began, our American leaders were quick to point out that the United States must continue to recognize that our

strength is not to be measured by arms alone. They emphasized that our ability to join in a common defense of peace rests also on the energies of people and on how much they can produce. "People" means you and me, as well as all the rest of the folks at home.

Only three nations in the world—India, China, and the Soviet Union—outnumber the United States in total population. Communist China and the Soviet Union are lined up against the free world in support of aggression and Communist imperialism. This makes it important for us to exploit every possibility in the field of manpower and make intelligent and efficient use of our human resources. Every American has a job to do in these years when we must build our military strength for the sake of our country's security. Obviously, we cannot all bear arms, but we can in our various ways strive for our common goal—peace.

Your very presence at this meeting indicates that you are working toward this common goal. May I suggest how you can help even more—you can help solve the manpower shortage which is hampering both the industrial and Armed Forces defense efforts by advising our young women that it is the responsibility of every citizen—male or female—to serve our country in her time of need, and that time is now.

The Armed Forces' need for additional personnel is so urgent that all means must be taken to draw upon every possible source. The greatest single, potential source is the group of 8,500,000 women between the ages of 18–34. Of this group, census figures show there are more than 2,225,000 women who are high school graduates and without dependents under 18 years.

In view of this urgent requirement, the Department of Defense is undertaking a program to recruit 72,000 more women to serve with the WAC, WAVES, WAF, and Women Marines, Nurse Corps of Army, Navy and Air Force, and Women's Medical Specialist Corps of the Army and Air Force. The Defense Advisory Committee on Women in the Services, composed of 49 women leaders in the fields of education, business, journalism, theater, medicine, civil service, etc. has been formed at the direction of the Department of Defense. This committee has individually and collectively pledged responsibility for aiding the Department of Defense in:

1. Informing the American Public of the urgent manpower needs of which additional thousands of women in uniform comprise an indispensable part.

2. Creating further public acceptance of women in uniform, emphasizing to parents and families the sense of responsibility assumed by all components of the Department of Defense as to the welfare of women in services.

3. Helping to accelerate recruitment in quality and quantity, according to the respective requirements of the nine women's components.

In order that you may be better informed about women in the service, may I discuss with you the specific needs of the services, the standards for enlist-

ment and commissioning, and the broad established policies which guide the services in their administration and utilization of women personnel.

As has been stated, there is a real need for additional women in all services—the Army, the Navy, the Marine Corps, and the Air Force. Secretary of Defense, Robert A. Lovett, has said:

"Every American has a job to do in these tense years and we must build our military strength for the sake of our country's security. We must believe. We must work. We must serve.

"The Armed Forces have an urgent need for women in each branch of the military establishment. We are counting on many thousands of young women to volunteer for military service. They represent our greatest reservoir of human power, and I am confident that they will answer this call to share service for freedom."

I think that I can best summarize the standards for enlistment and commissioning of women in all military services by giving you a brief description of a typical service woman, a description, in short, of a kind of composite young woman in uniform. This portrayal is possible because the Army, Navy, Air Force and Marine Corps have much the same standards and requirements for enlistment and training as well as utilization policies for their women.

The age of my composite woman recruit is most likely to be somewhere between 18 and 22 years, a high school graduate, and if she is 20 or more, she is apt to have had a year or two of business experience. She is typically American in her interests and in her zest for living. To work side by side with men is no novelty; she has grown up with boys.

If she is between 21 and 29 years old and a college graduate, this typical American girl will probably decide she wants to be an officer. If she meets the physical, personal, and scholastic requirements and completes her officer training satisfactorily, she will receive a second lieutenant's or an ensign's commission, with the same pay and prerogatives as her male counterpart, and with the same opportunity for promotion and retirement if she decides to make the service her career. She may marry if she wishes, and probably will. She may remain in the service if she wants or in ordinary times she may request release from the service upon marriage.

Whether in enlisted ranks or as an officer, the young servicewoman today is representative of an average decent American home whether it be in the east, west, midwest, north or south. If she is an officer she will probably be a graduate of one of our accredited institutions—public or private, co-educational, or woman's college.

She accepts military discipline and restrictions as necessary and peculiar to the profession she has voluntarily chosen, and for the most part, she is tractable, industrious, independent, friendly, and eager to prove to her male colleagues that she can do any task to which she is assigned and for which she is trained. She asks and expects no quarter merely because she is a woman and is fiercely proud of the branch of service her uniform represents—which, incidentally, she undoubtedly considers the one most becoming to her. After working hours, she is equally pleased to lay her uniform aside and don her most feminine civilian attire.

I have gone to some length to portray what I consider to be a characteristic American service woman—be she in the Army, Air Force, Navy or Marine Corps—primarily to bring into clear focus the type of young woman who will be expected to contribute more and more in the months ahead to the nation's defense effort. I hope I have also indicated my own confidence in her ability to meet willingly and wholeheartedly any situation required of her....[2]

Certain broad established policies guide the four services in the administration and utilization of women personnel, just as certain restrictions on the use of women are imposed by law. For example, women in the Air Force, Navy, and Marine Corps may not serve on vessels except hospital ships and transports, and may not be assigned to duty in aircraft engaged in combat missions. For the WAC, the Secretary of the Army is the sole judge of where they may or may not serve. Aside from these not very limiting restrictions, women may be assigned within each service to any appropriate billet commensurate with physical capabilities.

In the interest of unification and uniformity, the four services have adopted certain overall administrative policies with respect to women. All require, for original enlistment or appointment, that a woman be unmarried and have no dependents under 18 years of age; all terminate the enlistment or appointment of a woman for pregnancy or if she acquires by marriage or adoption the custody of a minor child; none may confine women in brigs or military prisons. Aside from these obvious exceptions, all other regulations of each service are applicable equally to men and women. No longer is there any restriction on overseas duty, as there was in World War II for women in the naval services. Broadly speaking, they may be sent anywhere their services are needed. The Army, Air Force, and Navy are assigning increasing numbers of women to overseas billets. The Marine Corps is at present utilizing its women on continental United States posts and stations and in Hawaii.

I have attempted to give you a thumbnail sketch of the need for women in the service, the standards for women in the service and the broad established policies which guide the services in their administration and utilization of women personnel. Now, you are probably saying "Where do I come into the picture?" Let me answer that question by stating that the membership of this organization is composed of leaders who can recognize the high type of young women the Armed Forces need and deserve and it is my hope that my explanation of the need for women to share service for freedom may gain your interest and that you will help advise our young women of the need of their service in whatever way you find possible.

As Mr. Gill Robb Wilson has said, "In historic perspective, the women of America have never failed to meet their obligations."[3]

NOTES

1. Margaret M. Henderson Papers, Speeches 1952–1987, Southwest Collection, Texas Tech University, Lubbock, TX.

2. Here several pages of details on training have been omitted.

3. Gill Robb Wilson was a founder of the Civil Air Patrol as well as an author and poet, publisher, educator, and aviator.

Justine Wise Polier (1903–1987)

Justine Wise Polier was the first woman in New York appointed to a legal rank above magistrate. She served the city as a family court judge for thirty-seven years, from 1935 to 1972. Born in Oregon and educated at elite colleges in the Northeast, including Yale Law School, Polier's father was a well-known rabbi, and one of the founders of the NAACP, and a leader of the American Jewish Congress. Her mother, an artist, founded one of the first children's adoption agencies in 1916.[1] Polier began her own career in industrial labor law, but, in 1935, when Mayor LaGuardia of New York City appointed her to the Domestic Relations Court in Manhattan. She chose to make this her life's work. She resigned in 1973 at age 70, when she turned her attention to the Children's Defense Fund. Throughout her working life, Polier counted Eleanor Roosevelt as one of her closest friends and allies.

Polier's work in family and children's issues is best exemplified in her adoption work both as a judge and with the agency her mother, Louise Wise, founded in 1916, the Free Synagogue Child Adoption Committee, later renamed Louise Wise Services. Polier's position on child services and adoption was liberal and progressive. In particular, she advocated care for children as primary, placing the individual child's welfare before criteria of religious and racial matching. If such matching was possible, she supported it, but, according to Ellen Herman, Polier "adamantly opposed sustaining group rights at the expense of particular children and their search for a home....She abhorred the deployment of public resources to monitor group boundaries and referee group competition....It offended her most heartfelt convictions about children and what they needed. Difference made a difference, but only up to a point. When it came to kinship, all children deserved belonging, and they all deserved it equally."[2]

Polier has been characterized as "a forceful, even intimidating, person."[3] Her speeches reflect that strong persona, as well as her commitment to individual rights and freedoms. Her 1953 speech for Edward R. Murrow's radio program, *This I Believe*, is a personal testament to her parents' legacy. In this brief statement Polier defined freedom. She said: "From my earliest childhood I saw it through the eyes of my parents as both opportunity and challenge to do battle for those in bondage, to achieve freedom of the spirit and mind for one's self and one's fellow men."[4]

The speech included here was delivered in 1954 and focused, again, on the theme of freedom. Titled "Freedom—NOT Fear," the speech continued Polier's tribute to her parents, particularly her father Rabbi Stephen Wise. In this speech, Polier departed from her role as an advocate for children and families. Prompted by a statement of the U.S. House of Representatives Un-American Activities Committee that Rabbi Stephen Wise was a prominent Communist collaborator, Polier stepped into the political realm to express a straightforward indictment of the anti-Communist campaign led by Senator Joseph McCarthy.

After a powerful critique of the ways in which Congress was abusing the congressional committee, Polier offered an eight-point Code of Conduct for Congressional Committees. She reminded her audience of the tactics of Hitler and Stalin, and suggested that Senator McCarthy was adopting similar strategies, and challenged them to repudiate McCarthy and his supporters as "enemies of the American people, and the American way of life."

NOTES

1. Ellen Herman, "The Difference Difference Makes: Justine Wise Polier and Religious Matching in Twentieth-Century Child Adoption," *Religion and American Culture* 10 (2000): 3; see also Justine Wise Polier, *Juvenile Justice in Double Jeopardy: The Distanced Community and Vengeful Retribution* (Hillsdale: Lawrence Erlbaum, 1989).

2. Ibid., 24.

3. Ibid.

4. Justine Polier, *This I Believe*, Script 512, Schlesinger Library Manuscript Collections, 1, Harvard University, Cambridge, MA.

FREEDOM—NOT FEAR
ADDRESS BY HON. JUSTINE WISE POLIER,
PHILADELPHIA (FEBRUARY 1, 1954)[1]

Reprinted by Permission of the Schlesinger Library

It is inevitable that we who believe in America and the spirit of freedom which has made America great should be concerned with the present threats to spiritual, moral and intellectual freedom in this land today.

This is a time when little men are too often fearful, and when men who would destroy freedom are cloaking their attack on it in the name of anti-communism. Happily for America, there have been throughout its history courageous citizens who have refuted those who sought to turn brother against brother and uproot freedom in America. I would like to read to you the words of a great American:

"If we are to violate the Constitution, will the people submit to our unauthorized acts? Sir, they ought not to submit; they would deserve the chains that these measures are forging for them. The country will swarm with informers, spies, delators and all the odious reptile tribe that breed in the sunshine of a despotic power... the hours of the most unsuspected confidence, the intimacies of friend-ship, or the recesses of domestic retirement afford no security. The companion whom you must trust, the friend in whom you must confide, the domestic who waits in your chamber, all are tempted to betray your imprudent or unguarded follie; to misrepresent your words; to convey them, distorted by calumny, to the secret tribunal where jealousy presides—where fear officiates as accuser and sus-picion is the only evidence that is heard...

"Do not let us be told that we are to incite a fervor against a foreign aggression to establish a tyranny here at home; that we are absurd enough to call ourselves free and enlightened, while we advocate principles that would disgraced [sic] the age of Gothic barbarity."

These are the words of Edward Livingston uttered on the closing day of the Alien and Sedition Acts Debate in 1798. The words are true again today. America again has need of men and women who have the courage to protect it against both external foes and internal foes. Freedom has never been won or maintained by fearful men, would-be inquisitors or tyrants. These must be resisted today as they were in the early days of early American history. It is tragic that the words of Edward Livingston should so aptly describe the procedures used and the atmosphere created by too many of our Congres-sional Committees during the past few years. Anyone familiar with the his-tory of Congressional investigation must be aware of the important and valuable role they have oftimes played in securing the basic information on which proposals for Federal legislation should be considered. Frequently, Congressional hearings have provided the forum in which citizens could petition their government to correct wrongs including corruption in govern-ment and to provide legislative measures to meet new problems of the growing and ever more complex problems of this country.

Our concern with Congressional investigations today is that they have become perverted by men who would use them not to secure knowledge so that they may legislate more wisely, but as platforms for their own demagoguery, as public pillories for those with whom they disagree, and as a public stage show in which as actors with or without a supporting cast, they can invade the province of both the Executive and Judicial branches of our Government.

Our concern stems from the current misuse of the Congressional Com-mittee, its secret one-man hearings, its employment of informers, its defi-ance of the bulwarks of freedom lodged in our Bill of Rights, its bullying tactics against citizens and other Departments of Government, its assaults on intellectual freedom and its defilement of the independent spiritual leaders of America in order to spread an atmosphere of fear and hysteria.

As Representative Jacob I. Javits recently noted, last year there were 236 separate Congressional investigations as compared to 25 some thirty years ago; the legislative work of Congress which is its primary responsibility is too often put aside or relegated to an unimportant position in favor of Congressional investigations on matters which are unrelated to its responsibility to legislate. It is [sic] almost become accepted that political success or preferment depends on getting into one of those acts rather than on making a sound contribution to the development of needed and wise legislation. Here one finds a serious default or avoidance of a public and governmental responsibility.

This situation has become possible and profitable because of those who would sell fear at the price of freedom and destroy the qualities of faith, courage and the will to build a stronger, nobler America that has made it great among the nations of the world.

Americans who came to this country to avoid religious and political persecution not only dreamed of a land of freedom in which the dignity, intellectual and moral freedom of the individual should be safeguarded. They drew upon their experience under tyranny to establish safeguards against the destruction of freedom for themselves and their children for which they were ready to lay down their lives. Some of our Congressional Committees have in recent years created procedures and used methods which repudiate every safeguard of freedom established under the Bill of Rights. This has been accomplished under the leadership of men who would restrain others but know no self-restraint.

Congressional Committees have gone beyond the area of their authority and responsibility to investigate for the purpose of securing information necessary to the intelligent and effective formulation of legislative recommendations. The questioning of a private citizen as to his private and political beliefs, the sources of material for a book privately published with the threat of contempt proceeding and jail if he refused to disclose such information to Senator Joseph McCarthy can hardly be regarded as within the proper scope of a legislative Committee. The slander against and public attempts to degrade and intimidate known anti-Communists who have publicly expressed their disapproval of McCarthy methods, as in the case of James Wechsler, Editor of the New York Post, in an effort to terrorize the press is not within the function of a Congressional Committee. Here the price exacted for making the record public was disclosure of the names of associates known twenty years before.

Congressional procedures have violated the Bill of Rights. They have sought to try and condemn men and thus render them outcasts without disclosing the full charges, the source of the charges, without providing a fair hearing, without permitting them counsel, without the right to confront witnesses or cross-examine those whose charges, if believed, would destroy their lives. All this has been justified on the ground that these were not criminal trials and as though the destruction of a man's reputation and life by

Congressional Committees were of less significance than conviction for such an offense as assault or petty larceny.

Dossiers are built up by Congressional Committees against men which include any and all derogatory information regardless of the reliability of the source of such information. These dossiers, as in the case of Bishop G. Bromley Oxnam, have been made available to anyone seeking information about him. It contained statements charging the Bishop association with forty odd allegedly "Communist front" organizations, although he was later to establish that he had never been associated with some and had quit others when he learned of their political leaning. This dossier also did not include the material showing the Bishop's great contribution to America, his strong anticommunist stands, or the responsible and sensitive tasks which he had undertaken on behalf of his country. Bishop Oxnam was able after a time to secure a public hearing. He was able, since he had a full record of his correspondence and actions, to refute the fantastic charges made against him. He had distinguished counsel, church support and public prestige as well as his own moral strength to help him in securing a public hearing. But while Bishop Oxnam's great contribution to the cause of freedom is unquestioned, the necessity of his exposure to ten hours of examination before a Congressional Committee, in order to defend himself, reveals not only the depths to which Congressional Committees have sunk but the insupportable burden now being placed on less famous or great men whose freedom and reputation is equally important not only to themselves but to this country.

Congressional Committees have come to endanger freedom in America in part because they have also ceased to be Committees composed of representatives of both major parties except in name. Too often they have become one-man forays or attacks on individuals or groups with whom an individual congressman either disagrees or whom he regards as good bait for self-aggrandizement. Thus not only does McCarthy become the sole actor repeatedly, but by his misuse of his chairmanship of a subcommittee he has hired irresponsible and disreputable staff to serve as his personal lackeys without consultation with or regard for the wishes of his fellow committee members.

Unverified and false charges against individuals and government agencies have been leaked to the press without clearance with committee members. Fellow committee members have not even been given adequate notice of hearings. So, too, Mr. Velde issued subpoenas to President Truman, a Justice of the Supreme Court and a former Secretary of State without consultation with or notice to his Committee. In each case public headlines were captured, and a body blow was dealt to the safeguards for orderly and responsible government action and to the American tradition of fair play.

In the mad race for scalps by some Congressional Committees the reckless use of informers smacks of Stalin's Russia and Hitler's Germany. In our Courts the public interest in the use of informers to prosecute criminals is judicially balanced against the demands of fair play for the defendants. This is not true in their use by Congressional Committees. Dossiers are compiled including information not revealed to the person under attack and oftimes concealing the identity of the informer. The reliability of the informer and his information are not checked. The right to cross-examine the informer is not allowed. Frequently a Committee hearing such informers does not even question the informer or the information before publicizing it.

Regardless of the motives of Senator McCarthy in embracing and employing J. B. Matthews, who grossly slandered the Protestant clergy of this country, the fact remains that his unholy smear was given circulation through the Congressional Committee. Later it was revealed that Benjamin Gitlow, former head of the Communist conspiracy was called before the House Committee on Un-American Activities to inform against or vilify the Protestant clergy. In Executive session this same informer in July 1953 alleged:

"Before the creation of the front organizations the ministers who carried out the instructions of the Communist Party or collaborated with it were limited in number.

"The outstanding ones among them were...Rev. Judah L. Magnus, Rev. John Haynes Holmes...Rabbi Stephen S. Wise."

This vilification released by the Committee in September revealed that not a single question had been put to the "informer" Gitlow concerning any of these distinguished Ministers. Nor had he been asked to provide one scintilla of evidence to substantiate these charges. The Committee had not even seen fit to inform the Ministers thus charged who were still living of the charges or to give them the opportunity to answer the charges before they were released for distribution to the press. The danger of giving such credence to professional witnesses and cloaking their lies with immunity is to be seen this instance. When Mr. Gitlow was confronted with his statement in his own community he crawled and partially recanted, saying:

"It was the purpose of this testimony to show how the Communist movement, from its very inception—though anti-religious and in principle atheistic—was able to attract a number of well-meaning, liberal and social-minded religious leaders such as Rabbis Magnus and Wise. The charge was not made that they were ever communists or members of the Communist Party."

Whether Mr. Gitlow was bid to spice the attack on Protestantism with the names of two distinguished leaders of the Jewish Ministry no longer alive I do not know. I do know that he lied and that he knew he lied about them, as he did about John Haynes Holmes, a noble spirit, who, unlike Gitlow has ever been a foe of totalitarianism of every kind, black, brown and red. In the light of my father's lifelong devotion and service to America and Americans of all races and faiths the revulsion to the attack upon him was inevitable. He needs no defense by me or any man. I rather feel that if he knew that this attack upon him had helped to awaken Americans to the threat to their freedom and to meet it more courageously he would have welcomed it.

America has many tasks ahead if it is to eliminate from public life men and methods that endanger freedom. The largeness of this task must not discourage us. There are many ways in which each of us who cares can help.

There are concrete tasks to be done. Among them is the task of ending the excesses of Congressional Committees which have debated the meaning of the Bill of Rights.

Happily, more and more citizens including members of Congress of both parties are determined to secure Federal legislation that will impose a code of fair procedure on all Congressional Committees. Such a code can do much to end the ugly abuses we have witnessed without in any way impairing the proper functions of our Congressional Committees. Such a code should provide that:

1. Inquiries should be directed to gather information for legislative purposes and for checking on the administration and enforcement of law. They should not seek to function as a grand jury nor seek to expose individuals.

2. Material not included in Committee reports should be held as confidential except that it can be made available to Federal and State Investigation and Intelligence agencies for official purposes. There should be no public comment on a person or organization under investigation by a Congressional Committee member or staff person until the inquiry is completed.

3. One-man investigating Committees should be prohibited. All phases of investigations including the authorization of subsidiary inquiries, the hiring of staff, the scheduling of hearings, the subpoenaing of witnesses and the release of public statements and reports should represent the considered judgment of the majority of the committee. To this end all members should receive due notice of meetings and other Committee action. Adequate provision must be made for effective minority reports.

4. Members of a Committee and persons employed by it should not speak or write for compensation while an investigation is in progress.

5. Material reflecting adversely upon persons living or dead should not be made public before an opportunity has been given to them or their representatives to reply. Such answers should be released with the publication of the adverse material.

6. Whenever charges are made against a person or organization at a public hearing they should be afforded an early opportunity to publicly present their side of the case. They should have the opportunity to cross-examine witnesses against them.

7. Constitutional objections and questions of privilege raised by witnesses should be tested through summary judicial procedures rather than by defense in criminal actions.

8. The Rules Committee in each House of Congress should be empowered to receive and investigate complaints of abuses by Congressional Committees and report findings with recommendations to Congress.

Such a code would provide one concrete answer to the question "Freedom or Fear?" But the attack on freedom and the divisiveness of and slavery to fear comes from many sources and in many ways. Censorship of books, of plays, of pictures, of teaching, attacks on our schools have become the pastime of a horde of self-appointed men who would enforce conformity on America. There are those who again would imprison the inquiring mind and return America to an age of superstition and inquisition.

This we shall resist. We have seen Hitler who, in the name of the Master Race, first made Germans suspicious of one another; who evoked hatred and fear through the use of the big lie—the conscious and deliberate repetition of lies on the assumption that repetition would lead to acceptance; who then destroyed all who dared oppose him; who attacked and subjugated neighboring lands, and finally plunged the world into war.

We have seen Stalin turn his country into a land of informers and counter-informers, where purge succeeded purge and fear became ruler.

And now we see the germs of the same disease that destroyed freedom in Germany and Russia being injected into our body politic in the name of anti-communism. We have seen the Lustron [lustral] but not lustrous figure from Wisconsin strut across the stage, aping the tactics of Hitler and Stalin. The words of Louis the Fifteenth, "I am the State" are now paraphrased by his lackeys to read "If you oppose McCarthy you are a Communist or a dupe of Communism." Recently, he not only attacked a General who questioned his conduct at the Monmouth inquiry but demanded an explanation from West Point as to why the General had been permitted to speak. Not being satisfied with the roles of French King and Grand Inquisitor he has also recently assumed the role of Marc Antony. In the famous funeral oration, after inflaming the mob against Brutus, he kept repeating "But Brutus is an honorable man." In similar vein, McCarthy attacks President Eisenhower, even questioning the veracity of reports from the White House concerning the number of McCarthy inspired telegrams received and then hastens to add, "If there was a mistake, it's an honest one."

America has rarely been cursed with would-be dictators or know-nothing leaders. We cannot afford to be fooled or frightened even for an hour by the antics of such men. They must be repudiated as enemies of the American people and the American way of life. Our answer must be Freedom, not fear.

NOTE

1. Typescript with handwritten revisions. "Freedom—NOT Fear," Justine (Wise) Polier Papers, Schlesinger Library, Harvard University, Cambridge, MA.

Katie Louchheim (1903–1991)

Katie Louchheim's extensive activism on behalf of the Democratic Party took her to the height of national party politics. She first gained prominence as the District of Columbia delegate to the Democratic National Convention in 1948 and 1952; then served as Director of Women's Activities of the National Democratic Party (1953–1960); vice chair of the Democratic National Committee (1956–1960); and finally as Deputy Assistant Secretary of State for Educational and Cultural Affairs under Lyndon B. Johnson. Long active in party politics, a prolific writer and speaker, Louchheim campaigned extensively during the 1950s and 1960s for Democratic causes. In her two books, *By the Political Sea* (1970) and *The Making of the New Deal* (1983), she articulated her political philosophy and provided a lively account of her experiences in public life.

In the tradition of Carrie Chapman Catt, Louchheim believed that women should roll up their sleeves and directly engage in the nuts and bolts of partisan party politics. As she stated in a speech before the Democratic National Committee, "—Too many women exhibit a preference for working in community improvement associations, non-partisan, or bi-partisan women's groups. They fail to graduate even from such a helpful school of politics as the League of Women Voters into the real world of politics—the political party."[1] As the following speech illustrates, she did not hesitate to lambaste her Republican opponents or use Cold War rhetoric to sway her audience. With oratorical flourish, she championed the cause of the Democratic Party. On the road constantly during the 1950s and 1960s, a typical few months might include speeches in several states given before such organizations as the Women's National Democratic Club, the Springfield Massachusetts Adult Education Council, the American Friends Service Committee of Philadelphia, Denison University in Ohio, and the New Hampshire Democratic State Committee.[2]

Although Louchheim's public activism challenged conventional gender notions during the 1950s, she did rely upon the rhetoric of sexual difference in her efforts to persuade women to step into the political fray. Employing an updated version of "political motherhood," she argued that women, because of their nurturing and reproductive capacities, brought special qualities to bear on public life. In the following 1954 speech, given before the National Conference of Jewish Women, Louchheim enunciated the gendered politics of the day. A woman's home "is the world," she declared, and one that needs women to act as "guardian" and protector. This speech, like many Louchheim delivered, served as her opening volley at the outset of a debate with a Republican counterpart. In the 1950s, many women's organizations arranged gala events that highlighted such debates between prominent political women. Louchheim kept abreast of a wide array of campaign issues, making the case for the Democratic platform with regard to the economy, employment, taxes, education, housing, and foreign policy. The persuasive power of her speeches also relied upon her ability to tie Cold War concerns to gender politics. Comparing the "isolated homemaker" to the "untouched atom," she urged women to join with others—to get involved with politics—and like the atom "expend [their] energies to change the world."

NOTES

1. Katie Louchheim, "Speech by Mrs. Katie Louchheim," given in California (audience unknown), May 11, 1955. Papers, "Speeches in California," C49, Library of Congress, Washington, DC.

2. Katie Louchheim, "Speaking Engagements, November 1953 through November 2, 1954," Louchheim Papers, Library of Congress, Washington, DC.

STANDARD STUMP SPEECH
BEFORE NATIONAL CONFERENCE OF JEWISH
WOMEN, CHICAGO (SEPTEMBER 20, 1954)[1]

It is a pleasure to be with you today. We are all proud of the excellent work you do and of the education and public affairs programs of the Conference of Jewish Women's organizations. Many other groups could learn from your example.

Today you are indicating your earnest interest in examining political issues. I am delighted to appear with Mrs. Cathcart on this program. I have been advised that she is an able and challenging debater.

I expect we will find we have many differences of opinion so before we begin to enumerate those differences, I think I should point out that we also have many viewpoints in common.

We both think *our* Party is the best Party. We both think *our* candidates are the best candidates. And, we both want *our* side to win the election this November. So you see, Mrs. Cathcart and I are in complete agreement up to a point—the point of the pencil in the voting booth and where it makes the X.

I think, too, that we would agree that women play an increasingly important role in politics—not only by getting out the vote but by participating in all kinds of political activity.

We like to think of ourselves as homemakers first—but today's housewife is not only the guardian of her home. In the broader sense, she is the guardian of the future. For a woman's home today is the world.

And if you wonder what you—one lone woman—can do about the world, just consider the atom.

The isolated homemaker, like the untouched atom, remains insignificant. But like the explosive atom, you can expand your energies and change the world.

This November we will have a chance to change the world by going to the polls and voting for the candidates and party of our choice.

But it seems to me that women today have more of a duty than voting. The biggest part of a woman's job is to get out the thought as well as the vote.

Behind the Iron Curtain they get out the vote but they are very careful not to encourage people to think. The thought behind each ballot cast in America is the margin of difference between our elections and theirs.

So often I'm asked what issues women are interested in. My answer is: All the issues. I'm convinced there is no such thing as a woman's issue.

I am certain you will want to know: What is happening to our National economy? To our relations with other countries? To our conservation and welfare programs? You will want to know what kind of people are running for public office and what has been accomplished by this 93rd Congress.

Glittering generalities about peace and prosperity are fine for campaign oratory but they remain meaningless unless the Party in power is prepared to take action. In politics, promises are but daydreams—it is enacted legislation that counts.

In 1952 we had no way of knowing what the Republicans would do. They had been out of power for 20 years.

They promised to do a great many things. They promised a change. Let's take a good look at what has been changed.

First, you'll recall we got the change to a hard money policy. It caused a virtual panic in government bonds and threatened to plunge the entire country into serious trouble. It had to be changed back because it was soon apparent that hard money was altogether too hard to get.

The Republicans did succeed in changing our economy in other ways. In Democratic Administrations we became accustomed to an ever increasing national income—the pie was bigger every year. Not only was it bigger but larger slices were going to the people who needed the most—the average consumer. As their purchasing power grew, prosperity increased.

Now this distribution of income has changed. Payrolls are off seven billion dollars. As a result, the principal consumers are getting a smaller piece of a smaller pie while a larger piece is going to recipients of rents, royalties, dividends and high salaries.

What does this mean to the average businessman—not the corporation—the average small businessman? It means fewer customers with money to buy. It means higher interest rates on loans for the purchase of goods or for renovation. In some cases, it means business failure. In 1953, the rate of business failures rose 70 per cent.

Today there are upwards of three and a half million unemployed and many thousands more are sharing jobs in order to stay on industrial payrolls part-time. Those are people who know that there has been a change.

We're going to hear a lot in the coming campaign about how the Republicans changed the Tax bill. They are taking credit for reducing taxes seven billion, 400 million. The President recently pointed out exactly how much tax relief has gone to the little fellow—to those with dependent children, people who hire baby sitters, retired folks, farmers who practice soil and water conservation, those who can claim depreciation and those who are unfortunate enough to have medical expenses.

We added up those tax reliefs and used the President's own figures. We got 821 million dollars. You don't have to be a mathematician to subtract from the 7 billion, 400 million and find you still have 6 billion, 574 million to account for. And you don't need an elephant's memory to recall that nearly 5 million of this difference is tax relief voted by the last Democratic Congress. The rest of it was tax relief which this Republican Congress granted to corporations and the 8 per cent of the population who drew dividends.

This, more than anything else illustrates the difference of approach to problems by the two political parties. The Republicans sincerely believe in the trickle down theory. They sincerely believe that if you make the affluent and privileged more privileged and more affluent, prosperity will surely trickle down to all the rest of us.

Democrats have a different attitude and philosophy on taxation. We believe that taxes should be reduced fairly and equitably for all taxpayers—not just for selected classes of individuals. That is why the Democrats proposed raising the exemption for the taxpayer and his dependents as the basis for tax reduction.

I do not think it fair to question the sincerity of people in either party. I think we must understand the basic difference in philosophy and judge accordingly.

Another example of this difference is evident in the farm program. Although the Republicans did not hesitate to subsidize big business, their Secretary of Agriculture has gone on record that subsidies to farmers are immoral. Why is it that to the Republicans it is immoral to subsidize the farmer and not immoral to subsidize business? The answer lies in Secretary of Interior McKay's statement: "We're here in the saddle of an Administration representing business and industry."

The President, too, enunciates the Republican philosophy when he says he is conservative in economic matters but liberal in human affairs. We Democrats do not understand this kind of a pronouncement. Isn't this a distinction without a difference? We Democrats have always believed the right to earn a decent living is a human affair.

While we're about it, let's see how liberal the Republicans have been in other human affairs. Take our schools. We are hundreds of thousands of classrooms and teachers short. We know that one child in every five goes to school in a fire-trap. What liberal action did the Republicans take? Well— they didn't take any action. They are going to make a study to find out why so many children can't study at all.

In estimating our housing needs, the Administration has been extremely conservative—more conservative than the late Senator Taft. Senator Taft fought before his death for 135 thousand public housing units. Without the strong hand of Senator Taft to support it, the public housing program of the Administration slumped to a mere 30 thousand units. Meanwhile, slums are still gaining on us. High interest rates have made the cost of privately built homes so high that middle income families cannot afford to build them.

The Republicans have made many humanitarian gestures. A typical example of this is the President's proposed health insurance program. This was said to be a measure to help the millions of families who cannot pay their medical bills. But, of course, it wasn't. It was designed to guarantee private insurance companies against loss. Fortunately, the Congress did not even waste its time on this one.

Another much vaunted humanitarian gesture was the bill to admit 214 thousand refugees. It is on the record but so far, because of so much red tape, only a trickle of refugees have been admitted. At the rate we are going, it will take 97 years to admit the entire 214 thousand.

Even the Republicans have told me that the failure to administer this act has lost us friends. To oppressed peoples everywhere, America used to hold out the hope of freedom and opportunity—even to those who would never realize the dream of coming here. But now we have cruelly crushed all their hopes. America no longer has a place in their dreams or their affections.

Meanwhile, the President has really been conservative in economic affairs.

We have seen the Republicans attempt the biggest give away of all times. They have sought to turn over to private industry future control of atomic energy, public grazing lands, public power sites and industrial plants built at the taxpayers' expense.

This is the Republican definition of being conservative but to us Democrats it does not add up to conservation of people's resources.

The issue of foreign policy is certainly one that concerns us all. In no other field have the Republicans been so inept or so divided. Their guiding formula—if they have one—has been to talk tough and carry a twig. The result has been exactly what we might expect. The tough talk has frightened our friends and the twig—the whittled down version of our defense program— has been a consolation to our enemies.

Under Democratic administrations we built up a careful system of alliances and friendships. We recognized that some of our friends lacked military and economic strength so we initiated a program of assistance which included not only armaments but the means to rebuild their economies. We also had trade programs to stimulate recovery—programs appealing enough to offset the temptation to carry on extensive trade with Russia and Red China.

We have seen the Republican Administration surrender to the GOP protectionists in Congress by abandoning all proposals for lowering tariffs. Foreign aid funds were slashed. Point Four—which had us so many friends—became Point Two and a Half and cut our friendships accordingly.

Republicans in Congress successfully blocked all efforts to establish a forward looking trade program. The most they would give the President was a one year extension of the Democratic reciprocal trade program. Remember in 1952 President Eisenhower said: "Our foreign trade is not just the frosting on our economic cake, but one of its essential ingredients." This is still true— all that's needed now is a Democratic baker.

Speeches by various Republican spokesmen have had the ferociousness of an Indian war dance. They have threatened massive retaliation, withdrawal from the UN, severing of relations with Russia. No wonder our allies are frightened. This kind of talk sounds as if we were willing to plunge into world war three and take everyone with us.

The Chicago Daily News summed it up:

"If you add up all the statements made by Eisenhower, the Vice-President, the Secretary of State, the military and assorted Republican leaders, the sum total is bluff, bluster, backdown and baloney."

The Republicans have played penny-ante with our defenses and monopoly with our foreign policy. There has been no bi-partisanship in the sense that Democrats were consulted before policy decision were made.

When the Democrats were in power, there was consultation with leading Republicans prior to the making of major foreign policy decisions including such programs as aid to Greece and Turkey, the Marshall plan, the North Atlantic Treaty and the decision to intervene in Korea.

The American people have become so accustomed to our having a bi-partisan foreign policy that it is hard for many of them to believe that we no longer have one.

There are other things that are hard for people to understand. We couldn't even come close to getting statehood for Alaska and Hawaii, but we have had a Senator from Formosa shouting loudly for a new protective war in the far east. The China lobby and its trigger happy friends might appropriately be classified as the fourth branch of government. Their antics have caused us to lose face first in Indo-China and now in Quemoy.

The sorry state of our foreign affairs puts us in real danger. The two factions of the Republican Party have been so busy fighting about who will seize the initiative in foreign affairs that neither has done so. What we need is a Democratic Congress that will really go ahead and seize the initiative and knows an initiative when it sees one.

At this point, if you will permit, I would like to go from the general to the particular. We cannot discuss issues and ignore candidates. I'm sure you would not expect me to pass up the opportunity to talk about a truly outstanding Democrat—Senator Paul H. Douglas.

He has consistently backed resistance to Communist aggression through as much collective action as possible, through reciprocal trade and by efforts to build strong national defense.

On the home front he has shown a deep and sympathetic understanding for the problems of the farmer, the wage earner and the small businessman. He is, in fact, a trained economist who has foreseen and pointed out the dangers in the Administration's economic polices.

If you will look at Senator Douglas's record, you will find that at all times he has conducted himself as a statesman. Unlike his opponent, he has never been a spokesman for private interests. Paul Douglas is the kind of senator people from both political parties can be proud to have represent them in the Senate.

And let me add that you are doubly fortunate here in Illinois to have so many other fine Democratic candidates. I can't begin to tell you the contributions your Democratic Congressmen have made to the welfare of the nation. I urge each of you to look into their records. I have no fear of urging you to do so for you will find them men of the very highest caliber.

I have tried to outline what I believe are the issues vital to our national existence. I have endeavored to show you how the basic differences between the two parties have been reflected in the course of events. I have not hesitated to point out that we Democrats believe our future is threatened.

As women, you and I are particularly concerned with the future. We do not want to be bungled into either war or depression. We want to continue the spiral of prosperity for all begun under Democratic Administrations. We want the kind of national leadership that promised expanding opportunities for ourselves and future generations.

We know we can afford neither timid leaders who ask hesitantly nor thoughtless leaders who act unwisely. We cannot afford them because they diminish the stature of Democracy in the eyes of the world.

Sometimes we content ourselves with wishing for a better future. We tend to take for granted our great American heritage not realizing the importance of the way we vote or the importance of participation in politics. The right to political participation is one of the many strands of freedom that make up our heritage. To grasp this strand with visible hands and weave it into the fabric of our heritage is to act with bold resolve to mold things nearer to our hearts' desire, always seeking a better world.

NOTE

1. Louchheim Papers, Library of Congress, Washington, DC. The copyright of Katie Louchheim's unpublished writing is dedicated to the public.

Dorothy Shaver (1889–1959)

Dorothy Shaver's life epitomizes the classic American story of the "self-made man"—but for a woman, and a woman of the 1950s. Shaver started out in a small southern town, Carter Point, Arkansas, (population 300), but after attending the Universities of Arkansas and Chicago, left them behind for the excitement of New York City. Arriving in New York with her sister Elsie, she began an ascent to what would ultimately lead to the pinnacle of corporate success. In 1945, Shaver became the first female president of the Lord & Taylor department store.

She began her career at Lord & Taylor by way of family ties and sharp business acumen. Upon their arrival in New York, Dorothy and Elsie Shaver were soon in business together. Elsie, an aspiring painter, designed dolls that Dorothy, with the encouragement of Samuel Reyburn, a fellow Arkansan and family acquaintance, and fortuitously, the president of Lord & Taylor, marketed and sold in the store's windows. While their financial prospects soared, the work was all-consuming and since Elsie wanted to pursue painting full-time, the sisters dissolved their doll business after three years.

But Dorothy Shaver had only begun her foray into corporate life. Shaver had impressed Samuel Reyburn. Not wanting to lose her talents but not entirely sure of them either, he hired her on a per-fee basis to conduct an analysis of Lord & Taylor's comparative business bureau. As Shaver recounted, her report concluded that it was only a "complicated espionage system set up to report on the merchandise of other stores" and therefore "a waste of time." She suggested that instead "Lord & Taylor forget competitors and concentrate on designing the right things to begin with."[1] This incisive report demonstrated the creativity and independent flair that would mark her career. In 1924, Reyburn hired her to establish a bureau of stylists at Lord & Taylor. Three years later Shaver became a member of the board of directors; by 1931, she was elected a vice president; in 1937, first vice-president; and in 1945, president.

Shaver played a major role in shaping the development of the modern department store. Under her direction, Lord & Taylor emphasized artistic presentation and created separate departments that catered to distinct segments of the population. In what would become a staple of department store design, Shaver split Lord & Taylor's floor plan into separate shopping areas for teenagers, college women, budget shoppers, brides, petite women, and pregnant women. She also expanded Lord & Taylor beyond Fifth Avenue, supervising the opening of six suburban branches.

Shaver championed an "American style" and promoted American designers at a time when most retailers still deferred to Paris and Europe. She instituted the annual Lord & Taylor American Design Awards in achievements which she celebrated four Americans for their creative achievements. Recipients included fashion designers, artists, business entrepreneurs, and such figures as Edward R. Murrow and Albert Einstein. In the 1930s, she promoted such young American designers as Adrian Clare Potter and Claire McCandell. Shaver received numerous awards herself including honorary doctorates from Bates College and New York University, the Associated Press's "Outstanding Woman in Business" in 1941 and 1947, as well as the French Cross of Chevalier. In 1958, New York Governor Averell Harriman appointed her to the State Commerce Department's Business Advisory Council.

A popular speaker throughout her career, Shaver addressed many professional and business groups, including the National Conference of Christians and Jews, the Annual American Design Awards luncheons, and the Museum of Modern Art. She also spoke at all her store openings and in 1954 delivered a speech on Edward Murrow's radio series, *This I Believe*.[2] In the following speech, Shaver illustrates her devotion to American style and design but does so within the 1950s Cold War context. Making a comparison reminiscent of Richard Nixon and Nikita Khrushchev's famous "kitchen debate," Shaver argued that the American look did not sacrifice fashion to function, as did Soviet styles, but instead through a "mass market for good taste," combined them, making American women "the best dressed in the world." In contrast to the rhetoric of 1950s domesticity, Shaver emphasized that the new "American look" catered to the needs of modern women, who, while still tending the home, had moved into public life and the professions. Unlike the Soviets, however, American fashion still allowed women to appear feminine and beautiful.

NOTES

1. Margaret B. Parkinson, "How Did She Get There?" *Charm*, December 1955, 122, 141.
2. "Obituary," *New York Times*, 29 June 1959.

ADDRESS BEFORE THE PHILADELPHIA FASHION
GROUP (FEBRUARY 7, 1955)[1]

Reprinted by Permission of the Schlesinger Library

I have been asked to talk about American fashion and American fashion designers. The great American fashion industry as we know it today did not exist a generation ago. The word "American" and the word "designer" had not been introduced to one another. Today the fashion industry is the third largest industry in the United States. The number of American designers has jumped from zero to over two thousand. America and Paris share the fashion leadership of the world.

Even in this land where success stories abound, the story of the American fashion industry is extraordinary. It is no wonder, for behind it are three extraordinary partners: the American designer, the American manufacturer and the American retailer. Together they form an historic triumvirate. Their achievement explodes all theories that good taste must be exclusive and expensive. They have demonstrated in dollars and cents that objects in good taste can be successfully mass-produced and successfully mass-marketed.

The proof of this is everywhere in America, in every city and every village, in every home and every office. For American women, at every income level, are the best dressed in the world.

Neither the retailer, nor the manufacturer, nor the designer could have done this alone. Though each has had a definite function, all were interdependent. Frequently the functions have overlapped, and this is good, for it reflects the interplay and the understanding of each other's problems, which were vitally necessary to build our great fashion industry.

The designers' function was to create beautiful clothes, which met the requirements of a new way of life for women. In their designs they had to capture the essence of a whole social revolution, a revolution which has engulfed us all. As women our lives have been radically changed because of it. In business, in civic life and in the home, we are fulfilling roles which were little more than a dream a generation ago.

As doctors, bankers, manufacturers, scientists, yes, even store presidents, we figure importantly in business and in the professions. In civic affairs, as clubwomen, school board chairmen, members of Philadelphia's city council, we're a definite force. And at home, as mistress of the house, how well we know that often we're also cook, governess, laundress and chauffeur.

It's inevitable that with these new roles our clothing needs should be different from what they were twenty years ago. We must have clothes that can go places and do things. But as a certain Philadelphia magazine has put it, never underestimate the power of a woman. None of these activities has displaced one iota of our femininity.

We want clothes that are functional, yes, but we also want them to be beautiful. We want clothes that are washable and durable but also charming. In fact, our desire to look attractive is probably greater than it was twenty years ago because now we are on view more of the time. It isn't only when we go to a ball that we want to look well, it's also when we're typing, cooking, golfing, voting.

Our designers have fulfilled these demands. They have discarded frivolity but not femininity. They have simplified lines without making them stark. They have provided comfort without sacrificing smartness. They have remembered that fashion has a dual purpose; to serve, of course, but also to enhance.

But it was up to our manufacturers to produce the goods, literally and figuratively. And they have. They produced, by machine, elegance and quality no machine had ever before approximated. The cut, the drape, the finish associated only with handwork, became their domain. They created the most delicate look from the sturdiest fabrics. They kept pace with every advance in dyes, in natural and synthetic fibres. And because of mass-production, the price of beautiful clothes, for the first time, was within every woman's reach.

Suddenly a new kind of fashion market had to be created; a mass market, and more than that, a mass market for good taste. This was the retailers' function. It required a deep understanding of people and of the social and economic and cultural forces working upon them. It meant raising the public standard of taste.

Running a store means dealing with people, all kinds of people and I have learned that there is no man or woman who does not respond to beauty, whether in a dress, a car, an advertisement, or a window display. Even the craze for the Model T died when better designed cars became available— even though they cost a little more.

The double job of the retailers, through their advertising, their windows, their merchandising displays, was first to indoctrinate the American woman to buy with good taste, and second, to offer her clothes which satisfied not only her physical needs but also her emotional needs: in other words, clothes which she needed plus clothes which she couldn't resist.

As a retailer, I must pay tribute here to the fashion press of America. Our great fashion magazines, our newspapers, the radio, and most recently television, have superbly carried out their job of bringing the fashion news to the buying public. Mass production means millions of dresses, and millions of dresses need millions of customers. The press has been on the job constantly, expanding, educating, and exciting the consumer market. It has been both critic and friend to the fashion industry.

All of us are so close to the fashion industry and so busy working with it in one way or another, that we may not have had the time or the perspective to examine the underlying reasons for our success. Yet those reasons hold the clues to our future growth.

We have succeeded because we have tried to keep our taste level high, no matter what the price level. We have succeeded because we have tried to give the best quality possible at every price. With new technological advances every day, this is a never ending job.

We have succeeded because our fashions are a valid and honest expression of American living. They have a look which symbolizes a way of life. It's The American Look, as we named it at Lord & Taylor many years ago and as it has come to be known around the world.

To me all American fashions share this look. It's implicit in the style, the fabric, the workmanship, yet it transcends them all. To strangers it tells at a glance that we are a free people, a prosperous people, a young people. It tells more of our production methods than a dozen lectures on technology and economics. It reflects our demand for functionalism but also our yearning for beauty. It is an unmistakable announcement of the difference between Communist rule and democratic government.

These are the reactions I have heard whenever I have gone abroad or whenever foreign visitors have come here. To the rest of the civilized world American fashions are a symbol of our democracy, proof that here one need not be rich to be well dressed, proof that in America equality and independence live together.

This is a country full of ideas, full of warmth, full of dreams. If we in the fashion industry can continue to express them, our opportunities are unlimited and our greatest glories yet before us.

NOTE

1. Typescript. Dorothy Shaver Papers, 1947–1959, Schlesinger Library, Radcliffe Institute, Harvard University, Cambridge, MA.

Fannia Cohn (1885–1962)

From 1918 until the year of her death, 1962, Fannia Cohn led the Education Department of the International Ladies Garment Workers Union (ILGWU). Under her leadership, her union developed the most extensive workers' education program in the nation. Born in Russia in 1885, Cohn was the daughter of middle-class Jewish parents. She attended a private school in Russia and became a socialist revolutionary during her teens; but after a brother was nearly killed in a pogrom, she came to the United States with the financial assistance of a relative in New York. Once in the United States, relatives offered her further financial assistance to continue her education. However, Cohn sought to raise the working class from within and became a garment worker. At twenty, she was already an older worker in that time and industry. She became a mentor and teacher to younger workers. In so doing, Annelise Orleck tells us, Cohn had "created the role that she would play throughout her career: an educator to younger workers."[1]

Cohn was a prolific writer on worker's education and women's roles in the labor movement and a frequent public speaker. Her published articles and speeches were typically made into pamphlets. Examples include: *The Uprising of the Sixty Thousand*, honoring a 1933 strike; *Can Women Lead*, which describes obstacles to female leadership within unions and ways the obstacles might be overcome; and *We Kept Our Faith*, a memorial to the Triangle victims.[2]

The speech included here was given at an ILGWU convention in 1956. It is noteworthy that Cohn, a devoted unionist who had served her union for three decades, was given just ten minutes to speak.[3] In the speech Cohn described the union as "pioneers in adult education" and gave examples of its programs. She discussed union values, and aligned those values with the Bill of Rights and with the United Nations. Finally, she praised the worker's education movement as a dynamic, persistent, but nurturing manifestation of those values.

NOTES

1. Annelise Orleck, *Common Sense and a Little Fire: Women and Working-Class Politics in the United States, 1900–1965* (Chapel Hill: University of North Carolina Press, 1995), 38.

2. Fannia Cohn, *The Uprising of the Sixty Thousand*, reprinted from *Justice*, September 1, 1933; *Can Women Lead*, reprinted from *Justice*, February 15, 1936; *We Kept Our Faith*, reprinted from *Justice*, 1961.

3. Still later, her time limit was reduced even further to only five minutes, as evidenced in papers contained in the UNITE (Successor to ILGWU) archives at the Kheel Center, Cornell University, Ithaca, NY.

A TALK DELIVERED BY FANNIA M. COHN AT THE ILGWU CONVENTION (MAY 14, 1956)[1]

Reprinted by Permission of Cornell University on behalf of UNITE

It would take much more than ten minutes to tell the dramatic story of the early days of the ILGWU Educational Department. I will rather confine myself to the goals, to the ideas behind it.

It was a social, intellectual, and human purpose which inspired the pioneers in adult education—this means the ILGWU. In those days, new pioneers were flocking into the United States—pioneering never ends in the New World. They came to this country to enjoy the blessings of democracy. Instead, they were immediately involved in a struggle against the sweatshop. But after the bitter struggles of the Uprising of the 20,000—the general strike of the dressmakers of 1909—and the Great Revolt—the general strike of the cloakmakers, of 1910—and the general strike of the women in the garment industry in 1913—after partial victories were won, unions established, the workweek shortened, there arose the question, "How to utilize this precious, newly-gained leisure?"

As a partial answer to this question the ILGWU Educational Department was established. A program for this newly established office had to be worked out. The task immediately facing us was that of integrating these victorious workers into their adopted country. First of all, they had to be taught the language of their new country—English. For this purpose were established educational, recreational, and social centers in 9 public schools in New York City, as well as in Philadelphia and Chicago. The English teachers in these centers were on the payroll of the Board of Education, but the privilege of selecting them was granted by the Board to us. One evening a week, we conducted our own program, whose goal was to enrich the lives of our people and help them to develop their personalities. Then, as now, we had faith in their innate capacities for growth and development. We believed then, as now, that human nature and human behavior are not static, but are constantly changing. We felt it to be our mission to help to develop enlightened, understanding, imaginative citizens who could participate creatively in the affairs of their union, the larger labor movement, the state, and the nation. Therefore, we also arranged special instruction in citizenship, and tens of thousands of our members became citizens of their adopted country, with our help.

But our educational department was not static. It adapted itself to new conditions, to a changing world, keeping pace with the growth of our members. We kept a constant eye on promising students. For them, we arranged special courses for "Active Members," which were also attended by executive board members. We know that full-time officers have little spare time in which to follow world events, so we conducted a program for our officers in which competent educators analyzed and evaluated current events and the more important problems which confronted the labor movement, the community, and the nation. This was a rewarding experience. A program was also provided for wives and children of members, and this program led to the establishment of a pioneer youth camp.

Unity House, our ILGWU vacation country place, was not overlooked. An interesting, enjoyable cultural program was conducted there. We had outstanding personalities among the lecturers.

Those who completed satisfactorily the work at the social and educational centers were offered an advanced program at Washington Irving High School, where the adult university was established. History repeats itself: we are again conducting a program in a center of higher education. For many years, we conducted an education program at the Washington Square branch of New York University, and now for the last few years, our Saturday program has been conducted at Hunter College, where stimulating and thought-provoking cultural activities are carried on. Our program includes music appreciation, interpretations of literature, American history, the drama, and other subjects which stimulate broad cultural interest in our members during their leisure hours.

To make it possible for our members to enjoy the best in literature, the ILGWU Book Division was established. Not only did the Division select good titles, but the department also contributed generously toward the purchase cost.

The Activity called KNOW YOUR CITY, which consists in Saturday visits to local points of interest, was begun thirty years ago, and developed into a class on wheels. Instead of lectures on art, natural history, science, industry, educational, social, and governmental institutions and scenic and historic points, specific museums, factories, universities, and so on are visited with suitable teachers. Instead of an abstract impression, our members are given an immediate first-hand experience of the subject under consideration. This of course brings us into closer contact with the life of the community, and encourages a more active participation in this life.

We have always arranged activities under the auspices of our local unions. These have been conducted in five languages (Italian, Russian, Spanish, Yiddish, and English) to meet the needs of our own United Nations.

As we know, man lives in the present, but also in the past and in the future. In the present, we take lessons from the past, that we may better plan for the future, for the generations who will follow us. The memory of the past and our goals for the future combine to make our present faith. We may not always live up to the Bill of Rights, but it embodies our deepest faith, a faith which the Educational Department is constantly seeking to express and implement in action. We desire, for instance, to deepen our understanding of the problems of the world of which we are a part, and we appreciate the aspirations of the various peoples around the earth for independence and self-government. In answer to this strong desire, the Educational Department arranges institutes in the United Nations headquarters in which outstanding leaders of the world organization participate. To explore community, national, and current world problems, the Educational Department arranges annual open discussions in which leading educators participate.

Thus, I think it fair to say that the inspiring traditions of our union, and the idealism of our people have found expression in our Educational Department. Even in the most trying days in the history of the ILGWU, when the union was threatened by destructive forces, and during the frightful depression of the thirties when we hardly had enough money to pay for our telephone service, we held on to the Educational Department. We preserved the continuity of this important educational labor institution which influenced the whole idea of the importance of adult education. Many of the leaders in the field of adult education were inspired by the early experiments made in our department. We are happy in the thought and take pride in the fact that the ILGWU nurtured the workers' education bureau which was later taken over by the AF of L and then developed into an important and effective AFL-CIO department of education.

NOTE

1. Typescript with handwritten revisions. Fannia Cohn Collection, Kheel Center, Cornell University, Ithaca, NY.

Rachel Louise Carson (1907–1964)

Author-biologist Rachel Louise Carson is best known for her book *Silent Spring* (1962). A compelling indictment of chemical pesticides, the book was not only an inspiration for the American environmental movement of the late twentieth century, it also prompted significant legislation, including banning the pesticide DDT.[1] Carson was born on May 27, 1907, in rural Springdale, Pennsylvania. Her family lived in a farmhouse surrounded by woods and meadows. Carson reportedly knew as a child that writing was her vocation. Her mother is credited with nurturing Rachel's interests in both books and nature. She began writing at an early age, becoming a prize-winning, published author of short fiction, in children's magazines such as *St. Nicholas*, by the age of ten.[2]

After graduating from high school, Carson attended Pennsylvania College for Women (now Chatham College), where she majored in English until her junior year, when she took a course in biology that was a life-changing experience.[3] She changed her major to zoology, graduating magna cum laude in 1928, and spent the summer after graduation studying at the Marine Biological Laboratory in Woods Hole, Massachusetts. She earned a Master of Arts in Marine Biology at Johns Hopkins University while working two part-time jobs academic to help support her family.

Carson continued teaching part-time to help alleviate her family's financial hardships during the depression. After the deaths of her father and her older sister, Carson started work as a radio scriptwriter for the United States Bureau of Fisheries. She passed the civil service test and became a full-time junior aquatic biologist for the Bureau of Fisheries—the first female biologist the Bureau had ever hired. She worked for the Bureau (which evolved into the Fish and Wildlife Service) for sixteen

Rachel Louise Carson speaking before Senate Government Operations subcommittee studying pesticide spraying. Bettman/Corbis.

Library of Congress, Prints and Photographs Division, NYWT&S Collection, United Press International photo, [reproduction number LC-USZ62-11207].

years. During that time she was promoted to the grade of biologist and became editor-in-chief of the Information Division. The success of her book *The Sea Around Us* (1951), which she wrote while still working full time for the Fish and Wildlife Service, made it possible for Carson to leave government employment and dedicate her life to writing.

The success of her book also had at least one other important impact on Carson's life, however; it virtually required her to become a public speaker. As Carson once told an audience:

I have found that the writing of books has many unexpected consequences. One of the things I didn't anticipate when I wrote *The Sea Around Us* was that I should ever be called upon to make a speech! In fact....I still resist the idea, although with the passage of time I have become a little more resigned....[4]

The speech included here was given in response to an award, the Achievement Award of the American Association of University Women (AAUW) in 1956. It is reprinted with the capitalization and indentation of the podium copy included in Carson's papers at Yale University. Similar patterns are seen in some of her other speaking notes and manuscripts.

While it is a complete manuscript, rather than a keyword outline, it may have functioned somewhat like an outline in helping her keep her place and maintain her chosen pace.

The speech focused upon three interrelated ideas: (1) that she viewed the award she received as endorsement of her work and encouragement to continue her roles as a communicator and interpreter of scientific information, (2) that she perceived the writing profession as essentially lonely and pioneering, but one that friendly acknowledgment, such as this award, made happier, (3) that the subjects about which she had written and expected to write in the future had "in some mysterious way" chosen her. Among those subjects, by the time of this speech, were the sea, the seashore and the animal and plant life found there. Like Cassandra or Jeremy, ancient prophets truthful but reviled, Carson accepted her "hermeneutical" destiny. Her masterpiece, *Silent Spring,* is a twentieth-century jeremiad by the remarkable, sensitive, humble women who spoke the following words upon receiving an AAUW Achievement Award in 1956.

NOTES

1. *Silent Spring* was ranked among the top ten nonfiction books of the twentieth century, earning Carson a ranking among *Time* magazine's top 100 scientists and thinkers of the twentieth century. See the Modern Library Board's list of the 100 Best Nonfiction Books of the Twentieth Century (www.randomhouse.com /modernlibrary/100best); and *Time* 100: Scientists and Thinkers (www.time.com /time/time100/scientist/profile/carson03.html).

2. Lisa Budwig, "Breaking Nature's Silence: Pennsylvania's Rachel Carson," October 22, 1997 (www.dep/state.pa.us/dep/PA_Env-Her/rachel.htm); Christine Oravec, "Rachel Louise Carson," in *Women Public Speakers in the United States, 1925–1993,* Karlyn Kohrs Campbell, ed. (Westport, CT: Greenwood Press, 1994), 72–89.

3. Budwig, "Breaking Nature's Silence," 2–3.

4. Speech before AAUW (Virginia Association) December 8, 1959. Rachel Carson Papers, Beinecke Rare Book and Manuscript Library, Yale University, New Haven, CT.

ACCEPTANCE OF AAUW ACHIEVEMENT AWARD (1956)[1]

I DOUBT THAT ANY WORDS I might chose [sic] would express adequately
my appreciation of this award.
By conferring it upon me, you have not only made me feel one
of you,

but from this time forward I shall be conscious
 of your friendly interest
 and even your participation in all that I am doing.
WRITING IS A LONELY PROFESSION AT BEST.
 Of course there are stimulating and even happy
  associations with others, as friends or colleagues.
But during the actual work of creation the writer cuts
 himself off from all others and confronts his
 subject alone.
He moves into a realm where he has never been before
 —perhaps where no one has ever been.
 It is a lonely place—and even a little frightening.
 But if he carries with him into that realm of mental
  solitude a warm glow of frinedship [sic] and of appreciation
  such as you have signified by this award—
  his task is made immeasurably happier.
NO WRITER CAN STAND STILL.
 He continues to create or he perishes.
 Each task completed carries its own obligation to go on
  to something new.
I AM ALWAYS MORE INTERESTED in what I am about to do
 than in what I have already done.
 I interpret this Achievement Award, not only as
  approval of what my work has stood for in the past
 but as an expression of your belief that I may go on to
  do other things that are worth doing.
SO PERHAPS IT IS APPROPRIATE to suggest very briefly tonight
 the area of my present thought and work—
 the area in which your award will assist me—
 materially and intangibly.
OVER THE YEARS I have developed certain beliefs about the
 relation between the writer and his subject.
 I believe, for example, that in some mysterious way the
  subject chooses the writer—not the other way around.
 To illustrate: I cannot explain my own preoccupation with
  the sea. The fascination was always there—
  calling me—long before I had seen the ocean.
AFTER DEALING FIRST IN MY BOOKS WITH THE physical realities of
 the sea,
 I came naturally enough to consider its amazing and
 abundant life—
 especially as revealed most accessibly at the meeting
  place of sea and land.
 Then it seemed inevitable that the *central riddle of life*
  itself should begin to possess my mind:
  how, in the dim past of our earth, living things first arose;
  how they evolved;
  and what their future may be.
 This will be the general subject of my next book.

AS I HAVE PONDERED THESE QUESTIONS I have become aware
    that in biology, as in physics and astronomy,
    new horizons have been established.
Today we are gaining wholly new conceptions,
    and these are leading toward the understanding of life
    processes that heretofore have remained in the realm of mystery.
THE OLD BARRIERS BETWEEN THE BRANCHES OF SCIENCE—
    and they were man-made ones after all—
    are breaking down.
        whatever else life may be,
        it is to an important extent a chemical and physical process.
    Biologists now freely use the tools provided by chemistry
        and physics.
    By doing so, they are opening doors that had remained
        closed throughout the centuries
        of human intellectual effort.
UNTIL RECENTLY, I HAD BEEN ONE OF THOSE
    who believed we should never be able to penetrate
    the mystery of how life arose.
    Now, studying the work of some modern pioneers
    in biochemistry,
    I have come to believe science can at least form a
        reasonable theory to account for that mystery of all mysteries.
    I believe we shall come to understand, too, exactly how
        the gene exerts its control over heredity—
        directing the development of the cell and of the whole organism
        through complex chemical action.
AND WHO, A GENERATION AGO, would have dared believe that
    groups of molecules having the basic characteristics of living
    things might one day be synthesized in the laboratory?
    Today, the possibility is there—if we will look at it.
ALL THIS MEANS THAT BIOLOGY HAS MOVED FORWARD INTO A NEW
    PHASE of its development
    Its leaders are men and women who have had the courage
    to abandon preconceived ideas.
    They seek truth—whatever truth may prove to be.
IT IS A PRIVILEGE to be a biologist in this particular
    era of expanding horizons.
    I consider it my especial privilege to have the
    opportunity to INTERPRET some of these discoveries
        for those who are not scientists.
    They do have meaning and significance for us all.

NOTE

    1. Note cards. Rachel Carson Papers, Series I, Folder 1829, Beinecke Rare
Book and Manuscript Library, Yale University, New Haven, CT.

Martha May Eliot (1891–1978)

Martha Eliot was a pediatrician who devoted her practice to a lifetime of public service at local, national, and international levels. She graduated from Radcliffe College and then the Johns Hopkins School of Medicine in 1918. After serving a number of internships/residencies, and doing some teaching at Yale University School of Medicine, Eliot joined Grace Abbott at the federal Children's Bureau in 1924. In addition to her work there, which included helping Director Abbott draft a version of Title V of the Social Security Act, she was acclaimed for her pioneering research on the children's disease rickets.[1]

When Abbott retired as bureau chief, her primary assistants, Katharine Lenroot and Eliot, were both contenders as her replacement. However, Lenroot, a social worker like Abbott, had served as acting Chief in Abbott's absence and was appointed to the position. Under Lenroot, Eliot continued to demonstrate leadership, particularly in developing the Emergency Maternal and Infant Care (EMIC) program, modeled on Julia Lathrop's War Risk Insurance idea from World War I.[2] Eliot also helped found UNICEF and the World Health Organization (WHO), serving as Assistant Director of WHO from 1949 to 1951. In 1951, Eliot left WHO and was persuaded to take over as chief of the Children's Bureau, Lenroot having been forced out by officials in the Truman administration. In 1957, Eliot resigned to become a professor of Child and Material Health at the Harvard School of Public Health.

Eliot was an active speaker throughout her career. Two radio series in particular, *The Child Grows Up* and *Children in Wartime*, regularly featured remarks by Eliot during the 1930s and 1940s. A powerful intellectual,

Eliot never published her work. Thus, her collected speeches held at the Schlesinger Library, are an important record of Eliot's work and thought on issues of public health from 1924 into the 1960s.

The speech included here was delivered shortly after Eliot retired as chief of the Children's Bureau. It is a 1958 commencement address to graduating nurses at Beth Israel Hospital in New York. In this speech Eliot characterized many of the ways in which American society changed during the postwar years, and she challenged student nurses to be prepared for a new array of child welfare and health care issues arising from the "population explosion" of the 1950s. With remarkable foresight, Eliot urged the graduating nurses to be ready for health and welfare problems associated with deteriorating urban areas, suburban conformity and intolerance, and child care for working mothers, as well as issues related to increasing numbers of unmarried mothers.

NOTES

1. Jacqueline K. Parker, "Women at the Helm: Succession Politics at the Children's Bureau, 1912–1968," *Social Work* 39 (September 1994): 554; see also materials in the Martha May Eliot Papers, Schlesinger Library Manuscript Collections, Harvard University, Cambridge, MA.

2. Ibid., 554–555.

THE COMMUNITY AND ITS CHILDREN
1958 COMMENCEMENT ADDRESS OF THE BETH
ISRAEL HOSPITAL SCHOOL OF NURSES[1]

Reprinted by Permission of the Schlesinger Library

I am happy to be here tonight to speak to you who are about to be graduated from this School of Nursing and to enter a new life of independent action. Though the channels that will give direction and inspiration to that action have been forming for all the years of your lives, they have, no doubt, become deeper and broader during your three years at this School. What you have gained here in knowledge and wisdom will serve you long and well. As you go about your new tasks you will time and again look back, as I have looked back all my life at my educational experience, and realize how meaningful your work here at the School has been for each future event and how each future experience enriches that which has come before. From tonight on, each of you will become a responsible member of some community and will be seeking ways, as members of the old and honorable profession of nursing, to render service to the people of those communities. The traditions and the prestige of your profession will open many doors to you for such service and most, if not all, of you will sooner or later find yourselves involved in activities with the community's children. It is fitting, therefore, that we should consider tonight some of the facts of child life in our communities today and a few aspects of community action that may be of concern to you in meeting the needs of children.

May I remind you first, however, that the foundation patterns of your own lives, that have made each of you what you are today, were laid down first in your earliest years and were woven, in large part, from the warp and woof of the family and community culture into which each of you were born and in which you spent those early formative years. The variations in your individual family customs and mores, in the social and psychological attitudes of parents, and in your own individual reactions to them, together with the changes that took place in your family structure, have no doubt placed their marks deeply on each of you. Within this family structure and culture each of you was nurtured; out of it each of you, through the process of growth and development, has emerged as an individual.

As you grew the impact upon you of the community in which your family lived became stronger and stronger. In your earliest years the influence of the community reached you through your parents. No doubt your parents had many contacts in the community. Their friends, their relatives, their intimate advisors; the representatives of the organized community services, physician, nurse, teacher, religious counselor; the casual contacts of the neighborhood in which you lived; all these and more had their influence on your parents when you were young and served to strengthen, mold, and modify your family life and the goals and attitudes of your parents in that most important of all tasks—the task of rearing children.

As you grew, each to become the individual person that you are, you acquired the fundamental characteristics of personality that you have. Each of you has passed with greater or less success through the seven successive stages of growth and development, described so understandably by Erikson, to arrive today at that last stage in which you will now be taking your own places as responsible, mature members of some community.

The world into which you are emerging is indeed a new and different one from that of twenty or even ten years ago. It is a world of rapidly increasing population, of tremendous speed in communication and transport, of miracles in the physical and biological sciences, of struggle of the social sciences to keep pace with the natural sciences, of unprecedented movements of population, of automation in industry and business, of conformity to social pressures, of too frequent family breakdown and serious emotional disturbances among young people, of international tension and increased individual anxiety. For many people, it is a world of movies and television, of processed foods, of automobiles and electric refrigerators, of electric irons and washing machines, of gadgets of every description, and of relative health and happiness. But for millions of other people, those who live in the so-called underdeveloped countries, it is still a world of hunger, bad housing, inadequate clothing, sickness and premature death, of hard and prolonged hours of work that provide only for the merest existence. And everywhere the tensions brought about by international rivalries and disagreements add to the qualms of conscience and the individual fears and anxieties that nearly all of us have carried forward from our childhood as a result of the need to conform often unreasonably, it seems, to the demands of our culture.

This in a few words is the world in which you will be taking your places; in which new families are being formed, in which a new generation of children are growing up. It is no easy task that parents have today. It is no easy task for doctors, and nurses, teachers and social workers, and others who seek to help parents in their job of rearing children.

To some who have watched this new world a'coming over many years the task of accommodating old ways to new may seem staggering, bewildering, unsurmountable in its on-rush of scientific achievement. In their anxiety and ignorance of what it means and how the new knowledge can be used to aid rather than to destroy mankind, many people may see only confusion and ultimate disaster.

But to those of you who have grown up during this period of rapid change the task is indeed different. To you the great advances in science will serve as a stimulant to seek new solutions to many age old problems. Upon you, and the millions and millions of other young people like you in the world, rests the task of fitting into this new world, and, each in your own way, understanding the contribution that you can make either in your own families or through community action to the present and the coming generation of children.

What, then, is the situation with respect to our children? What are some of the community problems with which you and your colleagues in the whole nursing profession will have to wrestle? There is time to speak of only a few. The facts that I shall give you are generally national in scope, but like all national data they are compiled from the local communities and from the States, and so may be thought about in each community.

Let us look first at our burgeoning child population and at some of its characteristics that make child health and child welfare work complex.

In 1957, the Census Bureau estimated that we had more than 59 million children and youth under 18 years of age in this country, an increase of some 19 million (47%) since 1940; twelve million of this increase or 25% has occurred since 1950. By 1960, the Census Bureau estimates this child population will have been increased by nearly 5 million more. This so-called "population explosion" has exceeded all previous records and has affected many of our public and voluntary programs for families and children. The unprecedented shortage of teachers and classrooms in our schools is perhaps our most pressing current problem growing out of this population rise. But it is only one of many with which you should be familiar.

I am thinking of the hundreds of thousands of low-income families who have migrated from rural areas to our central city slums, so recently vacated by the mass movement of city families to suburbia. The bad social and health conditions of these deteriorated city districts foster discontent, anxiety, family break-up, dependency, neglect, delinquency. Even in the mushrooming suburbs, to which so many families have moved hoping to find space, sunlight, health, good schools, congenial neighbors, and good recreation facilities, conditions disadvantageous to the health, welfare, and education of children exist. One of the problems of these new suburbs that concern many child health and welfare workers is the over-emphasis on conformity that is so prevalent in them. Sometimes these conforming groups are justified as natural gatherings of like with like, but the isolation of children in the community and in school from children who come from families of other cultural backgrounds is a real deprivation in their social growth and development. The detrimental effect on their personality development may well be reflected, not in an increase of tolerance for people of different cultures, but in greater intolerance and discrimination. I do not have to dwell on the desperate need we have in this country to take steps that will tend to dispel rather than increase intolerance and discrimination. The damage done to the developing personalities of the intolerant is far more devastating to our national life and international relations than is the damage done to those against whom discrimination is shown.

Housing problems have for many decades involved us as a people in actions that have consciously or unconsciously influenced children and young people adversely with respect to this question of understanding the variation and the strengths and value of different cultures and groups. Policies of segregation, zoning laws, and the attitudes of owners of property have ingrained in children in their most impressionable years the habit of associating only with children and families of their own or similar culture. The current problems in the hundreds of new suburban communities are no exception. For those of us who are committed to fostering international understanding among peoples, the development of these one-culture conforming type of communities, whether in central cities or in the new suburbs, is a serious backward step. It is an area of community action in which each of us should have the deepest concern and be prepared to take our individual positions courageously.

For you who will be taking your places in the community as nurses, whether in hospitals, public health programs, or as informed citizens, there is another major problem arising out of the population explosion that inevitably will be of concern to you. I am thinking now of what the community must to do help parents more effectively than we do today to understand and to foster healthy personality development in infancy and the pre-school years. Each year now more than 4 million babies are born; more than 4 million families have the responsibility of starting them on the road to healthy personality development.

The Midcentury White House Conference on Children in 1950 took as its main theme and centered its reports around this question of how a healthy personality in the child can be achieved. This is, no doubt, a matter of education of the public, and in particular of young parents, in what is required to assure satisfactory all around growth and development of children. It involves many new concepts of the role of medicine, psychology, sociology, and cultural anthropology. It involves a new look at our social behavior and at those deeply imbedded aspects of our various cultures that have forced us, and will force our children to conform to tradition, taboos, superstitions, prejudices, and other concepts that have no scientific evidence to substantiate them and that are the underlying and unconscious cause of many of the individual anxieties and fears.

Health personnel generally, and doctors and nurses in particular, have an important role to play in this business of parent education, for it is they who are often the first to have an opportunity to counsel with young parents before or at the time when the first baby is expected in a new family. The influence of even a few words at this time is well known. That these words should be imbued with wisdom based on facts and scientific knowledge would, I believe, be generally accepted by our colleagues in medicine.

It is also generally accepted that health personnel require thorough basic training in child growth and development if they are to be successful in this field of parent education. Facts we may learn; the wisdom that we need will be acquired through experience, especially that which is gained under the supervision of a counselor who is himself wise in the understanding of human behavior and interpersonal relations. Of those of you who graduate today there is presumably not one who will not need this kind of wisdom in the career of your choice. As members of a community, be it as a hospital nurse, a public health nurse, a private duty nurse, or as an administrator, you will sooner or later have the opportunity to learn what the resources of the community are to foster the kind of parent education that we want.

I have time for only one more aspect of the community's concern for its children, namely, that of services in the social welfare field. Child welfare programs came into being many decades ago in response to the demands of citizens that the community's children should have as much protection from abuse, neglect, and dependency as were then being provided for animals by the humane societies. The story of how a great reform movement which resulted in the creation of the first society for the prevention of cruelty to children grew out of the efforts of a single citizen in New York to protect one child who was being abused by her parents is often told as an illustration of the influence and power that can be exerted for the good of a community by one determined member of society. Sometimes, today, such reformers are laughed at, but on the whole those in authority who hold the responsibility to act in the common good, at least secretly and often openly, applaud the leadership of citizens who help steer the course of such action by communities. Many times groups of disadvantaged people have had their load lightened because of the efforts of a small number of informed citizens who have learned how to get the facts, how to bring them to the attention of the authorities, and the public at large, and who refuse to drop the issues until action is taken. When the issue relates to the welfare or health of children the goals have wide-spread interest and may in the long run serve to create comparable concern for and public interest in reform measures more difficult of accomplishment.

Though we have gone a long way in assuming public responsibility for the protection of children through State and national action, there are still countless communities in our country where well established principles of child welfare have not been applied. In this area of children's needs, as in the field of child health, there is still great opportunity for action by well-informed citizens.

The first step for any interested person is to get at the facts. There are many questions that we can ask ourselves. What, for example we may ask, is happening to children of working mothers in my community? Have the authorities, whether public or voluntary, supplied enough day-care centers to meet their needs? Are they near enough to the family homes so that it is practical for the mothers to use them? What is the quality of care provided? Is nursery education part of that care? How well trained are the workers? Who can help us answer these questions?

Or, we may ask: What is happening to the unmarried mothers in our community? Are we making adequate maternity care freely available to these young women in ways that they can accept it? What is happening to their babies? How satisfactory are the adoption policies in our community? Are babies being passed from family to family without regard for the baby's need of a single, loving, warm-hearted mother-person who can substitute for the child's own mother until decisions are reached with respect to permanent care? Are the State laws adequate for the protection of these babies, their natural parents, and their future adoptive parents? Are the medical and legal professionals cooperating with the social workers to assure adequate service and care? How well are the laws carried out? To whom can we turn for answers to these questions?

These and many other matters affecting the health and welfare of children spring quickly to mind when we stop to consider what the community is doing for its children. They are but a few examples that could be drawn from a long list of children's needs of which we, as members of a health profession, must be aware. Once we join one of the health professions, as you are tonight, new obligations automatically come to rest upon us to accept a share in the responsibility of the public for its children. Because you are young and new at your chosen work does not relieve you of this obligation. On the contrary, your youth, your newly acquired knowledge, and the traditional concern of the nursing profession for service, increase your obligation to extend yourselves into the community in which we have chosen to live and to give it your knowledge and strength in partial return for what it has given you. To do so will bring to you in the years ahead not only the satisfactions that come from providing the best possible care to an individual patient, but also those which come from sharing in our common responsibility for the good of all children.

NOTE

1. Typescript with handwritten revisions. Martha May Eliot Papers, Schlesinger Library, Harvard University, Cambridge, MA.

Pauli Murray (1910–1985)

Pauli Murray was a Renaissance woman—writer, political activist, and spiritual leader.[1] She was raised by her grandparents in North Carolina and graduated with a degree in English from Hunter College in 1933. During this period she worked for the WPA and the Workers' Defense League. Murray met Eleanor Roosevelt in 1940 and they became close friends. She attended Howard University Law School, then received an M.A. from the U.C. Berkeley School of Law in 1945. During World War II she was instrumental in organizing the first sit-ins leading to successful integration of lunch counters near the Howard University campus in Washington, DC. Her survey of racial laws in the United States, which she wrote in 1950, was an important document for the 1954 *Brown vs. Board of Education* Supreme Court decision, which denied the legitimacy of schools segregated by race.

Murray lived in Brooklyn, New York, and worked as a lawyer, and for many liberal causes throughout the 1950s. At the beginning of this period, her close friend Maida Springer-Kemp urged her to run for city council on the Liberal ticket. With Springer as her campaign manager, Murray ran a strong campaign, which, though unsuccessful, was an important breakthrough for African Americans. As the 1950s moved along, however, Murray grew more and more discouraged by the racism in the United States. She finally accepted a position teaching law at the University of Ghana. In 1965, Murray returned to the United States, having learned she was more American than African. She wrote that her experience led her to "understand that I am the product of a new history which began on African shores but which has not been shared by Africans, a history accompanied by such radical changes in a new environment that over time it produced a new

Pauli Murray, 1946.

Library of Congress, Prints and Photographs Division, NYWT&S Collection,
[reproduction number LCUSZ62-109644].

identity."[2] Upon returning to the United States, Murray completed a second
law degree at Yale University in 1965. In addition, she served on the Civil
and Political Rights Committee of President Kennedy's Commission on the
Status of Women. She eventually joined other women from the Commission
to found the National Organization for Women. In 1968, she accepted a faculty position at Brandeis University. And, finally, at age 63, Murray entered
the seminary and became the first black woman Episcopal priest in 1977.

The speech included here was delivered in 1959. Murray consciously placed herself and her audience at the middle of the twentieth century, focusing her remarks on civil rights. Murray was about to emerge as a national leader in the revived women's movement. The speech illustrates her determination to fight for justice, but her emphasis was on love and compassion, not anger and hatred. Murray transcended difference in her call to action, rather than demanding people take sides in a winner/loser confrontation.

NOTES

1. Biographical information is from Pauli Murray, *The Autobiography of a Black Activist, Feminist, Lawyer, Priest, and Poet* (Knoxville, TN: University of Tennessee Press, 1987); Murray, *Proud Shoes: The Story of An American Family* (New York: Harper and Brothers, 1956); Sonja K. Foss, "Pauli Murray," in *Women Public Speakers in the United States, 1925–1993*, Karlyn Kohrs Campbell, ed. (Westport, CT: Greenwood Press, 1994), 319–330; Casey Miller and Kate Swift, "Pauli Murray," *Ms.*, March 1980, 60–64; and the Pauli Murray Papers, Schlesinger Library Manuscript Collection, Harvard University, Cambridge, MA.

2. Murray, *Autobiography*, p. 332.

BEING GOOD NEIGHBORS—THE CHALLENGE OF THE MID-TWENTIETH CENTURY, POUGHKEEPSIE NEIGHBORHOOD CLUB (FEBRUARY 12, 1959)[1]

Madam President, Helen Lockwood, members and friends of the Poughkeepsie Neighborhood Club:

We meet tonight on the 150th anniversary of the birth of Abraham Lincoln, who, in the words of Carl Sandburg, his biographer, "looms colossal in American history or in world annals." We mark this event symbolically by having a banquet in celebration of the Lincoln–Douglas debates which took place one hundred years ago. The words of Douglas have gone down into obscurity. They had no lasting value. The words of Lincoln still light our troubled pathway of the mid-Twentieth Century. He said:

"As I would not be a slave, so I would not be a master. This expresses my idea of democracy. Whatever differs from this, to the extent of the difference, is no democracy."

He also said:

"In giving freedom to the slave, we assure freedom to the free. * * * Our reliance is the love of liberty which God has planted in our bosoms. Our defense is in the preservation of the spirit which prizes liberty as the heritage of all men, in all lands, everywhere."

Those of us here in this room who have suffered humiliation can take courage from Lincoln's own experience, when he remarked:

"I have endured a great deal of ridicule without much malice; and have received a great deal of kindness, not quite free from ridicule. * * * It is difficult to make a man feel miserable while he feels he is worthy of himself and claims kindred to the great God who made him."

The final tribute to Abraham Lincoln at his burial vault in Springfield, Illinois, May 4, 1865, by Bishop Matthew Simpson, was a prophecy which applies to our own time. He said:

"There are moments which involve themselves in eternities...Such a moment came in the tide of our time to our land, when a question must be settled, affecting all the powers of the earth. The contest was for human freedom, not for this republic merely, not for the Union simply, but to decide whether the people, in their entire majesty, were destined to be the Government, or whether they were to be subjects to tyrants or aristocrats, or to class rule of any kind * * * and the result of this contest will affect the ages to come. If successful, republics will spread, in spite of monarchs, all over this earth."

Last week, we witnessed a triumph of the principles for which Lincoln lived and died—"That this nation, under God, shall have a new birth of freedom, and that government of the people, by the people, for the people shall not perish from the earth."

In the great state of Virginia, "massive resistance" finally bowed to the supreme law of the land and the Federal Constitution. In my own heart, and I am sure in your hearts as well, there was quiet rejoicing that the American dream of liberty and the Constitution which guarantees that liberty had survived one of its severest ordeals of our time.

We also meet tonight a few days after the 77th anniversary of the birth of another great American—your own friend and neighbor, Franklin D. Roosevelt—whose shadow lengthens across the Twentieth Century. Here, too, was a man who rose to national leadership at a time of deepening crisis and whose personality profoundly influenced the history of the world.

It was Roosevelt who brought courage and hope to a nation in the depths of economic and political crisis with the words of his first Inaugural Address, March 4, 1933:

"Let me assert my firm belief that the only thing we have to fear is fear itself."

And further, in the same address:

"In the field of world policy, I would dedicate the nation to the policy of the good neighbor."

In his State of the Union message of January 6, 1941, Roosevelt uttered those inspiring words that found electrifying response in the hearts and minds of men in every corner of the earth. He said:

"In the future days, which we seek to make secure, we look forward to a world founded upon four essential freedoms.

"The first is freedom of speech and expression—everywhere in the world.

"The second is freedom of every person to worship God in his own way—everywhere in the world.

"The third is freedom from want.

"The fourth is freedom from fear."

As we pause in our deliberations to pay tribute to the memory of these two men, we realize afresh the richness and wide range of the American dream of liberty and democracy. In externals, they present the widest contrast—one a man of humble origins and a Republican, the other born to wealth and prestige and a Democrat. Yet both had a common vision and a common love for humanity and both rose to the challenge of inspired leadership at a time of fateful decision. They represent the best in our common heritage, for in history they belong to no political party or single nation. They belong to mankind.

The strident tones of the debate over freedom are still echoing over our land. There are the inheritors of Douglas who defend the substitute for slavery—racial superiority and racial segregation. And there are the voices of men like Lincoln and Roosevelt who are passionately resolved that human liberty shall not perish from the earth.

And there are those of us who stand at the center of this turmoil—not quite one hundred years, only four generations removed from chattel slavery. Yet nowhere on the earth has a group of people come so far, so fast, with so little and against such odds. The bitterness of opposition to our advance in some parts of our country is the measure of our progress. And our sudden breakthrough into so many areas of American life hitherto closed to us is a measure of the vitality of the American dream.

I must say here, parenthetically, that despite Lincoln's devotion to the ideal of liberty, he was limited by the times in which he lived. As late as September, 1862, when he issued his preliminary Emancipation Proclamation, Mr. Lincoln believed that colored people could not live side by side with white people on a basis of equality and prefaced his proclamation with a statement of intention to continue his efforts to colonize Negroes elsewhere. What abject degradation must have been the lot of the human being in chattel slavery that Lincoln could not see in our slave ancestors the potential Ralph Bunches, Marian Andersons, Jackie Robinsons, Thurgood Marshalls, Mary McLeod Bethunes and countless others if given even half a chance!

I shall not attempt to document our progress, for we have lived through it together. I prefer to direct our attention to the unfinished tasks at hand.

In this connection, it is fitting that we come together under the auspices of the Poughkeepsie Neighborhood Club. The very name is symbolic, for the planet on which we live has now shrunk until the entire world is a neighborhood. What happens in Little Rock, Arkansas, or in Virginia, is on the front pages of the daily newspapers in every country. In fact, our desegregation troubles accounted for one of the world's ten top news stories of 1958. It was voted first place by the editors of the United Press International taking precedence over the November elections, the Middle East Crisis, the Adams–Goldfine story, the death of Pope Pius, and so on.

In a world of jet planes, intercontinental missiles and space probes, man's survival—barring cosmic catastrophe—depends in large measure upon how quickly he can learn a fundamental respect for human life and human dignity everywhere to the same degree that he has for his own immediate family and his neighbor next door.

We are spending billions of dollars to probe outer space. We talk of visiting other planets. We seek to master the whole universe. Yet, for all our daring we are off-balance. We have not learned to master our own primitive hatreds and prejudices. And this is a sickness of which we are all victims whether we belong to a dominant majority or a disadvantaged minority. I am sometimes appalled at expressions of anti-Semitism and derogatory statements about other groups among Negroes, who should know better.

There are times when we ask ourselves in the words recorded by St. Matthew: "What is a man profited, if he shall gain the whole world and lose his own soul?" Or, to paraphrase it in terms of our current national and international scene—to what avail are our scientific discoveries and our ventures into outer space, if we have not learned to live alongside our neighbor next door who happens to have a different color, religion or national origin from our own?

To be a good neighbor is the great moral challenge of the mid-Twentieth Century. And the aspirations of this Neighborhood Club are also the aspirations of the world community—that men, women and children everywhere can walk and talk together as equals and feel that they belong in the community in which they live and in the family of nations; that they are neither fenced out nor fenced in; that they are free to fulfill their individual destinies and that they are judged by their individual worth.

None of us can escape this challenge. The very essence of democracy and the Judeo-Christian faith which we have inherited is not only individual right but individual responsibility. As Adlai Stevenson said recently,

"Freedom demands infinitely more care and devotion than any other political system. * * * The natural government of man is servitude, tyranny. It is only by intense thought, by burning idealism and unlimited vision that freedom has prevailed."

The first step in being a good neighbor is to clean up one's own back yard and to tidy one's own lawn. A neighbor may accept a cup of sugar which we lend in an emergency, and yet be contemptuous of the slatternly way in which we live.

Let us, therefore, direct our attention to America's back yard—her continuing problem of racial and religious bigotry. The issue of race is enmeshed in every social, economic and political question of our time. It lies heavily upon the hearts and minds of each of us. There is little surcease from the cold war of nerves at home which keeps pace with the cold war abroad. The printing and circulation of hate literature is at a post-war high. In many areas, respect for law and order has given way to general lawlessness and violence such as the bombing of homes, schools, churches and synagogues. Efforts to deal with the problem on a Federal level have too often been throttled in Congress by the threat of filibuster and the abdication of moral principles to personal ambition and political expediency. A vacuum in presidential leadership has only aggravated the situation.

This is no longer our private affair. Every American traveler abroad is beset by embarrassing questions about our race problem. Our Federal Government is bedeviled by it in every aspect of our international affairs. As one writer has put it, "the whole machinery of our international propaganda has to be given over to defensive explanations...there are times when the race issue all but dominates the incoming cable files," and in the words of one high official, "it interlards almost everything we do" both in the State Department and the U.S. Information Agency.

The intense international concern over American racial affairs is crucial to world peace and to our position as a world power. In the aftermath of World War II come a world-wide social and political revolution. As Harold R. Isaacs, a student of public affairs, put it, the United States has found itself competing for power and leadership in a world "where the white man no longer walks as master. In vast parts of the world that have suddenly become so important to us, there are people who have had the experience of Western white racism, whose whole lives and personalities, indeed, were largely shaped by it. These people have ceased allowing themselves to be demeaned by white foreigners in their own countries and they are acutely sensitive to the race aspect of all their new relationships, especially with Americans, heirs to the declining power of Western white man."

Note the volcanic explosiveness with which African nationalism is erupting all over that continent and the glacial-like lethargy with which the Western mind is reacting to this thrust toward equality of treatment and the overthrow of colonial rule. Some 200,000,000 African natives are involved in this massive awakening. In a year's end roundup a few weeks ago, Charles Collingwood, veteran CBS correspondent, predicted that Africa will assume the crucial importance in world affairs during the next ten years which the Middle East has held during the past ten years. And a State Department official stated bluntly a few weeks ago that our racial troubles at home were hampering our relations with the emerging African nations.

We in the United States are shaping the ultimate choice which the peoples of the world will make between two systems—that of democracy with its emphasis upon the individual or that of totalitarianism with its emphasis upon the all-powerful state. We are desperately trying to complete by constitutional and democratic means a social and political revolution which erupted into a civil war to abolish chattel slavery a hundred years ago. It was then paralyzed for a half century following Reconstruction. It surged forward with new impetus during and after World War II. Other social revolutions of modern times have been punctuated by prolonged periods of violence, repression and dictatorship. Moreover, we are learning that the emerging peoples of Asia and Africa are not sold on our western forms of democracy, nor do they have the same instinctive distaste for Soviet Communism that we do. Leaders of African territories are being trained in Moscow as well as in Oxford or Harvard. And there are signs—as in the riots of the Belgian Congo—that the Africans are increasingly impatient at those so-called peaceful methods which seem to obstruct and delay their strides toward self-rule. The Soviet bloc, meanwhile, boldly exploits our vulnerable racial troubles on the one hand while it seeks on the other hand to influence rising African nationalism with offers of trade and aid.

Hence, our form of democracy is facing the stresses and strains of its severest inner test at precisely the time when our greatest rival is bidding for world supremacy on several fronts by other than democratic means. Which system shall triumph? The moral certainty that ours deserves to triumph is by no means unassailable. Take note of Adlai Stevenson's authoritative warning recently that "between a chaotic, selfish, indifferent society and the iron discipline of the Communist world...outer tyranny with purpose may well triumph over the inner purposeless tyranny of a confused way of life."

If I have painted a somewhat gloomy picture, it is done so that we may face unflinchingly the dimensions of our challenge. I am not unmindful of those positive and creative forces which are coming to the surface and in which our hope for solution lies. I shall mention only two.

One is the increasing national awareness of our racial problem and the intense soul-searching which the vast majority of Americans are presently undergoing. In our own lifetime we have seen the conspiracies of silence and evasion torn away, revealing the depth of our turmoil. No longer do we have to shout in vain to get a hearing. In fact, the most conspicuous phenomenon in our current situation is the relative silence of Negro Americans and the violent debates among white Americans on the subject.

This self-examination has created tensions, of course, but I like to think of these as the crisis of growth which attends all social change in a vigorous society rather than the death rattle of a dying society. If one result in this reexamination of basic democratic principles has been "massive resistance" to the supreme law of the land, another far more important and lasting result has been the realignment of the law of the land so that it is consistent with the Constitution and with those principles of justice and equality for all. Moreover, we are feeling the influence of this realignment of practice with principles throughout the land, not only in corrective state and local legislation but in the reexamination and change of the policies of private organizations, institutions and individuals.

The second force is the role which the American Negro is playing in this crisis. It is our destiny as the largest and most controversial minority in the United States to be the barometer of the state of democracy in our own country. We were the physical embodiment of the issue of the mid-Nineteenth Century: That a nation cannot exist half-slave and half-free. We remain the embodiment of the issue in its mid-Twentieth Century form. We are the symbol of the world fermentation into which all nations have been caught up. We have reacted to it with a new self-image which is the common heritage of all Americans. Our intensity of purpose born of repression is not unlike that of the African colonials. We, of course, are committed to Western democracy and disciplined to the rigors of our minority status. We recognize that standing alone we cannot solve the grave issues of human freedom in our country. We can only raise them. But raise them we must, for we are not one whit less determined than the peoples of Asia and Africa to achieve the equality of status which we have so long been denied. Having raised them, however, the major burden of solution shifts to our white fellow citizens. For as Adlai Stevenson has said:

" 'The unfinished work' which Lincoln left us, of creating a society in which all men can hold up their heads as equals and self-respecting citizens, can never be accomplished unless there are enough white men and women who resist to the core of their being the moral evil of treating any of God's children as essentially inferior."

Recently, Chet Huntley, NBC Televsion news commentator, touched off a heated debate by suggesting that the present deadlock in the school situation in the South might be broken if the NAACP and the "militant Negro leadership" withdrew from the school desegregation issue. He continued, and I quote, "I am sure that if the Negroes of America stand—as they can—on the law of the land, the result will be continuing tension and the destruction of at least part of our school system." The storm of protest which following this telecast brought Thomas Waring, Editor of the Charleston, S.C., *News and Courier*, and Roy Wilkins of the NAACP together last Sunday evening for a televised statement of the segregationist and the NAACP positions. Mr. Waring echoed the view of Mr. Huntley in saying that "public education is bound to suffer" as a result of school integration. He continued, *"Local self-government through division of State powers is the Keystone of the Republic. It is being torn apart for the sake of a sociological experiment."*

What Mr. Waring and those who adhere to his view fail to realize is that the very birth and development of our American form of democracy is a "sociological experiment," but we believe it represents the great hope of mankind everywhere.

The Huntley debate, however, has raised a question to which we must give our most thoughtful consideration. History has thrust upon Negro Americans the difficult role of raising unpleasant issues which bring inner conflicts, tensions, turmoil, political crisis and the constant threat of violence. We believe, of course, that we have no choice; for our own sakes and the sake of our country's future we must raise these issues. And whether we raise them vocally or not, our very presence is an issue in America. How can we admirably acquit ourselves in this historical role? How can we set the example of neighborliness which will convert ever larger numbers of Americans to total commitment to our cause?

I have talked about the Four Freedoms. In closing, may I briefly suggest *Four Dedications* to which we should commit ourselves.

The first is *determination*: a resoluteness of purpose to exercise our rights and shoulder our responsibilities in every avenue of our community life.

In the words of Roy Wilkins who answered Mr. Huntley's challenge: "If it is contended that Negro Americans should renounce their constitutional rights, and the redress of their grievances in the courts, we believe this is more than anyone has the right to ask of any people...We cannot do it. We will not do it. We should have no right to be Americans or to enjoy the respect of our fellows, or to receive the love and honor of our children if we voluntarily accepted a lesser status."

Only as we exercise the rights of democracy do they flourish. Disuse brings tyranny. The right to vote is the most solemn obligation of citizenship. In New York, our civil rights in employment, education, public accommodations and publicly-assisted housing are defined by law and protected by remedies under the jurisdiction of the State Commission Against Discrimination. It is our duty to pursue these remedies wherever these rights are violated, for only as we invoke these remedies do we keep an alert public conscience.

The second is *inspiration*: that "burning idealism and unlimited vision" of which Adlai Stevenson talked. To inspire is to stimulate and arouse people to some creative effort. The example of the nine Little Rock youngsters last year who walked with dignity and restraint amid violence and repeated humiliations was an inspiration to every thoughtful American and to millions of people abroad. We, too, have that ability to inspire our fellow Americans by the example of dignity under all circumstances, and must instill this dignity in our children and they in their children.

The third, and in some ways the most important task to which we must dedicate ourselves, is that of *qualification*. I cannot stress this point too much to the young people in this audience. You must gain that knowledge, skill and experience to fit yourselves for the positions of opportunity which are opening to you as barriers of discrimination fall. We are asking that there be no double standards in our society. We must therefore be prepared to meet the most exacting requirements of a single-standard society. *You must be qualified*. As one of my employers told me, "You must be better than good—you must be at your very best."

We must be willing to pay the price of equal opportunity—the keen competition with the best minds and talents our country has to offer. We are asking our fellow Americans to pluck out deep-rooted ways of thinking about us and to accept us as colleagues and equals. We, too, must cast out deep-rooted ways of thinking about ourselves, of expecting too little of ourselves, of doubting ourselves. We must raise our sights, broaden our vision, aspire to the Presidency of the United States, the Supreme Court bench, the Governor's mansion. Only as we have noble aims will our performance rise above mediocrity. And only as we accept responsibility for the welfare of the whole community will our thinking become integrated rather than segregated. For integration is a matter of the mind and the spirit as well as the body.

And finally, we must dedicate ourselves to the task of *conciliation*. To conciliate does not mean to make concessions of principle. It means to win over to principle, to gain by friendly acts, to reconcile and make consistent.

All America is now engaged in various stages of reconciling its practices and making them consistent with the American Dream. We have it in our power to help ease the tensions which necessarily accompany the great social experiment of which we are a vital part. I have long thought that overcoming a deep-rooted prejudice of race or religion is a deeply emotional experience, like being converted to religion or even falling in love. Too often we react to humiliations with resentment and belligerence. If we could learn the technique of converting our resentments into creative and friendly responses, we could go far in reducing tensions and hastening the day of conciliation in the South as well as elsewhere. We got a brief glimpse at such a technique in the Montgomery boycott. Let us find other techniques and use them.

I am reminded of the story of a father whose family had moved into a new neighborhood in a city in California and whose little daughter looked out to see a cross burning on the lawn. In response to her question about it, he replied, "It is only some Christian who has lost his way."

Let us rededicate ourselves tonight to the unfinished tasks of Lincoln and Roosevelt, so that our great country may find her way to that position of trust, respect and esteem accorded to a good neighbor in a world neighborhood.

NOTE

1. Typescript. Pauli Murray Papers, Schlesinger Library, Harvard University, Cambridge, MA.

Suggested Readings, 1945–1960

Crawford, Vicki L., Jacqueline Anne Rouse, and Barbara Woods. *Women in the Civil Rights Movement: Trailblazers & Torchbearers 1941–1965* (Bloomington, IN: Indiana University Press, 1994).

Evans, Sara. *Personal Politics: The Roots of Women's Liberation in the Civil Rights Movement and the New Left* (New York: Knopf, 1979).

Friedan, Betty. *The Feminine Mystique* (New York: Norton, 1963).

Glendon, Mary Ann. *A World Made New: Eleanor Roosevelt and the Universal Declaration of Human Rights* (New York: Random House, 2001).

Harvey, Anna L. *Votes Without Leverage: Women in American Electoral Politics, 1920–1970* (Cambridge: Cambridge University Press, 1998).

Harvey, Brett. *The Fifties: A Woman's Oral History* (New York: ASJA Press, 2002).

Horowitz, Daniel. *Betty Friedan and the Making of* The Feminine Mystique: *The American Left, The Cold War, and Modern Feminism* (Amherst, MA: University of Massachusetts Press, 1998).

Kaledin, Eugenia. *Mothers and More: American Women in the 1950s* (Boston: Macmillan, 1984).

Kerber, Linda K., Alice Kessler-Harris, and Kathryn Kish Sklar, eds. *U.S. History as Women's History: New Feminist Essays* (Chapel Hill, NC: University of North Carolina Press, 1995).

Lynn, Susan. "Gender and Post-World War II Progressive Politics: A Bridge to Social Activism in the 1960s U.S.A.," *Gender and History* 4 (Summer 1992): 215–239.

Meyerowitz, Joanne. "Beyond the Feminine Mystique: A Reassessment of Postwar Mass Culture, 1946–1958," *The Journal of American History* (March 1993): 1455–1482.

Meyerowitz, Joanne, ed. *Not June Cleaver: Women and Gender in Postwar America, 1945–1960* (Philadelphia: Temple University Press, 1994).

Moody, Anne. *Coming of Age in Mississippi* (New York: Dell, 1975).

Murray, Margaret A. M. *Women Becoming Mathematicians: Creating a Professional Identity in Post-world War II America* (Cambridge, MA: MIT Press, 2000).

Olson, Lynne. *Freedom's Daughters: The Unsung Heroines of the Civil Rights Movement from 1830 to 1970* (New York: Simon and Schuster, 2001).

Orleck, Annelise. *Common Sense and a Little Fire: Women and Working-Class Politics in the United States, 1900–1965* (Chapel Hill, NC: University of North Carolina Press, 1995).

Rosen, Ruth. *"Dawn of Discontent," The World Split Open: How the Modern Women's Movement Changed America* (New York: Penguin Books, 2001): 3–36.

Rupp, Leila J., and Taylor, Verta. *Survival in the Doldrums: The American Women's Rights Movement, 1945–1960s* (New York: Oxford University Press, 1987).

Weigand, Kate. "The Red Menace, the Feminine Mystique, and the Ohio Un-American Activities Commission: Gender and Anti-Communism in Ohio, 1951–1954," *Journal of Women's History* 3 (Winter 1992): 70–94.

Weigand, Kate. "Vanguards of Women's Liberation: The Old Left and the Continuity of the Women's Movement in the United States, 1945–1970s," Ph.D. dissertation, Ohio State University, 1995.

Epilogue

The historical record to which this volume contributes demonstrates that women acted on their own and in the nation's political behalf throughout the twentieth century. It is imperative that we study and analyze these words because they document women's long history of political rhetoric and activism as well as trace the roots of the modern women's liberation movement. As we sift through women's public discourse, in debating the merits of the speakers' eloquence, style, intent, and import, the complex nature of women's development as citizens and public speakers begins to emerge. Though *always* speaking as women, they not only spoke on "women's issues" but also responded to any and all substantive matters of the day, whether the issue was child care, party politics, or international diplomacy.

In the early 1960s, the nation once again began to reassess gender definitions and women's place in American society. One reason for the public nature of this discussion was that long-time labor activist and consumer advocate Esther Peterson convinced newly elected President Kennedy to establish a Presidential Commission on the Status of Women. Peterson was put in charge of running the commission, which was chaired by Eleanor Roosevelt. It is important to note that a commission of this sort could not have been established without the existence of a pool of women who could lay claim to strong records of accomplishment in the public sphere. This group, with state-by-state counterparts, provided the essential raw data that documented women's inequality across all socio-economic sectors. Armed with this data and employing Cold War rhetoric (we must use all of our talents to compete with the Soviet Union), women began to organize feminist campaigns at the national level. In 1963, female activists, primarily from the network of state Commissions, established NOW, the National Organization for Women. NOW adopted a reformist agenda consistent with the generally middle-class status of its members. Other, more radical groups of reformers organized separately. Unfortunately, members of these groups were often unaware of the persistent activism of so many women who preceded them.

Fear of nuclear war and communism continued to dominate political discussion in the 1960s, leading women to engage in debates about the arms race, the Nuclear Test Ban treaty, and the hard-line response to the Cold War as waged in Cuba and Southeast Asia. Women also initiated and joined a range of other social movements, including trade unionism, the early environmental movement, and consumer activism. Most prominently, after almost a decade of constant political agitation, led and staffed in large part by African American women from the South, Congress passed the Civil Rights and Voting Rights Acts, which secured *legal equality* for African Americans. At the same time, activist Pauli Murray and Senator Margaret Chase Smith turned their attention to women's equality. They made sure that the word "sex" remained in the Civil Rights Act of 1964, which therefore outlawed discrimination in public accommodation and employment based on race, national origin, religion, and *sex*.

By the late 1970s, the fight for women's rights returned to the national stage. Americans focused on women's public activities, which again ranged from orderly legislative campaigns to outrageous street theater. As scholars emerged from this movement, they began to want to know more about their own history—the history of women of all races and classes—throughout American life. Bit by bit, activists and academics began to fill in the gender gaps that existed in most traditional historical narratives. The speeches contained in this volume aid that process. With this collection, activists, students, and researchers now have materials to explore women's rich history of political rhetoric and activism between 1920 and 1960. If nothing else, this volume illustrates that women's well-publicized 1960s activism was not spontaneously generated, but rather built upon women's long political history, including that of delivering vital, dynamic speeches in the public domain.

To truly know this history, more research needs to be done. Archival research is certain to uncover additional noteworthy speeches. We plan to continue searching, and we hope that this volume will encourage others to take up the challenge.

Appendix: Speeches by American Women Published in *Vital Speeches of the Day*, October 8, 1934–December 31, 1959

Ahlgren, Mrs. Oscar A., President, General Federation of Women's Clubs
    "Challenge of Democracy," 18 (1952–53): 756.
Alexander, Dr. Ruth, Lecturer and Columnist
    "Post-war America That America Does Not Want," 9 (1943–44): 171.
    "Which Way America?" 15 (1949–50): 301.
    "Mid-century World," 17 (1951–52): 242.
    "What Price for the Welfare State?" 18 (1952–53): 199.
    "Formula for Freedom," 20 (1954–55): 150.
    "What Price the Fatted Calf?" 22 (1956–57): 460.
Allen, Florence E., U.S. Circuit Court Judge
    "Bridge to the Future," 11 (1945–46): 390.
Anderson, Mrs. Eugenie (Moore), U.S. Ambassador to Denmark
    "How Our Foreign Policy Is Working," 18 (1952–53): 134.
Austin, Mrs. Jean
    "Alone Together," 3 (1936–37): 136.
Banning, Margaret Culkin, Novelist and Specialist in American Women's Activities
    "War and the Family," 9 (1943–44): 442.
Beals, Mrs. Norman K., Vice President, High School Parent Teachers Association, Franklin, PA
    "Free Man vs. Puppet Man," 15 (1949–50): 725.
Bolton, Francis P., Representative from Ohio to U.S. Congress (Rep)
    "Fundamental Defenses," 14 (1948–49): 503.
Bonny, Mrs. J. B., President, National Association of Pro America
    "Women's Heritage: Beware of Propaganda," 15 (1949–50): 594.
Buck, Pearl S., Author
    "Asiatic Problem," 8 (1942–43): 303.
    "Heart of Democracy," 8 (1952–53): 395.

Bush-Brown, Mrs. James, Director, Pennsylvania School of Horticulture for
        Women, Ambler, PA
        "Rewarding Satisfactions," 16 (1950–51): 699.
Crain, Lucille Cardin, Editor, *The Educational Reviewer*
        "What Are Our Schools Teaching about Business?" 16 (1950–51): 657.
Donlon, Mary H., Chairman, New York State Workman's Compensation Board
        "Get into Politics up to Your Ears," 16 (1950–51): 282.
Douglas, Helen Gahagan, Representative from California to the Democratic
        National Convention
        "Freedom Cannot Be Inherited," 10 (1944–45): 632.
Dulles, Mrs. Eleanor Lansing, Special Assistant to the Director, Office of German
        Affairs, U.S. Department of State
        "Education, Communist Style, American Style," 23 (1957–58): 590.
        "The Challenge of the Western Policy for Germany," 25 (1959–60): 324.
DuMars, Miriam Richardson, American War Mothers
        "No Rocking Chair Age," 17 (1951–52): 341.
Dunne, Irene, Actress and Delegate to the United Nations
        "Freedom is Responsibility," 25 (1959–60): 283.
Fenner, Mrs. Merwyn, Hilton Institute on World Affairs
        "Mice or Men?" 17 (1951–52): 684.
Fisher, Ella W., Associate Professor of Physical Education, Savannah State College
        "Action Scale to Finer Womanhood," 23 (1957–58): 403.
Gambrell, Mary Latimer, Department of History, Hunter College
        "Old Wine in New Bottles," 8 (1942–43): 667.
Glueck, Eleanor T., Research Associate for the Institute of Criminal Law, Harvard
        University
        "Family, the School, and Crime," 1 (1934–35): 516.
Graves, Mrs. Jennie H., President, Vogue Dolls
        "Impact of Taxation on Small Business," 23 (1957–58): 214.
Gruber, Ruth, Field Representative, U.S. Department of the Interior
        "Rediscovery of Alaska," 10 (1944–45): 181.
Hickey, Margaret A., Chairman, Women's Advisory Committee, War Manpower
        Division
        "Bound for the Future," 10 (1944–45): 49.
Hobby, Oveta Culp, Secretary, Department of Health, Education and Welfare
        "Citizen Responsibilities," 21 (1955–56): 905.
Hoppock, Anne, Assistant Director of Elementary Education, New Jersey Depart-
        ment of Education
        "No Time for Panic," 24 (1958–59): 499.
Horton, Mildred McAfee, President, Wellesley College
        "Woman's Responsibility Today," 13 (1947–48): 504.
        "Predictions for the Unpredictable Future," 17 (1951–52): 617.
Houghton, Dorothy D., Assistant Director for Refugees, Migration and Voluntary
        Assistance, U.S. Foreign Operations Administration
        "World Challenges American Educators," 21 (1955–56): 1168.
Hurst, Fannie, Novelist
        "Crisis in the History of Women," 9 (1943–44): 479.
Jacobs, Jane, Associate Editor, *Architectural Forum*
        "Downtown Planning," 25 (1959–60): 190.

Kenny, Sister Elizabeth, Founder of the Elizabeth Kenny Institute
    "Many Shall Walk Again," 10 (1944–45): 26.
Leopold, Alice, Assistant U.S. Secretary of Labor
    "The Challenge of Tomorrow," 24 (1958–59): 478.
Luce, Clare Boothe, Representative from Connecticut to U.S. Congress (Rep) and
    Ambassador to Italy
    "America in the Post-war Air World," 9 (1943–44): 331.
    "Search for an American Foreign Policy," 10 (1944–45): 550.
    "Greater and Freer America," 10 (1944–45): 586.
    "Waging the Peace," 11 (1945–46): 43.
    "News Blackout of the Fifth Army," 11 (1945–46): 305.
    "America and World Communism," 11 (1945–46): 647.
    "China's Government," 12 (1946–47): 94.
    "Saintly Scientist: George Washington Carver," 13 (1947–48): 241.
    "Chamber of Commerce and Communism," 13 (1947–48): 465.
    "Italy in 1955," 21 (1955–56): 1070.
    "Permanent Revolution," 21 (1955–56): 1415.
Lyells, Mrs. Ruby B. Stults, President, Mississippi State Federation of Colored
    Women's Clubs
    "New Emancipation," 10 (1944–45): 349.
    "Accent on Youth," 12 (1946–47): 156.
    "Woman-Power for a Better World," 14 (1948–49): 217.
    "Look Ahead," 15 (1949–50): 659.
Mann, Mrs. Marty, Executive Director, National Committee for Education of
    Alcoholism
    "What Shall We Do about Alcoholism?" 13 (1947–48): 253.
Sister Mary Jeanne, Editor in Chief, *Catholic Art Quarterly*
    "Art in Christian Education," 19 (1953–54): 478.
McCormick, Mrs. Anne (O'Hare), Member of the *New York Times* Editorial Board
    "U.S. as a World Leader," 13 (1947–48): 432.
McIntosh, Millicent C. (Mrs. Rustin), Dean, Barnard College
    "Goals of Progressive Education Not Sufficient Today," 15 (1949–50): 90.
    "Can the Intellect Survive?" 15 (1949–50): 559.
    "New Horizons for Women," 19 (1953–54): 311.
McLemore, Ethel Ward, Wife of a Corporate Official, Fort Worth, Texas
    "Restoring Stability to the Family," 21 (1955–56): 1330.
Meyer, Mrs. Annie Nathan, Senior Trustee of Barnard College, Author and Play-
    wright
    "Do We Need Emerson Today?" 5 (1938–39): 261.
Meyer, Mrs. Eugene, Journalist
    "British Home Front Compared with Ours," 9 (1943–44): 459.
    "Modern Curriculum in American Education," 15 (1949–50): 100.
Morrissey, Elizabeth, Professor of Economics, College of Notre Dame, Baltimore
    "Status of Women," 15 (1949–50): 55.
Newcomer, Mabel, Professor and Chair of Economics, Vassar College
    "How Are We Going to Pay for Defense?" 7 (1941–42): 343.
    "Economics of Disarmament," 23 (1957–58): 230.
Norton, Mary T.
    "Wage and Hour Legislation: Object of the Law," 4 (1937–38): 485.

Palffy, Eleanor, Vice Chairman, Red Cross Nurses' Aid Corps
    "Art of Living for Woman Today," 8 (1942–43): 224.
Pannell, Anne G., President, Sweet Briar College
    "Nation's Strength Begins in the Home," 18 (1952–53): 145.
Perkins, Frances, Secretary of Labor
    "Social Security Act," 1 (1935): 792–4.
Porter, Sylvia, Syndicated Columnist
    "Charter of Economic Human Rights," 23 (1957–58): 678.
Reed, Anna Y.
    "Is Guidance a Racket?" 4 (1937–38): 636.
Rogers, Agnes, Author
    "Elegance Is Not Undemocratic," 16 (1950–51): 126.
Rogers, Edith Nourse
    "Tragedy of the Highways," 2 (1935–36): 439.
Rooney, Miriam Therese, Associate Professor of Law, Catholic University of
    America
    "Kinds of Government and the Growth of isms," 15 (1949–50): 107.
Roosevelt, Mrs. Franklin Delano, Delegate to the United Nations
    "UN and You," 12 (1946–47): 444.
Roosevelt, Mrs. Theodore J.
    "Sino-Japanese Dossier," 3 (1936–37): 697.
Sampson, Mrs. Edith S., Attorney and Member of the U.S. Delegation to the
    United Nations
    "Show the East How the Freedom Revolution Works," 17 (1951–52): 272.
    "Equal Opportunity: Equal Responsibility," 23 (1957–58): 519.
Skinner, Cornelia Otis, Actress and Author
    "Life is Simple," 16 (1950–51): 661.
Smith, Lillian Eugenia, Author
    "Ten Years from Today," 17 (1951–52): 669.
Smith, Mrs. Margaret Chase, U.S. Senator from Maine (Rep)
    "Growing Confusion," 16 (1950–51): 552.
    "Woman, the Key Individual of Our Democracy," 19 (1953–54): 659.
    "Impatience and Generosity," 21 (1955–56): 1230.
Springer, Adele I., Attorney, Past President, National Association of Women
    Lawyers
    "Woman's Role in the Machinery of Government," 23 (1957–58): 373.
Stevenson, Mary L.
    "We, the Public," 25 (1959–60): 664.
Stricker, Margery, Editor, *Alumni News*, New Rochelle College.
    "The Intellectual," 24 (1958–59): 701.
Sturtevant, Sarah M.
    "Change and the Student," 2 (1935–36): 112.
Thompson, Dorothy (Mrs. Sinclair Lewis), Journalist
    "Propaganda in the Modern World," 2 (1935–36): 66.
    "Woman and Freedom in Our Society," 2 (1935–36): 154.
    "Death of Democracies," 3 (1936–37): 354.
    "A Nation of Speculators," 3 (1936–37): 450.
    "Freedom's Back Is Against the Wall!" 3 (1936–37): 546.

"Sino-Japanese Dossier: Background and Personalities," 3 (1936–37): 698.

"Nazi Foreign Missions," 3 (1936–37): 712.

"The Liberal Spirit," 4 (1937–38): 98.

"Stopping Propaganda," 5 (1938–39): 494.

"Let's Face the Facts: There Are No Neutral Hearts," 6 (1940–41): 345.

"Future World Order: The Idea of the United Nations," 7 (1941–42): 533.

"Power to Maintain Peace," 10 (1944–45): 81.

"State in a Democracy," 14 (1948–49): 394.

"Axioms of Global Policy," 15 (1949–1950): 433.

"Greece Today," 16 (1950–51): 200.

"Which Way America?" 16 (1950–51): 548.

"Middle East Problem." 20 (1954–55): 295.

Valentine, Mrs. Helen, Editor, *Charm* Magazine

"How to Keep More of the Money You Earn," 20 (1954–55): 506.

Verona, Sister M., Vice President, College of St. Scholastica, Duluth, Minnesota

"New Dimensions! New Challenges!" 24 (1958–59): 300.

Vining, Elizabeth Gray

"Educated Heart," 20 (1954–55): 600.

Walker, Mabel L., Executive Director, Tax Institute, Inc.

"American City Is Obsolescent," 13 (1947–48): 697.

Willoughby, Gertrude

"Stability of the Family," 19 (1953–54): 158.

Wood, Mrs. W. T., First Vice President, Parents Council for Education, Eugene, Oregon

"How Well Are Our Schools Doing the Job?" 18 (1952–53): 308.

Woolley, Mary E., Expert on International Affairs

"Progress, Man's Distinctive Mark Alone," 4 (1937–38): 656.

"Crisis and Our Responsibility," 6 (1939–40): 205.

About the Authors

SANDRA J. SARKELA is Professor of English and Communication at the State University of New York, Potsdam.

SUSAN MALLON ROSS is Associate Professor of English and Communication at the State University of New York, Potsdam.

MARGARET A. LOWE is Associate Professor of History at Bridgewater State College.